MESSIANIC

SPRING HOLIDAY HELPER

MESSIANIC
SPRING HOLIDAY HELPER

edited by Margaret McKee Huey

Messianic Spring Holiday Helper

Published by Messianic Apologetics, a division of Outreach Israel Ministries
P.O. Box 850845
Richardson, Texas 75085
(407) 933-2002

www.outreachisrael.net
www.messianicapologetics.net

originally produced by TNN Press 2010 in Kissimmee, Florida

Table of Contents

Introduction ix

1   A Summarization of Purim Traditions 1
by Margaret McKee Huey and J.K. McKee

2   The Message of Esther 5
by J.K. McKee

3   A Summarization of Passover Traditions 13
by Margaret McKee Huey and J.K. McKee

4   Passover: A Sign to Remember 23
by Mark Huey

5   The Restoration of Passover 33
by Mark Huey

6   The Message of Exodus 39
by J.K. McKee

7   The Song of Moses and God's Mission for His People 53
by J.K. McKee

8   "Everyone Is Wrong But Me!" 67
by J.K. McKee

9   The Last Seder and Yeshua's Passover Chronology 71
by J.K. McKee

10   Some Features of the Ancient Passover Seder 139

11   What is the Problem With Easter? 143
by J.K. McKee

12   Passover: Paradox or Outreach? 153
by Mark Huey

13   Celebrating Passover Today 161
by Margaret McKee Huey

14   A Summarization of Shavuot Traditions 167
by Margaret McKee Hueyy and J.K. McKee

15   The Message of Ruth 173
by J.K. McKee

16   The Gospel According to Torah: It Happened at Shavuot! 177
by J.K. McKee

17   The Work of the Holy Spirit: Perfection of the Heart................187
by J.K. McKee

18   The Work of the Holy Spirit: Perfection of the Mind 197
by J.K. McKee

FAQs on the Spring Holiday Season 209

KOSHER YOUR PLATE **245**
    Purim 247
    Passover 248
    Shavuot 252

LITURGICAL RESOURCES **255**

    The Role of Liturgy 257
    Using these Liturgies 259
    Liturgical Resources for the Spring Appointed Times 259

    Before and After the Reading of the Megillah of Esther 261
    A Passover Haggadah for Messianic Believers 265
    Hallel for Passover 301
    Counting the Omer to Shavuot 305
    Hallel for Shavuot 309

About the Editor 313

Bibliography 317

Abbreviation Chart and Special Terms

The following is a chart of abbreviations for reference works and special terms that are used in publications by Outreach Israel Ministries and Messianic Apologetics. Please familiarize yourself with them as the text may reference a Bible version, i.e., RSV for the Revised Standard Version, or a source such as *TWOT* for the *Theological Wordbook of the Old Testament*, solely by its abbreviation. Detailed listings of these sources are provided in the Bibliography.

Special terms that may be used have been provided in this chart:

ABD: *Anchor Bible Dictionary*

AMG: *Complete Word Study Dictionary: Old Testament, New Testament*

ANE: Ancient Near East(ern)

Apostolic Scriptures/Writings: the New Testament

Ara: Aramaic

ATS: ArtScroll Tanach (1996)

b. Babylonian Talmud (*Talmud Bavli*)

B.C.E.: Before Common Era or B.C.

BDAG: *A Greek-English Lexicon of the New Testament and Other Early Christian Literature* (Bauer, Danker, Arndt, Gingrich)

BDB: *Brown-Driver-Briggs Hebrew and English Lexicon*

BECNT: *Baker Exegetical Commentary on the New Testament*

BKCNT: *Bible Knowledge Commentary: New Testament*

C.E.: Common Era or A.D.

CEV: Contemporary English Version (1995)

CGEDNT: *Concise Greek-English Dictionary of New Testament Words* (Barclay M. Newman)

CHALOT: *Concise Hebrew and Aramaic Lexicon of the Old Testament*

CJB: Complete Jewish Bible (1998)

DRA: Douay-Rheims American Edition

DSS: Dead Sea Scrolls

ECB: *Eerdmans Commentary on the Bible*

EDB: *Eerdmans Dictionary of the Bible*

eisegesis: "reading meaning into," or interjecting a preconceived or foreign meaning into a Biblical text

EJ: *Encylopaedia Judaica*

ESV: English Standard Version (2001)

exegesis: "drawing meaning out of," or the process of trying to understand what a Biblical text means on its own

EXP: *Expositor's Bible Commentary*

Ger: German

GNT: Greek New Testament

Grk: Greek

halachah: lit. "the way to walk," how the Torah is lived out in an individual's life or faith community

HALOT: *Hebrew & Aramaic Lexicon of the Old Testament* (Koehler and Baumgartner)

HCSB: Holman Christian Standard Bible (2004)

Heb: Hebrew

HNV: Hebrew Names Version of the World English Bible

ICC: *International Critical Commentary*

IDB: *Interpreter's Dictionary of the Bible*

IDBSup: *Interpreter's Dictionary of the Bible Supplement*

ISBE: *International Standard Bible Encyclopedia*

IVPBBC: *IVP Bible Background Commentary (Old & New Testament)*

Jastrow: *Dictionary of the Targumim, Talmud Bavli, Talmud Yerushalmi, and Midrashic Literature* (Marcus Jastrow)

JBK: New Jerusalem Bible-Koren (2000)

JETS: *Journal of the Evangelical Theological Society*

KJV: King James Version

Lattimore: The New Testament by Richmond Lattimore (1996)

LITV: *Literal Translation of the Holy Bible* by Jay P. Green (1986)

LS: *A Greek-English Lexicon* (Liddell & Scott)

LXE: *Septuagint with Apocrypha* by Sir L.C.L. Brenton (1851)

LXX: Septuagint

m. Mishnah

MT: Masoretic Text

NASB: New American Standard Bible (1977)

NASU: New American Standard Update (1995)

NBCR: *New Bible Commentary: Revised*

NEB: New English Bible (1970)

Nelson: *Nelson's Expository Dictionary of Old Testament Words*

NETS: New English Translation of the Septuagint (2007)

NIB: *New Interpreter's Bible*

NIGTC: *New International Greek Testament Commentary*

NICNT: *New International Commentary on the New Testament*

NIDB: *New International Dictionary of the Bible*

NIV: New International Version (1984)

NJB: New Jerusalem Bible-Catholic (1985)

NJPS: Tanakh, A New Translation of the Holy Scriptures (1999)

NKJV: New King James Version (1982)
NRSV: New Revised Standard Version (1989)
NLT: New Living Translation (1996)
NT: New Testament
orthopraxy: lit. "the right action," how the
    Bible or one's theology is lived out in the
    world
OT: Old Testament
PreachC: *The Preacher's Commentary*
REB: Revised English Bible (1989)
RSV: Revised Standard Version (1952)
t. Tosefta
Tanach (Tanakh): the Old Testament
Thayer: *Thayer's Greek-English Lexicon of the
    New Testament*
TDNT: *Theological Dictionary of the New
    Testament*

TEV: Today's English Version (1976)
TNIV: Today's New International Version
    (2005)
TNTC: *Tyndale   New   Testament
    Commentaries*
TWOT: *Theological Wordbook of the Old
    Testament*
UBSHNT: United Bible Societies' 1991
    Hebrew New Testament revised edition
v(s). verse(s)
Vine: *Vine's Complete Expository Dictionary of
    Old and New Testament Words*
Vul: Latin Vulgate
WBC: *Word Biblical Commentary*
Yid: Yiddish
YLT: Young's Literal Translation (1862/1898)

Introduction

"These are the appointed times of the LORD, holy convocations which you shall proclaim at the times appointed for them. In the first month, on the fourteenth day of the month at twilight is the LORD's Passover. Then on the fifteenth day of the same month there is the Feast of Unleavened Bread to the LORD; for seven days you shall eat unleavened bread. On the first day you shall have a holy convocation; you shall not do any laborious work. But for seven days you shall present an offering by fire to the LORD. On the seventh day is a holy convocation; you shall not do any laborious work. Then the LORD spoke to Moses saying, 'Speak to the sons of Israel, and say to them, "When you enter the land which I am going to give to you and reap its harvest, then you shall bring in the sheaf of the first fruits of your harvest to the priest. And he shall wave the sheaf before the Lord for you to be accepted; on the day after the Sabbath the priest shall wave it…It is to be a perpetual statue throughout your generations in all your dwelling places"'" (Leviticus 23:4-11, 14b).

One of the most exciting things that is happening in this present season of spiritual renewal, as the Messianic movement grows and expands, is the restoration of the appointed times of the Lord for *all* of His people! His festivals are being recognized by Believers all around the world to be special seasons in which all who follow the God of Israel should actively participate! It is wonderful to hear the reports of how the Father is restoring the truths found in being obedient to His Instruction, as we observe and remember our Hebraic heritage, and consider His plan of salvation history in a very real and tangible way.

Perhaps the most recognizable of the appointed times of the Lord, given to us in the Torah, occur in the Spring. Anyone who is familiar with the Bible's account of redemption knows about the Exodus and the giving of the Ten Commandments. The plagues dispensed upon Ancient Egypt, and God's deliverance of the Israelites via the Passover lamb and through the Red Sea, are paralleled in the Apostolic Scriptures by the sacrifice of Yeshua the Messiah (Jesus Christ) at Golgotha (Calvary), and the final atonement that He has provided—vindicated by His resurrection from the dead. In the past twenty years, evangelical Christians have been exposed to the Passover *seder* in significant numbers, and are embracing it as a very meaningful and significant part of their faith. This has helped to expand the growth of the Messianic movement, perhaps more than anything else—**as born again Believers really want to learn to do something that Jesus did!**

To help you and your family during this special season, we have included a variety of important articles on how to deal with your participation in the Spring holidays. We have included articles on Passover, the Festival of Unleavened Bread, what to do about Easter, and *Shavuot* or Pentecost. Many of these teachings come from our Virtual Spring Holiday series from over the past few years. These articles address the importance of remembering both the Exodus and the resurrection of Yeshua, and how you can properly commemorate these events with your family, focusing on the truths of the Scriptures. We have a practical guide that includes kosher recipes and a Haggadah for Passover, which you can adapt for your family or congregation. And as an added bonus, we have included articles on the often overlooked holiday of *Purim*, which precedes the Passover season by a month. Common issues and controversies that can arise during the Spring holiday season— both externally *and* internally—are also addressed, as fairly as possible.

Our family believes that the restoration of the Spring holidays is a blessing to us! We, who are to walk as Messiah Yeshua walked, must reach out to others in love at this time when the Father is restoring His appointed times to His people. Yeshua told us that others would know that we are His disciples by the love that we have for one another (John 13:35). We encourage you to love your family and friends in such a way concerning these feasts that they will be drawn to us, and not repelled. Invite your family and close friends to your home, **to join you** for your Passover *seder*, or to your Messianic congregation or fellowship for a real hands on, educational experience. As you purchase various kosher items for your Passover *seder*, you will likely encounter Jewish people who do not yet know Messiah Yeshua, and this will be a unique testimony to them of your obedience to the God of Israel.

Dear friends, it is only through our unconditional love for our Christian brethren that one day they will want to know what we know about walking like the Messiah. One day they will want to know why we have become thoroughly Messianic, and what they can learn from us. Likewise, only by Jewish people witnessing Messianics obeying the statutes of God's Torah, will they be provoked to considering the claims of the gospel, and recognize Yeshua as Israel's Messiah.

Let us rejoice in the true understanding that Yeshua not only actively participated in the Spring Feasts of the Lord, but that He was indeed the Passover Lamb Himself! Let us be a positive witness to all we encounter during the Spring holiday season.

Chag Sameach!
Margaret McKee Huey

~ 1 ~

A Summarization
of Purim Traditions

Margaret McKee Huey and J.K. McKee

The holiday of *Purim* (פּוּרִים) is a relatively minor festival in the Tanach (Old Testament), yet it portrays a very important story that all of God's people need to understand. Having been dispersed into Babylonian exile in 585 B.C.E., the Jewish people now find themselves under Persian rule. While many find their new Persian rulers more tolerant than the Babylonians, the Jews are still a minority and often find themselves subject to harassment and persecution. In the Book of Esther, King Ahasuerus' (or Xerxes') grand vizier, the evil Haman, devises a plot to kill the Jews when he is not worshipped by Mordecai. But Ahasuerus' new wife, the Jewess Esther, is placed in just the right position at just the right time to see that this scheme does not come to pass. Instead, Haman is executed using the very means that he intended to use against the Jews.

As can be imagined, a great sense of relief engulfed the Jewish people in Persia when Haman's plans were thwarted. God's people were preserved from mass genocide. Esther 9:20-28 summarizes how the festival of *Purim* was instituted by Mordecai to celebrate the Jews' deliverance from Haman:

"Then Mordecai recorded these events, and he sent letters to all the Jews who were in all the provinces of King Ahasuerus, both near and far, obliging them to celebrate the fourteenth day of the month Adar, and the fifteenth day of the same month, annually, because on those days the Jews rid themselves of their enemies, and *it was a* month which was turned for them from sorrow into gladness and from mourning into a holiday; that they should make them days of feasting and rejoicing and sending portions *of food* to one another and gifts to the poor. Thus the Jews undertook what they had started to do, and what Mordecai had written to them. For Haman the son of Hammedatha, the Agagite, the adversary of all the Jews, had schemed against the Jews to destroy them and had cast Pur, that is the lot, to disturb them and destroy them. But when it came to the king's attention, he commanded by letter that his wicked scheme which he had devised against the Jews, should return on his own head and that he and his sons should be hanged on the gallows. Therefore they called these days Purim after the name of Pur. And because of the instructions in this letter, both what they had seen in this regard and what had happened to them, the Jews established and made a custom for themselves and for their descendants and for all those who allied themselves with them, so that they would not fail to celebrate these two days according to their regulation and according to their appointed time annually. **So these days were to be remembered and celebrated throughout every generation, every family, every province and every city; and these days of Purim were not to fail from among the Jews, or their memory fade from their descendants."**

Concerning the observance of *Purim*, v. 22 is most significant: "They were to observe them as days of feasting and merrymaking, and as an occasion for sending gifts to one another and presents to the poor" (NJPS). *Purim* was to be a time of rejoicing and doing good to one another, as God's faithfulness was revealed to the Jewish people through the actions of His followers. Even though "God" or "the Lord" is not mentioned specifically in the Book of Esther, one undoubtedly sees Him work through individuals who are committed to Him.[1]

The Formation of Purim

The term *Purim* (פּוּרִים) is actually derived from the Semitic (probably Akkadian) term *pur* (פּוּר),[2] meaning "lot." It denotes the lots cast by Haman to determine when the mass execution of the Jews in Persia was to occur, as Esther 3:7 indicates, "In the first month, which is the month Nisan, in the twelfth year of King Ahasuerus, **Pur, that is the lot**, was cast before Haman from day to day and from month *to month*, until the twelfth month, that is the month Adar," with the 13th of Adar chosen as the date to enact the executions (Esther 3:13). The 14th of Adar occurring immediately thereafter is designated as the day to commemorate *Purim*, although on leap years it is celebrated in the month of II Adar. *Purim* will often fall in either late February or early March on the Gregorian calendar. Although one would think that commemorating *Purim* and the almost destruction of one's people would be something negative, the Talmud explains, "when Adar comes, rejoicing increases" (b.*Ta'anit* 29a).[3]

In the Apocrypha *Purim* is called "Mordecai's day" (2 Maccabees 15:36), indicating that it was being celebrated as an important festivity several centuries before the ministry of Yeshua the Messiah. Traditionally, *Purim* is to be a time when the Jewish community believes that a person's joy is to increase. The tractate *Megillah* in the Mishnah details the celebration of *Purim* and some of the critical lessons it is to teach us. In Jewish tradition, *Purim* "is a minor festival in that work on it is permitted, but it has been joyously celebrated in Jewish communities as a reminder of God's protection of His people" (*EJ*).[4] It is customary that *Purim* not fall on the Sabbath.

---

[1] It is notable that God is specifically mentioned in the Apocryphal Additions to the Book of Esther, seen in the Greek Septuagint.

[2] Ludwig Koehler and Walter Baumgartner, eds., *The Hebrew & Aramaic Lexicon of the Old Testament*, 2 vols. (Leiden, the Netherlands: Brill, 2001), 2:920.

[3] *The Babylonian Talmud: A Translation and Commentary*. MS Windows XP. Peabody, MA: Hendrickson, 2005. CD-ROM.

[4] Louis Jacobs, "Purim," in Encyclopaedia Judaica. MS Windows 9x. Brooklyn: Judaica Multimedia (Israel) Ltd, 1997.

Assorted Customs of Purim

The main feature of *Purim* by far is the study of the Book of Esther. Some Jewish Rabbis such as Moses Maimonides afforded Esther a place in the Hebrew canon second only to the Torah. The study of Esther during *Purim* is frequently done with a special *megillah* (מְגִלָּה) scroll in Hebrew. Of particular interest to *Purim* is that it calls members of the Jewish community to remember the trials that they have faced and God's faithfulness through those trials, especially the ones encountered in the Diaspora. Haman beguiled King Ahasuerus with the word, "There is a certain people scattered and dispersed among the peoples in all the provinces of your kingdom" (Esther 3:8), and this has caused many Jews to think of themselves and the additional places they have been scattered throughout history. Ronald L. Eisenberg remarks,

"All too frequently, Jews have faced a variety of Hamans, but in most instances (unlike in the *Megillah*) the conclusion of the story has not been happy. The triumph of the weak over the powerful recounted in the Book of Esther has been enormously uplifting to Jews throughout their long exile."[5]

Jewish theology has always considered *Purim* important because it typifies the salvation history of God, where He interjects Himself into the world of mortals and is able to act on their behalf, providing deliverance. Consequently, many Christian theologians likewise value the themes of the Book of Esther, and how we see God performing these actions through normal human vessels who are called by Him and empowered by His Spirit.

A major feature of *Purim*, detailed in Esther 9:22, is the encouragement for one to give to the poor. This is partially because when one has experienced God's deliverance, he or she should then be grateful to provide out of His abundance for those who have little or nothing. Varied Jewish traditions include the giving of certain kinds of foods based on specific interpretations of the themes of *Purim*.

The centerpiece of the modern observance of *Purim* is what was originally known as the *Purim-spiel*. This custom arose in Ashkenazic Jewish communities in Europe to give a performance for one's family or community to remember the story of Esther. Over time, however, this has developed into a very elaborate "*Purim* play" or dramatic presentation, often with young girls in the community dressing up with fancy gowns and makeup in honor of Queen Esther.

Today, there are some who surmise that under the influence of the Italian Carnival in the Middle Ages, the *Purim* play came about. However, it is more likely that "Under the influence of the Italian carnival...men [were] permitted to dress as women and women as men" (*EJ*).[6] This would primarily have included "masquerading."[7] In this kind of *Purim* reenactment, the gender roles may have been reversed for the play to add a comic element, with men dressing up as Queen Vashti and Esther, and women dressing up as King Ahasuerus and Haman. This is, notably, not something that we see in *Purim* reenactments today, as mostly children are those who play the characters with the gender roles intact.

---

[5] Ronald L. Eisenberg, *The JPS Guide to Jewish Traditions* (Philadelphia: Jewish Publication Society, 2004), 255.

[6] Jacobs, "Purim," in *EJ*.

[7] Eisenberg, 258.

Traditional Foods

Eating is undoubtedly a major part of celebrating *Purim*, with a variety of traditional foods. One of the most common centerpieces of *Purim* are *Hamantashen* or Haman hat cookies. These are pastry cookies usually filled with fruit. Frequently, this is one of the foods that is made for and given to poor people for *Purim*.

During *Purim*, some Jewish communities observe vegetarian meals, due to the belief that Esther and Mordecai were vegetarian and did not eat from the Persian table. However, most Jews today disregard this custom.

There is some notable controversy surrounding a Rabbi Rava's teaching in the Talmud that one should get so drunk on *Purim* that he cannot tell the difference between Mordecai or Haman when their names are spoken during the reading of Esther (b.*Megillah* 7b). Following this example has led some to believe that *Purim* is not a time of seriousness, when one recalls the salvation history of God, but instead that it is a holiday of frivolity and lewdness. Thankfully, there are Jewish teachers who have led by an example of encouraging *Purim* to not be a time of drunkenness, but instead sober severity and piety (and even fasting).

When we celebrate *Purim* as Messianic Believers today, we have an opportunity to pause for a moment and consider how our Heavenly Father has worked, and continues to work, through human beings who are faithful to Him. We get to consider that if Esther and Mordecai had not stopped Haman's rampage, that the hope of our Messiah Yeshua entering into the world through the Jewish people would not be realized. While *Purim* gives us a time to have fun with one another, it should be through that humor and irony when God is able to communicate to us in a unique way, and we recall the miracles that He has performed for us—not just in ancient times, *but also today!*

~2~

The Message of Esther

J.K. McKee

The Book of Esther is one of the most important books in the Bible. While Esther is commonly considered during the season of *Purim*, the specific concepts it communicates often go under-appreciated. Esther is much, much more than just cheering when the name "Mordecai" is mentioned or booing to "Haman" when the story is shared in the congregation, or dressing up and participating in a play. Esther gives us a snapshot of the Diaspora Jewish community following the fall of the Babylonian Empire, the complexities of the Jews having to live under Persian rule, the antiquity of anti-Semitism long preceding the time of Yeshua, the workings of God behind the scenes through normal people, and most especially how God uses women to accomplish His tasks. Esther also tells us what happens after God's people are spared from certain doom, and how they are to protect themselves.

The story of Esther begins during the reign of the Persian King Ahasuerus or Xerxes, who reigned between 486-465 B.C.E. While Bible readers most often know this king for the role he plays in the Book of Esther, history at large knows Xerxes as the Persian king who failed to conquer Greece.[1] The account of Esther opens up when Xerxes intends to display "the vast wealth of his kingdom and the splendor and glory of his majesty" for "a full 180 days" (Esther 1:4). In the midst of a great banquet he holds after the time of celebration (Esther 1:5-8), the intoxicated king intends to display his wife Vashti to those gathered. Nothing is stated in the Biblical text regarding why he asks of this—only saying that Xerxes wanted to "display her beauty" (Esther 1:11)—but one can only imagine a woman walking into a crowd of drunken men and what they were thinking, perhaps wanting to rip her clothes off (if she were not already nude). Vashti, as one can only expect, refuses the request of the king who "became furious and burned with anger" (Esther 1:12).

King Xerxes consults with his closest advisors, wanting to know what is to be done with his wife (Esther 1:14-15). They tell him that if something is not done, wives all over Persia and Media will imitate Queen Vashti, and there will be gross disrespect of husbands and men in general (Esther 1:17-18). They rule that Queen Vashti not be allowed into his presence again, and specifically that "the king give her royal position to someone else who is better than she" (Esther 1:19). So

---

[1] Duane A. Garrett, ed., et. al., *NIV Archaeological Study Bible* (Grand Rapids: Zondervan, 2005), 716; note on Esther 1:1.

significant was this, that "He sent dispatches to all parts of the kingdom, to each province in his own script and to each people in its own language, proclaiming in each people's tongue that every man should be ruler over his own household" (Esther 1:22).

After this declaration and with his own anger subsided, King Xerxes is advised, "Let a search be made for beautiful young virgins for the king" (Esther 2:2), and commissioners are sent to the provinces of the Persian Empire to search for a new queen. In the capital city of Susa, a Jewess named Hadassah, "also known as Esther, [who] was lovely in form and features" (Esther 2:7), had been taken by her older cousin Mordecai as a daughter. The search commences, and she was found to have all the right qualities and won the favor of the leader of the king's harem. Leaving, Mordecai tells her not to reveal her Jewish heritage (Esther 2:10). We are told that Esther "had to complete twelve months of beauty treatments prescribed for the women...And this is how she would go to the king" (Esther 2:12, 13). Esther was the one woman who "the king was attracted to...more than any of the other virgins" (Esther 2:17), being made queen.

As these events occur at the palace, Mordecai was sitting outside at the gate (Esther 2:19). Minding his own business, perhaps wondering what is going on inside, he overhears a conversation between two of the king's officers. These two men, Bigthgana and Teresh, "became angry and conspired to assassinate King Xerxes" (Esther 2:21). Mordecai relays the news to Esther, who reports it to the king on his behalf (Esther 2:22). As a result, the two were executed and their bodies publicly displayed or "hanged" (Esther 2:23).

Following this we are introduced to Haman, one of the Persian nobles, and a man whom the author of Esther considers to be an Agagite.[2] King Xerxes honors Haman, yet "Mordecai would not kneel down or pay him honor" (Esther 3:2). Mordecai enraged Haman, who was promptly told that "he was a Jew" (Esther 3:4). "When Haman saw that Mordecai would not kneel down or pay him honor, he was enraged" (Esther 3:5), and rather than wanting to just do damage to Mordecai or bring him harm, "Instead Haman looked for a way to destroy all Mordecai's people, the Jews, throughout the whole kingdom of Xerxes" (Esther 3:6). The scheming Haman then goes before his king, and speaks the insidious words,

"There is a certain people dispersed and scattered among the peoples in all the provinces of your kingdom whose customs are different from those of other people who do not obey the king's laws; it is not in the king's best interest to tolerate them. If it pleases the king, let a decree be issued to destroy them, and I will put ten thousand talents of silver into the royal treasury for the men who carry out this business" (Esther 3:8-9).

King Xerxes promptly gives Haman his signet ring in approval (Esther 3:10). Ironically enough, it was not the style of the Persians to exterminate people, as the Persians were widely known for their tolerant attitudes, unlike the Assyrians or Babylonians who had preceded them. Haman receiving Xerxes' immediate approval is a testament to his ability to connive and manipulate with lies, some of the distinct qualities of (state) anti-Semitism seen throughout later history. We are told, "Dispatches were sent by couriers to all the king's provinces with the order to destroy, kill and annihilate all the Jews—young and old, women and little

---

[2] Agag was the deposed king of the Amalakites, whom King Saul let live (1 Samuel 15).

children…A copy of the text of the edict was to be issued as law in every province and made known to the people of every nationality so that they would be ready for that day" (Esther 3:13-14).

Upon hearing about this genocidal plot against his people, Mordecai "tore his clothes, put on sackcloth and ashes, and went out into the city, wailing loudly and bitterly" (Esther 4:1). It is also recorded, "In every province to which the edict and order of the king came, there was great mourning among the Jews, with fasting, weeping and wailing" (Esther 4:3). Esther herself "was in great distress" (Esther 4:4). Mordecai relays what has happened to Esther via her servant, and how Haman was at the center of the plot to kill all the Jews in Persia. Mordecai "urge[d] her to go into the king's presence to beg for mercy and plead with him for her people" (Esther 4:8).

Just going before the king of Persia was not an easy thing to do, even for his queen. Esther relays the message to Mordecai, "All the king's officials and the people of the royal provinces know that for any man or woman who approaches the king in the inner court without being summoned the king has but one law: that he be put to death. The only exception to this is for the king to extend the gold scepter to him and spare his life" (Esther 4:11). Esther knows the gravity of going before King Xerxes. Yet, Mordecai is sure that she is told: "if you remain silent at this time, relief and deliverance for the Jews will arise from another place, but you and your father's family will perish. **And who knows but that you have come to royal position for such a time as this?**" (Esther 4:14, emphasis mine). Mordecai is confident that the Jewish people will not be exterminated, but if Esther fails to act there will be a price to pay as her family will die. Esther asks Mordecai for the Jews in Susa to fast for her, as she contemplates what is to be done.

After three days, Esther "stood…in front of the king's hall. The king was sitting on his royal throne…When he saw Queen Esther standing in the court, he was pleased with her and held out to her the gold scepter" (Esther 5:1-2). Esther was indeed in the right place at the right time, and King Xerxes is so happy to see her, that he says, "What is your request? Even up to half the kingdom, it will be given you" (Esther 5:3). Rather than telling the king right then and there the problem her people were facing, she asks if she can hold a banquet for the king and Haman (Esther 5:5), and it is granted.

During this banquet, both King Xerxes and Haman are found drinking wine. The king once again asks Esther what her request is, and she asks them if they can have another banquet the following day (Esther 5:7). As he leaves, "Haman…went out in high spirits. But when he saw Mordecai at the king's gate and observed that he neither rose nor showed fear in his presence, he was filled with rage. Nevertheless, Haman restrained himself and went home" (Esther 5:9-10). When he arrived home, Haman "boasted…about his vast wealth" and specifically "all the ways the king had honored him and how he had elevated him above the other nobles and officials" (Esther 5:11). Even more interesting, Haman specifically says, "I'm the only person Queen Esther invited to accompany the king to the banquet she gave" (Esther 5:12). Yet this is followed by the perturbed remark, "all this gives me no satisfaction as long as I see that Jew Mordecai sitting at the king's gate" (Esther 5:13). Haman's wife asks that they build a structure[3] up to seventy-five

---

[3] In v. 14 Zeresh says "Have a gallows built," yet the Hebrew source text reads ya'asu etz or "Let them prepare a tree" (YLT), or "wood."

cubits high on which to display Mordecai's corpse. We are told: "**This suggestion delighted Haman**" (Esther 5:14, emphasis mine).

While Haman continues in his schemes to destroy the Jews, King Xerxes could not sleep. As a sure remedy, "he ordered the book of the chronicles, the record of his reign, to be brought in and read to him. It was found recorded there that Mordecai had exposed Bithgana and Teresh…who had conspired to assassinate him" (Esther 6:1-2). The king asks what kind of honor had been bestowed upon Mordecai for his act of preservation, and is told that nothing had yet been done (Esther 6:3-4). While this is happening, "Haman is standing in the court" (Esther 6:5), and upon entering the king asks him, "What should be done for the man the king delights to honor?" (Esther 6:6a). And as it is said, "Haman thought to himself, 'Who is there that the king would rather honor than me?'" (Esther 6:6b). Haman was so self-consumed that it was only natural that any reward dispensed by the leader of the Persian Empire could go to *him*. Haman tells the king,

"For the man the king delights to honor, have them bring a royal robe the king has worn and a horse the king has ridden, one with a royal crest placed on its head. Then let the robe and horse be entrusted to one of the king's most noble princes. Let them robe the man the king delights to honor, and lead him on the horse through the city streets, proclaiming before him, 'This is what is done for the man the king delights to honor!'" (Esther 6:7-9).

Perhaps thinking that he will be paraded around the city in the Fifth Century B.C.E equivalent of a ticker-tape parade, King Xerxes tells Haman, "Get the robe and the horse and do just as you have suggested for Mordecai the Jew, who sits at the king's gate. Do not neglect anything you have recommended" (Esther 6:10). In a twist of complete irony, rather than having this honor done to *himself*, Haman must parade the man he hates with a passion—Mordecai—around the city on horseback. He has to proclaim to the city: "This is what is done for the man the king delights to honor!" (Esther 6:11). Humiliated, Haman rushes home and reports what has taken place (Esther 6:12). Haman's wife gives him some sound advice: "you cannot stand against [Mordecai]—you will surely come to ruin!" (Esther 6:13), and following this Haman is prepared to go to Esther's second banquet.

As King Xerxes "and Haman went to dine with Queen Esther…the king again asked, 'Queen Esther, what is your petition? It will be given you?'" (Esther 7:1). With her husband and Haman right there, and with Haman likely unsure of what is going on, having had some wine, Esther is direct with her response:

"If I have found favor with you, O king, and if it pleases your majesty, grant me my life—this is my petition. And spare my people—this is my request. For I and my people have been sold for destruction and slaughter and annihilation. If we had merely been sold as male and female slaves, I would have kept quiet, because no such distress would justify disturbing the king" (Esther 7:3-4).

The king is naturally astonished, asking Esther, "Who is he? Where is the man who has dared to do such a thing?" (Esther 7:5). Esther's answer is to the point: "The adversary and enemy is this vile Haman" (Esther 7:6).

Haman probably did not know what to do, and we can only imagine the kinds of bodily reactions he had when signaled out as the culprit against Esther and her people. Did he vomit? Did his stomach churn? Did he lose his voice or get a sudden headache? One thing is certain, as King Xerxes ran out of the banquet furious, "Haman, realizing that the king had already decided his fate, stayed behind to beg Queen Esther for his life" (Esther 7:7b). Returning to address Haman, the king sees him in a prostrated position before Esther. All he has to say is, "Will he even molest the queen while she is with me in the house?" (Esther 7:8b). Upon saying this, one of the king's eunuchs informs him that a structure seventy-five cubits high has been built on which Mordecai's corpse was supposed to be displayed (Esther 7:9). The king's words are direct: "Hang him on it!" (Esther 7:10). And so "the king's fury subsided" (Esther 7:10).

This is normally where the common *Purim* play ends the story—with the death of Haman. Yet the Book of Esther still has three more chapters, each of which tells us more about what happened. After Esther has just pleaded for her life, Mordecai is brought in before King Xerxes, is formally introduced, and is given Haman's estate (Esther 8:1-2). Esther, having been saved, pleads for the lives of all the Jews throughout the Persian Empire (Esther 8:3-5), telling him "For how can I bear to see disaster fall on my people? How can I bear to see the destruction of my family?" (Esther 8:6). Having just called for the death of Haman, the king is moved to make another ruling:

"Now write another decree in the king's name in behalf of the Jews as seems best to you, and seal it with the king's signet ring—for no document written in the king's name and sealed with his ring can be revoked" (Esther 8:8).

A new ruling in favor of the Jews was sent throughout the empire— "Mordecai's orders to the Jews, and to the satraps, governors and nobles of the 127 provinces stretching from India to Cush[4]" (Esther 8:9). Mordecai's ruling was sent in the languages of all, with the direct approval and signet stamp of King Xerxes (Esther 8:9b-10). The Jews were given permission to defend themselves against any aggression, and a set date was given "so that the Jews would be ready on that day to avenge themselves on their enemies" (Esther 8:13). Far be it from the Jewish people in the empire being the victims; they are now authorized to go and root out potential foes. As a consequence, the text tells us "many people of other nationalities became Jews[5] because fear of the Jews had seized them" (Esther 8:17). Somehow, these people realized that the Jewish people were going to take the decree seriously, and whether or not they "converted," they certainly did their best to *blend in.*

This edict was to be carried out on the 13th of Adar, and although "the enemies of the Jews...hoped to overpower them...the tables were turned and the Jews got the upper hand over those who hated them" (Esther 9:1). "The Jews assembled in their cities in all the provinces of King Xerxes to attack those seeking their destruction. No one could stand against them, because the people of all the other nationalities were afraid of them" (Esther 9:2). In the day of the Jews' vengeance, the administrators of Persia actually helped them because Mordecai had replaced Haman in Xerxes' government (Esther 9:3-4)! "The Jews struck down all

---

[4] Or, Ethiopia.

[5] Heb. *yahad.*

The verb *yahad* is rendered with *Ioudaizō* in the Septuagint, employed in Paul's rebuke of Peter in Galatians 2:14. Peter's behavior in separating to the conservative Jews from Jerusalem, dividing the assembly in Antioch, would require the non-Jews to undergo ritual proselyte conversion in order for unity to be restored. Paul would have nothing of this, as unity and inclusion in the assembly are to be based on the work of Yeshua for all people.

For a further discussion, consult the article "The Message of Galatians" and the commentary *Galatians for the Practical Messianic,* by J.K. McKee.

their enemies with the sword, killing and destroying them, and they did what they pleased to those who hated them" (Esther 9:5), and we are specifically told that the ten sons of Haman met their death (Esther 9:6) and whose corpses were displayed (Esther 9:13-14). A great number of the Jews' enemies were killed during this day.[6]

On the day following, the 14th of Adar, the Jewish people throughout the Persian Empire "rested and made it a day of feasting and joy" (Esther 9:17). The Jews had been saved from complete obliteration, and their enemies had been routed out. The people could now live in peace, wherever they were located, and could remember how Queen Esther was placed by God in the Persian court. This festival was to be "a day for giving presents to each other" (Esther 9:19), and was recorded for posterity by Mordecai (Esther 9:20). It was to be celebrated "annually…as the time when the Jews got relief from their enemies" (Esther 9:22). It was called *Purim*, as Haman had "cast the *pur* (that is, the lot) for their ruin and destruction" (Esther 9:23). However, the Jews throughout the empire had been delivered, and were specifically admonished to remember this time of deliverance "every year…at the time appointed" (Esther 9:27).[7] As it was decreed:

"These days should be remembered and observed in every generation by every family, and in every province and in every city. And these days of Purim should never cease to be celebrated by the Jews, nor should the memory of them die out among their descendants" (Esther 9:28).

The Biblical text is very clear on the need to celebrate Purim *b'kol dor v'dor* or "in all generation and generation" (my translation). "Esther's decree confirmed these regulations about Purim, and it was written down in the records" (Esther 9:32).

Mordecai is attested to have been alongside King Xerxes (Ahasuerus) in "all his acts of power and might," and he is listed "in the book of the annals of the kings of Media and Persia" (Esther 10:2). He, as Jew who was once designated for execution, "was second in rank to King Xerxes, preeminent among the Jews, and held in high esteem by his many fellow Jews, because he worked for the good of his people and spoke up for the welfare of all the Jews" (Esther 10:3).

The narrative of Esther when taken as a whole has much more to teach us than the common *Purim* play does it justice. Far be it from Esther being some kind of ironic comedy, the Book of Esther adroitly displays themes common to the human condition such as: love, oppression, goodness, evil, and justice for those who would harm others. While there is no direct mention of God in the account, one can certainly see how the Lord works through the various characters with the Jewish people in the end being saved from certain extinction. As Mordecai clearly told Esther, "perhaps you have attained to royal position for just such a crisis" (Esther 4:14, NJPS). You may have used this sort of expression before and did not know where it came from. Better yet, perhaps you have been in the right place at the right time, and have been able to be used by God for some kind of important service.

---

[6] Esther 9:16 specifically says that seventy-five thousand were killed, but this could obviously be a rounded number. Furthermore, it is not improbable that being aided by the Persian government, the Persians themselves were responsible for eliminating the Jews' enemies and any other criminal elements that plagued them.

[7] Heb. *v'kizmanam b'kol shanah v'shanah*, "according to their season, in every year and year" (YLT).

Looking at the place of Esther in the whole of Scripture, it is obvious that there are connections between the figure of Haman and the coming antimessiah/antichrist. Haman was a man filled with self-love and self-worship. He could only think about himself. While the text does not say so explicitly, were the would-be assassins of King Xerxes in Haman's close confidence? Did Haman as a noble of Persia possibly ever see himself as deposing the king and being installed as a monarch himself? Haman was undoubtedly a man consumed with ambition, and whose negative traits have lived on throughout history.

Anti-Semitism in the world pre-dated the arrival of Yeshua the Messiah by many centuries. The Book of Esther only gives us a small snapshot of the attitudes that other people have had toward the Jews. Haman manipulated King Xerxes to get him to sign the Jews' death warrant. But in the end as the Jews are saved, they stand up for themselves and are authorized by the government to take care of their enemies. The Jews do not play the role of the victim, instead taking preemptive action and targeting those who would do them harm. What might this teach us about not only when Jews stand up for themselves today—here on the other side of the Holocaust—but when we as Believers might be tempted to be a little too pacifistic? What might this teach us about our spirituality as Messianics, when we might be tempted to victimize ourselves because we have been treated badly? What kinds of specific actions can we take to defend ourselves?

Perhaps the most overlooked theme is the role that Esther plays not only as the person able to save her people, but as a woman. Throughout the history of the Bible, it is not as though God *will* use women; **God uses women.** Esther is one of many significant heroines in the Scriptures who are used by the Lord in a mighty way. Yet, far from Esther being a radical feminist, she works within the rules laid out by the Persian establishment, winning the favor of the king. Esther uses her God-given intellect to lay a clever trap for Haman. And, at the end Esther is able to introduce King Xerxes to Mordecai who is then placed in a position second only to his own. The Book of Esther should teach every Messianic male to respect women and highly value the role that they play, as Esther was directly responsible not only for the salvation of the Jewish people—but for eliminating a direct threat to her husband in Haman. Without Esther, the Jewish people could have been annihilated and there would have been no Messiah Yeshua born to save the world!

As you can see, the Book of Esther teaches us much, much more than what is captured in the *Purim* play. While it is good to have a laugh, and indeed God gave us as human beings a sense of humor, Esther is still a very serious story. Esther is a life and death account about how easy it was for the Persian king to be manipulated into thinking that the Jews must be eliminated. Esther teaches us about a very old problem in anti-Semitism that continues to this very day. Yet, it also shows how God orchestrates things behind the scenes, and uses willing vessels to accomplish His salvation history. Like Esther and Mordecai, each one of us can be used by Him for circumstances that require a voice of reason, a temperament of compassion, or a fiery protester who will stand firm for what is right. What message does the Book of Esther teach you? Is it something that will last far behind the holiday of *Purim*?[8]

---

[8] Consult the entry for the Book of Esther in *A Survey of the Tanach for the Practical Messianic* for a summary of its date, composition, etc.

Messianic Spring Holiday Helper

~3~

A Summarization
of Passover Traditions

Margaret McKee Huey and J.K. McKee

The Spring festivals of Passover and Unleavened Bread are an extremely important time of observance and reflection in Jewish communities all over the world. It is a time of both communal and family fellowship, where one often observes the Passover meal with a congregation or synagogue, in addition to extended family. This is the time when the Jewish people commemorate *zeman heruteinu* or the "Season of our freedom." Every morning Exodus 20:2 is to be remembered, which admonishes us, "I am the LORD your God, who brought you out of the land of Egypt, out of the house of slavery." Even though non-Jewish Believers, who were not raised in the Synagogue or necessarily exposed to Passover since their youth, can feel separated during this time of traditional observance, Rabbi J.H. Hertz indicates that the story of the Passover is something that all of humanity partakes of in one way or another. He observes,

"The primal word of Israel's Divine Message is the proclamation of the One God as the God of Freedom. The recognition of God as the God of Freedom illumines the whole of human history for us. In the light of this truth, history becomes one continuous Divine revelation of the gradual growth of freedom and justice on earth."[1]

Certainly, when Believers in Messiah Yeshua sit down to partake of the Passover meal, we are not just remembering the Exodus of the Ancient Israelites and the plagues that God dispensed upon the Egyptians. We are sitting down to remember great events in the salvation history of the world. The primary event we remember is the slaying of the Passover lamb, God's mercy toward His people in Egyptian bondage, and how He led them to freedom through the Red Sea. This is a heritage that all those who follow the God of Abraham, Isaac, and Jacob partake of, as the Apostle Paul writes, "For I do not want you to be unaware, brethren, that our fathers were all under the cloud and all passed through the sea" (1 Corinthians 10:1).

---

[1] J.H. Hertz, ed., *Pentateuch & Haftorahs* (London: Soncino Press, 1960), 295.

But Passover takes on an all new depth and dimension for us when we understand that Yeshua and His Disciples partook of the *seder* meal prior to His arrest and crucifixion. And of course, the elements of the Passover typify His redemptive sacrifice for us on the cross. But how did Yeshua actually observe Passover? Biblically speaking, there are only two principal elements of the Passover meal: the lamb (Leviticus 23:5; Numbers 28:16) and *matzah* or unleavened bread (Leviticus 23:6; Numbers 28:17). Of course, by the First Century C.E. some distinct traditions regarding Passover had advanced, which found their way onto the *seder* plate of Yeshua. Certainly since then, as the Second Temple was destroyed and as the Jewish people have been dispersed all over the world, new traditions have developed in the new places where many found themselves. As Messianic Believers, what place are these traditions to have in our Passover observance? How important is it for us to understand some of them, so that we might be enriched and encouraged?

The Search for Leaven

The observance of Passover often begins several days before the day of Passover with a search for leavened items in one's home that are to be removed. Exodus 12:19-20 clearly admonishes us, "Seven days there shall be no leaven found in your houses; for whoever eats what is leavened, that person shall be cut off from the congregation of Israel, whether *he is* an alien or a native of the land. You shall not eat anything leavened; in all your dwellings you shall eat unleavened bread." The eating of unleavened items is a memorial to the Exodus, where the Israelites had to eat *matzah* (מַצָּה) because not enough time was available to allow bread to rise (Exodus 12:34). The possession of *chametz* (חָמֵץ) or leaven[2] in one's home is forbidden, although various traditions have arisen to account for how this is to be observed. Some of these traditions bear in mind how sanitization has changed since the time of the Exodus.

An educational custom that has developed in the Jewish community is *bedikat chametz* or the "search for leaven." The Mishnah specifies "On the night preceding the fourteenth [of Nisan] they seek out leaven by the light of a candle" (m.*Pesachim* 1:1).[3] It dates back to Second Temple times as an activity often to participate in with small children. While most of the leaven in one's house has already been removed, parents will often hide pieces of bread or leavened items for the children to find. The search for leavened items in ancient times often was undertaken with the use of a candle, feather, and wooden spoon, even though a flashlight is often substituted today for safety. Customarily, after the leaven is gathered, it is either thrown out or burned in a fire. In more modern times, however, "Many religious Jews simply seal cupboards that contain hametz (leaven) with tape, unsealing them again when the festivities are over."[4]

In Jewish thought, the presence of leaven is often likened to the presence of sin in one's life or household. Ronald L. Eisenberg notes, "The Rabbis regarded

---

[2] Also known in the Hebrew Scriptures as *seor* (שְׂאֹר); in the Greek LXX and Apostolic Scriptures as *zumē* (ζύμη).

[3] Jacob Neusner, trans., *The Mishnah: A New Translation* (New Haven and London: Yale University Press, 1988), 229.

[4] Marlena Spieler, *Jewish Cooking: The Traditions, Techniques, Ingredients, and Recipes* (London: Hermes House, 2003), 31.

hametz as the symbol of the evil inclination."[5] Rabbinical tradition regards leaven as sin, because just as the presence of yeast can cause fermentation to occur in dough, so can the presence of sin in one's heart cause one to puff up and become prideful, haughty, and arrogant. The Talmud explains this further:

"*And when R. Alexandri had finished saying his Prayer, this is what he said:* Lord of the ages, it is perfectly obvious to you that our will is to do your will. But what prevents it? **It is the leaven in the dough, the subjugation to the pagan kingdoms.** May it be pleasing before you, O Lord our God, to save us from their power so that we may return to carry out the rules that please you with a whole heart" (b.*Berachot* 17a).[6]

This concurs precisely with what the Apostle Paul writes the Galatians, *prior to the composition of the Talmud*, in his reflection of their "Torah observance" with improper intentions: "A little yeast leavens the whole batch of dough" (Galatians 5:9, NRSV).[7] In his admonitions to the Corinthians, he emphasizes that when one observes Passover, a person must strive to eliminate sin—represented by leaven—because Yeshua has come to remove the leaven from us by His sacrifice:

"Clean out the old leaven so that you may be a new lump, just as you are *in fact* unleavened. For Messiah our Passover also has been sacrificed. Therefore let us celebrate the feast, not with old leaven, nor with the leaven of malice and wickedness, but with the unleavened bread of sincerity and truth" (1 Corinthians 5:7-8).

Even though diligent searches are often made for leaven in Jewish homes during Passover, certain practices have arisen in various communities that may be considered of a "questionable nature" by some. One occurrence, in particular, is the practice of selling leaven to a Gentile through an intermediary such as a rabbi. A person or family may collect all leavened items from one's house and then sell it, for a limited time, to a non-Jew, only to buy it back when Passover is completed. But before you condemn this as being an outright circumvention of the Torah, how this custom possibly developed is detailed in the Talmud:

"*For* said Rabin bar R. Ada, 'There was the case of someone who deposited a saddlebag full of leaven with Yohanan of Haquq, and rats made holes in it, and leaven burst out. He came before Rabbi. At the first hour, he said to him, "Wait," at the second, "Wait," at the third, "Wait," at the fourth, "Wait", at the fifth, "Go, sell it in the market."' *Doesn't this mean, to gentiles, and the ruling accords with the position of R. Judah?* Said R. Joseph, 'No, it means, to Israelites, in accord with the position of R. Meir.' *Said to him Abbayye, 'If it is to Israelites, then why shouldn't he keep it for himself?'* It is because of suspicion [that he doesn't keep it for himself], for it has been taught on Tannaite authority: **If the charity fund collectors run out of poor among whom to distribute the money, they change the small change into large coins [to protect the money] with outsiders, but not out of their own funds.** If supervisors of the soup kitchen run out of poor to feed, they may sell the food to others but not to themselves, since it is said, 'And you shall be guiltless towards the Lord and towards Israel' (Num. 32:22). *Said R. Ada bar Mattenah to R. Joseph, 'You*

---

[5] Eisenberg, 269.

[6] *The Babylonian Talmud: A Translation and Commentary.*

[7] The Galatians' improper Torah observance is explored in the commentary *Galatians for the Practical Messianic* by J.K. McKee.

explicitly said to us: **Go and sell it to gentiles**, in accord with the position of R. Judah'" (b.*Pesachim* 13a).[8]

What we see here is that the custom of selling leaven to Gentiles before Passover was originally intended to be an alternative practice, when such items could not be given to the poor. Originally, leavened items were to be given to the poor outside the community of Israel, and if not given, could be sold, but subsequent later generations interpreted these rulings as allowing for a temporary sale.

Of course, the ramifications for us today regard what we are to do when we remove the leavened items from our homes as Messianic Believers. Are we simply to throw them all away, assuming that we do not eat them several weeks before Passover? Or, are there needy people or food banks that we could donate these items to? That is certainly what the original purpose of the Talmud's ruling on leaven was intended to consider.

The Seder Centerpiece

The principal elements of observing Passover by far are found on the *seder* plate. The Hebrew word *seder* (סֵדֶר) literally means "order," as we recall the story of Passover and its significance. In the Book of Exodus, only two specific commands are given regarding the *seder*. We are first told to eat *matzah* or unleavened bread for a period of seven days: "In the first *month*, on the fourteenth day of the month at evening, you shall eat unleavened bread, until the twenty-first day of the month at evening" (Exodus 12:18). Secondly, we are told to recall the events that have taken place leading up to this observance: "You shall tell your son on that day, saying, 'It is because of what the LORD did for me when I came out of Egypt'" (Exodus 13:8).

Additional Rabbinical injunctions, most of which were present during the time of Yeshua, add the elements of drinking four cups of wine (b.*Pesachim* 99b), eating *maror* (מָרוֹר) or bitter herbs (b.*Pesachim* 116b), and finally reciting praise or *hallel* (הַלֵּל) at various times during the meal (b.*Pesachim* 117b).

We see these various elements present in the Passover *seder* of Yeshua, although perhaps not as refined as they are today in the Jewish community. Yeshua and His Disciples drink wine at their *seder* (Matthew 26:27), they would have partaken of the bitter herbs as did the rest of the Jews of the time, and they sang a designated praise after their meal (Matthew 26:30; Mark 14:26). We see these same things present in the *seder* services throughout the Messianic community today, as Messianic Judaism has largely adapted these traditions, and new traditions that have been added since the First Century, and re-interpreted them in a Yeshua-oriented light.

There are some major symbols of Passover that are present on *seder* plates all throughout the Jewish community. The first of these is the *zeroa* (זְרוֹעַ) or shankbone of a lamb. The Hebrew term *zeroa* has a variety of meanings, including, "**arm, shoulder, strength**" (*BDB*).[9] The Talmud rules, "R. Joseph says, 'There have to be two kinds of meat, one in memory of the Passover-offering, the other in

---

[8] *The Babylonian Talmud: A Translation and Commentary.*

[9] Francis Brown, S.R. Driver, and Charles A. Briggs, *A Hebrew and English Lexicon of the Old Testament* (Oxford: Clarendon Press, 1979), 283.

memory of the festal-offering.' *Rabina said, 'Even a bone and its broth'"* (b.*Pesachim* 114b).[10] The shankbone is placed on the *seder* plate in memory of the Lord's decree that "I will also redeem you with an outstretched arm and with great judgments" (Exodus 6:6). The Hebrew for "outstretched arm" is *zeroa netuyah* (זְרוֹעַ נְטוּיָה).

It is notable that there are divergent practices among the Sephardic and Askenazic Jewish communities as it relates to Passover and whether or not lamb is allowed to be eaten. Ashkenazic Jewry (Northern, Central, and Eastern European) does not eat lamb at Passover. This is based on the Biblical command, "You are not allowed to sacrifice the Passover in any of your towns which the LORD your God is giving you; but at the place where the LORD your God chooses to establish His name, you shall sacrifice the Passover in the evening at sunset, at the time that you came out of Egypt" (Deuteronomy 16:5-6). Because this is a clear reference to the Temple in Jerusalem, and since the Temple has been destroyed, Ashkenazic Jewish *halachah* prohibits the consumption of lamb at Passover, and instead allows for poultry. Sephardic Jewry (Spain, North Africa, and Arab lands) does permit lamb to be eaten at Passover, as a memorial to the Exodus. Messianic Jewish practice is often divided as to whether or not someone was raised Ashkenazic or Sephardic. A viable *halachah* for Messianic non-Jews is frequently debated.

Other objects placed upon the *seder* plate include *karpas*, a fresh green vegetable, typically parsley. Often dipped in salt water early in the Passover meal, it is to symbolize the new life that came forth from the tears of the Ancient Israelites (b.*Pesachim* 114a). *Charoset* (or *charoses*) is a paste of chopped fruit, nuts, wine, and spices (with many variant recipes), symbolizing the mortar that was used by the Ancient Israelites to make bricks. The *beitzah* or roasted egg symbolizes the hardness of Pharaoh's heart, employing a widely-available element that all Jewish communities could agree was "kosher" for Passover.

In the *seder* service itself, a common practice is for all the participants to wash their hands, indicating that one has eliminated impurities (b.*Pesachim* 115a). Throughout the meal, the *magid* is a recitation of the events of the Exodus, and in some Jewish communities the *seder* plate is lifted up to reveal the *matzah* hiding underneath. In Second Temple times, what would become known as the *Rabban Gamaliel Hayah Omeir* or "Rabban Gamaliel would say," was a required act where the three main elements of the *seder* would be explained: the Passover sacrifice, the unleavened bread, and the bitter herbs (m.*Pesachim* 10:5). Of course, what is notable about this instruction, is that it was delivered by the principal teacher of the Apostle Paul (Acts 22:3). Certainly, in any Messianic teaching on Passover, we need not overlook these three things.

Wine (Heb. *yayin*, יַיִן) is a major element during the *seder* meal, obviously as it is to symbolize the blood of the Passover lamb. In the Passover traditions of Second Temple times, four cups of wine were to be consumed by participants in the meal (m.*Pesachim* 10:1). There are a variety of views in the Jewish community as to what these cups mean. The Midrash holds to the principal view among the Rabbis (*Exodus Rabbah* 6:4), which is that they represent four different expressions of God's deliverance used in the Exodus: (1) removal from burden, (2) deliverance from bondage, (3) redemption, (4) restoration. These are derived from Exodus 6:6-

---

[10] *The Babylonian Talmud: A Translation and Commentary.*

7, where the Lord tells Israel He will remove them from Egypt, and fulfill His promises to their ancestors:

"Say, therefore, to the sons of Israel, 'I am the LORD, and I will bring you out from under the burdens of the Egyptians, and I will deliver you from their bondage. I will also redeem you with an outstretched arm and with great judgments. Then I will take you for My people, and I will be your God; and you shall know that I am the LORD your God, who brought you out from under the burdens of the Egyptians.'"

There are some other views of what the four cups of wine at Passover represent, including the four times that Pharaoh's cup is mentioned in the story of the butler, who brought Joseph before him to accurately interpret his dreams (Genesis 40:11, 13). Another view is that they represent the four kingdoms (Babylon, Persia, Greece, and Rome) that oppressed Israel. An additional interpretation is that they represents four worlds: this world, the days of the Messiah, the revival of the dead, and the world to come. One common practice during the *seder* is to drip drops of wine onto one's plate to remember the ten plagues that God delivered upon Egypt (Exodus 7:14-11:10; 12:29-33).

In more modern traditions, a fifth cup of wine has been added called the Cup of Elijah, who is to come and herald the Messianic Age (cf. Malachi 4:5). Messianic Believers sometimes will include the Cup of Elijah, as it is believed that Elijah or a type of Elijah will be one of the Two Witnesses of Revelation, but is not always included as others think that the typology has been completely fulfilled by John the Baptist (cf. Matthew 17:10-13; Mark 9:11-13).

In the specific *halachah* pertaining to the wine and Passover *seder*, red wine is preferred as it mimics the appearance of blood (b.*Pesachim* 108b). However, white wine is not prohibited as some Jewish communities in Europe had various "blood" accusations levied against them during the Middle Ages, and found it easier to use white wine for the *seder* meal.

In the *seder* meal, it is also not uncommon to consume the *korech*, a sandwich that is made of *matzah* and *moror*, in observance of Numbers 9:11: "In the second month on the fourteenth day at twilight, they shall observe it; they shall eat it with unleavened bread and bitter herbs." This practice was instituted by Rabbi Hillel (b.*Pesachim* 115a), who pre-dated Yeshua the Messiah, thus making it a common institution in Second Temple times (and hence the common nomenclature for it, the "Hillel sandwich"). The Apostle Paul certainly would have been trained to partake of the *korech* in his Rabbinical training by Gamaliel, who was Hillel's grandson.

It is notable that three pieces of *matzah* are placed on the *seder* table and are present throughout the entire meal. What these three pieces represent has been interpreted differently in the Jewish community as possibly representing the three divisions of Israel (*cohen*/priest, Levite, Israelite), the three Patriarchs (Abraham, Isaac, and Jacob), and the "three measures of fine flour" (Genesis 18:6) used by Sarah to make cakes for the three Divine visitors (Genesis 18:6), who according to tradition came on what would become the night of Passover.

Messianic views surrounding what the three *matzot* mean often concur with the third view, and are commonly reinterpreted as representing the Divine manifestations of Father, Son, and Holy Spirit in the Godhead.[11] In some Jewish communities today, however, a fourth piece of *matzah* has been added, sometimes representing "those Jews who still live under oppressive regimes and lack the freedom to openly practice their religion."[12] At the beginning of the *seder* meal, the leader is to take the middle *matzah* and break it in two. Half of this broken *matzah* is hidden and it becomes the *afikoman*. In the Messianic community, this has been interpreted as representing Yeshua's death, burial, and resurrection for us, as the *afikoman* is to come forth at the end of the meal. It is thought that at the end of the meal, Yeshua held up the *afikoman* and said "This is My body."

The most important aspect of Passover as emphasized in the Jewish tradition is stated in the Mishnah. It is the belief that "In every generation a person is duty-bound to regard himself as if he personally has gone forth from Egypt...therefore we are duty-bound to thank, praise, glorify, honor, exalt, extol, and bless him who did for our forefathers and for us all these miracles. He brought us forth from slavery to freedom, anguish to joy, mourning to festival, darkness to great light, subjugation to redemption, so we should say before him, Hallelujah" (m.*Pesachim* 10:5).[13] When you celebrate Passover, personalize what you are remembering not only for what it means to be delivered from Egypt, but what it means to be delivered from the bondage of sin to the freedom you now experience in the Lord Yeshua.

The Haggadah

Each person partaking of the *seder* meal is often given his or her own *haggadah*, or order of service, to follow, based on the command of Exodus 13:8 for parents to tell their children about Israel's deliverance from Egypt. Between the first Passover in Egypt to the Passovers kept in the Land of Israel, coupled with the division and dispersion of Israel, and later with a vast Diaspora Jewish community by the time of Yeshua, the celebration of Passover advanced substantially. By the time of Yeshua, the specific order of service for Passover became codified in the Haggadah of Passover, first referred to in the Mishnah. This was focused around a midrashic interpretation of Deuteronomy 26:5-9, which allowed for one to recline and remember the mighty deeds God performed before the Egyptians in delivering Israel:

"You shall answer and say before the LORD your God, 'My father was a wandering Aramean, and he went down to Egypt and sojourned there, few in number; but there he became a great, mighty and populous nation. And the Egyptians treated us harshly and afflicted us, and imposed hard labor on us. Then we cried to the LORD, the God of our fathers, and the LORD heard our voice and saw our affliction and our toil and our oppression; and the LORD brought us out of Egypt with a mighty hand and an outstretched arm and with great terror and with signs and wonders; and He has brought us to this place and has given us this land, a land flowing with milk and honey.'"

We see elements of the traditional Jewish Passover of the First Century included in Yeshua's Last Supper, and some slight deviations. The *Dictionary of*

---

[11] Consult the FAQ on the Messianic Apologetics website, "Trinity." Also to consider is Brian Edgar, *The Message of the Trinity* (Downers Grove, IL: InterVarsity, 2004).

[12] Eisenberg, 285.

[13] Neusner, *Mishnah*, 250.

Judaism in the Biblical Period summarizes the central elements of Passover contained in the Haggadah:

"The ritual found in the Haggadah is first referred to in M. Pesaḥim, chapter 10, which describes a festival meal marked by a set order of foods and a required liturgy (seder). At the heart of the meal is an explanation of the significance of three foods (unleavened bread, bitter herbs, and the passover offering) and the recitation of the Hallel-psalms. In early Amoraic times, this basic ceremony was embellished through the addition of a discussion of Israelite history, leading up to and including captivity in Egypt. In later developments, continuing to the present, liturgical poems and other homilies have been added to the basic format set in talmudic times."[14]

Today, we obviously see a wide variation of Passover customs and traditions present in the Jewish community and in Messianic Judaism. There are significant variations between Sephardic and Ashkenazic Jews, as well as between Orthodox, Conservative, and Reform (or Progressive) Judaism. The Passover *haggadah* (הַגָּדָה) is something that has been adapted and changed by each denomination of Judaism, as some *haggadah*s include an all-night service, where one stays awake and focuses on certain Scriptures, to those that are only focused around a meal at one's home with family and close friends. There are traditions present in Passover today that are unique to the lands where the Jewish people have been scattered. Messianic Judaism has adapted many of these traditions to form its own Passover *haggadah*s, which demonstrate how we are to rejoice in God delivering Israel from Egypt, and Yeshua delivering us from the bondage of sin.

The Four Questions

A significant part of the *seder* that dates back to Second Temple times (m.*Pesachim* 10:4) is the recitation of the four questions, all asked with the Hebrew phrase *mah nishtanah*, "What is different?" While these questions are customarily asked by small children today or the youngest participant in the *seder*, originally they were probably asked by the leader of the *seder*, in order for the adults to contemplate throughout the service. There are some varied Ashkenazic and Sephardic rituals observed when these four questions are asked. The Ashkenazic order of these questions is the more common one practiced in American Jewry, and consequently also the Messianic movement. Each one of these questions focuses around the *seder* meal and its uniqueness:

1. On all other nights we eat either *chametz* or *matzah*. Why, on this night, do we eat only *matzah*?
2. On all other nights we eat all kinds of vegetables. Why, on this night, must we eat bitter herbs?
3. On all other nights we do not usually dip vegetables even once. Why, on this night, do we dip twice?
4. On all other nights we eat sitting upright or reclining. Why, on this night do we eat reclining?[15]

In the Sephardic tradition, "the order of the four questions is dipping, matzah, bitter herbs, and reclining."[16] Regardless of how these four questions are ordered,

---

[14] Jacob Neusner and William Scott Green, eds., *Dictionary of Judaism in the Biblical Period* (Peabody, MA: Hendrickson, 2002), pp 266-267.

[15] Op. cit. in Eisenberg, pp 277-278.

they have developed as a way of instructing children to reflect on the significance of Passover. What is notable, is that as these four questions are asked, participants in the *seder* meal are to customarily recline, even though at the first Passover the Israelites were to eat with their loins girded and in haste (Exodus 12:11). As Eisenberg explains, "during the celebration of freedom at the seder, Jews...dramatize their status as free human beings."[17] Those who are in slavery do not have the luxury of reclining at the table as being free from bondage. This is a custom that the Messiah Himself practiced, as the Gospels attest, "Yeshua was reclining *at the table* with the twelve disciples" (Matthew 26:20; cf. Mark 14:18; Luke 24:30) during His Last Supper Passover observance.

Miscellaneous Traditions

There are some miscellaneous traditions that also exist in the Jewish community, but are not practiced by all during the Passover season. Those who hold to an allegorical interpretation of the Song of Songs will often meditate on this text as it is perceived as being a "love story" between God and Israel.[18] The *dayenu* song of "it is enough" is commonly sung at most Passover *seders*, recounting in musical form the hardships of the Israelites and the thankfulness that we are to have for God delivering us from bondage.[19] Finally, almost all *seders* would be incomplete without the *nirtzah* prayer, a concluding plea to God to send the Messiah so that all in the Jewish community might be able to celebrate it in Jerusalem next year.[20]

Of these three final traditions, the most significant for us as Messianic Believers is the prayer for the Messiah to come soon. Unlike most in the Jewish community, we know that the Messiah has come in the Person of the Lord Yeshua. He observed Passover with His Disciples the evening He was betrayed, only to later be tried as a common criminal and executed upon a Roman cross. Yeshua in His death became our Passover Lamb, slain for the sins of the entire world. As He said on that evening almost 2,000 years ago, "But I tell you, from this moment I will not drink of this fruit of the vine until that day when I drink it in a new way in My Father's kingdom with you" (Matthew 26:29, HCSB; cf. Mark 14:25; Luke 22:18). We are still awaiting to find out what that "new way" actually is.

Between now and then, as the emerging Messianic movement grows and expands, many questions will be asked about how we are to observe Passover, what traditions we should incorporate into our celebration, whether or not Ashkenazic or Sephardic *halachah* is best for us, and of course many unforeseen things that we can presently only speculate about. There will be variance in the Messianic community and among Messianic brothers and sisters about how Passover is to be observed. There are many Jewish customs and traditions that are

---

[16] Ibid., 278.

[17] Ibid.

[18] Traditional Christian exegesis of Song of Songs similarly regards it as a "love story" between "Christ and His church." Eisenberg is keen to note that "some modern scholars reject this idea because of the complexity of its language" (p 271), and instead accept it as being a love poem between Solomon and his wives. The authors of this article lean very heavily toward this interpretation as well. Consult the entry for Song of Songs in *A Survey of the Tanach for the Practical Messianic*.

[19] Joseph Tabory, *JPS Commentary on the Haggadah* (Philadelphia: Jewish Publication Society, 2008), pp 97-98.

[20] Ibid., pp 122-135.

edifying to the Body of Messiah that ministries like ours believe should not be ignored, and have been integrated into our commemoration.

Just like every Jewish family or community has developed its own Passover customs, in the many diverse lands to which the Jewish people have been spread, do not hesitate to develop some of your own traditions, recipes, or customs if you are not Jewish. If you do this, however, recognize the freedom that others have to adopt an Ashkenazic-style or Sephardic-style *halachah*. More than anything else, whatever you do, do it to the glory of the Lord, and let Him be the focus of your observance. Remember the Last Supper He conducted with His Disciples, and in your partaking of the Passover meal, do it to His glory!

~4~

Passover: A Sign to Remember

Mark Huey

"The blood shall be a sign for you on the houses where you live; and when I see the blood I will pass over you, and no plague will befall you to destroy *you* when I strike the land of Egypt. Now this day will be a memorial to you, and you shall celebrate it *as* a feast to the LORD; throughout your generations you are to celebrate it *as* a permanent ordinance" (Exodus 12:13-14).

When we consider the Spring feasts of the Lord, which begin with the remembrance of Passover and the Festival of Unleavened Bread, we are reminded that one of the reasons that we observe these holidays is because it is a sign of our obedience to God's commandments. In the Book of Exodus, we are introduced to the "sign" depicted in the appointed time that has been called *Pesach* (פֶּסַח) or Passover, and it is to be remembered "as an institution for all time" (NJPS).[1]

Amazingly, in spite of the clear language stated in this passage about the concept of "forever," or perhaps "perpetual" (NRSV), a significant number of those who serve the God of Abraham, Isaac, and Jacob—unfortunately do not follow the prescription to remember the Passover. This tragedy is one that is quite perplexing. Thankfully, in recent years the re-introduction of Passover *seders*, and an overall renewed interest in the Old Testament on the part of many evangelical Christians, is being used by the Ruach HaKodesh or Holy Spirit to ignite an insatiable blaze for truth inside the hearts of many.

What is it about this particular sign that in and of itself is so life changing? Is it possible that the Holy One really does want His children to remember the trauma of the Ancient Israelites' Exodus from Egypt—and what it required in terms of human life—in order to get our undivided attention? Certainly, there are few things as moving as the mental image of an unblemished, innocent lamb being slaughtered, in order to prevent the angel of death from visiting your home. To have this lamb's blood painted on the doorposts and lintels of your home as an act of obedience, and a sign that this home has been protected, is extremely thought provoking. **It is an extremely powerful image of the work accomplished by our Messiah Yeshua at Golgotha** (Calvary).

One should clearly see that God in His infinite wisdom knew that the repetitive nature of the annual Festival of Unleavened Bread, preceded by the

---

[1] Heb. *chuqqat olam techagguhu* (חֻקַּת עוֹלָם תְּחָגֻּהוּ).

celebration of Passover, would for generations be a wonderful illustration pointing directly to the required sacrificial work of Yeshua. Each year as the families of Israel would gather to remember the deliverance from their bondage as slaves in Egypt, these observances would focus their attention upon the Lord's hand of salvation, and the various initial steps taken to receive His loving protection. The timing of this sign of remembrance is coordinated with the physical reality of the renaissance that takes place each Spring. When you read about the Exodus and the details of what the Israelites did as they prepared to depart Egypt, you can glean the steps that are often included in various Jewish *haggadahs* that have been compiled to follow during the order of service, or *seder* (סֵדֶר), that commemorates these events.

Lamentably, not all followers of the God of Israel over the centuries have been faithfully following the command to remember this event, even though it is critical instruction from the heart of our Heavenly Father. The enemy of our souls, knowing the power of the repetitive celebration of Passover with all its imagery, has worked diligently to rob many of the blessings that come from observing it. HaSatan knows that if the community of faith discontinues this permanent sign of God's faithfulness, the possibility of deterring His true works is increased dramatically. He also knows that to the Jewish people, "signs" have always meant something, as Paul indicates in 1 Corinthians 1:22, "Jews demand miraculous signs and Greeks look for wisdom" (NIV).

It is signs like Passover, circumcision (Genesis 17:11), the *Shabbat* rest (Exodus 31:13), the virgin birth of the Messiah (Isaiah 7:14), and a multitude of others that declare that the LORD God is the Creator of the universe. This is one of the reasons why the enemy does not want us to remember Passover. The enemy wants us to be weak, and not be enriched in our faith.

Passover Hiatus

When we go back and analyze some of the history of remembering Passover, we discover that the people of Israel neglected this celebration for long periods of time in the Bible. This is perhaps understandable because one of the last references to the Passover that is recorded in the Torah comes when Moses gives more specific instructions about where it is to be celebrated. Two times Moses states that the Passover sacrifice should be made in the place of the Lord's choosing:

"Observe the month of Abib and celebrate the Passover to the LORD your God, for in the month of Abib the LORD your God brought you out of Egypt by night. **You shall sacrifice the Passover to the LORD your God from the flock and the herd, in the place where the LORD chooses to establish His name.** You shall not eat leavened bread with it; seven days you shall eat with it unleavened bread, the bread of affliction (for you came out of the land of Egypt in haste), so that you may remember all the days of your life the day when you came out of the land of Egypt. For seven days no leaven shall be seen with you in all your territory, and none of the flesh which you sacrifice on the evening of the first day shall remain overnight until morning. **You are not allowed to sacrifice the Passover in any of your towns which the LORD your God is giving you; but at the place where the LORD your God chooses to establish His name, you shall sacrifice the Passover in the evening at sunset, at the time that you came out of Egypt**" (Deuteronomy 16:1-6).

Do you think that the Ancient Israelites were somewhat confused about the celebration of the Passover in any other place than where God had established Himself? We know that this is a reference to what would later be the Temple Mount in Jerusalem. So today, does this mean that the *only* place we can celebrate the Passover is in Jerusalem, where the Tabernacle/Temple once stood before the Lord? *I do not think so.* We might not sacrifice a lamb to remember the Passover, but we should make an effort to memorialize the work of God.

Surely over the centuries, these verses have been used by some to justify eliminating the celebration of Passover unless you can physically be in Jerusalem on the Temple Mount, conducting the prescribed sacrifice of an unblemished lamb, in order to comply with all of the originally-stated requirements. But as we know, ignoring the Passover completely would take away from the imperative for God's people to remember the events of the Exodus as a memorial throughout their generations. The practical need and benefits of having a Passover meal, in one's home or with one's fellowship or congregation as a permanent ordinance, would be eliminated from the community of Israel scattered abroad.

As we search a little further into the Biblical record, we discover that in the days of Joshua, the Israelites observed the Passover on the plains of Jericho. Initially, as they were first conquering the Promised Land, the memorial was honored:

"While the sons of Israel camped at Gilgal they observed the Passover on the evening of the fourteenth day of the month on the desert plains of Jericho. On the day after the Passover, on that very day, they ate some of the produce of the land, unleavened cakes and parched *grain*" (Joshua 5:10-11).

We do not see a further reference to the Passover in the Scriptures until the reign of King Hezekiah, who ruled the Southern Kingdom of Judah from approximately 727-696 B.C.E. But this does not mean that the celebration of the Passover and the Festival of Unleavened Bread did not re-occur until the reign of King Hezekiah. Two references from the time of King Hezekiah, and his great-grandson King Josiah, seem to indicate that the observance of Passover continued until the time that Israel was transitioning from a nation served by judges, to one ruled by a physical king:

"Surely such a Passover had not been celebrated from the days of the judges who judged Israel, nor in all the days of the kings of Israel and of the kings of Judah" (2 Kings 23:22).

"There had not been celebrated a Passover like it in Israel since the days of Samuel the prophet; nor had any of the kings of Israel celebrated such a Passover as Josiah did with the priests, the Levites, all Judah and Israel who were present, and the inhabitants of Jerusalem" (2 Chronicles 35:18).

If you will recall the history of Ancient Israel, the Prophet Samuel was essentially the bridge between the period of the judges of Israel and the kings of Israel. During his lifetime, he anointed King Saul and King David. He was raised in the house of Eli, the high priest of Israel, and was the last "judge" of Israel. When you read the two verses that are reflections of what had happened before the Passover celebrations during the reigns of Kings Hezekiah and Josiah, you might conclude that the last times of celebrating Passover could have been in the era of Saul, David, or perhaps even Solomon. But whatever you conclude, Passover memorials were definitely stopped for a number of generations between the time of those kings and Hezekiah.

Hezekiah Reinstates Passover

King Hezekiah was responsible for reinstating the Passover among the people of the Southern Kingdom. Here are some opening words recorded in 2 Chronicles 29:1-11:

"Hezekiah became king *when he was* twenty-five years old; and he reigned twenty-nine years in Jerusalem. And his mother's name *was* Abijah, the daughter of Zechariah. He did right in the sight of the LORD, according to all that his father David had done. In the first year of his reign, in the first month, he opened the doors of the house of the LORD and repaired them. He brought in the priests and the Levites and gathered them into the square on the east. Then he said to them, 'Listen to me, O Levites. Consecrate yourselves now, and consecrate the house of the LORD, the God of your fathers, and carry the uncleanness out from the holy place. For our fathers have been unfaithful and have done evil in the sight of the LORD our God, and have forsaken Him and turned their faces away from the dwelling place of the LORD, and have turned *their* backs. They have also shut the doors of the porch and put out the lamps, and have not burned incense or offered burnt offerings in the holy place to the God of Israel. Therefore the wrath of the LORD was against Judah and Jerusalem, and He has made them an object of terror, of horror, and of hissing, as you see with your own eyes. For behold, our fathers have fallen by the sword, and our sons and our daughters and our wives are in captivity for this. Now it is in my heart to make a covenant with the Lord GOD of Israel, that His burning anger may turn away from us. My sons, do not be negligent now, for the LORD has chosen you to stand before Him, to minister to Him, and to be His ministers and burn incense."

Here we are told about the righteousness that Hezekiah desired to bring back to the Southern Kingdom of Judah. This led to the reinstatement of Passover during his reign:

"Now Hezekiah sent to all Israel and Judah and wrote letters also to Ephraim and Manasseh, that they should come to the house of the LORD at Jerusalem to celebrate the Passover to the Lord GOD of Israel. For the king and his princes and all the assembly in Jerusalem had decided to celebrate the Passover in the second month, since they could not celebrate it at that time, because the priests had not consecrated themselves in sufficient numbers, nor had the people been gathered to Jerusalem. Thus the thing was right in the sight of the king and all the assembly. So they established a decree to circulate a proclamation throughout all Israel from Beersheba even to Dan, that they should come to celebrate the Passover to the Lord GOD of Israel at Jerusalem. For they had not celebrated *it* in great numbers as it was prescribed" (2 Chronicles 30:1-5).

Interestingly, if you take into consideration the timing of these events and what is being said, you realize that King Hezekiah was actually making the first concerted attempt to reunite an Israel that had been divided. The text states that Hezekiah sent couriers all throughout, from Beersheba to Dan, not only proclaiming that Passover was to be celebrated—but he invites those of the conquered Northern Kingdom who had not been captured by the Assyrians:

"The couriers went throughout all Israel and Judah with the letters from the hand of the king and his princes, even according to the command of the king, saying, 'O sons of Israel, return to the LORD God of Abraham, Isaac and Israel, that He may return to those of you who escaped *and* are left from the hand of the kings of Assyria. Do not be like your fathers and your brothers, who were unfaithful to the Lord GOD of their fathers, so that He made them a horror, as you see. Now do not stiffen your neck like your fathers, but yield to the LORD and enter His sanctuary which He has consecrated forever, and serve the LORD your God, that His burning anger may turn away from you. For if you return to the LORD, your brothers and your sons *will find* compassion before those who led them captive and will return to this land. For the LORD your God is gracious and compassionate, and will not turn *His* face away from you if you return to Him.' So the couriers passed from city to city through the country of Ephraim and Manasseh, and as far as Zebulun, but they laughed them to scorn and mocked them. Nevertheless some men of Asher, Manasseh and Zebulun humbled themselves and came to Jerusalem. The hand of God was also on Judah to give them one heart to do what the king and the princes commanded by the word of the LORD. Now many people were gathered at Jerusalem to celebrate the Feast of Unleavened Bread in the second month, a very large assembly. They arose and removed the altars which *were* in Jerusalem; they also removed all the incense altars and cast *them* into the brook Kidron. Then they slaughtered the Passover *lambs* on the fourteenth of the second month. And the priests and Levites were ashamed of themselves, and consecrated themselves and brought burnt offerings to the house of the LORD" (2 Chronicles 30:6-15).

Even though the feast was being remembered on the fourteenth day of the second month due to the unclean status of many (v. 17), the Scripture states that some survivors from Asher, Manasseh, and Zebulun humbled themselves and came to Jerusalem for the Passover. It must be noted that, "The hand of God was on Judah, too, making them of a single mind [*lev echad*, לֵב אֶחָד] to carry out the command of the king and officers concerning the ordinance of the LORD" (v. 12, NJPS). Judah initiated the reinstitution of the celebration, and they sincerely wanted the Northern Kingdom survivors, recently devastated by Assyria, to come back into fellowship by remembering Passover. **In some respects, this is almost a foreshadowing of what is taking place today around the world, as more and more Messianic Jews are being asked to perform Passover *seders* for many Christians.** I believe that the restoration of Israel that King Hezekiah was by no means able to accomplish, has actually begun in our day.

In fact, when you read a little further, you find that the celebration was so well received by those gathered from Judah, Asher, Manasseh, and Zebulun, that they extended the celebration for an additional seven days:

"Then Hezekiah spoke encouragingly to all the Levites who showed good insight *in the things* of the LORD. So they ate for the appointed seven days, sacrificing peace offerings and giving thanks to the Lord GOD of their fathers. Then the whole assembly decided to celebrate *the feast* another seven days, so they celebrated the seven days with joy. For Hezekiah king of Judah had contributed to the assembly 1,000 bulls and 7,000 sheep, and the princes had contributed to the assembly 1,000 bulls and 10,000 sheep; and a large number of priests consecrated themselves. All the assembly of Judah rejoiced, with the priests and the Levites and all the assembly that came from Israel, both the sojourners who came from the land of Israel and those living in Judah. So there was great joy in Jerusalem, because there was nothing like this in Jerusalem since the days of Solomon the son of David, king of Israel. Then the Levitical priests arose and blessed the people; and their voice was heard and their prayer came to His holy dwelling place, to heaven" (2 Chronicles 30:22-27).

This extended celebration is referred to as bringing great joy and exuberation to all who participated in it: "There was great rejoicing in Jerusalem, for since the time of King Solomon son of David of Israel nothing like it had happened in Jerusalem" (v. 26, NJPS). This statement indicates that there were probably Passover celebrations in the time of Solomon, but none are recorded in the Bible itself. (Although we do have some descriptions of the Temple dedication and other times when Solomon presided over great feasts). Hezekiah was able, for a short season, to bring elements of Israel together to celebrate the Passover, and as a result all those who participated in it were blessed.

Josiah's Renaissance

The next time we discover Passover being celebrated is during the reign of another king, Josiah, who reigned over the Southern Kingdom from approximately 640-609 B.C.E. Between the reigns of Hezekiah and Josiah, ruled two evil kings, Manasseh (697-642 B.C.E.) and Amon (642-640 B.C.E.). During their reigns, the return to idolatry was unchecked. Being evil, they personified what the Southern Kingdom became during their lifetimes. The next significant Passover celebration occurred during the eighteenth year of the reign of King Josiah:

"So all the service of the LORD was prepared on that day to celebrate the Passover, and to offer burnt offerings on the altar of the LORD according to the command of King Josiah. Thus the sons of Israel who were present celebrated the Passover at that time, and the Feast of Unleavened Bread seven days. There had not been celebrated a Passover like it in Israel since the days of Samuel the prophet; nor had any of the kings of Israel celebrated such a Passover as Josiah did with the priests, the Levites, all Judah and Israel who were present, and the inhabitants of Jerusalem. In the eighteenth year of Josiah's reign this Passover was celebrated" (2 Chronicles 35:16-19).

Here we read how during the reign of King Josiah, the celebration of Passover had taken a hiatus since the days of the judges of Israel. But previously, we read the testimony of the fourteen-day Passover celebration during the reign of King Hezekiah some 80-100 years earlier. The Chronicler may not consider the celebration of Passover during the reign of Hezekiah to be a legitimate celebration, as it was late, or he may be working on different traditions being compiled into Biblical history.[2] Another possibility is that this was a very special Passover celebrated, labeled *k'Pesach* (כַּפֶּסַח)—meaning that it had great significance for Josiah's generation. Nevertheless, it is important to note that Passover was reinstituted for a season:

"Then the king commanded all the people saying, 'Celebrate the Passover to the LORD your God as it is written in this book of the covenant.' Surely such a

---

[2] Consult the entries for the Books of Kings and the Books of Chronicles in *A Survey of the Tanach for the Practical Messianic* for a summary of their dates, compositions, comparison and contrast, etc.

Passover had not been celebrated from the days of the judges who judged Israel, nor in all the days of the kings of Israel and of the kings of Judah. But in the eighteenth year of King Josiah, this Passover was observed to the LORD in Jerusalem" (2 Kings 23:21-23).

Earlier in his life, when King Josiah heard the words of the Torah, it so pierced him that he tore his clothes in anguish: "It happened that when the king heard the words of the Scroll of the Torah, he rent his garments" (2 Kings 22:11, ATS). Josiah was so moved by hearing the Word that he began to clean up much of the idolatry that had crept into the Southern Kingdom. Then, when he heard the instruction of the Torah (probably from the Book of Deuteronomy)[3] read to the inhabitants of Jerusalem, he vowed to keep it with all his heart and soul:

"The king went up to the house of the LORD and all the men of Judah and all the inhabitants of Jerusalem with him, and the priests and the prophets and all the people, both small and great; and he read in their hearing all the words of the book of the covenant which was found in the house of the LORD. The king stood by the pillar and made a covenant before the LORD, to walk after the LORD, and to keep His commandments and His testimonies and His statutes with all *his* heart and all *his* soul, to carry out the words of this covenant that were written in this book. And all the people entered into the covenant" (2 Kings 23:2-3).

These events eventually led to the reinstatement of Passover that was referred to earlier. **Can you begin to see that the observance of Passover is something that the enemy wants to stop?** This is the annual sign that reminds us as God's people of His deliverance via the blood of the Lamb. There is no more important theme for us as Believers to understand!

Ezra's Generation

Following the return of the Southern Kingdom of Judah from Babylon, we find righteous men and women of God returning to the celebration. In the Book of Ezra, we are told that the Jewish exiles began to celebrate the Passover and the Festival of Unleavened Bread:

"The exiles observed the Passover on the fourteenth of the first month. For the priests and the Levites had purified themselves together; all of them were pure. Then they slaughtered the Passover *lamb* for all the exiles, both for their brothers the priests and for themselves. The sons of Israel who returned from exile and all those who had separated themselves from the impurity of the nations of the land to *join* them, to seek the Lord GOD of Israel, ate *the Passover*. And they observed the Feast of Unleavened Bread seven days with joy, for the LORD had caused them to rejoice, and had turned the heart of the king of Assyria toward them to encourage them in the work of the house of God, the God of Israel" (Ezra 6:19-22).

Here, we see that during the Festival of Unleavened Bread, the people rejoiced because the king of Assyria had actually encouraged them to work on the house of God.

This is the last reference in the Tanakh of Passover celebration. As you can read, Israel's obedience to the commandment to keep Passover is definitely challenged by its own disobedience, but at times by the external authorities in place. We read in the Book of 1 Maccabees, in the Apocrypha, that the ordinances

---

[3] For a further discussion, consult the article "The Message of Deuteronomy" by J.K. McKee.

and commandments to observe the Sabbath and feasts were definitely forbidden during the Syrian-Greek invasion:

"And the king sent letters by messengers to Jerusalem and the cities of Judah; he directed them to follow customs strange to the land, to forbid burnt offerings and sacrifices and drink offerings in the sanctuary, to profane sabbaths and feasts, to defile the sanctuary and the priests, to build altars and sacred precincts and shrines for idols, to sacrifice swine and unclean animals, and to leave their sons uncircumcised. They were to make themselves abominable by everything unclean and profane, so that they should forget the law and change all the ordinances. And whoever does not obey the command of the king shall die" (1 Maccabees 1:44-50).

The Jewish people were absolutely forbidden on the threat of death if they disobeyed the king's orders. But we know that from our knowledge of the time between the return from exile and the coming of Messiah Yeshua, the Maccabees were able to rise up against the Seleucids, and return the people to the adherence of these commandments.[4]

Yeshua: The Passover Lamb

During the time of Yeshua, we see the celebration of Passover spoken of throughout the Apostolic Scriptures (New Testament), notably by how His family was following the commandment to make the Passover a memorial feast:

"Now His parents went to Jerusalem every year at the Feast of the Passover. And when He became twelve, they went up *there* according to the custom of the Feast" (Luke 2:41-42).

Yeshua not only celebrated Passover, **but He was actually called the Lamb of God,** sacrificed for the redemption of sinful humanity. As John the Immerser declared when he encountered Yeshua at the waters of the Jordan, "Behold, the Lamb of God who takes away the sin of the world!" (John 1:29). Later in His life, Yeshua observed a unique Passover as He prepared to be the sacrificial Lamb Himself, instructing two of His Disciples to prepare the Passover meal for all of them:

"Then came the *first* day of Unleavened Bread on which the Passover *lamb* had to be sacrificed. And Yeshua sent Peter and John, saying, 'Go and prepare the Passover for us, so that we may eat it'" (Luke 22:7-8).

Throughout His life, the Messiah observed and remembered the command to participate in the Passover. As the sacrificial Lamb of God, He fulfilled His word to Nicodemus when He said that He Himself must be lifted up on the cross to die, which would, in and of itself, be a "sign" to all those who had eyes to see and ears to hear: "As Moses lifted up the serpent in the wilderness, even so must the Son of Man be lifted up" (John 3:14).

Remember that Moses lifted up a brazen serpent in the desert to bring healing to those who looked upon it. Those who followed the command to look upon this standard lived. This was a "sign" that, when complied with, healed the venomous bite of the poisonous snakes: "And Moses made a bronze serpent and set it on the standard; and it came about, that if a serpent bit any man, when he looked to the bronze serpent, he lived" (Numbers 21:9).

---

[4] For a further discussion, consult the relevant chapters of the *Messianic Winter Holiday Helper.*

As you can see, "signs" and adherence to them, *can mean the difference between life and death*. Or, they can at least mean the difference between us understanding life and death, and how God's work via His Son, has brought us final deliverance.

The "Signs" We See Today

Believers today are once again considering the Ancient Israelites' Exodus from Egypt, and what it means to those of us who have been delivered from the power of sin by Yeshua. Keep in mind that the born again Believers, ten days after Yeshua's ascension to the right hand of the Father, were then endowed with the indwelling presence of the Holy Spirit or Ruach HaKodesh. Getting these Spirit-filled followers of the Messiah of Israel to stop remembering the "sign" of the first major deliverance after His crucifixion and resurrection, was going to be difficult. Because the new Believers had the supernatural empowerment to obey God's commandments and fulfill Yeshua's Great Commission in the Earth, was there any way to change and/or alter the command?

As the Apostles died off in the First Century, and new leadership came to the emerging Christian Church, the community of Believers steadily veered away from the Hebraic Roots of the faith. Substitute celebrations that recognized the resurrection of the Messiah, but replaced or downplayed the original themes of Passover, began to be instituted.[5] This was complicated by anti-Semitism in the Roman Empire and a strong hostility from the Jewish community to Believers in Yeshua. The replacement of Passover by what we now call "Easter," caused much of the Second and Third Century Church to discard the commandment to keep Passover, one that we are told is to be observed perpetually. It is extremely sad that this tragic series of circumstances took place, and took us away from blessings that come from obedience to our Heavenly Father.

In our day, around the globe, the Lord is restoring to His people the benefits of spending the time to observe and remember what He has accomplished for them. The Father is restoring forgotten truths to His people in the emerging Messianic community, who are being called to partake of the *seder* meal that is once again becoming a "sign" to us all. The Lord is preparing a people who obey His commandments and have a salvation testimony in Yeshua (Revelation 12:17; 14:12). Are you going to be a part of that people? Will you take Passover seriously? What new things might you learn about what He has done for us?

---

[5] Consult the entries "Easter," in David W. Bercot, ed., *A Dictionary of Early Christian Beliefs* (Peabody, MA: Hendrickson, 1998), pp 223-224; "Paschal Controversy," in Ibid., pp 500-501; "Passover, Jewish," in Ibid., 501.

~5~

The Restoration of Passover

Mark Huey

In this hour of restoration, the Holy One of Israel is forging ahead using a variety of circumstances to bring His people into a fuller understanding of Him and His Word. The festival of Passover, or *Pesach* (פֶּסַח) in Hebrew, is being utilized as one of the principal magnets for restoring the Body of Messiah. Yeshua described the reality that the true sheep will hear His voice, to various Pharisees and Disciples gathered centuries ago:

"I am the good shepherd, and I know My own and My own know Me, even as the Father knows Me and I know the Father; and I lay down My life for the sheep. I have other sheep, which are not of this fold; I must bring them also, and they will hear My voice; and they will become one flock *with* one shepherd" (John 10:14-16).

The Lord has never annulled the instruction for His people to remember the Exodus of Ancient Israel from Egypt. The Scriptures are very clear about this commandment, but as history and tradition have revealed, the replacement of a Passover observance by Easter via the Christian Church, has obscured the great blessings that come by obeying this remembrance (Leviticus 23:6-14). Passover and the Feast of Unleavened Bread, which take up eight days in the Spring, have been replaced by one day that recalls the resurrection of the Messiah Yeshua.

The problem is simply this: although the resurrection of our Messiah is of paramount importance in our spiritual understanding, **and remembering it is certainly worthy of our time and reflection,** it would be *far better* to follow our Creator's plan for celebrating this awesome reality. He knows our hearts and proclivity to wander, and He commanded a time of remembrance that would engage our bodies, souls, and spirits over a period of several days, rather than just a few hours of recollection. As Believers today are being exposed to the Biblical admonition to observe Passover and the Feast of Unleavened Bread, the wisdom of following His ways becomes crystal clear. The Lord has been using the proliferation of Passover *seder*s throughout the Christian world to ignite significant interest in Believers' Hebraic Roots, and bless many people in unfathomable ways.

For the past several decades, as the Messianic Jewish movement has gained momentum and exposure, the Holy Spirit has been moving upon many Believers from all types of evangelical denominational backgrounds, to participate in these annual convocations along with Jewish Believers. Dedicated Messianic teachers have been asked to conduct Passover *seder*s in a variety of settings. When the

Messiah's work as the Lamb of God is properly conveyed, these presentations become quite an eye-opener to many who are seeking the ancient paths of the Patriarchs and the Hebraic Roots of our faith.

Testimonies abound from Messianic Believers about how the Lord used a Passover *seder* at a church to encourage further examination and investigation into other topics, such as observing *Shabbat* or the dietary laws. Over the past several years, a rule of thumb that I have personally witnessed is that when ten new people are exposed to a Passover *seder* at a church, at least one of the attendees wants more information concerning the Hebraic Roots of his or her faith. Now, the Spirit of God is amplifying the call to His people, and it appears that the percentages are increasing. Today, many Messianic fellowships and congregations often use these events for an outreach to their communities with varying degrees of success.

A few extremists contend that the Passover is strictly for the family of Believers who are physically circumcised. Arguments can be made for both perspectives.[1] If there is a concern or strong debate, then the recommendation from me would be to encourage family *Pesach* gatherings, preceding a more open communal event. This may be one way to circumvent the problem of those who should and who should not attend.

The firsthand evidence we have witnessed does suggest that many of those first exposed to a Passover *seder* have later been drawn into the Messianic movement. In his letter to the Romans, the Apostle Paul seems to suggest, that by using different events to preach the good news of the Messiah, the Lamb of God, the lost will be found:

"For there is no distinction between Jew and Greek; for the same *Lord* is Lord of all, abounding in riches for all who call on Him; for 'WHOEVER WILL CALL ON THE NAME OF THE LORD WILL BE SAVED.' **How then will they call on Him in whom they have not believed? How will they believe in Him whom they have not heard? And how will they hear without a preacher?** How will they preach unless they are sent? Just as it is written, 'HOW BEAUTIFUL ARE THE FEET OF THOSE WHO BRING GOOD NEWS OF GOOD THINGS!' However, they did not all heed the good news; for Isaiah says, 'LORD, WHO HAS BELIEVED OUR REPORT?'" (Romans 10:12-16).[2]

I believe it is up to the individual assemblies of Believers as to how they believe the Father would have them approach this blessed appointed time of convocation. Yet, Passover is a significant time that Christians can be exposed to our Hebraic Roots—*and* the Messianic community can provoke non-believing Jews to jealousy for faith in Messiah Yeshua!

Pesach and Our Jewish Brethren

While studying through the Torah portions on the annual Rabbinical calendar, you will discover that the Jewish Sages have augmented the importance of Passover and the Feast of Unleavened Bread with some instructive traditions. To the Messianic community of faith, the Jewish people, who were entrusted with the

---

[1] Consult the article "Is Circumcision for Everyone?" by J.K. McKee for a further examination of this divisive topic.

[2] Cf. Joel 2:32; Isaiah 52:7; 53:1.

oracles of God (Romans 3:2), continue to share their wisdom for approaching the Holy One and His precepts.

The remembrance of the Exodus from Egypt is one of the most important events in the annual life of the Jewish community. As the cyclical Torah portions have been synchronized over the ages, the passages which deal specifically with the Exodus just happen to line up with the months preceding Passover. This specific timing allows Torah teachers and students to study and prepare in advance for the yearly remembrance. By considering some specific passages during the Winter months before the month of Aviv/Nisan, hearts are being prepared for the *seder* meal, as Spring arrives and the Earth returns to a newness of life.

To compliment these traditional Torah readings from the Book of Exodus, the Rabbis have recommended a set of Haftarah readings that fall on four designated Sabbaths for special consideration. These are labeled: *Shabbat Shekalim, Shabbat Zachor, Shabbat Parah*, and *Shabbat HaChodesh.* Interestingly enough, when you analyze the timing and the subject matters of these additional Haftarah selections,[3] you can discern that the Lord was indeed guiding the Sages' selection in order to enhance the Passover season.[4]

Shabbat Shekalim
2 Kings 11:21-12:16

First, on the Sabbath that precedes or coincides with the New Moon initiating Adar, the month prior to Aviv/Nisan, *Shabbat Shekalim* (shekels) is celebrated. The Haftarah reading is 2 Kings 11:21-12:16, which is usually complimented by an additional reading of Exodus 30:11-16. The subject being discussed is the commandment regarding the Temple tax of a half-shekel, that in many ways serves as a form of a census of the Israelite males who are twenty years of age and older. If you will recall, the half-shekel tax is not to be burdensome, and is small enough to be affordable to all regardless of their economic status. By making this contribution, which was designated for the service of the Tent of Meeting, the contributors indicate their allegiance to the established order as determined by God.

When you contemplate the choice of the 2 Kings passage that deals with the reinstitution of this "temple tax" by the high priest Jehoaida, some other thoughts intrude. Here we discover that Athaliah, the daughter of Ahab and Jezebel, ruled the Southern Kingdom of Judah for six years after the death of her husband Jehoram and her son Ahaziah. Many forget that the House of David's rule over Judah was interrupted until Joash, the seven-year old son of Ahaziah who was protected from the murderous Queen Mother Athaliah, was crowned king. The wise high priest Jehoaida reestablished the half-shekel contribution as a way to determine who sided with the young king. In many respects, as the Jewish people reflect on this treacherous time and the steps that were taken by the Levites, they can be reminded of the constant perils that seek to destroy the heritage of the Patriarchs.

---

[3] 2 Kings 12:1-12:17; 1 Samuel 15:2-15:34; Ezekiel 36:16-36:38; Ezekiel 45:16-46:18.

[4] Consult Nosson Scherman and Meir Zlotowitz, eds., *Complete ArtScroll Siddur, Nusach Ashkenaz* (Brooklyn: Mesorah Publications, 1984), pp 870-911, for a summary of some traditional Orthodox Jewish liturgy employed during this time.

Shabbat Zachor
I Samuel 15:2-34

In a like manner, on *Shabbat Zachor* (Remember), the Sabbath that precedes the celebration of *Purim*, the concept of remembrance is reinforced. The Haftarah portion that is read is from 1 Samuel 15:2-34, with an additional reading from the Torah (Deuteronomy 25:17-19). The reminder that the Amalekites are always going to seek to destroy Israel is discussed. The 1 Samuel passage deals with King Saul's unwillingness to destroy the Amalekites as instructed by God. As you come to the end of the episode, the Prophet Samuel demonstrates the proper way to handle the demise of King Agag.

But, Agag's fall does not occur—as some Jewish commentators have speculated[5]—until he sires a child who became the forefather of the wicked Haman, who centuries later seeks to destroy the Jewish people throughout the Persian Empire. The Book of Esther, the basis for the upcoming *Purim* celebration, is contemplated as the realities of Amalek's desire to destroy Israel are considered. Finally, the following passage from the Torah is discussed to emphasize the need to remember:

"Remember what Amalek did to you along the way when you came out from Egypt, how he met you along the way and attacked among you all the stragglers at your rear when you were faint and weary; and he did not fear God. Therefore it shall come about when the LORD your God has given you rest from all your surrounding enemies, in the land which the LORD your God gives you as an inheritance to possess, you shall blot out the memory of Amalek from under heaven; you must not forget" (Deuteronomy 25:17-19).

Shabbat Parah
Ezekiel 36:16-38

The third of these special Sabbaths to prepare the heart for Passover, *Shabbat Parah* (Red Heifer/Lots), is celebrated on the week immediately following *Purim*. The two readings that are considered are Numbers 19:1-22, which deal specifically with the admonitions about the purification required by the ashes of the red heifer, and Ezekiel 36:16-38, which touches on the issues of a clean heart of flesh washed by the waters of purification. Once again, preparation for the upcoming Passover season is in mind, as these passages prepare the hearts of the faithful for the specific requirements of *Pesach* and the Feast of Unleavened Bread. Here, just after the *Purim* reminder, the focus is personal purification, and yet, the entire red heifer ceremony is something inexplicable to human reasoning. It is simply required by the Lord for the Tabernacle/Temple service, obeyed by faith in order to comply with His Instruction.

Interestingly, much of this particular ordinance has to deal with the problems associated with handling dead people. Of course, this can be a delicate subject when you consider comments from Yeshua that described the dead in this manner: "Follow Me, and allow the dead to bury their own dead" (Matthew 8:22). Is it possible He was stating that those without eternal life are essentially dead? And if so, does that mean that as we deal with people without spiritual life, we are handling the dead, and hence are in constant need of purification? When you

---

[5] Nosson Scherman and Meir Zlotowitz, eds., *ArtScroll Tanach* (Brooklyn: Mesorah Publications, Ltd., 1996), 680.

compliment this consideration with the words of Ezekiel 36, some other thoughts come to mind. Here, the Prophet Ezekiel begins a discussion about our need to be cleansed by the waters of purification, by likening Israel to a woman in her menstrual cycle, or a period of continual uncleanness:

"Son of man, when the house of Israel was living in their own land, they defiled it by their ways and their deeds; their way before Me was like the uncleanness of a woman in her impurity. Therefore I poured out My wrath on them for the blood which they had shed on the land, because they had defiled it with their idols. Also I scattered them among the nations and they were dispersed throughout the lands. According to their ways and their deeds I judged them" (Ezekiel 36:17-19).

When we approach the Passover season, we can contemplate the possibility that due to such a state of impurity, we might not be ready to be fully one with our Messiah. As Ezekiel continues prophesying, the waters of purification—sprinkled on a heart of flesh—brings the required state into being:

"Then I will sprinkle clean water on you, and you will be clean; I will cleanse you from all your filthiness and from all your idols. Moreover, I will give you a new heart and put a new spirit within you; and I will remove the heart of stone from your flesh and give you a heart of flesh. I will put My Spirit within you and cause you to walk in My statutes, and you will be careful to observe My ordinances. You will live in the land that I gave to your forefathers; so you will be My people, and I will be your God. Moreover, I will save you from all your uncleanness" (Ezekiel 36:25-29a).

Shabbat HaChodesh
Ezekiel 45:16-46:18

Finally, the Sabbath that precedes the New Moon of Aviv/Nisan is the fourth and last special week, called *Shabbat HaChodesh*. This Sabbath actually commemorates the first commandment given to the Israelites to begin the countdown to the fourteenth of Aviv/Nisan and the Passover season. Consequently, this Sabbath's reading goes back to Exodus 12:1-20 and recalls the Angel of Death. The Haftarah portion which compliments it comes from Ezekiel 45:16-46:18. Here, the concurrent theme appears to be the New Moon and the need to acknowledge it.[6] We may be reminded of how the Seleucids attempted to stop this remembrance when they were temporarily in power over Jerusalem (cf. 1 Maccabees 10:34). By stopping this annual rite, the momentum of following the rest of the *moedim* or appointed times of the Lord could be stopped.

So once again, the hearts of God's people are being prepared for the coming of the Passover season. The additional reminder that the first of Aviv/Nisan has arrived now puts one on notice that the night of remembrance is approaching. As you can see, each of these special Sabbaths creates an atmosphere of expectation that is carried forward into the celebration of Passover.

Passover Restored

It is difficult to ascertain how many Messianic communities of faith incorporate these additional readings into their weekly examination of the Torah as

---

[6] Consult the FAQ entry on the Messianic Apologetics website "New Moon."

the Passover season approaches. Certainly, as the celebration of the Biblical holidays continues to grow through time and our faith community expands, many will employ some of these traditions to prepare hearts for a more meaningful time of remembrance. Eventually, as the Prophet Jeremiah tells us, the commemoration of the Exodus will be altered as a greater Exodus will occur at some future time. We get our first glimpse of what Jeremiah is referring to when he admonishes God's people for their lack of observance of the Passover, and other basic commandments:

"Now when you tell this people all these words, they will say to you, 'For what reason has the LORD declared all this great calamity against us? And what is our iniquity, or what is our sin which we have committed against the LORD our God?' Then you are to say to them, '*It is* because your forefathers have forsaken Me,' declares the LORD, 'and have followed other gods and served them and bowed down to them; but Me they have forsaken and have not kept My law. You too have done evil, *even* more than your forefathers; for behold, you are each one walking according to the stubbornness of his own evil heart, without listening to Me. So I will hurl you out of this land into the land which you have not known, neither you nor your fathers; and there you will serve other gods day and night, for I will grant you no favor. **Therefore behold, days are coming,' declares the LORD, 'when it will no longer be said, "As the LORD lives, who brought up the sons of Israel out of the land of Egypt," but, "As the LORD lives, who brought up the sons of Israel from the land of the north and from all the countries where He had banished them." For I will restore them to their own land which I gave to their fathers.** Behold, I am going to send for many fishermen,' declares the LORD, 'and they will fish for them; and afterwards I will send for many hunters, and they will hunt them from every mountain and every hill and from the clefts of the rocks. For My eyes are on all their ways; they are not hidden from My face, nor is their iniquity concealed from My eyes'" (Jeremiah 16:10-17).

Jeremiah rebukes his listeners for not obeying God's Torah, and as a result, the people will be scattered into the nations. But note that he declares how one day they will no longer talk about the Exodus out of Egypt, but will recall a gathering when the banished return from all the countries of the world. Today, this is occurring as many Jewish people are returning from Russia and the lands to the north, in partial fulfillment of this prophecy. But he further states that others, various fishers and hunters, will go out and seek the last remnants of Israel as well.

If we are in the Last Days, or are at least approaching them, then a clarity of understanding needs to come forth, as these prophecies are probably beginning to come to pass in some way. It is beneficial to consider some of the practices that have been employed over the years to encourage a more serious focus during Passover and the Feast of Unleavened Bread. We need to become more serious about remembering the Exodus from Egypt. Perhaps when we sit in God's Kingdom one day in the future and talk about the work He has done, we will not be completely ignorant as we have learned what the Greater Exodus was through our commemoration of Passover.

~6~

The Message of Exodus

J.K. McKee

The Book of Exodus is one of the most important, yet controversial books of the entire Bible, and certainly the most important book of the Torah. Commentator John I. Durham confidently asserts, "The Book of Exodus is the first book of the Bible."[1] This is because without an Exodus of Israel from Egypt, there is no people to preserve and testify to the traditions regarding Creation, Noah, Abraham and the Patriarchs, and the faithfulness of God toward these individuals. In other words, without the Book of Exodus you have no Book of Genesis. And this is only one of the obvious themes that gets overlooked when one considers the significance of Exodus.

Every year in the Spring, sometime between Passover or Easter (or Easter and Passover depending on the year), the Exodus usually gets a great deal of publicity. There are many questions and debates surrounding the Exodus. When did it take place? How many people were actually involved? What was the route of the Exodus and the real location of Mount Sinai? Who was the Pharaoh of the Exodus? Why is there no Egyptian record surrounding it? And while it may be good to engage with these discussions from time to time, too frequently people take their eyes off of the Biblical text and the significant message(s) that Exodus has for us as people of faith, and away from the unique character forming ability that the Book of Exodus so aptly possesses. Furthermore, as Messianics who often examine Exodus every year, are there any things that we overlook regarding this critical text of God's revelation?

The Hebrew title of the Book of Exodus is *Shemot*, meaning "Names," as the text begins with "These are the names of the sons of Israel" (Exodus 1:1), testifying how the Patriarch Jacob and his sons entered into Egypt, and have now "multiplied greatly and became exceedingly numerous, so that the land was filled with them" (Exodus 1:6). While Joseph had been used in the past to deliver Egypt through a time of famine and trial, making a great name for himself (Genesis chs. 39-50), a new Egyptian dynasty and a new Pharaoh had come to power "who did not know about Joseph" (Exodus 1:8). Not knowing about Joseph, this dynasty found the Semitic Israelites to be a convenient workforce, and they were concerned "if war breaks out, [they] will join our enemies, fight against us and leave the country"

---

[1] John I. Durham, *Word Biblical Commentary: Exodus*, Vol. 3 (Waco, TX: Word Books, 1987), xix.

(Exodus 1:10).[2] The Israelites in Egypt, while having greatly multiplied, found themselves pressed into deep servitude to Egypt, as the Egyptians "made their lives bitter with hard labor in brick and mortar and with all kinds of work in the fields" (Exodus 1:14).

In spite of the Israelites being placed in slavery to Egypt, the Egyptians were still worried as they did multiply. The Pharaoh thus rules that Israelite males who are born are to be killed (Exodus 1:16), and sees to it that a search be made for infant males to be thrown into the Nile (Exodus 1:22).

A Levite woman conceives, giving birth to a son, and is able to actually hide him for three months (Exodus 1:2). Yet she is unable to hide him indefinitely, and so "she got a papyrus basket for him and coated it with tar and pitch. Then she placed the child in it and put it among the reeds along the bank of the Nile" (Exodus 1:4; cf. Hebrews 11:23). The boy's sister watches this from a distance (Exodus 1:5), and then sees it actually floating to where the Pharaoh's daughter is bathing. The Pharaoh's daughter recognizes the child as one of the Hebrew babies, but is intent to take it for her own. "She named him Moses, saying, 'I drew him out of the water'" (Exodus 1:10). The prince Moses is raised as a member of the Egyptian court.

Somehow, although raised Egyptian, Moses knew that he was different. "One day, after Moses had grown up, he went out to where his own people were and watched them at their hard labor. He saw an Egyptian beating a Hebrew, one of his own people. Glancing this way and that and seeing no one, he killed the Egyptian and hid him in the sand" (Exodus 2:11-12). Having been enraged at the terrible treatment toward the slaves, he reaches a point of decision and somehow recognizes that he too was a Hebrew. This murder is known by two Hebrews the next day (Exodus 2:11-12), and news also gets back to Pharaoh (Exodus 2:15). Presumably, Moses as a prince of Egypt and grandson of Pharaoh could have killed a common Egyptian and easily gotten away with it. But the revelation that he was actually a Hebrew changed everything. Moses quickly had to flee to Midian for his own life.

Moses' life in Midian certainly did not have the luxuries he experienced in Egypt. He becomes acquainted with the priest of Midian, Jethro, whose daughter, Zipporah, he marries (Exodus 2:20-21). Moses becomes a shepherd. While in this time of exile, "the king of Egypt died. The Israelites groaned in their slavery and cried out...God heard their groaning and he remembered his covenant with Abraham, with Isaac and with Jacob" (Exodus 2:23-24). As he tended the flock of Jethro at Mount Horeb, Moses witnesses a burning bush, exclaiming "I will go over and see this strange sight—why the bush does not burn up" (Exodus 3:3). The Lord cries out to Moses from the bush, and Moses simply responds with *hinneni*, "Here I am" (Exodus 3:4). Moses removes his sandals on the holy ground (Exodus 3:5), and the Lord identifies who he is by telling Moses that He knows of the suffering of Israel and that He will deliver them into the land promised to their forefathers (Exodus 3:7-8): "[T]he cry of the Israelites has reached me, and I have seen the way the Egyptians are oppressing them. So now, go. I am sending you to Pharaoh to bring my people the Israelites out of Egypt" (Exodus 3:9-10).

---

[2] Consult the FAQ entry on the Messianic Apologetics website "Exodus, Pharaoh who did not know Joseph."

Moses is not entirely convinced that returning to Egypt and speaking to a people whom he barely knows will work. Moses does not even know the proper name of the God to whom he is speaking, who will promptly tell him "I AM WHO I AM" (Exodus 3:14), *ehyeh asher ehyeh.*[3] He then gives him a special name, that not even the Patriarchs knew (cf. Exodus 6:3), YHWH (HaShem),[4] to designate Himself from the many gods of Egypt (Exodus 3:15). Moses is to tell the Egyptian Pharaoh to let the Israelites go for a three-day journey to worship Him, but instead he will resist. The Lord says, "I know that the king of Egypt will not let you go unless a mighty hand compels him. So I will stretch out my hand and strike the Egyptians with all the wonders that I will perform among them. After that, he will let you go" (Exodus 3:19-20). The Israelites will leave Egypt with a great number of spoils (Exodus 3:21-22).

Moses, still not entirely sure, is shown the power of the Lord right before his eyes. His staff turns into a snake (Exodus 4:3-5), and his hand turns leprous as he inserts it into his cloak (Exodus 4:6-8). The Lord speaks to Moses about the kinds of mighty acts he will be responsible for unleashing upon Egypt (Exodus 4:8-10). And worried about his speaking abilities, the Lord, although irritated with Moses, tells him that his brother Aaron will be used as a spokesman (Exodus 4:11-16). Coming down from the mountain, Moses returns to his enslaved people in Egypt (Exodus 4:18-20) to face a new Pharaoh and the biggest challenge of his life (Exodus 4:21-22).

Aaron is led into the wilderness to meet Moses on his return to Egypt (Exodus 4:27-28), and both of them demonstrate the Lord's signs before the Israelite elders (Exodus 4:29-31). Convinced of their cause, Moses and Aaron go before Pharaoh for the first time, commanding that the people be allowed to go into the desert to worship before HaShem for a three-day festival (Exodus 5:1-3). The Pharaoh refuses because he is unwilling to stop the Israelites' labor (Exodus 5:4-5), and he then issues the order that they not be given straw to make their required allotment of bricks (Exodus 5:6-19). The people were furious with Moses in disbelief, clamoring, "May the LORD look upon you and judge you! You have made us a stench to Pharaoh and his officials and have put a sword in their hand to kill us" (Exodus 5:21). Moses beseeches the Lord, expressing some doubts (Exodus 5:22-23) as the Israelites deride him. Under extreme stress, the Lord repeats the great calling that He has given Moses to free His people (Exodus 6:1-8),[5] and He tells him to go again before Pharaoh.

Once again Moses must go before Pharaoh, but this time God says "I will harden Pharaoh's heart" (Exodus 7:3). Even though Moses and Aaron must obey the command of the Lord to go before Egypt's king, he will still not listen to them (Exodus 7:4), requiring Divine judgments upon Egypt to know that HaShem is the God of the universe (Exodus 7:5). Moses and Aaron perform their first "miracle" (Exodus 7:9) before Pharaoh when Aaron's staff is transformed into a snake. The

[3] The Hebrew *ehyeh asher ehyeh* was rendered as *egō eimi* or "I AM" in the Greek Septuagint. *Egō eimi* is used numerous times in the Gospels pointing to the Divinity of Yeshua the Messiah (cf. Matthew 14:24-33; Mark 14:61-63; Luke 22:70-71; John 8:56-59; 18:4-6).
[4] In this article, when wanting to point people to the Divine Name of God, I will simply refer to YHWH as HaShem, concurrent with the traditional Jewish interpretation of the Third Commandment (Exodus 20:7; Deuteronomy 5:11; cf. m.*Yoma* 6:2), adhered to by Yeshua and His Apostles (cf. 3 John 7).
[5] In the text of Exodus following (6:14-27), a Levite genealogical chart is given, validating Moses' leadership.

Pharaoh is not impressed as his magicians can do the same thing (Exodus 7:11), even though "Aaron's staff swallowed up their staffs" (Exodus 7:12). Pharaoh's heart is hardened (Exodus 7:13). What follows are a series of distinct encounters between Moses and Pharaoh, and great ecological plagues are unleashed upon Egypt.

The tension between Moses as leader of Israel and the Pharaoh of Egypt is obvious: "Pharaoh's heart is unyielding; he refuses to let the people go" (Exodus 7:14). Moses is commanded by God to turn all of the water in Egypt into blood, and it is so bad that even the fish of the Nile die (Exodus 7:16-21). The Pharaoh is still not convinced, as his own magicians can replicate the act (Exodus 7:22).

A week later Moses goes before the Pharaoh again, repeating God's request that His people be allowed to worship Him for three days in the wilderness (Exodus 7:25-8:1). He is threatened with a plague of frogs, which will come out of the Nile and overwhelm the people as an annoying menace (Exodus 8:2-5). Even though Moses and Aaron are able to call the frogs upon Egypt, so can Pharaoh's own magicians (Exodus 8:7). For the first time, though, Pharaoh actually asks Moses and Aaron to "Pray to the LORD to take the frogs away from me and my people, and I will let your people go to offer sacrifices to the LORD" (Exodus 8:8), as he is at least beginning to recognize that HaShem has some power. The next day, the plague of frogs stops (Exodus 8:10-11), as "They were piled into heaps, and the land reeked of them" (Exodus 8:14). Pharaoh hardens his own heart (Exodus 8:15).

The third plague comes without an initial clash with Pharaoh, as the Lord simply commands Aaron to "'Stretch out your staff and strike the dust of the ground,' and throughout the land of Egypt the dust will become gnats" (Exodus 8:16). This is the first plague that the magicians of Egypt were *unable* to reproduce (Exodus 8:18), who are forced to tell their king "This is the finger of God" (Exodus 8:19a). Still, the Pharaoh "would not listen, just as the LORD had said" (Exodus 8:19b).

The next encounter with Pharaoh comes with the decree that if he does not let the Israelites go worship HaShem in the wilderness for three days, "I will send swarms of flies on you and your officials, on your people and into your houses. The houses of the Egyptians will be full of flies, and even the ground where they are" (Exodus 8:20). Included in this warning is that the Israelites in Goshen will not have this plague affect them (Exodus 8:22), as the Lord says "I will make a distinction between my people and your people" (Exodus 8:23). As the flies are unleashed upon Egypt, Pharaoh actually extends permission to Moses, "Go, sacrifice to your God here in the land" (Exodus 8:25), as he is still at least beginning to recognize that HaShem has some power. Yet, Moses insists that God will only allow the sacrifices outside of Egypt (Exodus 8:26-27), so Pharaoh says that they can do it "but you must not go very far. Now pray for me" (Exodus 8:28). Yet, as the flies leave Egypt, Pharaoh once again hardens his heart (Exodus 8:32).

Each plague gets more and more intense. The Pharaoh is once again told that if he does not allow the Israelites to worship God in the wilderness, severe consequences will be unleashed. This time, a major catastrophe will be unleashed against Egyptian livestock (Exodus 9:1-3), but not against the livestock of the Israelites (Exodus 9:4). "Pharaoh sent men to investigate and found that not even one of the animals of the Israelites had died. Yet his heart was unyielding" (Exodus 9:7).

The fifth plague comes when God commands Moses and Aaron, "Take handfuls of soot from a furnace and have Moses toss it into the air in the presence of Pharaoh. It will become fine dust over the whole land of Egypt, and festering boils will break out on men and animals throughout the land" (Exodus 9:8-9). This was yet another plague that the magicians of Egypt could not replicate (Exodus 9:11), and so the Lord hardens Pharaoh's heart (Exodus 9:12).

The next encounter with Pharaoh is even more intense. If the Pharaoh does not let the Israelites go into the desert to worship the Lord, He says "this time I will send the full force of my plagues against you and against your officials and your people, so you may know that there is no one like me in all the earth. For by now I could have stretched out my hand and struck you and your people with a plague that would have wiped you off the earth. But I have raised you up for this very purpose, that I might show you my power and that my name might be proclaimed in all the earth" (Exodus 9:14-16). HaShem promises to "send the worst hailstorm that has ever fallen on Egypt, from the day it was founded till now" (Exodus 9:18). The hail, along with significant thunder and lightning, descends upon Egypt (Exodus 9:22-25), but not upon the Israelites in Goshen (Exodus 9:26). The Pharaoh pleads with Moses and Aaron, "This time I have sinned…The LORD is in the right, and I and my people are in the wrong" (Exodus 9:27), agreeing to let them go to worship Him (Exodus 9:28). However, once the plague subsides Pharaoh recants, this time "He and his officials hardened their hearts" (Exodus 9:34) refusing to let Israel go.

For some reason or another, the Pharaoh of Egypt and his court fail to realize that by refusing the request of HaShem they are plunging their country into utter ruin. God subsequently tells Moses and Aaron to once again go before him, asking him "How long will you refuse to humble yourself before me? Let my people go, so that they may worship me" (Exodus 10:3). The Lord says that if Pharaoh does not allow this, locusts will be unleashed upon the Egyptians, and "They will cover the face of the ground so that it cannot be seen" (Exodus 10:5). Pharaoh's officials exhibit some common sense: "How long will this man be a snare to us? Let the people go, so that they may worship the LORD their God. Do you not yet realize that Egypt is ruined?" (Exodus 10:7). Pharaoh agrees to let *only* the Israelite males go worship Him, and that the whole population including females and small children is not allowed to go (Exodus 10:8-10). By refusing the Lord's request, locusts are unleashed upon Egypt (Exodus 10:12-15). Pharaoh confesses once again that he has sinned against Him, and a strong wind takes all of the locusts into the Red Sea (Exodus 10:16-19). Still, Pharaoh hardens his heart (Exodus 10:20).

There is no encounter with the Pharaoh as the ninth plague manifests itself upon Egypt. Moses is simply told by the Lord, "Stretch out your hand toward the sky so that darkness will spread over Egypt—darkness that can be felt" (Exodus 10:21). This *choshek* engulfed Egypt for three days, although not the dwellings of the Israelites (Exodus 10:23). Pharaoh summons Moses and appears to capitulate, this time allowing the women and children to go with them into the wilderness to worship God. He does, though, say "only leave your flocks and herds behind" (Exodus 10:24). This is unacceptable as those animals are needed to offer burnt offerings to the Lord (Exodus 10:25-26). God thus hardens Pharaoh's heart, and he forcibly tells Moses, "Get out of my sight! Make sure you do not appear before me again! The day you see my face you will die" (Exodus 10:28).

The tenth and final plague upon Egypt is the most severe and serious. HaShem says, "After that, [Pharaoh] will let you go from here, and when he does, he will drive you out completely" (Exodus 11:1). Far be it from just being able to go worship the Lord in the wilderness, the Israelites will be let go completely from the bonds of Egypt (cf. Exodus 11:3), and they will leave with a great amount of spoil (Exodus 11:2). The Lord intends to "go throughout Egypt. Every firstborn son of Egypt will die, from the firstborn of Pharaoh, who sits on the throne, to the firstborn son of the slave girl, who is at her hand mill, and all the firstborn of the cattle will die. There will be loud wailing throughout Egypt" (Exodus 11:4-6).

The command is given in Exodus for the Israelites to commemorate this event by remembering the Passover. Prior to the plague of the firstborn being unleashed upon Egypt, the Israelites were told to take the blood of a lamb "and put it on the sides and tops of the doorframes of the houses" (Exodus 12:7). They were also to eat its meat, along with bitter herbs and unleavened bread (Exodus 12:8). The original Passover meal was to be eaten in haste, as the promised departure from Egypt was imminent (Exodus 12:11).

In the plague upon Egypt's firstborn, HaShem is clear in saying "I will bring judgment on all the gods of Egypt" (Exodus 12:12), but also that "The blood will be a sign for you on the houses where you are; and when I see the blood, I will pass over you. No destructive plague will touch you when I strike Egypt" (Exodus 12:13). So significant is this Passover event, "This is a day you are to commemorate; for generations to come you shall celebrate it as a festival to the LORD—a lasting ordinance" (Exodus 12:14). The Festival of Unleavened Bread is also to be commemorated for the week following, as one contemplates the departure from Egypt (Exodus 12:15-20; 13:7-10) and eats nothing with yeast. Critical lessons are to be taught to each generation as one remembers the deliverance of God (Exodus 12:24-27, 43-50).

As the Israelites assemble to have a very sacred and sober meal of lamb, bitter herbs, and unleavened bread, "At midnight the LORD stuck down all the firstborn in Egypt...Pharaoh and all his officials and all the Egyptians got up during the night, and there was loud wailing in Egypt, for there was not a house without someone dead" (Exodus 12:29-30).

The Egyptian Pharaoh, leader of the Thirteenth Century B.C.E. superpower, is now completely humiliated before the power of HaShem the God of Israel. He summons Moses and Aaron, telling them "Up! Leave my people, you and the Israelites! Go, worship the LORD as you have requested" (Exodus 12:31). "The Egyptians urged the people to hurry and leave the country. 'For otherwise,' they said, 'we will all die!'" (Exodus 12:33). The Israelites gather spoil of "silver and gold and...clothing" (Exodus 12:35), and several hundred thousand people make their way from Ramses to Succoth (Exodus 12:37).

The Israelites find themselves nestled in a camp on the shores of the Red Sea, as God prohibited them from traveling to Canaan via the dangerous Philistine country, lest they desire to return to Egypt (Exodus 13:17-18). With them are the mummified remains of the Patriarch Joseph (Exodus 13:19; Genesis 50:26). The Lord appears to them "in a pillar of cloud to guide them on their way and by night in a pillar of fire to give them light, so that they could travel by day or night. Neither the pillar of cloud by day nor the pillar of fire by night left its place in front of the people" (Exodus 13:21-22).

While the Israelites are encamped with their backs to the sea (Exodus 14:1-2), the Lord still desires to communicate something to the Egyptian Pharaoh. "Pharaoh will think, 'The Israelites are wandering around the land in confusion, hemmed in by the desert'" (Exodus 14:3). God asserts, "I will harden Pharaoh's heart, and he will pursue them. But I will gain glory for myself through Pharaoh and his army, and the Egyptians will know that I am the LORD" (Exodus 14:4). When Pharaoh hears that the Israelites have gone, he is furious and declares "What have we done? We have let the Israelites go and have lost their services!" (Exodus 14:5). Pharaoh sends the Egyptian army after these rabble to the seaside where they are gathered (Exodus 14:7-9).

The Ancient Israelites, having seen the plagues that the Lord enacted upon Egypt, see the Egyptian chariots "marching after them. They were terrified and cried out to the LORD" (Exodus 14:10). But then they chastise Moses, "Was it because there were no graves in Egypt that you brought us to the desert to die? What have you done to us by bringing us out of Egypt? Didn't we say to you in Egypt, 'Leave us alone; let us serve the Egyptians'? It would have been better for us to serve the Egyptians than to die in the desert!" (Exodus 14:11-12). Answering the clamor of people, Moses says *hityatzbu u're'u et'yeshuat ADONAI*: "stand firm and see the salvation of the LORD" (Exodus 14:13, RSV). "The LORD will fight for you" (Exodus 14:14). Up to this moment, the focus of disobedience and rebellion to HaShem has been on the Egyptian Pharaoh; now it shifts to the people of Israel themselves and whether they will believe in their God and His power.

We all know the scene far too well. At the moment of disbelief for the Israelites, "Moses stretched out his hand over the sea, and all that night the LORD drove the sea back with a strong east wind and turned it into dry land. The waters were divided, and the Israelites went through the sea on dry ground, with a wall of water on their right and on their left" (Exodus 14:21-22). The horde of several hundred thousand makes their way, albeit carefully, on the land provided to them. The pillar of fire and cloud keeps the Egyptian army at bay (Exodus 14:24), and they recognize "Let's get away from the Israelites! The LORD is fighting for them against Egypt" (Exodus 14:25).

Still, the stupidity of the Pharaoh compels the Egyptians to follow in after the Israelites (Exodus 14:28). The Lord commands Moses, "Stretch out your hand over the sea so that the waters may flow back over the Egyptians and their chariots and horsemen" (Exodus 14:26), and the force is decimated with not one of them surviving. One can now validly wonder why there is no record of the Exodus in Egyptian history. The god Pharaoh was defeated by HaShem the God of Israel—a God of slaves—in battle. Gods do not make mistakes, and so why would Egypt want to remember such catastrophes, failures, and blunders brought on them by Pharaoh, the son of Ra? Yet for His people, "when the Israelites saw the great power of the LORD displayed against the Egyptians, the people feared the LORD and put their trust in him and in Moses his servant" (Exodus 14:31). Miriam and the women of Israel begin dancing in praise to Him (Exodus 15:20-21).

A song, the *shirat ha'yam* or the Song of the Sea, is commissioned to remember what happened to the Egyptian armies. It proclaims "The LORD is my strength and my song; he has become my salvation" (Exodus 15:2), speaking of the fall of Pharaoh's chariots (Exodus 15:4-5) and the great majesty of God (Exodus 15:7). HaShem as Creator has dominion over the sea to swallow up His enemies

(Exodus 15:8), as the people ask "Who among the gods is like you, O LORD? Who is like you—majestic in holiness, awesome in glory, working wonders?" (Exodus 15:11). So significant is this Song of the Sea, that it even conveys a message to the Canaanites whose land has been promised to Israel (Exodus 15:14-17; cf. Joshua 2:10).[6]

While the Israelites are a free people on the opposite shores of the Red Sea, **the process of their salvation has only begun.** Only three days into their journey, after seeing the mighty acts of deliverance via the hand of God, they start complaining. They wish to have sweet waters (Exodus 15:23-25). At this time, the people are first told "If you listen carefully to the voice of the LORD your God and do what is right in his eyes, if you pay attention to his commandments and keep all his decrees, I will not bring on you any of the disease I brought on the Egyptians, for I am the LORD, who heals you" (Exodus 15:26). Obedience to HaShem is now a clear requirement of His people. As they learn to obey Him, they will not face the same kinds of adversities that the Egyptians faced when God judged them for being obstinate.

This still does not phase the Israelites. Just about a month out of Egypt and in the Wilderness of Sin, the people again complain against Moses and Aaron, "If we had died by the LORD's hand in Egypt! There we sat around pots of meat and ate all the food we wanted, but you have brought us out into this desert to starve this entire assembly to death" (Exodus 16:3). They do not appreciate the freedom that the Lord has given them, but as their Provider He gives them instructions on how to collect bread or the manna He sends from Heaven (Exodus 16:4-5), which would only last for an allotted time (Exodus 16:15-26). Moses still must remind the people that although they think of themselves as grumbling against him, they are actually grumbling against God (Exodus 16:6-8). The faithfulness of God is demonstrated, and so Moses is told "Take an omer of manna and keep it for the generations to come, so they can see the bread that I gave you in the desert when I brought you out of Egypt" (Exodus 16:33).

The initial challenges for the newly-free Israelites still keep coming. The Israelites complain because of lack of water: "Why did you bring us up out of Egypt to make us and our children and livestock die of thirst?" (Exodus 17:3). Moses is told by the Lord, "take in your hand the staff with which you struck the Nile, and go. I will stand there before you by the rock at Horeb. Strike the rock, and water will come out of it for the people to drink" (Exodus 17:6). While the thirst of the Israelites is quenched, Moses "called the place Massah and Meribah because the Israelites quarreled and because they tested the LORD saying, 'Is the LORD among us or not?'" (Exodus 17:7; cf. Psalm 95:8; Hebrews 3:8).

Now encamped at Rephidim, the Amalekites come and attack Israel. Joshua is told by Moses to take a force and go out and fight them, as he would stand on top of a hill watching, holding out the staff that God gave him (Exodus 17:8-9). The fight went well "As long as Moses held up his hands, the Israelites were winning, but whenever he lowered his hands the Amalekites were winning" (Exodus 17:11). "Aaron and Hur held his hands up…So Joshua overcame the Amalekite army with his sword" (Exodus 17:12, 13). Hence we see the beginnings of a long, protracted hostility between Israel and the Amalekites (Exodus 17:14-15).

---

[6] Consult this writer's article "The Song of Moses and God's Mission for His People."

Now approaching the third month out of Egypt, Moses and his father-in-law, Jethro the priest of Midian, have a reunion along with Moses' wife and sons (Exodus 18:2-8). He attests to have heard of the plagues HaShem dispensed upon Egypt, and the deliverance He had accomplished for the people of Israel (Exodus 18:1, 9-12). Jethro gives Moses advice on how to delegate responsibility among the leaders of Israel so he alone will not have to judge each individual dispute and be worn out (Exodus 18:13-26).

The Israelites finally arrive at Mount Sinai, *ha'har* or "the mountain" (Exodus 19:2). Moses ascends this mountain to speak to HaShem concerning His will for Israel. The Lord says "if you obey me fully and keep my covenant, then out of all nations you will be my treasured possession. Although the whole earth is mine, you will be for me a kingdom of priests and a holy nation" (Exodus 19:5). Although they do not yet understand it, **God is already speaking to Israel about their future service unto Him as His intermediaries to the world.** Returning to the people, the Israelite assembly unanimously declares "We will do everything the LORD has said" (Exodus 19:8). A very significant and awesome time of theophany then ensues, with the people of Israel being told to consecrate themselves (Exodus 19:10, 15, 22) as God's Divine presence will engulf the mountain before them. "Mount Sinai was covered with smoke, because the LORD descended upon it in fire. The smoke billowed up from it like smoke from a furnace, the whole mountain trembled violently, and the sound of the trumpet grew louder and louder. Then Moses spoke and the voice of God answered him" (Exodus 19:19). He goes up to the top of the mountain a second time, and one of the most important events in human history occurs.

The *aseret ha'devarim* or Ten Words (more commonly called the Ten Commandments) are the first that are delivered from God, to His servant Moses (Exodus 20:1-17). It is quite significant that while HaShem will punish those who commit idolatry against Him (Exodus 20:4), "to the third and fourth generation of those who hate me" (Exodus 20:5), He will show "love to a thousand generations of those who love me and keep my commandments" (Exodus 20:6). No deity in the Ancient Near East, either those of Egypt or of Canaan, would ever make such promises. The Israelites stand beneath Sinai in fear and at a distance (Exodus 20:18). They have told Moses, "Speak to us yourself and we will listen. But do not have God speak to us or we will die" (Exodus 20:19). Moses indicates, "God has come to test you, so that the fear of God will be with you to keep you from sinning" (Exodus 20:20).

While on Mount Sinai, Moses receives additional instructions from the Lord. These concern the construction of proper altars (Exodus 20:22-26), laws regarding servitude within Israel (Exodus 21:2-11), personal injuries and appropriate reparations (Exodus 21:12-36), a respect of property and warnings against theft and shortdealings (Exodus 22:1-15), various social responsibilities including proper sexuality among the people (Exodus 21:16-31), how the people are to respect justice (Exodus 23:1-9) and give their land a Sabbath rest (Exodus 23:10-13), and how the people are to gather three times a year for specific festivals (Exodus 23:14-17). The Lord promises to send His angel ahead of the people, and for them not to adopt the ways of the Canaanites and their gods (Exodus 23:20-32).

The seventy elders are allowed to come closer to Moses while on the mountain, and the people declare once again "Everything the LORD has said we will do" (Exodus 24:3), along with a written transcription (Exodus 24:4). An altar is built for HaShem and sacrifices are made. Blood from those sacrifices is sprinkled on the people, testifying to their commitment before Him (Exodus 24:6-8). The elders of Israel get to witness a greater manifestation of God's presence than they had ever seen before (Exodus 24:9-10). Moses goes up to the summit of Mount Sinai to receive the Ten Words written on stone (Exodus 24:12-14). "When Moses went up on the mountain, the cloud covered it, and the glory of the LORD settled on Mount Sinai…To the Israelites the glory of the LORD looked like a consuming fire on top of the mountain. Then Moses entered the cloud as he went up on the mountain. And he stayed on the mountain forty days and forty nights" (Exodus 24:15-18).

On Mount Sinai, Moses is surrounded by the presence of God. Not surprisingly, the commandments he is given by the Lord concern how His presence is to manifest itself in the midst of the congregation of Israel. Moses is told "have them make a sanctuary for me, and I will dwell among them. Make this tabernacle and all its furnishings exactly like the pattern I will show you" (Exodus 25:8-9).

The elements of the Tabernacle include: the Ark of the Covenant (Exodus 25:10-22), the Table of Showbread (Exodus 25:23-30), and the lampstand or *menorah* (Exodus 25:31-40). The Tabernacle, a traveling tent structure, is likewise to be constructed according to a pattern and be elaborate (Exodus ch. 26). There is to be an altar for burnt offerings (Exodus 27:1-8), and a courtyard (Exodus 27:9-19). Only consecrated oil is to be used in worship (Exodus 27:20), and the priests who serve in the Tabernacle are to be of the highest caliber with only the appropriate garments (Exodus chs. 28-29). Other elements such as the altar of incense (Exodus 30:1-10), special money (Exodus 30:11-16), a basin for washing (Exodus 30:17-21), anointing oil (Exodus 30:22-33), and incense (Exodus 30:34-38) all enhance the holiness of this enterprise. God gives a special knowledge to the craftsmen Bezalel and Oholiab to make the sacred objects (Exodus 31:1-11).[7]

Concurrent with His theme to dwell among His people, HaShem is sure to tell Moses, "You must observe my Sabbaths. This will be a sign between me and you for the generations to come, so you may know that I am the LORD, who makes you holy" (Exodus 31:12). Failure to observe the Sabbath meant certain death for the Ancient Israelites who transgressed (Exodus 31:14-16), as they would be skewing God's original desire in Creation for human beings to commune with Him (Exodus 31:17). Finally after emphasizing this, the Lord "gave [Moses] the two tablets of the Testimony, the tablets of stone inscribed by the finger of God" (Exodus 31:18).

As Moses is surrounded by the presence of the Eternal, the Israelites return to their cycle of being impatient and grumble. "When the people saw that Moses was so long in coming down from the mountain, they gathered around Aaron and said, 'Come, make us gods who will go before us. As for this fellow Moses who brought us up out of Egypt, we don't know what has happened to him'" (Exodus 31:1). Aaron succumbs to the people's demands, asking them to gather gold. He fashions

---

[7] While some try to find secret or hidden meanings behind every single design of the Tabernacle, it is better for us to remember that the Lord is working within the religious expectations of the people of the Ancient Near East. Far be it from the Tabernacle being the First Temple "read back" or "microscoped" into the "mythology" of the Exodus as purported by many past liberal theologians, there were many traveling tent shrines in the ANE. Furthermore, the great significance of the poles, rings, and ropes may just *actually be* that they kept the Tabernacle structure from falling down! The specificity and elaborate nature of the Tabernacle must first be understood as a testament to the holiness of the structure and how God expects it to reflect His majesty.

a golden calf, and perhaps intending it to be a representative for HaShem or some kind of consort for Him or any number of possible things, Aaron actually tells Israel "These are your gods, O Israel, who brought you up out of Egypt" (Exodus 31:4). He compounds his own sin by then declaring, "Tomorrow there will be a festival to the LORD" (Exodus 31:5), and so the Israelites rebel against the One True God and indulge themselves before the idol (Exodus 31:6).

The Lord promptly tells Moses, "Go down, because your people, whom you brought up out of Egypt, have become corrupt. They have been quick to turn away from what I commanded them" (Exodus 32:7-8a). A unique scene then takes place, as the Lord tells Moses, "Now leave me alone so that my anger may burn against them and that I may destroy them. Then I will make you into a great nation" (Exodus 32:10). Moses entreats his God, "why should your anger burn against your people, whom you brought out of Egypt with great power and a mighty hand? Why should the Egyptians say, 'It was with evil intent that he brought them out, to kill them in the mountains and to wipe them off the face of the earth'?" (Exodus 32:11-12). Did God deliver Israel only to wipe them out in the desert? What message would this send to the Egyptians? **It would not be consistent with the mercy of which He spoke when delivering the Ten Commandments** (cf. Exodus 20:5-6). Moses reminds God about the promises He made to multiply the Patriarchs' seed (Exodus 32:13), and so He does not destroy the people (Exodus 32:14).

Moses descends Mount Sinai, showing Joshua the tablets of the Ten Commandments (Exodus 32:15-16). The two of them encounter the Israelites in revelry before the golden calf, and so Moses' "anger burned and he threw the tablets out of his hands, breaking them to pieces at the foot of the mountain" (Exodus 32:19). The calf is taken and ground into powder, scattered into water for the Israelites to drink (Exodus 32:20). Aaron's response to *why* he had fashioned the calf is patently weak: "they gave me the gold, and I threw it into the fire, and out came this calf!" (Exodus 32:24). To quell any further rebellion against HaShem, Moses rallies the Levites to himself who are to go and kill those who "were running wild" (Exodus 32:25, cf. vs. 28-29). Moses returns to God's presence on Mount Sinai, and a plague is unleashed upon the Israelites because of their worship of the golden calf (Exodus 32:35). But most significantly, the fact that the Lord did not destroy *all of the people* because of their rebellion, **is a great indication that He is different from all of the other gods of Planet Earth.** All of the other Ancient Near Eastern deities would have wiped out their people without any second thoughts.

As things begin to stabilize in the camp of Israel, Moses sets up a special Tent of Meeting, where the business of administering Israel was to be conducted (Exodus 33:7-8). The presence of the Lord would frequently manifest itself at the Tent of Meeting (Exodus 33:9-11), and most of the intimate one-on-one communication He would have with Moses would occur here. HaShem clearly tells Moses, "My Presence will go with you, and I will give you rest" (Exodus 33:14). The leader of Israel will later get to actually see the "back" of God, but not His face, witnessing a greater manifestation of His goodness and compassion (Exodus 33:19-20).

The Lord does not cast aside His chosen people. He commissions Moses to once again ascend Mount Sinai, but this time chisel for himself a second set of Ten Commandments (Exodus 34:1-5). Moses recognizes what God is doing by proclaiming "The LORD, the LORD, the compassionate and gracious God, slow to anger, abounding in love and faithfulness, maintaining love to thousands, and forgiving wickedness, rebellion and sin. Yet he does not leave the guilty unpunished; he punishes the children and their children for the sin of the fathers to the third and fourth generation" (Exodus 34:6-7). We are disadvantaged as people in the Twenty-First Century to read these words, because too many place an emphasize on curses or punishments that are to only pass down to the third and forth generations, in light of what the mercy and compassion of God truly mean when set against the religious background of the Thirteenth Century B.C.E. *No other gods of the period offered such beneficence!* HaShem is truly unique by displaying these great qualities, and provides for forgiveness and restitution (cf. Exodus 34:8-9)!

It is at this point where God states His definitive intention to enter into a covenant relationship with Israel (Exodus 34:10). Their salvation thus far has been a very rocky road since the parting of the Red Sea, but now He is preparing to train the people as to what it means to be His holy witnesses in the world. By obeying Him, the pagan inhabitants of Canaan will be driven out (Exodus 34:11). But Israel is reminded, "Break down their altars, smash their sacred stones and cut down their Asherah poles. Do not worship any other god, for the LORD, whose name is Jealous, is a jealous God" (Exodus 34:13; cf. 17). HaShem desires the complete and total loyalty of His people! He then repeats to Israel some of the important things of what it means to be His people (Exodus 34:17-26), and these things are all transcribed in the official record (Exodus 34:27). When returning from the mountain, Moses shines with the glory of God so significantly that he must place a veil over his face (Exodus 34:29-35).

The remainder of the Book of Exodus describes how the Tabernacle was constructed, the materials used were collected, and how some specific people were used in its assembly (Exodus chs. 35-40). One year from their departure from Egypt, the Tabernacle of the Lord is finally consecrated (Exodus 40:17), and the people of Israel have a sanctuary in their midst with which they can formally relate to their God. After Moses completes the final work, "the cloud covered the Tent of Meeting, and the glory of the LORD filled the tabernacle...In all the travels of the Israelites, whenever the cloud lifted from above the tabernacle, they would set out; but if the cloud did not lift, they did not set out—until the day it lifted. So the cloud of the LORD was over the tabernacle by day, and fire was in the cloud by night, in the sight of all the house of Israel during all their travels" (Exodus 40:34, 36-38). **The Israelites were now ready to enter into the great purpose that God had for them**, following Him at His lead.

We reflect on these events 3,300 years after they took place. We are undeniably affected by films such as The Ten Commandments or Prince of Egypt, each of which gives an artistic interpretation of the events. But the Biblical text tells us things much more significant than Hollywood ever can! When examining the message of Exodus, we are given the two important sides to the salvation message. Salvation begins by the Lord God directly intervening in the lives of human beings via His deliverance through the Red Sea, and salvation continues by being brought to His mountain and given His Instruction for holy living. As we grow in faith, we are trained and molded by God so that we can serve as priests in the world—intermediaries between HaShem and the rest of the world commissioned to declare His goodness. We also remember that the Lord is very patient with us when we do falter, and He will often restrain the full force of His judgment.

Understanding the dynamic themes of the Book of Exodus is one of the most important things that today's Messianic movement can do. The unique messages that Exodus has, played an extremely important role in the development of Messianism and the concept of the Messiah serving as a "second Moses." They formed a substantial part of Messianic expectation and prophecy accomplished by Yeshua, and certainly Exodus helped inform the Apostles' worldview in the First Century. Yeshua the Messiah is certainly our Passover Lamb, but we have so much *more* to consider when it comes to Exodus, that it is overwhelming with all of the lessons to be considered and learned, although it is also very simple.

How are we to be led on our own exodus out of sin, into not only a new birth via the cross, but also a new life as we approach God's mountain? Exodus thematically teaches us about justification and sanctification—being forgiven of sin *and* growing in God's grace—concepts which we can never overemphasize! How we learn to appreciate the message of Exodus as today's Messianic community will not be a huge challenge if we truly desire to be a people who can accomplish the Lord's purpose for us.[8]

---

[8] Consult the entry for the Book of Exodus in *A Survey of the Tanach for the Practical Messianic* for a summary of its date, composition, etc.

~7~

The Song of Moses
and God's Mission for His People

J.K. McKee

The emergence of a Messianic community that advocates, or at the very least, is more highly conscious of the promised restoration of Israel and the Hebraic Roots of the faith, asks questions that most as of today are not aware of—much less prepared to answer. Non-Jewish Believers, for example, entering into today's Messianic movement and becoming Torah obedient, are not supposed to become Messianic so that they can feel "born again again." They are also not designed to fill a void in people's hearts that they feel has been missing in their faith. *Being spiritually regenerated can **only** be provided by the redeeming work of Yeshua the Messiah!* The promised restoration of God's people, rather, should give all people within the maturing Messianic movement a vision and focus for the future as we determine the mission that God has for us as His people **as originally given to Ancient Israel.**

As new Messianic Believers have been made aware of the fact that they are all a part of the Commonwealth of Israel (Ephesians 2:11-12) or the Israel of God (Galatians 6:16), too many do not know the full ramifications of this reality in their lives. What does it mean to actually be "Israel"? For many, this answer is found in a life of diligent Torah obedience. But is Torah obedience to be an end to itself? The Torah is *more* than just a listing of commandments and principles by which to live; the Torah contains key stories and foundational accounts that are to mold God's people for His service. I would submit that only when we all **know** what that service is to be—whether we are Jewish or non-Jewish Believers—then we can be those who are fully aware of what it means to be "Israel."

Many Messianics believe that we are living in the end-times. Some think Yeshua will return very soon, and others not so soon. Some think that they can actually calculate the time of the end, while others prefer to look at various signs and events in the world. Not enough consider a wider array of Biblical prophecies and phenomena which define what *God's people* are to be doing in the end-times—versus those of the world. Surely, as the major theme of the Last Days is, "Lord, is it at this time You are restoring the kingdom to Israel?" (Acts 1:6), our Heavenly Father will be more concerned about *His people* during this time, than the rise of the beast or the false prophet.[1] Few in the emerging Messianic community today are aware of the full ramifications of the following prophecy:

"And they sang the song of Moses, the bond-servant of God, and the song of the Lamb, saying, 'Great and marvelous are Your works, O Lord God, the Almighty; righteous and true are Your ways, King of the nations!'" (Revelation 15:3).

The Book of Revelation says that in the end-times, the saints will be those who "sing[2] the song of Moses, the servant of God, and the song of the Lamb" (RSV). Certainly, we should all agree that the Song of the Lamb represents the proclamation of the gospel, and the salvation that is available in Yeshua. This is fairly obvious, as the saints are also those "who keep the commandments of God and hold to the testimony of Yeshua" (Revelation 12:17; 14:12). To "sing" the Song of the Lamb is simply a poetic way of saying "proclaim the good news."

What it means for the end-time saints to sing the Song of Moses is actually much more complicated. By no means is it a popular praise song sung in today's Messianic world! "Singing" the Song of Moses means that **we are to embody the mission and purpose as seen in the Song of Moses.** In order to do this, we must identify what the Song of Moses actually is, interpret it properly against its ancient context, and then consider some of the specific things that are involved with the prophesied restoration of God's people. We may find that the Song of Moses is much more complicated than we originally thought, and that it is going to challenge us both in our approach to theology *and* in how we interact with the world at large. We may not actually be "singing" this song today in our approach to Biblical faith.

The Message of the Exodus

When a person thinks of the Song of Moses, immediately the Ancient Israelites' Exodus from Egypt should come to mind. Not only should the Exodus come to mind because it is the event that the Biblical authors most often associate with Moses, but also because the Song of the Lamb—the gospel—is typified by the Exodus.

Our mission as the people of God is easily embodied in the picture of the Exodus. The Lord miraculously intervenes for the sake of those in harsh bondage to slavery, and then delivers them through the Red Sea (picturing salvation from sin). As Paul can confidently tell the Corinthians,

"For I do not want you to be unaware, brethren, that our fathers were all under the cloud and all passed through the sea; and all were baptized into Moses in the cloud and in the sea; and all ate the same spiritual food; and all drank the same spiritual drink, for they were drinking from a spiritual rock which followed them; and the rock was Messiah" (1 Corinthians 10:1-4).

But God's salvation obviously did not stop on the opposite shores of the Red Sea. The Lord took the Ancient Israelites to His mountain to enter into covenant relationship with them, and gave them His Instruction to train them to fulfill His mission (picturing sanctification). Being redeemed *and* then being instructed and empowered for the Lord's service—are all a part of the salvation experience.

---

[1] For some further discussion, consult the book *When Will the Messiah Return?* by J.K. McKee.

[2] Grk. *adousin* (ᾄδουσιν), present active indicative or "sing," not necessarily "sang."

God Himself in the Person of His Son has had to directly intervene in the lives of each of us who were in harsh bondage to sin, delivering us on an exodus out of slavery to new life and redemption in Him. Yet, our salvation today does not end with a proclamation of faith in Messiah Yeshua (Christ Jesus), but in fact *begins* there. Our salvation continues as we learn more about the Lord, our relationship with Him grows and becomes more intimate, and as we mature spiritually we accomplish the tasks He has given us.

The Exodus of Ancient Israel was surely about much more than just deliverance from Egyptian servitude.[3]

The Song of the Sea

The Book of Exodus can be easily divided into two principal sections: Israel in bondage (Exodus 1-14) and Israel in the wilderness (Exodus 15:19-40:38). The first section records how Ancient Israel was in slavery to Egypt, the calling of Moses as God's deliverer, the plagues upon Egypt, and the departure from Egypt itself. The second section covers some of the early journeys of Ancient Israel, the awesome scene of Mount Sinai and giving of the Ten Commandments, the worship of the golden calf, and the regulations regarding the Tabernacle. All of Exodus has extremely important things to teach God's people today,[4] but the two large divisions of Exodus hinge on one critical section as seen in Exodus 15:1-18 or the Song of the Sea. In Jewish theology the Song of the Sea is often referred to by the Hebrew designation *shirat ha'yam* (שִׁירַת הַיָּם). All of us should be familiar with the Song of the Sea:

> "Then Moses and the sons of Israel sang this song to the LORD, and said, 'I will sing to the LORD, for He is highly exalted; the horse and its rider He has hurled into the sea. The LORD is my strength and song, and He has become my salvation; this is my God, and I will praise Him; My father's God, and I will extol Him. The LORD is a warrior; the LORD is His name. Pharaoh's chariots and his army He has cast into the sea; and the choicest of his officers are drowned in the Red Sea. The deeps cover them; they went down into the depths like a stone. Your right hand, O LORD, is majestic in power, Your right hand, O LORD, shatters the enemy. And in the greatness of Your excellence You overthrow those who rise up against You; You send forth Your burning anger, *and* it consumes them as chaff. At the blast of Your nostrils the waters were piled up, the flowing waters stood up like a heap; the deeps were congealed in the heart of the sea. The enemy said, 'I will pursue, I will overtake, I will divide the spoil; My desire shall be gratified against them; I will draw out my sword, my hand will destroy them.' You blew with Your wind, the sea covered them; they sank like lead in the mighty waters. Who is like You among the gods, O LORD? Who is like You, majestic in holiness, awesome in praises, working wonders? You stretched out Your right hand, the earth swallowed them. In Your lovingkindness You have led the people whom You have redeemed; in Your strength You have guided *them* to Your holy habitation. The peoples have

---

[3] For a further discussion, consult this writer's article "The Message of Exodus."

[4] Indeed, I would strongly agree with John I. Durham, who opens his commentary (in *WBC*) with the statement, "The Book of Exodus is the first book of the Bible" (*Exodus*, xix). This is because without an Exodus of Israel from Egypt, there is no people to preserve and testify to the traditions regarding Creation, Noah, Abraham and the Patriarchs, and the faithfulness of God toward these individuals. In other words, without the Book of Exodus you have no Book of Genesis.

heard, they tremble; anguish has gripped the inhabitants of Philistia. Then the chiefs of Edom were dismayed; the leaders of Moab, trembling grips them; all the inhabitants of Canaan have melted away. Terror and dread fall upon them; by the greatness of Your arm they are motionless as stone; until Your people pass over, O LORD, until the people pass over whom You have purchased. You will bring them and plant them in the mountain of Your inheritance, the place, O LORD, which You have made for Your dwelling, the sanctuary, O Lord, which Your hands have established. The LORD shall reign forever and ever" (Exodus 15:1-18).

Most of you are familiar with what the *shirat ha'yam* is, and whether you realized it or not—the Song of the Sea *is* the Song of Moses.[5] The sections, of course, that draw your immediate attention are the proclamations of the mighty acts of God in leading the Israelites and in destroying the Egyptian armies. Although most of you are familiar with the Song of the Sea, you are probably only that familiar with vs. 1-5:

"I will sing to *ADONAI*, for he is highly exalted: the horse and its rider he threw in the sea. *Yah* is my strength and my song, and he has become my salvation. This is my God: I will glorify him; my father's God: I will exalt him. *ADONAI* is a warrior; *ADONAI* is his name. Pharaoh's chariots and his army he hurled into the sea. His elite commanders were drowned in the Sea of Suf. The deep waters covered them; they sank to the depths like a stone" (Exodus 15:1b-5, CJB).

The references to the LORD being the salvation of Israel and delivering Israel by His right hand fit very nicely with knowing that Yeshua is our Ultimate Salvation and that He sits at the Father's right hand. It is also important for us to know that just as Pharaoh's army was defeated by God in the Red Sea, so will Yeshua return victoriously and defeat the armies of the antimessiah/antichrist (Revelation 19:15-19). Yet, if we stop at v. 5 we miss the remainder of the Song of the Sea and we miss the greater focus of what it means to truly "sing" the Song of Moses.

Just consider what God actually does to the Egyptian armies:

"With a blast from your nostrils the waters piled up—the waters stood up like a wall, the depths of the sea became firm ground. The enemy said, 'I will pursue and overtake, divide the spoil and gorge myself on them. I will draw my sword; my

---

[5] While one might be tempted to identify the Song of Moses not with the *shirat ha'yam* of Exodus 15, but instead with Moses' closing words in Deuteronomy chs. 32 & 33, the opinion of various commentators identifies the Revelation 15:1-4 Song of Moses with Exodus 15:1-18. Alan Johnson indicates, "The Song of Moses is in Exodus 15:1-18. It celebrates the victory of the Lord in the defeat of the Egyptians at the Red Sea. In the ancient synagogue it was sung in the afternoon service each Sabbath to celebrate God's sovereign rule over the universe" (Alan Johnson, "Revelation," in Frank E. Gaebelein, ed. et. al., *Expositor's Bible Commentary*, Vol 12 [Grand Rapids: Zondervan, 1981], 546). Loren T. Stuckenbruck further says in regard to Revelation 15:1-4, "'the song of Moses'...chant alludes to the song of deliverance sung by Moses and the Israelites at the Red Sea (Exod 15:1-18)" (in James D.G. Dunn and John W. Rogerson, eds., *Eerdmans Commentary on the Bible* [Grand Rapids: Eerdmans, 2003], 1559).

The reference to the Song of Moses as Exodus 15:1-18 can be found in the Jewish *siddur* as a part of the *shacharit* prayers: "To the Israelite, the Redemption from Egypt is the great evidence of the rule of God in the universe" (Joseph H. Hertz, ed., *The Authorised Daily Prayer Book*, revised [New York: Bloch Publishing Company, 1960], pp 100-105; cf. Scherman and Zlotowitz, *Complete ArtScroll Siddur*, pp 78-81). This indicates that the *shirat ha'yam* or Song of Moses is indeed something that is recited every day in the Jewish tradition, thus making it imperative for today's Messianics to understand its theological significance, living it out properly.

hand will destroy them.' You blew with your wind, the sea covered them, they sank like lead in the mighty waters. Who is like you, *ADONAI*, among the mighty? Who is like you, sublime in holiness, awesome in praises, working wonders? You reached out with your right hand: the earth swallowed them. In your love, you led the people you redeemed; in your strength, you guided them to your holy abode" (Exodus 15:8-12, CJB).

Furthermore, consider what this event is going to mean for further things involving Israel:

"In your love, you led the people you redeemed; in your strength, you guided them to your holy abode. The peoples have heard, and they tremble; anguish takes hold of those living in P'leshet; then the chiefs of Edom are dismayed; trepidation seizes the heads of Mo'av; all those living in Kena'an are melted away. Terror and dread fall on them; by the might of your arm they are still as stone until your people pass over, *ADONAI*, till the people you purchased pass over. You will bring them in and plant them on the mountain which is your heritage, the place, *ADONAI*, that you made your abode, the sanctuary, *Adonai*, which your hands established. *ADONAI* will reign forever and ever" (Exodus 15:13-17, CJB).

What makes the Song of the Sea so significant is that it has a profound Ancient Near Eastern (ANE) background that often gets overlooked, and is underappreciated by most of your average Bible readers. Both Jewish and Christians scholars have recognized the ANE background behind the *shirat ha'yam*, however, and it is affecting some views of what it means for God's people to "sing" the Song of Moses. Nahum M. Sarna rightly recognizes that "The Song of the Sea assumed a special place in the Jewish liturgy quite early,"[6] yet he also does not hesitate to inform us, "The language of the poem is thoroughly archaic, employing several features commonly found in Canaanite poetry."[7] The *New Oxford Study Bible* also indicates that the reference to HaShem as "a man of war" (Exodus 15:3, RSV)[8] is reminiscent of "Canaanite mythical motifs [which] are used to confess the Lord's saving action in behalf of Israel."[9]

Today's Messianic community—either Messianic Judaism or the independent Messianic movement—largely fails with viewing the Tanach in its Ancient Near Eastern context. (In fact, in most Messianic exegesis it is just summarily disregarded and the Rabbinic tradition is *exclusively* what is consulted.)[10] This is unfortunate, because there is much to gain in what the Tanach says when placed against the other societies and cultures contemporary to Ancient Israel.[11] Evangelical Christian scholarship is further ahead in considering the ANE in its Old Testament scholarship, but is having to catch up to critical scholarship. Liberal scholars have

---

[6] Nahum M. Sarna, *JPS Torah Commentary: Exodus* (Philadelphia: Jewish Publication Society, 1991), 76.

[7] Ibid.

[8] Heb. *ADONAI ish milchamah* (יְהוָה אִישׁ מִלְחָמָה).

[9] Herbert G. May and Bruce M. Metzger, eds., *The New Oxford Annotated Bible With the Apocrypha*, RSV (New York: Oxford University Press, 1977), 86.

[10] Please note that I am not at all against giving a place to the Rabbinic tradition in Messianic examination of the Tanach; I am only against it having the *only* place.

[11] Of course, I must sadly also observe that as of right now (2008), the Messianic community does not deal very well with the role of Greco-Roman classicism in the broad Mediterranean background of the Apostolic Scriptures. Consult this writer's article "The Role of History in Messianic Biblical Interpretation" for a further discussion.

been much more affluent in considering the parallels between ANE literature and the Tanach, largely attributing such continuity to Ancient Israel "copying" off the religion of their neighbors.[12]

Some parallels between ANE mythology and various Biblical accounts seen in the Tanach are undeniable.[13] But did the Ancient Israelites merely borrow the religious ideas of their neighbors, as liberals commonly suggest? Or, did the accounts that the Ancient Israelites carry with them of their God—while paralleling some of the beliefs of their neighbors—still starkly contrast in the substance of the message? Conservative scholarship today is much more honest in recognizing the parallels between ANE religion and the Ancient Israelites, but is also much more forthright in demonstrating how the Bible *has the edge* over paganism.

With this all said, we cannot overlook the fact that the Song of the Sea has a message that parallels, yet directly confronts, some of the Canaanite religious views of the Thirteenth Century B.C.E. The Baal Cycle or the Epic of Baal,[14] is an Ugaritic religious story dating from 1400-1350 B.C.E., the same time period with Israel still in bondage to Egypt, yet being prepared to be delivered by Moses.[15] A major part of the Baal Cycle is "the conflict between Baal, the storm god, whose name means 'Lord,' and his enemy, Yamm, whose name means 'Sea.'"[16] It is likely that many of the Israelites knew, or had heard of the Baal Cycle, especially as Egypt was the superpower of the time and certainly had relations with the nearby Canaanites.

Ugaritic is a Semitic language possessing many cognates with Biblical Hebrew, and "the knowledge of Ugaritic texts has…provided clarification for interpretation of the OT" (*ISBE*).[17] Many nouns common to the Hebrew language, are pronounced exactly the same and mean exactly the same among its Semitic relatives—yet are also the proper names of Canaanite deities.[18] Terms such as *ba'al*

---

[12] Consult the workbook *A Survey of the Tanach for the Practical Messianic* for specific examples of how this has affected much of Old Testament Biblical scholarship on a book-by-book basis.

[13] Consult this writer's article "Encountering Mythology: A Case Study from the Flood Narratives," for comparisons and contrasts between the Flood of Genesis 6-8 and the Epic of Gilgamesh.

[14] The complete text of the Baal Cycle is available for access online at: <baal.com/baal/about/BaalEpic.shtml> or <piney.com/BaalEpic.html>.

[15] Note that while most Messianics hold to a Fifteenth Century B.C.E. Exodus, thus making the Torah approximately 3,500 years old, I hold to a Thirteenth Century B.C.E. Exodus, making the Torah approximately 3,300 years old. For a summation of the different views, consult K.A. Kitchen, "Exodus, The," in David Noel Freedman, ed., *Anchor Bible Dictionary*, 6 vols. (New York: Doubleday, 1992), 2:700-708; J.H. Walton, "Exodus, Date of," in T. Desmond Alexander and David W. Baker, eds., *Dictionary of the Old Testament Pentateuch* (Downers Grove, IL: InterVarsity, 2003), pp 258-272.

Also see this writer's entries for Exodus and Numbers in *A Survey of the Tanach for the Practical Messianic*.

[16] Mark S. Smith, trans., "The Baal Cycle," in Simon B. Parker, ed., *Ugaritic Narrative Poetry* (Atlanta: Society of Biblical Literature, 1997), 82.

[17] M. Liverani, "Ugarit; Ugaritic," in Geoffrey Bromiley, ed., *International Standard Bible Encyclopedia*, 4 vols. (Grand Rapids: Eerdmans, 1988), 4:939.

[18] The fact that terms used in Biblical Hebrew are also used in its Semitic relatives such as Ugaritic to refer to pagan deities, is neither known nor understood by many teachers in today's Messianic movement, who often perceive of Hebrew as a so-called "holy tongue" based on a misunderstanding of Zephaniah 3:9 (where the "purified lips" are actually speaking of a manner of speech [cf. Ephesians 4:29], not a spoken language). Such a misunderstanding can lead to ridiculous conclusions such as,

"The Set-apart Spirit, inspiring all Scripture, would most certainly not have transgressed the Law of Yahuweh by 'inspiring' the Messianic Scriptures in a language riddled with the names of Greek deities and freely using the names of these deities in the text, no way!" (C.J. Koster, *Come Out of Her, My People* [Northriding, South Africa: Institute for Scripture Research, 1998], vi).

(בַּעַל) and *yam* (יָם) and *el* (אֵל) as seen in the Ugaritic Baal Cycle (and many more), are used as common vocabulary words throughout the Hebrew Tanach, meaning: "husband," "sea," and "G/god." Many scholars are now agreed that the *shirat ha'yam* or the Song of the Sea employs various terms as seen in the Baal Cycle, as the defeat of Egypt sends a message from the God of Israel to the Canaanite peoples occupying the Promised Land.[19]

The message of the Song of the Sea takes *and subverts* themes as narrated in the conflict between Baal and Yamm, the sea god. The scene opens up with the god El trying to moderate their dispute:

The Messengers Deliver Yamm's Message
Then Yamm's messengers arrive, the legation of Judge River. At El's feet they [do not] bow down, they do not prostrate themselves before the Assembled Council. Standing, they speak a speech, [reci]te their instructions. A flame, two flames they appear, their [ton]gue a sharp sword. They tell Bull El, his Father: "Word of Yamm, your Lord, Your [Master], Judge River: 'Give up, O Gods, the One you obey, the One you obey, O Multitude; give up Baal that I may humble him, the Son of Dagon, that I may possess his gold.'"

El and Baal Respond
[And] Bull El, his Father, [answers:] "Your slave is Baal, O Yamm, your slave is Baal, [O River,] the Son of Dagon, your captive. He will bring tribute to you, like the Gods, bring [a gift to you,] like the Holy Ones, offerings to you."

Then Prince Baal is shaken: [He seize]s with his hand a striker, in his right hand a slayer, the land he str[ikes.][20]

The narrative then continues, telling us how Baal prepares to fight Yamm and then defeats him in battle:

Kothar Prepares Two Weapons for Battle Against Yamm
Kothar fashions the weapons, and he proclaims their names: "Your name, yours, is Yagarrish: Yagarrish, drive Yamm, drive Yamm from his throne, [Na]har from the seat of his dominion. May you leap from Baal's hand, like a raptor from his fingers. Strike the torso of Prince Yamm, between the arms of [Jud]ge River."

The weapon leaps from Baal's hand, like a raptor from his [fin]gers. It strikes the torso of Prince Yamm, between the arms of Judge River....

The weapon leaps from Baal's hand, [like] a raptor from his fingers, it strikes the head of Prince [Yamm,] between the eyes of Judge River. Yamm collapses and

---

Such assertions fail to consider the relationship of Biblical Hebrew as a Semitic language, and terms common to Hebrew used as the proper names of pagan gods in languages such as Ugaritic—including the terms El (אל) and Elohim (אֱלֹהִים)—which are applied to YHWH in the Tanach (cf. Jack B. Scott, "ʼēl," in R. Laird Harris, Gleason L. Archer, Jr., and Bruce K. Waltke, eds., *Theological Wordbook of the Old Testament*, 2 vols. [Chicago: Moody Press, 1980], 1:42). If such a standard as proposed were applied to the whole of Scripture, neither the Hebrew Tanach nor Greek Messianic Writings could be considered inspired of the Almighty, as both languages include common vocabulary words used to refer to pagan deities.

[19] Cf. Brian D. Russell, *The Song of the Sea: the Date of Composition and Influence of Exodus 15: 1-21* (New York: Peter Lang, 2007).

[20] *Ugaritic Narrative Poetry*, pp 100-101.

falls to the earth, his joints shake, and his form collapses. Baal drags and dismembers Yamm, destroys Judge River.[21]

Defeating Yamm in battle, Baal is then declared as king[22] and holds a victory feast.[23]

The similarity between the Baal Cycle and the Song of the Sea in Exodus 15, is that Baal is seen fighting Yamm, but that HaShem is actually seen using *yam* (יָם). Water, represented by the deity Yamm, was a major force in the ANE, as John Goldingay attests, "Middle Eastern cultures often used waters as a symbol of overwhelming threatening forces. These waters are indispensable to earthly life, yet they also imperil it from time to time."[24] In the Canaanite mythology, Baal and Yamm are equal deities separated only by a battle in which Baal defeats Yamm and takes over his holdings. Yet in the Biblical record, it is HaShem the God of Israel who has dominion over *yam* and who actually uses the sea to defeat His enemies:

"The deeps covered them; they went down into the depths like a stone. Your right hand, O LORD, glorious in power, Your right hand, O LORD, shatters the foe! In Your great triumph You break Your opponents; You send forth Your fury, it consumes them like straw. At the blast of Your nostrils the waters piled up, the floods stood straight like a wall; the deeps froze in the heart of the sea" (Exodus 15:5-8, NJPS).

Ancient Israel's Subversion of the Baal Cycle

How does the Song of the Sea of Exodus 15 compare to the Baal Cycle? In the Song of the Sea, HaShem is portrayed as a warrior (Exodus 15:3) just as Baal. In the Song of the Sea, HaShem defeats His enemies with His right hand (Exodus 15:6) just as Baal defeated Yamm. The key contrast between the Song of the Sea and the Baal Cycle is that **the God of Israel does not fight the sea!**

Exodus 15:4 says *markevot Par'oh v'chelo yara b'yam* (פַּרְעֹה וְחֵילוֹ יָרָה בַיָּם מַרְכְּבֹת), or "Pharaoh's chariots and army He threw in the sea" (ATS). In particular, it is recorded in v. 5 that "The deeps" or *tehemot* (תְּהֹמֹת) "cover them," which according to Durham were "the great primordial ocean waters held in restless impotence by [God] save when, as here, he turns them to his purposes."[25] HaShem exercises a complete and total control over *yam*, and uses *yam* for whatever He sees fit. Unlike the gods Baal and Yamm being equals, HaShem the God of Israel has no equals.

The Ancient Israelites declare before Him, "Who is like You, O LORD, among the celestials; who is like You, majestic in holiness, awesome in splendor, working wonders! You put out Your right hand, the earth swallowed them. In Your love You lead the people You redeemed; in Your strength You guide them to Your holy abode" (Exodus 15:9-13, NJPS). They praise HaShem for the mighty acts of deliverance He has demonstrated, and the awesome power that He displays over

---

[21] Ibid., pp 103, 104.

[22] Ibid., 105.

[23] Ibid., 106.

[24] John Goldingay, *Old Testament Theology: Israel's Gospel* (Downers Grove, IL: InterVarsity, 2003), 88.

[25] Durham, 206.

His Creation. Yet the message of HaShem's complete control was *not only* for the Ancient Egyptians, as the Song of the Sea continues:

"The peoples hear, they tremble; agony grips the dwellers in Philistia. Now are the clans of Edom dismayed; the tribes of Moab—trembling grips them; all the dwellers in Canaan are aghast. Terror and dread descend upon them; through the might of Your arm they are still as stone—till Your people cross over, O LORD, till Your people cross whom You have ransomed" (Exodus 15:14-16, NJPS).

The Ancient Israelites were going to enter into a Promised Land that had, as its then-present occupants: the Philistines, Edomites, Moabites, and Canaanites. All of these people, to some degree or another, recognized Baal as their principal deity, believing him to have defeated Yamm. Sarna is right to assert, "God's mighty deeds on Israel's behalf strike terror in the hearts of Israel's neighbors, their potential enemies."[26] The Ancient Israelites, being prepared to enter into the Promised Land, actually have a subversive message for the Canaanites: **You fear Baal and Yamm, yet our God is superior to them as He controls them!**

Baal, being the supreme deity of the Canaanites, set himself upon a mountain so that the peoples would all come to him and be in bondage to him as his slaves. In fact, most deities in the ANE had a mountain by which he/she could rule over the people subjugated as slaves. Yet, it is only HaShem in contrast to those false gods **who actually asks people to come to His mountain to join with Him in communion.** This too is a major feature of the Song of the Sea:

"You will bring them and plant them in Your own mountain, the place You made to dwell in, O LORD, the sanctuary, O LORD, which Your hands established. The LORD will reign for ever and ever!" (Exodus 15:17-18, NJPS).

B'har nachalatkha (בְּהַר נַחֲלָתְךָ) or "on your own mountain" (ESV) is where God plans to live and rule and reign over His people. The significance of HaShem having His own mountain is fully realized only against its ANE context. Sarna remarks that this "is a unique phrase in the Bible. It occurs in Ugaritic literature in relation to the sacred mountain *Ṣapon* on which stood the sanctuary of the Canaanite deity Baal. Here, this standard religious phrase, prevalent in the ancient Near East, is employed by the poet in monotheized form, totally emptied of its pagan content."[27] Apparently, HaShem taking over Baal's mountain was so important, that references to *Tzafon* (צָפוֹן) or the "north" are seen in the Book of Psalms:

"Great is the LORD, and greatly to be praised, in the city of our God, His holy mountain. Beautiful in elevation, the joy of the whole earth, is Mount Zion *in* the far north [*yarketei tzafon*, יַרְכְּתֵי צָפוֹן], the city of the great King" (Psalm 48:1-2).

"The heavens are Yours, the earth also is Yours; the world and all it contains, You have founded them. The north [*tzafon*] and the south, You have created them; Tabor and Hermon shout for joy at Your name. You have a strong arm; Your hand is mighty, Your right hand is exalted" (Psalm 89:11-13).[28]

The enemy of our souls has never had an original idea of His own; he has always been copying and mimicking God from the beginning, twisting God's truth

---

[26] Sarna, *Exodus*, 80.

[27] Ibid., 82.

[28] Note that just like Mount Zaphon being the mountain of Baal, Mounts Tabor and Hermon were also considered to be the habitations of Canaanite deities. Cf. Rafael Frankel, "Tabor, Mount," in *ABD*, 6:304-305; Rami Arav, "Hermon, Mount," in *ABD*, 3:158-160.

for his own ends. Yet the Lord has always been there to turn the tables on Satan, showing him up. The Song of the Sea is an excellent example of this. The enemy's demonic minions of Baal and Yamm, believed to possess mountains by which they can dominate human beings—are shown to be the frauds that they are by the message of Mount Sinai where HaShem asks the people to join Him in covenant relationship. Christopher J.H. Wright confirms,

"The use of this Canaanite imagery does not mean, of course, that the Old Testament *endorsed* the myths of...Baal. On the contrary, the faith of Israel subordinated any affirmations about these gods to the reign of YHWH. The Old Testament took over the language of Baal's kingship for the purpose of countering it by ascribing all rule in heaven and on earth to YHWH alone."[29]

Far from being slaves to the deity, the Lord asks Israel to be His servants in the world by declaring to the world His goodness and righteousness. Unless the Canaanites **would heed the message as declared by the Song of the Sea**, and possibly join with Israel as people like Rahab did,[30] then they would be consumed by their own sin. Before the Ancient Israelites enter into the Promised Land, God reminds them that it was because of the wickedness of the current inhabitants why they were to receive it:

"Do not say in your heart when the LORD your God has driven them out before you, 'Because of my righteousness the LORD has brought me in to possess this land,' **but *it is* because of the wickedness of these nations *that* the LORD is dispossessing them before you.** It is not for your righteousness or for the uprightness of your heart that you are going to possess their land, but *it is* because of the wickedness of these nations *that* the LORD your God is driving them out before you**, in order to confirm the oath which the LORD swore to your fathers, to Abraham, Isaac and Jacob" (Deuteronomy 9:4-5).

Truly, the Song of the Sea has much to teach us as Messianic Believers, and specifically the mission that the Lord has given us as He is in the process of restoring His people.

The Gospel as a Subversive Message

There are many more examples present in the Tanach where the message of the God of Israel directly subverts Ancient Near Eastern mythology: namely in that our Creator desires communion with His creatures, rather than the gods creating us only to make us their slaves. The Song of the Sea, *being the Song of Moses*, gives us an excellent picture of the mission that God's people are to perform. As a tribute to the Song of the Sea, Rahab testified, "For we have heard how the LORD dried up the water of the Red Sea before you when you came out of Egypt" (Joshua 2:10a), and she was "under the ban" (Joshua 6:17), being saved from the destruction of Jericho.

The need for God's people to communicate effectively to other cultures and societies is seen from the very beginning of Scripture, and is certainly seen in the Apostolic Scriptures. The Lord Himself appointed the Apostle Paul as "a chosen instrument of Mine, to bear My name before the Gentiles and kings and the sons of Israel" (Acts 9:15), and his unique training both as a Pharisee and Roman citizen

---

[29] Christopher J.H. Wright, *The Mission of God: Unlocking the Bible's Grand Narrative* (Downers Grove, IL: IVP Academic, 2006), 78.
[30] Joshua 2:1, 3; 6:17, 23, 25.

prepared him in advance to communicate the gospel effectively to the broad Mediterranean world. Paul had the training and the skills to go to the Synagogue and proclaim the gospel to Jews, and debate with Greeks and Romans in the marketplace about the futility of their religion. As he summarizes his ministry approach,

"I became to the Jews as a Jew, that Jews I might gain; to those under law as under law, that those under law I might gain; to those without law, as without law—(not being without law to God, but within law to Christ)—that I might gain those without law; I became to the infirm as infirm, that the infirm I might gain; to all men I have become all things, that by all means I may save some" (1 Corinthians 9:20-22, YLT).

Here, Paul is not saying that he keeps the Torah when around Jews and when around Greeks or Romans he disregards it. What he is saying is that he does his best to identify with his audience. To those Jews who are "under law" or subject to the Torah's penalties, being without faith in the Messiah, he does his best to consider their circumstances.[31] The same is true of pagans without God's Torah, which he *testifies to still follow* according to the Messiah's example (cf. Galatians 6:2). Likewise, Paul does his best to understand those with physical ailments. Paul did his best to consider the point of view of others—"With all kinds of people I have become all kinds of things" (CJB)—in order that he may see some come to saving faith.

The best kind of subversion we can directly see in the Apostolic Scriptures is probably witnessed in Paul's encounter with the Epicureans and Stoics at the Areopagus (Mars Hill) in Athens:

"Now while Paul was waiting for them at Athens, his spirit was being provoked within him as he was observing the city full of idols. So he was reasoning in the synagogue with the Jews and the God-fearing *Gentiles*, and in the market place every day with those who happened to be present…So Paul stood in the midst of the Areopagus and said, 'Men of Athens, I observe that you are very religious in all respects. For while I was passing through and examining the objects of your worship, I also found an altar with this inscription, "TO AN UNKNOWN GOD." Therefore what you worship in ignorance, this I proclaim to you. The God who made the world and all things in it, since He is Lord of heaven and earth, does not dwell in temples made with hands; nor is He served by human hands, as though He needed anything, since He Himself gives to all *people* life and breath and all things; and He made from one *man* every nation of mankind to live on all the face of the earth, having determined *their* appointed times and the boundaries of their habitation, that they would seek God, if perhaps they might grope for Him and find Him, though He is not far from each one of us; for in Him we live and move and exist, as even some of your own poets have said, "For we also are His children." Being then the children of God, we ought not to think that the Divine Nature is like gold or silver or stone, an image formed by the art and thought of man. Therefore having overlooked the times of ignorance, God is now declaring to men that all *people* everywhere should repent, because He has fixed a day in which He will judge the world in righteousness through a Man whom He has appointed,

---

[31] Consult this writer's article "What Does 'Under the Law' Really Mean?" for a further examination.

having furnished proof to all men by raising Him from the dead'" (Acts 17:16-17, 22-31).

In this classic scene from the Scriptures, Paul takes advantage of the situation presented to him in Athens. He is enraged at the idolatry present in the city, yet notices some kind of shrine dedicated to the "Unknown God." This he recognizes as being dedicated to the God of Creation, the God of Israel. Paul proceeds to say how He has blessed the Athenians in the past with life and sustenance, and is now taking an active interest in their lives. This God has now provided a means of complete satisfaction in One He has sent and resurrected from the dead.

Paul certainly had difficulty communicating the concept of resurrection to these Greeks. But, some of them seeking the "Divine Consciousness" were convinced that Paul had something to offer, testifying "We shall hear you again concerning this" (Acts 17:32). Paul was able to *validly subvert* something dedicated to what the Athenians knew as who-knows-what, and recognize that the God He knew had delivered Israel in the past—and had now sent His Son for the deliverance of sins—could offer them the same salvation that he had experienced. This was a transforming experience that the idols of Athens could not offer.

In the millennia since Paul debated in Athens, many Christians have done their best to subvert the native cultures into which they were planted. Some have done this with success, providing answers to pagans and skeptics and atheists, and have introduced them to Yeshua and have brought them redemption. Others have done this at the expense of practicing syncretism,[32] where Biblical concepts do not confront and subvert paganism, offering an alternative to Satan's lies, but instead find themselves fused and melded with native religion.

We have the advantage of history of being able to look back and discern the differences between cultural subversion and cultural syncretism as seen in both the Synagogue and the Church. How we do this as today's emerging Messianic movement, however, is a huge challenge.

"Singing" the Song of Deliverance

When Revelation 15:3 tells us that the end-time saints "sing" the Song of Moses, what it undoubtedly means is that these people will know how to embody the message of the *shirat ha'yam* of Exodus 15. The Song of the Sea contained a message to the inhabitants of the Promised Land that Israel was coming, and that Israel's God provided them something that neither the false gods Baal nor Yamm could.

Moving forward to today, in order to be molded into a people that can "sing" the Song of Moses, the emerging Messianic movement **must learn** to subvert the native cultures in which it finds itself. Unfortunately based on some of the current trends seen in the Messianic community, it may be a long time before we see this become reality. Whereas the Song of the Sea forces us to engage with the world

---

[32] The *Pocket Dictionary of Theological Terms* defines syncretism as, "The attempt to assimilate differing or opposite doctrines and practices, especially between philosophical and religious systems, resulting in a new system altogether in which the fundamental structure and tenets of each have been changed. Syncretism of the gospel occurs when its essential character is confused with the elements from the culture. In syncretism the gospel is lost as the church simply confirms what is already present in the culture" (Stanley J. Grenz, David Guretzki, and Cherith Fee Nordling [Downers Grove, IL: InterVarsity, 1999], 111).

and directly confront the world, disengagement and isolationism are largely seen in today's Messianic community.[33] Whereas the Song of the Sea forces us to recognize that Israel had a Divine mission to fulfill by proclaiming of the goodness of God, declaring our human "goodness" by keeping the Torah is what is commonplace in today's Messianic community (cf. Philippians 3:6-7).

Until we see a significant shift toward a more evangelistic, engaged, and above all spirituality edifying Messianic movement—that can be all the things that Ancient Israel was to be—we will not be able to "sing" the Song of Moses. And, this is surely complicated by a widescale inability to be well informed by a wider view of Biblical Studies, as demonstrated by comparing the Song of Sea to the Baal Cycle.

Singing the Song of Moses is not sitting in a congregation shouting out some praise song with Revelation 15:3 embedded in the chorus, any more than it is singing the words of Exodus 15. Singing the Song of Moses requires us as God's people **to embody the character and ethos of the Song of the Sea, and to live out its mission in our lives.** We have to demonstrate how our God is superior to all things.

How long will it be before the emerging Messianic movement can be a missional community that will be able to subvert the message of the world's cultures? When will we be able to recognize the needs of others, who are diligently searching for redemption, but will only be able to find it in Yeshua the Messiah? When will we be able to have those among us who can fulfill the prophecy of the hunters and fishers going forth to the nations, specifically to those who have accepted complete lies and who worship gods other than the God of Israel? As Jeremiah prophesied,

"'Behold, I am going to send for many fishermen,' declares the LORD, 'and they will fish for them; and afterwards I will send for many hunters, and they will hunt them from every mountain and every hill and from the clefts of the rocks'...O LORD, my strength and my stronghold, and my refuge in the day of distress, to You the nations will come from the ends of the earth and say, 'Our fathers have inherited nothing but falsehood, futility and things of no profit.' Can man make gods for himself? Yet they are not gods! Therefore behold, I am going to make them know—this time I will make them know My power and My might; and they shall know that My name is the LORD" (Jeremiah 16:16, 19-21).

These hunters and fishers, who I personally believe will be the 144,000 sealed servants from every tribe of Israel (Revelation 4:7-8), will have the ability to respond to the cries of the world's masses. They will be able to know the cultural and religious diversity of the audiences to whom they proclaim the goodness of the Lord of Creation, and properly present them with the message of salvation. They will be able to provide the answers that are so desperately sought and desired by such people.

The Song of the Sea asks today's Messianic movement some questions about who we are, and what lies ahead for us in the future. How we will be able to live out its message, though, is likely to be determined in the forthcoming years and decades, as we begin to mature both spiritually *and* theologically. Initially, it will not be easy, but in the long run God promises us that we will be able to "sing" His

---

[33] For a further discussion, consult this writer's article "How Are We to Live As Modern Messianics?"

song of deliverance to the entire world! I pray that each of us as individuals would learn to "sing" that song of deliverance *right now*, as we each work toward the restoration of His Kingdom.

~8~

"Everyone Is Wrong But Me!"

J.K. McKee

reproduced from the McHuey Blog

Passover is one of the most important times of year for the Messianic community of faith. The season of Passover and Unleavened Bread is so affluent with themes of God's salvation history it absolutely overwhelms the mind and inspires the soul. The Lord's plagues upon Egypt, the death of the firstborn, the Passover lamb, the deliverance through the Red Sea, and the onset of the Ancient Israelites sojourn in the desert immediately stir the senses and motivate us to action. The final time before Yeshua's crucifixion, His Last Supper, His prayers in the Garden of Gethsemane, His trial before the Jewish religious leaders, His encounter before Pilate and being beaten by the Romans, and finally His crucifixion and resurrection, are also remembered by the faithful as we contemplate the sufferings of our Lord. What all these things mean, how they connect together, and the significant role they play in the Bible and for us today—are really beyond comprehension.

Why does it seem that today's Messianic community in the early Twenty-First Century does not address these themes very well at this time of year?

All the way back in 1996 when I first started celebrating Passover as a Messianic Believer, things seemed so much easier than they seem today. I was a part of a vibrant Messianic Jewish congregation. We had a traditional *seder* in our home the first night of Passover. On the following night the congregation assembled at a hotel for a catered, sit down *seder* presentation that was also traditional. If I can recall correctly, there were at least 400 people in attendance, things went very smoothly, and many Christian visitors were exposed to the Messianic movement and to the significance of the Passover meal for the first time, in a very orderly and professional manner. I still think back on this first *seder* and consider it to be the ideal for every congregation and fellowship.

Since the late 1990s an incredible swell of non-Jewish Believers has entered into the Messianic movement, and issues that were not issues in Messianic Judaism have arisen to the surface. A great number of debates ensue this time of year that can cause a large amount of division and in-fighting among Messianic congregations and assemblies. They all concern the season of Passover. In the past three to four years (2004-2008), in particular, I have encountered far too many people utter the line: **"Everybody is wrong but me!"** People who are believed to have differing opinions, are at worst chastised as not truly following the Bible, or at best somehow not having the right "revelation." Where God's love, reason, and a fair-minded examination of the issues are I honestly do not know.

We start with the Passover *seder* itself: Are we to follow the traditional Jewish *seder* with the four glasses of wine or not? Or do we follow our own *haggadah*? Do we have lamb following Sephardic Jewish custom, or chicken following Ashkenazic Jewish custom? Do we eat with our "loins girded" (Exodus 12:11), or in a relaxed posture (Mark 14:18; Luke 22:14)? Do we allow for an egg to be on our Passover plates? Moving forward, to what degree do we consider what is "kosher for Passover"? Is Orthodox Jewish *halachah* sufficient, do we follow the lead of the more Centrist branches of Judaism, or do we make up our own rulings? And what about the season of counting the *omer* to *Shavuot*? Do we follow the traditional, Pharisaical method of determining when to celebrate *Shavuot*, follow its competing Saddusaical method, or even follow the Essenic method as attested in the Dead Sea Scrolls?

I think it is safe to say that far too much attention has been given to some of the minutiae of this season than is appropriate—at the expense of some of the much larger issues.

With a large number of non-Jewish Believers entering into the Messianic movement, and with the rise of an independent Messianic congregational phenomenon, during this season we will usually witness a great number of a-traditional ways to celebrate Passover. We will also witness a great number of congregational leaders asserting that their way of commemorating the Festival of Freedom is *the only way*, and some will even throw down the gauntlet and say that other ways are invalid and that others are not truly "keeping Torah" or thus commemorating Passover. When the Lord looks down on us from His throne in Heaven, what does He really think? Does He see men and women united around the two most important events in the entire Bible: the Exodus of Ancient Israel from Egyptian bondage *and* the final atonement offered for our sins? Better yet, what does the enemy think when he sees much of the Messianic movement this time of year? He is probably very pleased to see many people divided and harping on one another's ills, and that the greatest spiritual move since the First Century is ineffective to make a difference.

Is it possible, that when you sit down to remember this special season, we can all focus on some of the bigger concerns of Passover?

What does the Exodus mean to you? What does it mean to sacrifice a blameless lamb? What does it mean to be delivered via the Red Sea and brought to God's mountain? What does it mean for the King of Kings to be conducting an intimate meal with His chosen Twelve, as He prepares to be taken and executed on false charges the next day? What does it mean for the Savior of the world to be lifted up on a painful cross? What does it mean for Yeshua to be resurrected from the dead?

The book is far from closed on some of the debates that ensue this time of year. **Only** time, more research, a greater consideration for a broad array of hermeneutical factors, and reasonable people being problem solvers, will adequately answer them. But this season is not about whether you have lamb or chicken at your *seder* meal, or whether you are a designated Pharisee or Sadducee when it comes to counting the *omer*. This season is about our all-powerful and merciful God taking an interest in His creatures. It is about God directly intervening in the affairs of His people, delivering them into His salvation, and empowering them for new opportunities. How we learn to do this as the emerging Messianic movement remains a challenge, but not an impossible one if we are guided by His Spirit. But it will not be accomplished if we brazenly assert **"Everybody is wrong but me!"** during this special time of the year. Such a statement will only cause more problems, and is not solution oriented.

Oh, how I long for those simpler times of just twelve short years ago!

~9~

The Last Seder
and Yeshua's Passover Chronology

J.K. McKee

The season of Passover was my late father's favorite time of year, because being a licensed lay preacher at Christ United Methodist Church in Florence, KY, Holy Week was the time when he was able to conduct educational Passover *seders* and expose many evangelical Christians to their Hebraic Roots. Kimball McKee was able to show many how Jesus Christ held an intimate Passover *seder* meal with His Disciples prior to His death as the Lamb of God. He recited some of the various blessings, held up a piece of real unleavened bread or *matzah* to people who had never seen it before, and explained in a very edifying way the connection between the themes of the Exodus and the Messiah's work in delivering us from sin. The presentation would end with a communion service completely unlike what any of the attendees had ever participated in before.

I am very blessed to be able to think back on what my father did twenty years ago, in helping people see the relevance of Passover to their Christian faith. Looking at what has transpired since, especially that I am now a Bible teacher in the Messianic movement, the Passover is one of the most important aspects of our relationship with God. If we understand the Passover, we understand a huge part of His salvation history plan. Many Jewish people have been able to understand the sacrifice of Yeshua and His atoning work for sins, far more from the typological connections made via the traditional Passover *seder* than the standard Christian traditions of Holy Week. And, many Christians have been stimulated by the Holy Spirit to do far more than just attend a presentation on Passover, or even participate in the yearly *seder* of a local Messianic Jewish congregation—investigating their connection to the Torah and its commandments even further.

No Messianic Believer today denies that the Exodus, Passover, and this season of deliverance is important to our faith. **It is very important.** But twenty years ago, the controversy that my father witnessed was that there would be a few dissenting voices in the local church about why Christians would be considering something "Jewish." There would be people, obviously not attending his teaching presentation, who would very much frown upon evangelical Believers hearing about how the message of Jesus was seen in the Passover—even in spite of Paul's own word, "Christ our Passover also has been sacrificed" (1 Corinthians 5:7). Today, in our Messianic faith community, while the relevance of the Passover is not at all questioned, we nevertheless do commonly face some controversies when the Spring holiday season arrives.

What kind of issues present themselves when the Passover season arrives? Would you believe that there are some people in the Messianic community today who do not believe that the Last Supper was a real, or even a kind-of, *seder* meal? How many of you have been engulfed in the argument that we need to do exactly what Yeshua did, and not any "traditions of men,"[1] making Passover a bit unexciting? While there are longstanding disagreements on *halachah* between the Ashkenazic and Sephardic Jewish traditions on what is kosher for Passover, think about some of the new Messianic disagreements that have arisen on what actually took place in those days leading up to Yeshua's betrayal and execution. How long is three days and three nights? Was the Messiah really crucified, or put to death another away? And this is only a short list of what often gets discussed...

Reasonable theological inquiry and discussion are things that are very good, and as a teacher I encourage them. Every maturing Believer has a responsibility to go to the Biblical text, and do his or her best to interpret what is read, and when appropriate consider the relevant extra-Biblical histories or opinions of trusted scholarship. The challenge with today's Messianic generation, though, is that this is often not achieved. Because of the easy access to information on the Internet, blogs, YouTube, or discussion forums—many people, *including congregational leaders*, get their teachings from less-than-reliable sources. There might be a few things quite necessary for the discussion that get left out, as they may not be found in electronic venues, but rather in (expensive) physical books. Because of this, Messianic leaders and teachers may find the Passover season to have some "issues," which in the past might not have been issues.

Many Messianic congregations and fellowships truly make Passover into a blessed time for all who are involved. Jewish Believers get to once again connect with various traditions and customs that are familiar to them, being a part of their childhood. Non-Jewish Believers get to consider the Exodus and the deliverance of Ancient Israel is a much more tangible way, that simply reading something from Scripture does not fully convey. **Everybody gets to see connections to the gospel message of salvation, that they did not get to see before.** Some get to see aspects of deliverance and freedom, beyond that of just salvation from sin—such as helping the oppressed or impoverished—that they might not have thought of. Most of today's Messianics, including myself, do believe that the Last Supper was some kind of a Passover *seder* meal. For many of those same, when we "eat of the bread and drink of the cup" (1 Corinthians 11:28), we are reminded of many meaningful and supernatural things at such a solemn point in our commemoration.

I will not hide the truth from you: there are debates among interpreters as to what actually took place in the final moments prior to Yeshua's arrest. No one is fully agreed as to whether or not the Last Supper was a *seder* meal, or the exact day on which the Lord was executed. There are disputes over whether three days and three nights is a full 72 hours, a little over 36 hours, or some other time interval.

---

[1] I personally prefer the more inclusive language rendering of *tēn paradosin tōn anthrōpōn* (τὴν παράδοσιν τῶν ἀνθρώπων) as "human tradition(s)" (Mark 7:8; Colossians 2:8, NRSV/TNIV).

Some of today's Messianic leaders (even myself at times), quite sadly, have looked at the Passover season with a little bit of dread—not because of its great themes of salvation from sin, deliverance from bondage, etc.—but because there will be debates over issues like the Passover chronology, which in all likelihood may never be fully solved. *They want the Passover week to end as quickly as possible*, and get back to the normal routine. (Of course, even this is a bit of wishful thinking, considering the fifty-day counting of the *omer*, and whether it is to begin on the 16th of Nisan or the first Sunday after the weekly Sabbath of Unleavened Bread.)

We may not have all of the information that we need to support, with one-hundred percent accuracy, the opinions which we hold. And what happens when we get so focused on the minutiae of the chronology of the Last Supper, trial, execution, and resurrection of the Lord? **We run the risk of forgetting about the substance of what took place.** It is a salvation requirement that we affirm that Yeshua died and was resurrected (Romans 10:9); it is not a salvation requirement that we affirm that it took place on a particular day of the week, or even at a specific hour, minute, and second of the day.

I want all of us as Messianic Believers to step back from our opinions for a moment, and *focus first* on what we can agree upon. I think we can all agree that the substance of what we need to be considering is found in Peter's summary,

"Men of Israel, listen to these words: Yeshua the Nazarene, a man attested to you by God with miracles and wonders and signs which God performed through Him in your midst, just as you yourselves know—this *Man*, delivered over by the predetermined plan and foreknowledge of God, you nailed to a cross by the hands of godless men and put *Him* to death. But God raised Him up again, putting an end to the agony of death, since it was impossible for Him to be held in its power" (Acts 2:22-24).

We all agree that believing in the sacrificial death and resurrection of Messiah Yeshua is what is essential to our faith. I would submit that our attention during this season of Passover needs to be focused more on the severity of what took place, **so we do not forget what the Lord has accomplished for us.** *If* we can all recognize how He was scourged for our transgressions (Isaiah 53:5), then we should be able to reasonably offer some proposals for how it took place. The patterns of prophetic fulfillment admittedly might not be found in some nice little package with a big bow, or seen in a chart with 0 and 1s accuracy. We have to consider the perspectives of all four Gospels, and also recognize that Twentieth and Twenty-First Century vantage points of specificity are not the same as those of ancient times. We also have to recognize the uniqueness of the year Yeshua died for us, and how in the years following things returned to their relatively normal routine.

This article will consider various aspects of what many call the "Passion Week," or the final days before Yeshua's execution: the Last Supper meal, His prayer in the Garden of Gethsemane, His trial and humiliation, and His crucifixion and death, then followed by His resurrection. While I will be interjecting some of my own thoughts and opinions as to how and when this took place, we should be more concerned with recapturing an appreciation *for what actually occurred*, recognizing the timing of it as secondary.

During the Passover season, some of today's Messianic teachers and leaders could make all sorts of pulpit-pounding conclusions regarding Yeshua's Passover chronology—but not enough reflective thoughts on what He endured for us, and how we should live in response to His atoning work as faithful men and women of God, will probably be offered. *We should hope to see this trend altered.* It should be our desire to probe the multiple aspects of how Paul asserts, "Messiah died for our sins according to the Scriptures, and...He was buried, and...He was raised on the third day according to the Scriptures" (1 Corinthians 15:3).

The Lamb of God

A significantly important theme that controls how we look at Yeshua's death is the explicit assertion that He is the Lamb of God. As John the Immerser declared, "Behold, the Lamb of God who takes away the sin of the world!" (John 1:29). When we commonly think of sheep, we think of poor, helpless, and defenseless animals being ruthlessly killed by some kind of Big Bad Wolf—but that is not the image that the Scriptures intend to portray of Yeshua the Messiah. I.H. Marshall points out, "The description of Jesus as the Lamb of God belongs to the language of sacrifice which is no longer common currency today."[2] People who would be closely acquainted with the Levitical priesthood and prescribed animal sacrifices of the Torah, would be those most apt to make the appropriate typological connections between Yeshua as the Lamb of God, and what He has accomplished for us on the cross.

The first claim of Yeshua being the Lamb of God does not appear in a Passover-specific setting, although Isaiah's Suffering Servant being a "guilt offering" (Isaiah 53:10; Heb. *asham*, אָשָׁם) could be what is in view. It is undeniable that later in the Gospel of John, a direct appeal is made between Yeshua's sacrifice and the Torah's instructions regarding the lamb killed at Passover:

> "For these things came to pass to fulfill the Scripture, 'NOT A BONE OF HIM SHALL BE BROKEN'" (John 19:36).

> "It is to be eaten in a single house; you are not to bring forth any of the flesh outside of the house, nor are you to break any bone of it" (Exodus 12:46).

> "They shall leave none of it until morning, nor break a bone of it; according to all the statute of the Passover they shall observe it" (Numbers 9:12).[3]

An interesting connection between Yeshua's sacrifice and the Passover lamb can also be seen between the jar of sour wine and the hyssop used by the Ancient Israelites:

> "A jar full of sour wine was standing there; so they put a sponge full of the sour wine upon *a branch of* hyssop and brought it up to His mouth" (John 19:29).

> "You shall take a bunch of hyssop and dip it in the blood which is in the basin, and apply some of the blood that is in the basin to the lintel and the two

---

[2] I.H. Marshall, "Lamb of God," in Joel B. Green, Scot McKnight, and I. Howard Marshall, eds., *Dictionary of Jesus and the Gospels* (Downers Grove, IL: InterVarsity, 1992), 433.

[3] See also Psalm 34:20.

Cf. Kurt Aland, et. al., *The Greek New Testament, Fourth Revised Edition* (Stuttgart: Deutche Bibelgesellschaft/United Bible Societies, 1998), 399.

doorposts; and none of you shall go outside the door of his house until morning" (Exodus 12:22).

There are some parallels that are intended to be made between what occurred to Yeshua's body, and the killing of the original Passover lambs in Exodus. Of the four Gospels, John or the Fourth Gospel makes the point of portraying the Messiah as the One who accomplishes the grand fulfillment of what the original Passover lambs at the time of the Exodus could only foreshadow. As Paul M. Hoskins summarizes,

"The Passover context (19:14) and the mention of hyssop (19:29; Exod 12:22) are followed by the preservation of Jesus' legs from being broken and the piercing of his side (19:31-34). The blood of Jesus and the body/flesh of Jesus are both prominent in John's picture of Jesus on the cross. Given such a context, the Scripture quote in 19:36, 'a bone of him/it will not be broken' surely points to Exod 12:10, 46 and Num 9:12, even if it may also point to Ps 34:20. Thus Jesus' fulfillment of Scripture here signifies his fulfillment of the Passover lamb with respect to his body. The blood flowing out from his side also points to his fulfillment of the Passover lamb, whose blood is poured out."[4]

There are other places in the Apostolic Scriptures, of course, which make connections between Yeshua's sacrificial death and the Passover lamb. When Philip encounters the Ethiopian, he is seen reading from the Book of Isaiah: "Now the passage of Scripture which he was reading was this: 'HE WAS LED AS A SHEEP TO SLAUGHTER; AND AS A LAMB BEFORE ITS SHEARER IS SILENT, SO HE DOES NOT OPEN HIS MOUTH'" (Acts 8:32; cf. Isaiah 53:7). Philip asks him, "Do you understand what you are reading?", and is simply told, "Well, how could I, unless someone guides me?" (Acts 8:30, 31). When further asked, "Please *tell me*, of whom does the prophet say this? Of himself or of someone else?", "Then Philip opened his mouth, and beginning from this Scripture he preached Yeshua to him" (Acts 8:34, 35).

The Apostle Paul uses the image of Yeshua's sacrifice as Passover Lamb, and the themes of the Festival of Unleavened Bread, to motivate his Corinthian audience to ethical maturity. He writes them, "Your boasting is not good. Do you not know that a little leaven leavens the whole lump *of dough*? Clean out the old leaven so that you may be a new lump, just as you are *in fact* unleavened. For Messiah our Passover also has been sacrificed" (1 Corinthians 5:6-7). Their response to the sacrifice of the Lord should be one of fully changing any of their previous, ungodly habits: "Therefore let us celebrate the feast, not with old leaven, nor with the leaven of malice and wickedness, but with the unleavened bread of sincerity and truth. I wrote you in my letter not to associate with immoral people" (1 Corinthians 5:8-9). When the Corinthians come together for their Passover meal, they are to really consider how Yeshua's sacrifice for them is to motivate them to be holy and upstanding.

The theme of a lamb sacrificed is revisited later by John in the Book of Revelation, where Yeshua as the Lamb possesses extreme authority over the universe. This Lamb who was slain is given great glory and worship for what He has done, and what He is able to do, on behalf of the saints:

---

[4] Paul M. Hoskins, "Deliverance from Death by the True Passover Lamb: A Significant Aspect of the Fulfillment of the Passover in the Gospel of John" in Journal of the Evangelical Theological Society Vol. 52 No. 2 (2009):296.

"And I saw between the throne (with the four living creatures) and the elders a Lamb standing, as if slain, having seven horns and seven eyes, which are the seven Spirits of God, sent out into all the earth. And He came and took the book out of the right hand of Him who sat on the throne. When He had taken the book, the four living creatures and the twenty-four elders fell down before the Lamb, each one holding a harp and golden bowls full of incense, which are the prayers of the saints...Then I looked, and I heard the voice of many angels around the throne and the living creatures and the elders; and the number of them was myriads of myriads, and thousands of thousands, saying with a loud voice, 'Worthy is the Lamb that was slain to receive power and riches and wisdom and might and honor and glory and blessing.' And every created thing which is in heaven and on the earth and under the earth and on the sea, and all things in them, I heard saying, 'To Him who sits on the throne, and to the Lamb, *be* blessing and honor and glory and dominion forever and ever.' And the four living creatures kept saying, 'Amen.' And the elders fell down and worshiped" (Revelation 5:6-8, 11-14).

Today's evangelical Christians, and even Messianic Believers, often take for granted what it means for us to consider Yeshua the Messiah as the sacrificed Lamb of God. It is not only to motivate us to consider our human frailties and faults, driving us to our knees in worship—but it is also to really cause us to consider how as a man, Yeshua was brutally murdered for no just cause. Just as an innocent lamb would have to be killed, so was our Lord.

As important as the theme of Yeshua as the Lamb of God is for us as people of faith, we may not be aware of how there might be a slight theological issue with assuming that Yeshua's Passover sacrifice can suffice as a guilt offering. At the Last Supper He held with the Disciples, the Lord did say, "this is My blood of the covenant, which is poured out for many for forgiveness of sins" (Matthew 26:28; cf. Mark 14:24).[5] Yeshua's own claim is that the death He would soon experience would offer people a release from the punishment of sins. From the Torah, there are general instructions that we can consider in relation to animal sacrifice as they pertain to a sin offering (i.e., Leviticus 4:7; 17:3), that can be typologically connected to what Yeshua did at Golgotha. This is actually not the challenge. The possible issue is that corporate atonement and release from sins is to take place at *Yom Kippur* (Leviticus 16:34). Can Yeshua's sacrifice for humanity at Passover *also* fulfill the sacrificial expectations of the Day of Atonement?

Yeshua's sacrifice is definitely portrayed in the Scriptures as being something that is unique. 1 Peter 1:18-19 tells us, "you were not redeemed with perishable things like silver or gold from your futile way of life inherited from your forefathers, but with precious blood, as of a lamb unblemished and spotless, *the blood* of Messiah." The shed blood of the Messiah, permanently covering sins, does take the place of any animal sacrifice of the Torah, which at best could temporarily cover sin. Hebrews 9:26 asserts, "now once at the consummation of the ages He has been manifested to put away sin by the sacrifice of Himself." In fact, it can be rightfully thought that Yeshua's sacrifice offering permanent atonement for sins in place of animal sacrifices, is a reverse of how an animal sacrifice was offered in place of Isaac.

---

[5] Yeshua's words in Luke 22:20 are even more specific: "This cup which is poured out for you is the new covenant in My blood."

Consult the article "What is the New Covenant?" by J.K. McKee.

One of the reasons the Patriarch Abraham had great faith in God, is how he was prepared to fully go through with God's request to sacrifice his son, who was the child of promise (Genesis 21:12; Hebrews 11:18). Hebrews 11:19 says, "He considered that God is able to raise *people* even from the dead, from which he also received him back as a type." Abraham did not kill Isaac, but as he told his son, "God will provide for Himself the lamb for the burnt offering" (Genesis 22:8), and this is exactly what we see occur: "Then Abraham raised his eyes and looked, and behold, behind *him* a ram caught in the thicket by his horns; and Abraham went and took the ram and offered him up for a burnt offering in the place of his son" (Genesis 22:13). While the scene of Isaac's sacrifice is Mount Moriah in the future city of Jerusalem (Genesis 22:2), we are not given any clue as to when this actually took place. But what we do know is that Isaac's being substituted by a lamb/ram is a "figure" (Hebrews 11:19, KJV) depicting how the Messiah was to come and die.

When we consider what it means for something found in the Messiah's ministry to prophetically fulfill something seen in the Tanach Scriptures, what we primarily look for is that how God has acted in past history is manifested once again in the life and actions of the Messiah. A past event is to connect us to a unique activity the Messiah performs, but obviously the unique activity—while being continuous with a past activity—could not be unique unless there were something at least slightly different about it. This is where we have to consider how modern-day Western attitudes about "fulfillment" are not necessarily those of the ancients. It is easy for a critic of the Bible, or even a liberal theologian, to claim that Yeshua's death during the season of Passover would only fulfill the expectations of Passover. Yet Jews of the First Century could have seen it as being much more.

The First Century historian Josephus, writing about the Exodus, states how "when the fourteenth day was come, and all were ready to depart they offered the sacrifice, and purified their houses with the blood, using bunches of hyssop for that purpose, and when they had supped, they burnt the remainder of the flesh, when just ready to depart" (*Antiquities of the Jews* 2.312).[6] The sacrifice of the Passover lamb cleansed the homes of the Ancient Israelites. The background behind this cleansing of the houses, as provided by Josephus, could be Ezekiel 45:18-20:

"Thus says the Lord GOD, 'In the first *month*, on the first of the month, you shall take a young bull without blemish and cleanse the sanctuary. The priest shall take some of the blood from the sin offering and put *it* on the door posts of the house, on the four corners of the ledge of the altar and on the posts of the gate of the inner court. Thus you shall do on the seventh *day* of the month for everyone who goes astray or is naive; so you shall make atonement for the house."

Here, just as purification is offered for the homes of the Ancient Israelites at Passover (Exodus 12:27), so does the *Yom Kippur* sacrifice provide an atonement for God's House (Ezekiel 45:20; with the verb *kafar*, כפר actually employed in the text). Would it have been difficult for a First Century Jew to consider Yeshua's sacrifice for humanity at Passover, to in some degree accomplish the expectations of atonement for *Yom Kippur*—a sacred day which occurs seven months later? At least one First Century Jew, the author of Hebrews, had no problem recognizing

---

[6] Flavius Josephus: *The Works of Josephus: Complete and Unabridged*, trans. William Whiston (Peabody, MA: Hendrickson, 1987), 74.

that Yeshua's Passover sacrifice was "offered once to bear the sins of many," although He does acknowledge more on the salvation historical agenda: "[He] will appear a second time for salvation without *reference to* sin, to those who eagerly await Him" (Hebrews 9:28; cf. 10:12).[7]

Recognizing that Yeshua's sacrifice has prophetic ramifications beyond that of just Passover is possible not only because of the supremacy of God, but most especially because of how important the Exodus, the original Passover lambs, and God's deliverance of Ancient Israel from Egypt were to Second Temple Judaism. Up until the sacrifice of Yeshua, the major event that would have clearly defined Jewish identity would have been the Exodus. Following the sacrifice of Yeshua, Messianic Jewish identity—and indeed the identity for *all* of God's people on this side of the cross—would primarily have to be focused around Yeshua's atoning work. It is with this in mind that I think Paul says in Romans 3:21-22,

"But now {in an event} apart from the Law *the* righteousness of God has been manifested, being witnessed by the Law and the Prophets, even *the* righteousness of God through faith in Yeshua the Messiah [or: the faithfulness of Yeshua the Messiah, CJB][8] for all those who believe; for there is no distinction."

So great is God's righteousness manifested in Yeshua's sacrifice—something independent of, but surely expected by the Torah and the Prophets—that it has the capacity to reverse the effects of all people sinning (cf. Romans 3:23), with none having to perish (John 3:16).

Yeshua's sacrifice for humanity does occur during the season of Passover, and is intended to be connected to the Passover lamb. Yet it has effects which reach far beyond Passover, and into *Yom Kippur* or the Day of Atonement. While Western people might require Yeshua to have been sacrificed at *Yom Kippur* to fulfill the requirements of *Yom Kippur*, we have just cause to consider that the Passover sacrifice of the lamb is so significant, that it is **the prototype of all of the other animal sacrifices** which follow in the Torah. Hoskins notes how "Some conclude...that the Passover lamb was perceived by some first-century Jews, like John and Josephus, to be an atoning sacrifice."[9] If there is a major event that can prophetically fulfill the Passover sacrifice, then it stands to reason that such a sacrifice will have a resonating effect into the other sacrifices that are to be offered during the other appointed times. Hoskins offers us a good paragraph, further describing,

"Old Testament support for such a belief comes to light if one regards the Passover sacrifice (Exod 12:27) as a prototypical sacrifice. Then, sacrifices instituted later help somewhat in the interpretation of the character of the Passover sacrifice. The original Passover sacrifice consecrates or sanctifies the firstborn sons and animals so that they now belong to God (Num 3:13). Similarly, the ordination ram used in the sanctification of the priests, part of which they eat, is associated with making atonement for them (Exod 29:33). Hyssop appears elsewhere with respect to blood rites that cleanse from impurity and sin. In general, sacrifices, including peace offerings that resemble the Passover sacrifice, contribute to atonement even if some are more closely associated with it than others. The yearly sacrifice of the

---

[7] This obviously concerns the Second Coming and resurrection of the dead.

[8] Grk. *dia pisteōs Iēsou Christou* (διὰ πίστεως Ἰησοῦ Χριστοῦ).
Consult the article "The Faithfulness of Yeshua the Messiah" by J.K. McKee.

[9] Hoskins, in *JETS*, 52:287.

Passover in the Temple gives it a place in the sacrificial system, where atonement is a central concern and may suggest something about the original Passover (Deut 16:2). Finally, the Passover sacrifice spared the firstborn from a plague sent from God (Exod 12:12-13). Deliverance from a plague sent from God is elsewhere associated with atonement [Exod 30:11-16; Num 16:41-50, 25:7-13]. In light of this evidence, one can see why at least some Jews, like John and Josephus, could regard the Passover lamb as significant for atonement."[10]

It is quite important to recognize how imperative the controlling themes of the Passover and the Exodus were for Ancient Israel and Second Temple Judaism (cf. Acts 13:17; Jude 5)—as opposed to the themes of *Yom Kippur*, as important as they were. Yeshua's sacrifice had to be something **more significant** than Ancient Israel's deliverance from Egypt. As such, Yeshua as the Lamb of God does not only fulfill the sacrificial expectations of all of the appointed times by His single offering at Passover, but He also came to take away the sins of "the world" (John 1:29), and not just an exclusive segment of humanity. While that Jewish segment of humanity is surely to be honored (John 4:22), the Exodus and the supreme sacrifice of Yeshua as Passover Lamb affects everyone (1 Corinthians 10:1).

Also not to be overlooked, is that while Yeshua as the Lamb of God has fulfilled the sacrificial requirements of Passover and the appointed times, *more prophetic fulfillment* does await us in regard to the Passover as the Second Coming approaches (cf. Hebrews 9:28b).

The Last Supper

The Last Supper is one of the most spiritually significant parts of the Bible for those who have received Yeshua into their lives as Savior. In this scene depicted—from various vantage points in the Gospels—we witness a very intimate meal that our Master and Teacher holds with His Disciples, before later being arrested and executed by the Romans. While some Bible readers do wonder about what was being served and passed around at the table, what immediately jumps out at any of us is the Lord's claim, "Truly I say to you that one of you will betray Me—one who is eating with Me" (Mark 14:18; cf. Matthew 26:21). The response, "Surely not I, Lord?" (Matthew 26:22; cf. Mark 14:19) grabs our attention, as does Yeshua's slightly ambiguous remark, "*It is* one of the twelve, one who dips with Me in the bowl" (Mark 14:20; cf. Matthew 26:23). Admittedly for many Christians who have read about the Last Supper, their thoughts are probably focused a little more on how they know Judas Iscariot will be controlled by the Devil to betray the Messiah (Mark 14:21; Matthew 26:24-25; Luke 22:22; John 13:26-27). This is to be expected, because it forms a major part of the unfolding drama of history, and how the Lord's death would atone for humanity's sin.

Perhaps one of the most important things that draws evangelical Christians into the Messianic movement are the connections made between the Last Supper and the traditional Passover *seder* (סֵדֶר). When Christians begin to think of the bread and wine at the Last Supper as not just being any bread and wine, but actually the common elements of the Passover meal—they probably have enough knowledge of the Ancient Israelites' Exodus from Egypt to see the relevance. The Messiah is not just not dying some random death for the sins of the world, but He

---

[10] Ibid., 52:287-288.

has arrived on the scene at a moment in history that is to offer a kind of deliverance that the original Passover and Exodus—as important as they are—can only shadow. In Craig S. Keener's estimation, "By identifying his own mission with the Passover, Jesus indicates that he has come to enact the new redemption and new exodus promised by the prophets."[11]

Since the 1980s, more and more Christians have been attending Passover *seders*, either at a local Messianic congregation, or when a Messianic congregational leader holds one at his or her church. It has helped many Believers appreciate their spiritual heritage in the Torah, as well as their Jewish Roots. *They learn a great deal more about who the Jewish Jesus really is.* Furthermore, for those evangelical Believers who later become Messianic, the Passover is often a very special time—as they really get to consider not only the blessings of their salvation in Yeshua, but frequently how the themes of Passover got them to consider the further blessings of becoming Torah obedient.

Because of the special place that the original Passover and Exodus, and the Last Supper or *Seder*, hold for most of today's Messianic Believers, it comes as quite a shock when people hear views about the Last Supper not being some kind of Passover commemoration. The view of many in liberal scholarship is that the portrayal of the Last Supper as a kind of *seder* meal is one that is theological, not historical (cf. Mark 14:12-17; Matthew 26:17-20; Luke 22:7-14). Bruce Chilton concludes, "Recent scholarship has rightly seen that the identification of the Last Supper with Passover is theologically motivated...The basic elements of the Seder—lamb, unleavened bread, bitter herbs (see Exodus 12:8)—are notably absent at the Last Supper."[12] Chilton instead points to the Last Supper being one of the many Jewish *chavurot* or fellowship meals, attendant with bread and wine or *kiddush*, and for the Messiah how "eating socially with others in Israel was a parable of the feast in the kingdom that was to come."[13] Suffice it to say, the argument that the Last Supper meal of Yeshua was not really a Passover *seder* has been gaining some adherence. What this means in practice is that when some Messianic congregations and fellowships get together for their Passover commemoration—it is only to remember the original Passover—and not really any of the events surrounding the death and resurrection of the Lord.

No commentator reading the Gospels denies the fact that the three Synoptics consider the Last Supper meal to be a Passover *seder* (Mark 14:12; Matthew 16:17; Luke 22:7), but the Gospel of John states that Yeshua was sacrificed on "the day of preparation for the Passover" (John 19:14). Some choose to take John's statement as implying that the Last Supper meal was not a *seder*, and consider what the Synoptics have to say as not being quite accurate, or just being in outright error. Others, believing that all four Gospels are trustworthy accounts of the events, think that there is probably another solution to be found.

Anyone reading Mark 14:12-17; Matthew 16:17-20; Luke 22:7-14; and John chs. 13-17 can recognize how the three Synoptics briefly state that some kind of religious meal was held, and how the Fourth Gospel fills us in on some of the

---

[11] Craig S. Keener, *IVP New Testament Commentary Series: Matthew* (Downers Grove, IL: InterVarsity, 1997), 367.

[12] Bruce Chilton, "What Jesus Did at the Last Supper," in Molly Dewsnap Meinhardt, ed., *Jesus: The Last Day* (Washington, D.C.: Biblical Archaeology Society, 2003), 18.

[13] Ibid., 12.

teaching and discussion that took place during this meal. But was this just a special fellowship meal, with regular leavened bread and wine, or was it something rather unique? R.H. Stein describes, "If, as has been maintained, the Last Supper took place at a Passover meal, any proper interpretation must seek to understand it in light of this particular context. The Passover was an elaborate ritual full of symbolism and redemptive history....As the host of the Last Supper, Jesus would have been the one who retold the story."[14]

A significant Passover *seder*, held with His Disciples, is exactly what we should conclude took place—especially given the Lord's assertion, "I have earnestly desired to eat this Passover with you before I suffer" (Luke 22:15). Unless we look at Yeshua's reference to "eat" as something other than holding some kind of Passover meal, and deny that all of the Gospels include reliable history, then the Disciples really did hold a Passover *seder* with their Rabbi.

If Yeshua and His Disciples held a Passover *seder* for their Last Supper together, then this should be easily detectable from what is seen at their table. The three Synoptic Gospels of Mark,[15] Matthew, and Luke all succinctly record what takes place:

"As they were reclining *at the table* and eating, Yeshua said, 'Truly I say to you that one of you will betray Me—one who is eating with Me.' They began to be grieved and to say to Him one by one, 'Surely not I?' And He said to them, '*It is* one of the twelve, one who dips with Me in the bowl. For the Son of Man *is to* go just as it is written of Him; but woe to that man by whom the Son of Man is betrayed! *It would have been* good for that man if he had not been born.' While they were eating, He took *some* bread, and after a blessing He broke *it*, and gave *it* to them, and said, 'Take *it*; this is My body.' And when He had taken a cup *and* given thanks, He gave *it* to them, and they all drank from it. And He said to them, 'This is My blood of the covenant, which is poured out for many. Truly I say to you, I will never again drink of the fruit of the vine until that day when I drink it new in the kingdom of God'" (Mark 14:18-25).

"Now when evening came, Yeshua was reclining *at the table* with the twelve disciples. As they were eating, He said, 'Truly I say to you that one of you will betray Me.' Being deeply grieved, they each one began to say to Him, 'Surely not I, Lord?' And He answered, 'He who dipped his hand with Me in the bowl is the one who will betray Me. The Son of Man *is to* go, just as it is written of Him; but woe to that man by whom the Son of Man is betrayed! It would have been good for that man if he had not been born.' And Judas, who was betraying Him, said, 'Surely it is not I, Rabbi?' Yeshua said to him, 'You have said *it* yourself.' While they were eating, Yeshua took *some* bread, and after a blessing, He broke *it* and gave *it* to the disciples, and said, 'Take, eat; this is My body.' And when He had taken a cup and given thanks, He gave *it* to them, saying, 'Drink from it, all of you; for this is My blood of the covenant, which is poured out for many for forgiveness of sins. But I say to you, I will not drink of this fruit of the vine from now on until that day when I drink it new with you in

---

[14] R.H. Stein, "Last Supper," in *Dictionary of Jesus and the Gospels*, 447.
[15] Note how many New Testament theologians are in agreement that the Gospel of Mark was written first, and then expanded by Matthew in his Gospel composition.
Consult the entries for Mark and Matthew in *A Survey of the Apostolic Scriptures for the Practical Messianic* by J.K. McKee.

My Father's kingdom.' After singing a hymn, they went out to the Mount of Olives" (Matthew 26:20-30).

"When the hour had come, He reclined *at the table*, and the apostles with Him. And He said to them, 'I have earnestly desired to eat this Passover with you before I suffer; for I say to you, I shall never again eat it until it is fulfilled in the kingdom of God.' And when He had taken a cup *and* given thanks, He said, 'Take this and share it among yourselves; for I say to you, I will not drink of the fruit of the vine from now on until the kingdom of God comes.' And when He had taken *some* bread *and* given thanks, He broke it and gave it to them, saying, 'This is My body which is given for you; do this in remembrance of Me.' And in the same way *He took* the cup after they had eaten, saying, 'This cup which is poured out for you is the new covenant in My blood. But behold, the hand of the one betraying Me is with Mine on the table. For indeed, the Son of Man is going as it has been determined; but woe to that man by whom He is betrayed!' And they began to discuss among themselves which one of them it might be who was going to do this thing. And there arose also a dispute among them *as to* which one of them was regarded to be greatest. And He said to them, 'The kings of the Gentiles lord it over them; and those who have authority over them are called "Benefactors." But *it is* not this way with you, but the one who is the greatest among you must become like the youngest, and the leader like the servant. For who is greater, the one who reclines *at the table* or the one who serves? Is it not the one who reclines *at the table*? But I am among you as the one who serves. You are those who have stood by Me in My trials; and just as My Father has granted Me a kingdom, I grant you that you may eat and drink at My table in My kingdom, and you will sit on thrones judging the twelve tribes of Israel. 'Simon, Simon, behold, Satan has demanded *permission* to sift you like wheat; but I have prayed for you, that your faith may not fail; and you, when once you have turned again, strengthen your brothers.' But he said to Him, 'Lord, with You I am ready to go both to prison and to death!' And He said, 'I say to you, Peter, the rooster will not crow today until you have denied three times that you know Me.' And He said to them, 'When I sent you out without money belt and bag and sandals, you did not lack anything, did you?' They said, 'No, nothing.' And He said to them, 'But now, whoever has a money belt is to take it along, likewise also a bag, and whoever has no sword is to sell his coat and buy one. For I tell you that this which is written must be fulfilled in Me, "AND HE WAS NUMBERED WITH TRANSGRESSORS" [Isaiah 53:12]; for that which refers to Me has *its* fulfillment.' They said, 'Lord, look, here are two swords.' And He said to them, 'It is enough.' And He came out and proceeded as was His custom to the Mount of Olives; and the disciples also followed Him" (Luke 22:14-39).

What is narrated in the three Synoptic Gospels is obviously more concerned about how Yeshua is on the verge of being betrayed, via a conspiracy brought about by one of His own Twelve Disciples, than anything else. How can this be? How can someone who has spent more than three years with the Messiah, and who has seen Him perform miracles, cast out demons, walk on water, and exert supernatural power—**now deliver Him over to be murdered?** The reader is naturally inclined to think about *why* this would take place. The details of the kind of meal that Yeshua and His Disciples held, while important, are perhaps only a side feature of the events that are about to occur.

In conducting a Passover *seder* with His Disciples, then there are some serious typological connections that can be made regarding what Yeshua is about to experience in being betrayed and later murdered. For certain, the Lord's table included bread, wine, and some kind of dipping. But were these truly the elements of a *seder* meal, or just an ordinary meal?

There are aspects of the Last Supper which correspond to the customs witnessed in a traditional Jewish *seder* meal of the First Century, including:

- the meal is held within the city of Jerusalem (m.*Pesachim* 7:9)
- those present at the meal are reclining (Mark 14:18; Matthew 26:20; Luke 22:14; cf. m.*Pesachim* 10:1)
- the meal is held in the evening (Mark 14:17; cf. 1 Corinthians 11:23), as required by the Torah (Exodus 12:8)
- there are blessings over bread and wine (Mark 14:22-23; Matthew 26:26-27; Luke 22:17-19), a definite feature of the *seder* (m.*Pesachim* 10:2-3), including the drinking of the cup after the meal (m.*Pesachim* 10:6-7), likely the third cup of the *seder*, the Cup of Redemption
- the dipping into the bowl of salt water was a feature of the *seder*, including the bitter herbs and *charoset* (Mark 14:20; Matthew 26:23; cf. m.*Pesachim* 10:3)
- Yeshua's reference to His body and blood is likely reworked, or an addition to, the traditional Passover liturgy (Mark 14:22-24; Matthew 26:26-28; Luke 22:19-20; cf. m.*Pesachim* 10:5-6)
- the gathering is concluded with the singing of some kind of hymn (Mark 14:26; Matthew 26:30), and the Hallel (Psalms 115-118) is a part of the *seder*'s conclusion (m.*Pesachim* 10:6-7)[16]

While some of the details of the meal can seem a bit ambiguous, the testimony of Luke 22:15 is rather clear that when Yeshua sat down to eat, that He ate a Passover with His Disciples: "I have longed to eat this Passover with you before my death!" (NEB). And notably, this was the last Passover *seder* in which Yeshua partook, until His future arrival in the Kingdom: "for I say to you, I shall never again eat it until it is fulfilled in the kingdom of God" (Luke 22:16)—a very good indication that *beyond* the events of His death and resurrection, the Exodus and Passover account have important elements related to the Second Coming to be considered.

Even though Yeshua Himself says that the meal which He and the Disciples held was a Passover commemoration, there are some common objections made to it being some kind of *seder*. The three main elements of the *seder* would be "Passover {lamb}, unleavened bread, and bitter herbs" (m.*Pesachim* 10:5).[17] It is sometimes thought that while bitter herbs for Passover could be implied from the dipping into a bowl, that the other two elements are missing from this meal.

Proof for this conclusion is first made from the assumption that *matzah* (מַצָּה) or "unleavened bread" is rendered in the Septuagint (LXX) with *azumos* (ἄζυμος), but in all three Synoptics the more common word for bread, *artos* (ἄρτος), is

---

[16] Stein also adds how the giving of money to the poor (John 13:29) was common at Passover ("Last Supper," in *Dictionary of Jesus and the Gospels*, 446).

[17] Neusner, *Mishnah*, 250.

employed for the scene of the Last Supper.[18] *Artos* can be used for leavened bread, but then again it can just be a general term for bread either leavened *or* unleavened, and in a classical context meant "*a cake* or *loaf of wheat-bread*" (*LS*).[19] It is a mistake, though, for one to think that just because the more general term for "bread" is employed in the Synoptics that only leavened bread is intended. Stein points out how "The general term for 'bread,' whether the Greek *artos* or Hebrew *lehem* [לֶחֶם], was always used in the OT, the LXX, the Mishnah and the Targums to describe the shewbread, which consisted of unleavened bread."[20] Josephus actually referred to the shewbread as "twelve unleavened loaves of bread[21]" (*Antiquities of the Jews* 3.142).[22]

The other objection is that there is no specific reference to the eating of a Passover lamb, a definite feature of the *seder*. Yet, is this really proof that the meal was not a *seder*? Not at all. We do know that Jewish communities in the Diaspora would have observed Passover without the availability of a lamb slaughtered in Jerusalem, but certainly would have had the elements of unleavened bread and bitter herbs. Still, the omission of mentioning the lamb does not mean that it was not there. In fact, we have good reason to believe that a lamb was present for Yeshua's Last Supper. As Mark 14:12 points out, "On the first day of Unleavened Bread, when the Passover *lamb* was being sacrificed, His disciples said to Him, 'Where do You want us to go and prepare for You to eat the Passover?'" The Messiah held His meal during the period of this sacrificing,[23] a period of killing lambs that likely included not only the first day of the Passover week, but also some time immediately before—given the sheer amount of time it would take to properly handle the many tens of thousands of lambs which needed to be sacrificed.[24] Suffice it to say, it would have simply been understood—with all of the sacrificing going on—that Yeshua and His Disciples probably had a lamb.[25]

When denying that the Last Supper was a *seder* meal, the main alternative that interpreters have is in choosing to conclude that it was just a fellowship meal. The elements of bread and wine, while common to the *seder*, were apparently the common Jewish practice of *kiddush*. Stein rightly objects to the Last Supper just being some kind of *kiddush* meal. He observes, "The suggestion that the Last Supper was a *qiddûš*...and included a blessing over the bread and cup seems highly unlikely due to the numerous associations of the Last Supper with the Passover

---

[18] Mark 14:22; Matthew 26:26; Luke 22:19.

[19] H.G. Liddell and R. Scott, *An Intermediate Greek-English Lexicon* (Oxford: Clarendon Press, 1994), 121.

[20] Stein, "Last Supper," in *Dictionary of Jesus and the Gospels*, 446.

[21] Grk. *artous te dōdeka azumous* (ἄρτους τε δώδεκα ἀζύμους).

[22] *The Works of Josephus: Complete and Unabridged*, 88.

[23] Grk. *thuō* (θύω).

[24] Josephus (*Jewish War* 9.424) records how at one Passover there were as many as 256,500 lambs slain for the over 2,700,200 people in the environs of Jerusalem. Even if these numbers are a bit exaggerated, and the actual number of lambs was closer to the tens of thousands—it would probably have still taken more than 24 hours to appropriately slaughter lambs for all those who had come to Jerusalem for the Passover. The process probably involved some kind of spot check by the priest(s), a short prayer, and then the ritual killing, taking at least several minutes per lamb.

[25] It does have to be mentioned that following the destruction of the Temple in 70 C.E., the traditional Jewish *seder* was frequently observed without the lamb. In the Ashkenazic Jewish tradition especially up until modern times, lamb is not eaten at all during the season of Passover, and during the *seder* meal is often substituted by poultry.

celebration. Indeed, the traditional materials which inform us about the *qiddûš* are post-Christian...There is even a question as to whether the *qiddûš* was an actual meal or simply a blessing pronounced at a meal."[26] While the standard liturgy of "Blessed are You Lord our God..." is present in both the practice of *kiddush* and the Passover *seder*, there is simply too much in the Gospels that points to the Last Supper being a special Passover meal.

While Yeshua certainly held a Passover *seder* with His Disciples, there can be no doubting that it was not just a simple retelling of the Exodus story—with a few snippets here and there about His ministry. The very reason the Lord was so eager to have this meal with His Disciples, was to explain to them important realities about the Kingdom of Heaven. John chs. 13-17 inform us about some of the things that make the Last Supper rather unique, and the specific teachings Yeshua issued to His Disciples, as when He was gone they would be left to continue on with the mission. The Fourth Gospel details the important things that took place:

- Yeshua washed the Disciples' feet (John 13:5-20)
- Yeshua predicted His betrayal (John 13:21-38)
- Yeshua comforted His Disciples (John 14:1-6)
- Yeshua affirmed His oneness with the Father (John 14:7-15)
- Yeshua informed His Disciples that the Holy Spirit would come to them (John 14:16-31; 16:5-15)
- Yeshua described Himself as the Vine, and His followers as the branches (John 15:1-11)
- Yeshua told His Disciples about what it meant to love one another (John 15:12-17)
- Yeshua told His Disciples what it would mean for the world to hate them (John 15:18-16:4)
- Yeshua informed His Disciples about His death and resurrection (John 16:16-22)
- Yeshua spoke to His Disciples about the need for them to pray (John 16:23-33), then offering forth a long prayer on their behalf to the Father (John 17)

Many Believers today read this section of the Gospel of John because of important verses they find such as:

- "By this all men will know that you are My disciples, if you have love for one another" (John 13:35).
- "I am the way, and the truth, and the life; no one comes to the Father but through Me" (John 14:6).
- "Greater love has no one than this, that one lay down his life for his friends" (John 15:13).
- "I do not ask on behalf of these alone, but for those also who believe in Me through their word; that they may all be one; even as You, Father, *are* in Me and I in You, that they also may be in Us, so that the world may believe that You sent Me" (John 17:20-21).

---

[26] Stein, "Last Supper," in *Dictionary of Jesus and the Gospels*, pp 446-447.

How many of us forget that these things, and many others, were actually spoken by Yeshua to His Disciples during their conversations at the Last Supper and immediately afterward? The main theme of the Last Supper gathering is what the Disciples are supposed to do once their Lord is gone. When understood that this all took place during the midst of a Passover *seder*—with the elements of a *seder* all around them—it certainly should have caused them, and should cause *us today*, to take serious notice!

Most objections, that are actually issued against the Last Supper being a Passover *seder*, are not delivered from the substance of what occurred at the meal, but instead around the verses which introduce the scene for us. The Synoptics depict the Last Supper being a *seder* meal, and the Fourth Gospel depicts it as occurring before the Passover. The chart below lays out what Mark, Matthew, and Luke state, comparing it to John:

WAS THE LAST SUPPER A SEDER MEAL?		
MARK	**MATTHEW**	**LUKE**
On the first day of Unleavened Bread, when the Passover *lamb* was being sacrificed, His disciples said to Him, "Where do You want us to go and prepare for You to eat the Passover?" And He sent two of His disciples and said to them, "Go into the city, and a man will meet you carrying a pitcher of water; follow him; and wherever he enters, say to the owner of the house, 'The Teacher says, "Where is My guest room in which I may eat the Passover with My disciples?"' And he himself will show you a large upper room furnished *and* ready; prepare for us there." The disciples went out and came to the city, and found *it* just as He had told them; and they prepared the Passover. When it was evening He came with the twelve (Mark 14:12-26).	Now on the first *day* of Unleavened Bread the disciples came to Jesus and asked, "Where do You want us to prepare for You to eat the Passover?" And He said, "Go into the city to a certain man, and say to him, 'The Teacher says, "My time is near; I *am to* keep the Passover at your house with My disciples."'" The disciples did as Yeshua had directed them; and they prepared the Passover (Matthew 26:17-19).	Then came the *first* day of Unleavened Bread on which the Passover *lamb* had to be sacrificed. And Yeshua sent Peter and John, saying, "Go and prepare the Passover for us, so that we may eat it." They said to Him, "Where do You want us to prepare it?" And He said to them, "When you have entered the city, a man will meet you carrying a pitcher of water; follow him into the house that he enters. And you shall say to the owner of the house, 'The Teacher says to you, "Where is the guest room in which I may eat the Passover with My disciples?"' And he will show you a large, furnished upper room; prepare it there." And they left and found *everything* just as He had told them; and they prepared the Passover. When the hour had come, He reclined *at the table*, and the apostles with Him. And He said to them, "I have earnestly desired to eat this Passover with you before I suffer" (Luke 22:7-15).

THE DAY OF PREPARATION
JOHN
Now before the Feast of the Passover, Yeshua knowing that His hour had come that He would depart out of this world to the Father, having loved His own who were in the world, He loved them to the end. During supper, the devil having already put into the heart of Judas Iscariot, *the son* of Simon, to betray Him, *Yeshua*, knowing that the Father had given all things into His hands, and that He had come forth from God and was going back to God, got up from supper, and laid aside His garments; and taking a towel, He girded Himself (John 13:1-4).

The difference present, between the three Synoptics and the Fourth Gospel, is that the Synoptics state that the room was readied for Yeshua and His Disciples to eat the Passover (Mark 14:12, 14; Matthew 26:17-18; Luke 22:8,11), and John states that the meal was held before Passover (John 13:1) with the Lord crucified on "the day of preparation for the Passover" (John 19:14). There are those who believe that the Synoptics and the Fourth Gospel are in contradiction, and that we have to choose either one or the other. This would make one testimony in Scripture right, and one testimony in Scripture inaccurate, or just flat wrong. This obviously does not sit well with all interpreters—myself included—who believe that there is probably a fair way to synthesize the two perspectives.

One of the most common proposals for the Last Supper being held as a Passover *seder*, but with Yeshua's execution following taking place on the Day of Preparation for the Passover, is that there were competing religious calendars in usage in Judea. The Synoptic Gospels might represent the calendar of the sectarian Qumran community, which determined that the 14th of Nisan must always occur from Tuesday to Wednesday, this being an unofficial calendar that could have been followed by Yeshua and His followers. Then, following the more official and mainline calendar reckonings of the Temple authorities, Yeshua could have been sacrificed on the Day of Preparation of the Passover, as recorded in the Fourth Gospel.[27]

Another solution offered is that Yeshua and His Disciples held an actual *seder* meal on the 14th of Nisan, with the rest of the normal Jewish population. Yeshua being crucified on the Day of Preparation, is not the time immediately preceding the actual start of the Passover, but instead is "the day of Preparation of Passover Week" (John 19:14, NIV) for the weekly Sabbath that took place during Passover week (as proposed by at least one evangelical scholar in D.A. Carson in his commentary on John).[28] Yeshua would actually not have been sacrificed in conjunction with the Passover lambs, but instead with the offering at Unleavened Bread (Numbers 18:18-22). Yeshua would still be sacrificed as "the Passover" (cf. 1 Corinthians 5:7), although in a more general sense as a *chagigah* (חֲגִינָה) or festal offering.[29] From this perspective, Yeshua's *seder* meal was held on Thursday night, He was sacrificed on Friday before the weekly *Shabbat*, and then was resurrected Sunday morning—the traditional Good Friday-Easter Sunday scenario. Some Messianic ministries have adopted this perspective (discussed further).

Some are not convinced that the Day of Preparation is indicative of just the weekly Sabbath, but think that it can be used of High Sabbaths for Torah festivals as well, such as the first day of Unleavened Bread (Leviticus 23:7). John 19:14 does employ *paraskeuē tou Pascha* (παρασκευὴ τοῦ πάσχα), which is most literally "the preparation of the passover" (YLT). John 19:31 makes the point of how "the Jews, because it was the day of preparation, so that the bodies would not remain on the cross on the Sabbath (for that Sabbath was a high day), asked Pilate that their legs might be broken, and *that* they might be taken away." The Day of Preparation on which Yeshua was crucified, according to this, took place before the High Sabbath

---

[27] Cf. R.N. Longenecker, "Preparation, Day of," in *ISBE*, 3:953.

[28] Cf. W.E. Nunnally, "Preparation, Day of," in David Noel Freedman, ed., *Eerdmans Dictionary of the Bible* (Grand Rapids: Eerdmans, 2000), pp 1080-1081.

[29] Cf. Alfred Edersheim, *The Temple: Its Ministry and Services* (Peabody, MA: Hendrickson, 1994), 315.

of Passover. Certainly a High Sabbath could occur on the seventh day or a normal Saturday Sabbath, but not always. *LS* notably does define *paraskeuē* (παρασκευή) with the general definition, "among the Jews, *the day of Preparation*, the day before the sabbath of the Passover,"[30] which gives us room to think that the Day of Preparation was before a High Sabbath separate from the weekly Sabbath.

Consider how some of Yeshua's adversaries among the chief priests and Pharisees actually met with Pontius Pilate "on the next day, the day after the preparation" (Matthew 27:62). If the Day of Preparation were simply the time to prepare for the normal, weekly *Shabbat*, then why does Matthew 27:62 not just say that the chief priests and Pharisees met with Pilate on the Sabbath? Obviously they are in conspiracy to keep the Disciples from stealing Yeshua's body (Matthew 27:64)—and their sinister mission has caused them to overlook any kind of Torah keeping, be it on the weekly Sabbath or a separate High Sabbath.[31] But seeing how Matthew has referred to this as after the Day of Preparation, we should probably not view this as being a Saturday.

R.N. Longenecker adds to our discussion how the Passover, as a fixed day on the Hebrew calendar, "often coincided with the normal sabbath of the seventh day," further adding, "while Friday is the usual day of Preparation for the normal weekly sabbath, the precise dating of the preparation for the Passover sabbath mentioned in the Gospels depends on the dating of the Passover for that year" (*ISBE*).[32] It could very well be that the Day of Preparation occurred earlier than right before the normal weekly Sabbath, but still obviously affected the weekly Sabbath. If Yeshua's execution took place on a Thursday, and not the traditional Friday, then the Day of Preparation would be most especially a stringent time for getting ready—effecting both the High Sabbath and then the normal weekly Sabbath following.[33]

What makes the Messiah's crucifixion occurring on the Day of Preparation, before the actual day of Passover compelling, is how the Fourth Gospel makes a direct connection between Yeshua's death and the Passover lamb with quotations from the Torah (John 19:36; cf. Exodus 12:46; Numbers 9:12). Yeshua's crucifixion is intended to be directly associated with the killing of the lambs prior to the day of Passover on the 14th of Nisan, and not the festal offering of the 15th of Nisan (although if He were executed on this date, I believe the prophetic typology of the Passover lamb killed would still hold). An execution on the 14th of Nisan, among other things, would mean that when Yeshua died it did not occur during some kind of other offering made in the Temple, but rather the masses who were having their Passover lambs killed—most especially the priests—would had to have

---

[30] *LS*, 602.

[31] Whether the Day of Preparation occurred before a High Sabbath separate from or a normal weekly Sabbath that was also a High Sabbath, John Nolland's observations remain true:

"Is Matthew quietly saying that...the chief priests and Pharisees here had failed to do the preparing they deemed necessary and here are found doing it on the sabbath, in violation of at least its spirit and probably, in their own best lights, also its letter?" (*New International Greek Testament Commentary: The Gospel of Matthew* [Grand Rapids: Eerdmans, 2005], 1236).

[32] Longenecker, "Preparation, Day of," in *ISBE*, 3:953.

[33] This indicates that the usage of "Sabbath" we see (Mark 15:42; Luke 23:54; John 19:42) with the Day of Preparation takes on application not only for the High Sabbath of Unleavened Bread (Friday), but the weekly Sabbath that would follow (Saturday).

encountered the veil closing off the Holy of Holies torn at His death (Mark 15:38; Matthew 27:51).

So looking at the testimony of the Synoptics, which state that Yeshua held a *seder*, and the testimony of the Fourth Gospel, which states Yeshua was executed on the Day of Preparation—how could the Lord have actually held a Passover for the Last Supper? There is actually *a way* that we can consider Yeshua to have held a Passover *seder* meal, but then for Him to have been executed on the Day of Preparation following, with the official date of Passover following. Consider this proposal:

1. The historian Josephus records how at one Passover over 250,000 lambs were slaughtered for over 2.7 million people (*Jewish War* 9.424). Even if Josephus' figure is exaggerated, even killing several tens of thousands of lambs would probably have taken more than a full 24 hours. One can easily envision some lambs slaughtered immediately before (and maybe even after) the official start of Passover on the 14th of Nisan. The Mishnah indicates the possibility of a lamb slaughtered on the 13th of Nisan as being acceptable (m.*Zevachim* 1:3),[34] with early slaughter being allowed because of the sheer numbers of lambs.

2. Yeshua's Disciples found the room for their keeping of the Passover "On the first day of Unleavened Bread[35]" (Mark 14:12), with Matthew's later witness stating, "Now on the first...of Unleavened Bread[36]" (Matthew 26:17), omitting *hēmera* (ἡμέρα) or "day." This is likely indicative of the general start of the Passover season, and how preparations were underway prior to them actually occurring.[37] Claiming that Unleavened Bread started a little earlier than the 15th of Nisan (cf. Leviticus 23:6), is witnessed in Jewish literature (Josephus *Jewish War* 5.99).

3. Yeshua and His Disciples did not employ any kind of sectarian calendar in their keeping of Passover or the appointed times, but would have normally observed Passover on the 14th of Nisan with everyone else. Yet, because of the severity of the moment, and the Messiah's strong desire to celebrate Passover with them (Luke 22:15) knowing He was to be crucified, the Last Supper *seder* meal they all attended was deliberately held a day early.

The thought that Yeshua the Messiah would hold a Passover *seder* meal earlier than most everyone else, on the night of the 13th of Nisan, is a sensible and

---

[34] "The Passover which one slaughtered on the morning of the fourteenth [of Nisan] not for its own name ['under some other name']—R. Joshua declares valid, as if it were slaughtered on the thirteenth [of Nisan]" (m.*Zevachim* 1:3; Neusner, *Mishnah*, 699).

Also consult the relevant sections of Maurice Casey, "The Date of the Passover Sacrifices and Mark 14:12" in <u>Tyndale Bulletin</u> Vol. 48. No. 2 (1997). Accessible online at <http://www.tyndale.cam.ac.uk/>.

[35] Grk. *tē prōtē hēmera tōn azumōn* (τῇ πρώτῃ ἡμέρᾳ τῶν ἀζύμων).

[36] Grk. *Tē...prōtē tōn azumōn* (Τῇ...πρώτῃ τῶν ἀζύμων).

[37] Wise concurs how in Mark 14:12, "Mark is not using technical terminology here. In the more popular understanding this technical distinction was lost," suggesting how "Mark, in his description, has done what individuals today do when they speak of celebrating Christmas on Christmas Eve" ("Last Supper," in *Dictionary of Jesus and the Gospels*, 445).

reasonable solution—even if a bit obvious. The Master and His Disciples, especially considering the many tens of thousands of lambs that were probably being slain more than a day before the 14th of Nisan arrived, could certainly have had an authorized lamb for their Passover meal. The reason that Yeshua would have held this Passover early, would have been because "My time is near; I *am to* keep the Passover" (Matthew 26:18).

The suggestion that the Messiah would have deliberately held His Last Supper *seder* meal early, is notably one that is not popular with some of today's Messianics—especially those who hold to some rigid and inflexible applications of the Torah. A common value judgment made is that Yeshua would never have held His *seder* earlier, because that would be seen as nullifying or abolishing the Torah's instruction. In his lengthy paper "The Chronology of the Crucifixion," Tim Hegg just dismisses the thought that Yeshua's *seder* meal could have been held a day earlier, commenting,

"[S]ome would contend that Yeshua, as the Messiah, has the authority to change the timing of the Pesach meal and to hold it a day earlier. That, of course, is based upon the *mistaken* notion that Yeshua disregarded or otherwise considered the Torah to be obsolete in light of His having brought the Kingdom."[38]

These statements are a Messianic overreaction to some negative Christian views about the Torah, so that when special circumstances require there to be some flexibility in application, it is then incorrectly concluded that the Torah is invalidated. If we are a bit more reasonable about this, if Yeshua's *seder* meal were held a day early, then certainly the One who was Lord of the Sabbath[39] can surely also be allowed to be the Lord of the Passover. Yeshua was certainly doing the right thing making sure that His Disciples had a *seder* experience before His death—as He was the grand fulfillment in His very self of what the original Passover and Exodus represented.

I find no significant problems with the suggestion that Yeshua's Passover *seder* **on the year of His crucifixion** was held a little early—as it would enable Him to be killed on the actual day of lambs being offered, the 14th of Nisan, the Day of Preparation for the Passover. R.T. France's thoughts are appreciated:

"This particular group [Yeshua and the Disciples] would not differ outwardly from many other groups of pilgrims who had made arrangements to eat the meal together in Jerusalem at that time, except for one striking difference: according to the chronology for which I shall argue...they held it one day before the official date. Set within the Passover festival season, it was deliberately planned by Jesus as a Passover meal, but he knew that when the official time came the following evening, he would no longer be there to share it with them, and so he held it a day in advance. This in itself would give a special poignancy to the occasion, and what Jesus said once the meal began would lift it far out of the ordinary run of Passover celebrations."[40]

---

[38] Tim Hegg (2009). *The Chronology of the Crucifixion: A Comparison of the Gospel Accounts.* Torah Resource. Retrieved 22 January, 2010, from <http://www.torahresource.com>.

[39] Matthew 12:8; Mark 2:28; Luke 6:5.

[40] R.T. France, *New International Commentary on the New Testament: The Gospel of Matthew* (Grand Rapids: Eerdmans, 2007), pp 980-981.

The need for Yeshua as a Rabbi to hold a Passover *seder* with His Disciples, even if it might have been a little early, is quite apparent. Originally in Exodus, the Passover was to be a family affair, and at times could also include one's neighbors (Exodus 12:3-4). Yeshua and His Twelve Disciples did compose, in a matter of speaking, a kind of extended family (cf. Matthew 12:46-50)—and they did make the journey to be in Jerusalem for Passover. The testimony we see from the Synoptic Gospels and Fourth Gospel is not just a normal *seder* meal being held, but one where there are some significant teachings issued to those who would be carrying on the Messiah's work. If the meal were held on the evening of the 13th of Nisan, prior to the actual Passover on the 14th, it was for the unique needs of the moment—and by no means has to be considered any kind of abolishment of the Torah. As France recognizes,

"Of course it was strictly incorrect to hold a 'Passover' at any time other than the evening of Nisan 14/15, but Jesus was not one to be bound to formal regulations in an emergency situation."[41]

I believe that the easiest way to reconcile the surface differences between the Synoptic Gospels and the Fourth Gospel is to recognize that Yeshua's Last Supper meal was a Passover *seder* held a day earlier than everyone else's. **This is because on the actual day of Passover, Yeshua knew He would be dead.** The special circumstances present at this Passover season required a special accommodation. Yeshua wanted to be sure that before the actual Passover started, that His Disciples were given some critical teachings by Him, with all of the elements of the *seder* before them. It would be a scene that would be etched permanently in their minds, as they would have to take it with them for the rest of their lives—long after He was gone.[42]

The Last Supper as a Passover *seder* is something that is also to be permanently etched into our minds. Whether we consider His *seder* to have been held on the 14th of Nisan with the rest of the Jewish community in Jerusalem, or a little earlier on the 13th of Nisan with just the Twelve, **what is most important is that we pay attention to what He told His Disciples.** Do we really understand that as a result of His sacrificial work for us following, that the realization of great peace can be enacted with us? As our Lord said, "Peace I leave with you; My peace I give to you; not as the world gives do I give to you. Do not let your heart be troubled, nor let it be fearful" (John 14:27).

If we have the *shalom* of Yeshua present in our hearts, then we should be able to manifest it in our behavior to one another as sinners saved by His grace. Even though some useful theological discussions might take place over the details of the Last Supper meal, these discussions must occur in a manner that brings glory and honor to the One who conducted it. They must occur so that the joy we are to be experiencing in Him during this time might be filled and enhanced (John 15:11), not taken away.

Furthermore, if Yeshua did actually hold His *seder* meal a day early on the 13th of Nisan, He was not establishing a firm precedent for the later years following that

---

[41] R.T. France, *Tyndale New Testament Commentaries: Matthew* (Grand Rapids: Eerdmans, 1985), 365.

[42] While I do not share all of his conclusions, this section has taken into account some of the useful thoughts and references offered by Derek Leman of Messianic Jewish Musings <http://derek4messiah.wordpress.com>, in a series of postings offered from 09-11 March, 2009.

of His death. Messianic Believers today should commemorate the Passover *seder* on the 14th of Nisan as specified in the Torah, along with the worldwide Jewish community, recognizing the uniqueness of that one year in which the Lord was crucified.

The Bread and the Cup

What many Christians take away from the Last Supper is the understanding of Yeshua directing the Disciples' attention to the elements of bread and wine, and then connecting them to His forthcoming sacrifice. Yeshua directs His true followers to somehow eat of His flesh and drink of His blood in order to be reckoned as His:

"So Yeshua said to them, 'Truly, truly, I say to you, unless you eat the flesh of the Son of Man and drink His blood, you have no life in yourselves. He who eats My flesh and drinks My blood has eternal life, and I will raise him up on the last day. For My flesh is true food, and My blood is true drink" (John 6:53-55).

Originally spoken to a Jewish audience, these kinds of words could be viewed as being quite scandalous. The Torah forbids one from drinking blood and eating live flesh (Genesis 9:4; Leviticus 7:26; et. al.). Here, in teaching an audience that needs to be focused on who He is as the Messiah, Yeshua's words are stated so that they understand the degree to which they need to be considering Him. Literally speaking, people are not to either drink the Lord's blood or eat His flesh. Representatively speaking, people are supposed to meditate on how Yeshua's blood and His body are the tools by which full redemption is secured.

In the diverse traditions of Christianity today, many remember the scene of the Last Supper via the practice of communion: some kind of wine or grape juice, and some kind of bread, are consumed to remember the Lord's death. In the evangelical Methodist tradition in which I was raised, our church held communion on the first Sunday of every month. It was an open communion, meaning that everyone at the service could partake (and not just members of the United Methodist Church). It used grape juice and leavened bread. People most often took communion via intinction, meaning they would take a piece of the bread, and dip it in the cup of grape juice. When I would take communion, because my parents were active lay leaders and my father would teach on the Passover every year during Holy Week, I knew some rudimentary connections between it and the Passover. So important was communion to my family, that communion was actually offered at my father's funeral service.

The other main Christian tradition I have witnessed has been the administration of the Eucharist in the Anglican Church, as I have relatives who are evangelical Episcopalians. When I visit them, I will typically go to services with them on Sunday morning, where communion is offered at the close of every service. It is an open table for all Christians as well. There is more liturgy involved in the Anglican communion, than in the Wesleyan tradition (even though the Wesleyan movement arose from the Church of England). The elements do take on much more of a veneer of Catholicism, even though a kind of unleavened wafer, and real wine is used (in their church's case, a Port wine that has been diluted with water)—closer to what was actually served at the original Last Supper. And even though the Anglican communion is quite separated from any kind of First Century *seder*, the liturgy as employed from the Book of Common Prayer does include a quote from 1 Corinthians 5:7-8: "Christ our Passover is sacrificed for us; *Therefore let us keep the feast.*"[43]

These are two Protestant traditions[44] which try to honor the Last Supper, and how the Lord Yeshua really did shed His blood and was brutally beaten for the atonement of sins. Within the Gospels, there is no doubting how there is a special point in the meal Yeshua conducts, when He makes mention of a specific cup and some specific bread—which His Disciples are to take to serious heart:

"While they were eating, He took *some* bread, and after a blessing He broke *it*, and gave *it* to them, and said, 'Take *it*; this is My body.' And when He had taken a cup *and* given thanks, He gave *it* to them, and they all drank from it. And He said to them, 'This is My blood of the covenant, which is poured out for many. Truly I say to you, I will never again drink of the fruit of the vine until that day when I drink it new in the kingdom of God'" (Mark 14:22-25).

"While they were eating, Yeshua took *some* bread, and after a blessing, He broke *it* and gave *it* to the disciples, and said, 'Take, eat; this is My body.' And when He had taken a cup and given thanks, He gave *it* to them, saying, 'Drink from it, all of you; for this is My blood of the covenant, which is poured out for many for forgiveness of sins. But I say to you, I will not drink of this fruit of the vine from now on until that day when I drink it new with you in My Father's kingdom.' After singing a hymn, they went out to the Mount of Olives" (Matthew 26:26-30).

"And when He had taken a cup *and* given thanks, He said, 'Take this and share it among yourselves; for I say to you, I will not drink of the fruit of the vine from now on until the kingdom of God comes.' And when He had taken *some* bread *and* given thanks, He broke it and gave it to them, saying, 'This is My body which is given for you; do this in remembrance of Me.' And in the same way *He took* the cup after they had eaten, saying, 'This cup which is poured out for you is the new covenant in My blood'" (Luke 22:17-20).

When most of today's average Christians read what Yeshua did at the Last Supper, they rightfully acknowledge how the cup of wine and the bread that are served are to remind them of how His sacrifice has brought them redemption. The beauty of today's Messianic movement is that it emphasizes these things not as just common elements of any meal, but the main elements of the Passover *seder*. Messianic teachers rightly recognize that the bread Yeshua lifts up is likely that of the *afikoman*, and the cup would be the third cup of the traditional *seder*, the Cup of Redemption.[45]

At this point in the Last Supper, Yeshua has deliberately interrupted some of the normal liturgy and questions (cf. Exodus 12:26-27), to identify the elements of the *seder* with that of His own salvific work. The *lechem oni* (לֶחֶם עֹנִי) or "bread of affliction" (Deuteronomy 16:3), for example, now becomes associated with the soon to come breaking of His own body. Luke's testimony is most specific in the

---

[43] *The Book of Common Prayer* (New York: Oxford University Press, 1990), 364.

[44] Even though the Anglican Church does include many of the outward elements of Catholicism, the theology of the Church of England and its American Episcopalian counterpart is largely Protestant.

[45] Cf. David H. Stern, *Jewish New Testament Commentary* (Clarksville, MD: Jewish New Testament Publications, 1992), 80.

claim that Yeshua's sacrificial activity will be responsible for inaugurating the era of the New Covenant—prophesied in the Tanach as offering complete forgiveness for God's people, and the supernatural transcription of His commandments on the heart (Jeremiah 31:31-34; Ezekiel 36:25-27).

By the early Second Century, the emerging Christian Church would largely limit remembrance of the Last Supper by only employing the elements of wine and bread, in the Eucharist.[46] Some see hints in the Apostolic Scriptures themselves that remembering the cup and the bread *independent* of the Passover *seder* took on some focus for the *ekklēsia*. As Paul writes in 1 Corinthians 11:23-26,

"For I received from the Lord that which I also delivered to you, that the Lord Yeshua in the night in which He was betrayed took bread; and when He had given thanks, He broke it and said, 'This is My body, which is for you; do this in remembrance of Me.' In the same way *He took* the cup also after supper, saying, 'This cup is the new covenant in My blood; do this, as often as you drink *it*, in remembrance of Me.' For as often as you eat this bread and drink the cup, you proclaim the Lord's death until He comes."

No Biblical reader or commentator can deny how the cup which the Lord lifted up and the bread which He broke at the Last Supper—would have a definite impact on later generations of His followers, and how this was largely positive. The good Apostle Paul used the Last Supper to focus the spiritual attention of the Corinthians. When faithful Christians today partake of communion, their attention is also focused on the sacrifice of Yeshua for their sins. But was Paul actually reflecting on the tradition of the Eucharist—a religious rite designed to focus on the wine and bread consumed at the Last Supper—offered to Believers throughout the year, sometimes in religious services held daily? Or, is this to be something remembered at a very solemn and sacred moment in Believers' remembrance of the Passover *seder*?

How are we to view Paul's assertion "every time you eat this bread and drink this cup, you proclaim the death of the Lord, until he comes" (1 Corinthians 11:26, NEB)? Obviously, this is not a once-in-a-lifetime affair, as the cup and bread the Messiah employed at His Last Supper are to be remembered on some kind of regular basis. I am most inclined to think that the cup and bread that Believers are to partake of are those which Yeshua employed at His Passover *seder*, possessing significance far beyond what they originally entailed for those only remembering the Exodus. The Corinthians were notably those who were to celebrate the festival of Passover remembering Yeshua's sacrifice (1 Corinthians 5:7-8), and so the cup they would drink and unleavened bread they would eat, should be understood in this context. Anthony C. Thiselton's comments on 1 Corinthians 11:26 are quite poignant:

"...Paul...likens what the assembled congregation does in the actions of eating and drinking the bread and wine that makes believers contemporary with the cross *to the recital of the Passover Haggadah* as *gospel proclamation*. However, this is not simply a publishing of the objective event of the cross. It includes this **(the bread is broken** and **the cup** . . . *in the same way* . . .). Yet like those who recite the Haggadah of the Passover on the understanding that '*in every generation a man must*

---

[46] The term "Eucharist" is derived from the Greek *eucharistos* (εὐχάριστος), simply meaning "**being grateful,** *thankful*" (*BDAG*, 416).

Cf. "Eucharist," in Bercot, pp 251-252.

so regard himself as he came forth himself out of Egypt' (*m.Pesahim* 10:5), it *also* witnesses to *the participant's self-involving appropriation of the cross both for redemption and lifestyle* as those who *share Christ's death* in order to *share Christ's life.*"[47]

Here, Thiselton astutely identifies Yeshua's words about the cup and the bread specifically focused upon at the Last Supper—as being closely associated with the kind of liturgy employed within the Passover *seder*. Those who have personally identified with the meaning of the Exodus, are to now also personally identify with the meaning of the Messiah's death. When today's Messianic Believers arrive at that special point in the Passover meal—the eating of the *afikoman* and drinking of the third cup—is our Lord's redemptive work and teaching at the Last Supper at all remembered? Is there a solemn, silent moment, in either our home or congregational *seder* meals, when the redemption which He has accomplished is seriously reflected upon?

The Messianic movement has certainly inherited a Christian theological tradition for which communion on either a weekly or monthly basis is very important. Many churches today, wanting to more closely place communion within the context of Passover, actually use Jewish *matzah*. There is no uniform practice among Messianic congregations regarding communion. Some take Paul's words in 1 Corinthians 11:26 as being a normative practice for every worship service. Others take it as a reference to the yearly *seder* meal. Still, others will offer a kind of communion during various Messianic prayer services. And should they do this, *matzah* is rightly employed.

I come from a Christian background where communion was very important to the spiritual well being of the Church. Having been Messianic now for over fifteen years—while I greatly appreciate the Passover *seder* and the enrichment I have experienced in my faith—too frequently the eating of the *afikoman* and drinking of the Cup of Redemption, has not often been as spiritually enlightening as communion was in either my Wesleyan upbringing, or even when I partake of it now with my Episcopalian relatives. But I do not think this has anything to do with how the *afikoman* and Cup of Redemption are to focus our observance of Passover, nor how they are only considered once a year. I think it has to do with a failure on the part of many to consider the severity of this moment in the *seder*, and a lack of emphasis from the *seder*'s leader(s). Paul's words continue, telling us,

"Therefore whoever eats the bread or drinks the cup of the Lord in an unworthy manner, shall be guilty of the body and the blood of the Lord. But a man must examine himself, and in so doing he is to eat of the bread and drink of the cup. For he who eats and drinks, eats and drinks judgment to himself if he does not judge the body rightly" (1 Corinthians 11:27-29).

In the course of a home or congregational *seder*, there can be the tendency for people to get caught up in the eating of the meal, or the conversation of the guests, or in drinking a little too much wine—so that when the most important part of the evening arrives, **we may have lost our attention.** So if today's Messianics choose not to have a kind of weekly or annual communion, like their Christian counterparts—and I myself am inclined to only remember the Lord's Supper once a year at Passover—we have to make sure that we are doing it in a very reverent way. While

---

[47] Anthony C. Thiselton, *New International Greek Testament Commentary: The First Epistle to the Corinthians* (Grand Rapids: Eerdmans, 2000), 887.

we do not at all have to think that the bread and wine become the literal body and blood of the Lord, as the Roman Catholic doctrine of transubstantiation advocates—the Lutheran doctrine of consubstantiation, of the Lord's actual presence being there with the elements, might be something worthy of consideration. We do have to think that the Messiah Yeshua is sitting there with us during our *seder*, watching our every moves, and listening to our conversation (cf. 1 Corinthians 11:30-32).[48]

Yeshua's Prayer in the Garden of Gethsemane

While much of our attention as Messianic Believers is rightly focused on the Last Supper meal, and connections seen with the elements of the Passover *seder*—there is much more that has to be considered within the scope of Yeshua serving as a Passover sacrifice. Once the Last Supper concluded and the Disciples completed reciting Hallel (Psalms 115-118), things then began to take serious shape. They all depart for the Garden of Gethsemane, where we see some of the agony Yeshua has to experience, as He knows that He is about to be arrested and later unjustly executed.

The three Synoptics all record the scene that takes place in Gethsemane (Mark 14:32-42; Matthew 26:36-46; Luke 22:39-46), with the Fourth Gospel only telling us that Yeshua and His Disciples crossed over the Kidron ravine (John 1:1). The main point is that once their *seder* meal is concluded, the party all moves over to a place adjacent to the Mount of Olives. Luke's testimony is that this was "His custom" (Luke 22:39), which might be a good indication that in previous Passover commemorations, or other important gatherings, the Disciples had gone to this Garden of Gethsemane before (John 18:2). Then again, it may simply be an indication that after an important teaching gathering, it was Yeshua's custom for them all to go to a quiet place to reflect and pray. This is, after all, what they were supposed to be doing with the time of His death soon at hand.

Prior to leaving the place where they remembered the Passover, Yeshua makes a reference to Zechariah 13:7, which emphasizes "Strike the Shepherd that the sheep may be scattered" (cf. Mark 14:27; Matthew 26:31). At the death of the Messiah, His followers are likely going to react differently. Yeshua told Peter how he will deny Him, although Peter strongly protests to this, as do the other Disciples (Mark 14:29-31; Matthew 26:35). The Lord also makes the clear point to tell them, "But after I have been raised, I will go ahead of you to Galilee" (Matthew 26:32). While Yeshua has told them He will die, He also has told them He will be resurrected—and affirms to His Disciples how they will be reunited. But seeing this in the Gospels, the natural question we can ask is whether they really believed it before it took place.

Mark and Matthew both record the main substance of what transpired when Yeshua and the Disciples arrive at the Garden of Gethsemane. Yeshua tells His Disciples "Sit here while I go over there and pray" (Matthew 26:36; cf. Mark 14:32). Peter, James, and John all go with Him off to the side, and the Lord "began to be very distressed and troubled" (Mark 14:33; cf. Matthew 26:37). The agony Yeshua experiences is described as being to the point of death, and so He simply asks His

---

[48] Consult the FAQ entry on the Messianic Apologetics website, "Communion" (reproduced in this publication's section on "FAQs on the Spring Holiday Season").

three closest Disciples to be near Him (Mark 14:34; Matthew 26:38). One can think that Yeshua had a very high pulse, and was overwhelmed with anxiety—realizing that He was preparing to not just die and be humiliated like a common criminal— **but actually carry all of the sins of all humanity past, present, and future on His person.** Yeshua then goes off just by Himself, praying to the Father, "if it is possible, let this cup pass from Me; yet not as I will, but as You will" (Matthew 26:39; cf. Mark 14:36). Yeshua's reference to the cup He has to bear is no doubt connected to the imagery of the Passover dinner He and the Disciples have just concluded, and how He held up the cup representing the blood He would have to shed. Still, Yeshua's faithfulness unto death, in obedience to His Father, is realized.

Yeshua continues to pray (Mark 14:39), realizing He has to continue with the Father's will. But when He finishes, the Lord finds His Disciples asleep, something He is quite displeased about as they have only been there for about an hour (Mark 14:36-37; cf. Matthew 26:40-41). Yeshua returns to His praying, and still finds the Disciples asleep later, and they do not know what to do (Mark 14:38-39; Matthew 26:42-43). This repeats itself a third and final time, when all Yeshua can tell them is, "Are you still sleeping and resting? Behold, the hour is at hand and the Son of Man is being betrayed into the hands of sinners. Get up, let us be going; behold, the one who betrays Me is at hand!" (Matthew 26:45-46; cf. Mark 14:41-42). Yeshua was very concerned that in a drowsy state, His Disciples would fall into temptation, asserting how "the spirit is willing, but the flesh is weak" (Mark 14:38; Matthew 26:41). Some very important things were about to take place, and they would never again be able to be this close to their Rabbi until after His resurrection.

Luke's record adds some more specific details to the scene of what takes place in the Garden of Gethsemane. When Yeshua goes off to pray, He only "withdrew from them about a stone's throw" away (Luke 22:41), far enough away for some privacy, but probably not far enough to not be noticed or heard in some way. While praying, an angel appears before Yeshua to comfort Him with what He is about to endure (Luke 22:42-43). The most significant point that Luke makes is a physiological diagnosis of what Yeshua goes through: "And being in agony He was praying very fervently; and His sweat became like drops of blood, falling down upon the ground" (Luke 22:44). We should not think that Yeshua actually sweat blood, but what He did sweat would certainly have been a rather thick, very odorous perspiration, and quite indicative of one with a fast pulse and probably high blood pressure—even on the verge of a heart attack. Luke also observes that the Disciples were sleeping out of some kind of sorrow (Luke 22:45-46).

The prayer Yeshua offers to the Father in the Garden of Gethsemane is different than what is commonly called the High Priestly Prayer, offered at the end of the Last Supper in John 17. While John 17 is offered up on behalf of His Disciples, the agonizing prayer Yeshua issues here is on behalf of Himself. *He does not know if He can fully go through with it.* Within theological studies for many centuries, the prayer Yeshua delivers about not quite being able to bear "the cup" has caused some controversies. If Yeshua is God Incarnate, should He not be able to simply experience all of this, and not worry about it? Why demonstrate any kind of dread about having to be humiliated? The scene of the Garden of Gethsemane is a strident example of the humanity of Yeshua, His participation in the human experience, and how God entered the world of mortals as a mortal with the express purpose of redeeming mortals. Yeshua's prayer to the Father was a fully human response to what He was about to endure, one which He willingly went through, not at all asserting or claiming His privileges as God. As the *Carmen Christi* hymn affirms:

"[T]hough he was in the form of God, [he] did not regard equality with God as something to be exploited[49], but emptied himself, taking the form of a slave, being born in human likeness. And being found in human form, he humbled himself and became obedient to the point of death—even death on a cross" (Philippians 2:6-8, NRSV).[50]

While Yeshua was praying, His Disciples—even the three closest to Him— were off tired and asleep. We do not know if they had too much to eat or drink during the *seder* meal, and were now drowsy as a result. What we can deduce, especially from Yeshua's warning about them not falling into temptation (Mark 14:38; Matthew 26:41; Luke 22:40), is that demonic spiritual forces were out there having a negative affect on the Disciples. If they were not careful, it would impair their judgment in the events that would soon follow. The Mishnah actually includes some Passover instructions about falling asleep that could have a parallel with the Messiah's warning:

"And after the Passover meal they do not conclude with dainties. [If] some of those present fell asleep, they may eat [again]. But if all [fell asleep], they may not eat again. R. Yose says, '[If they merely] droused, they may eat again. But if they fell into a deep sleep, they may not eat again'" (m.*Pesachim* 10:8).[51]

There is no real indication that the Disciples fell into a deep sleep while Yeshua was praying. After consuming a *seder* meal with wine, having walked all the way to the Garden of Gethsemane, and with it being late and relatively dark— they all took little naps. There was *obviously* no after dinner coffee available, nor any other caffeine drink to keep them awake and at least artificially stirred for a little while. The warning we see in the Jewish tradition of Passover about not falling into a deep sleep should be well taken. Yeshua wanted the Disciples to be fully awake and alert, as His betrayal by Judas prepares to commence. It will be insufficient for His students to remember their Last Seder together, but then completely forget the events that follow. *The same is true for us as well.*

Yeshua's Betrayal by Judas Iscariot

One character whose actions feature prominently in the account of Yeshua's forthcoming execution is Judas Iscariot.[52] He has the unfortunate place in Scripture

---

[49] Grk. *harpagmos* (ἁρπαγμός); "someth. to which one can claim or assert title by gripping or grasping" (Frederick William Danker, ed., et. al., *A Greek-English Lexicon of the New Testament and Other Early Christian Literature*, third edition [Chicago: University of Chicago Press, 2000], 133).

Also, "Who, being in very nature God, did not consider equality with God something to be used to his own advantage" (TNIV).

[50] The *Carmen Christi* hymn continues, though, affirming the exaltation of Yeshua in Heaven as LORD, and how all of Creation will worship Him (Philippians 2:9-11; cf. Isaiah 45:23). In total, Philippians 2:5-11 demonstrates how Yeshua is both God and man, an early affirmation made by the First Century *ekklēsia* to be sure—but most importantly how His act of supreme sacrifice is to motivate His followers in proper service to one another.

For a further discussion, consult the commentary *Philippians for the Practical Messianic* by J.K. McKee. Also consult the excellent thoughts of Gerald F. Hawthorne, *Word Biblical Commentary: Philippians*, Vol. 43 (Waco, TX: Word Books, 1983), 78.

[51] Neusner, *Mishnah*, 251.

[52] Grk. *Ioudas ho Iskariōtēs* (Ἰούδας ὁ Ἰσκαριώτης).

as being known as the one who betrayed Yeshua.[53] The Gospels tell us that Judas was controlled by Satan (Luke 22:3; John 13:2). The Lord Himself said of Judas, "It would have been good for that man if he had not been born" (Matthew 26:24; cf. Mark 14:21)—clearly not the greatest of epitaphs. During the Last Supper, Yeshua's announcement that He is to be betrayed comes as a total shock to those in attendance (Mark 14:18-21; Matthew 26:21-23; Luke 22:21-23).

Judas Iscariot betrayed Yeshua for money, as the priests wanted Him dead (Mark 14:10-11; Matthew 26:14-16; Luke 22:2-5), with their payment of thirty pieces of silver sometimes connected to Zechariah 11:12.[54] Judas being paid to betray his Rabbi could be the result of him having been the treasurer for Yeshua and His band of Disciples (John 12:4-6; 13:29), although this is not conclusive because one who handled money needed to be impeccably responsible and trustworthy.

As Yeshua and His Disciples finish their discussions in the Garden of Gethsemane, Judas leads a group with swords and clubs up to Him, sent by the high priests and elders (Mark 14:43; Matthew 26:47; Luke 22:47a), specified to actually be a Roman cohort (John 18:3). Judas had informed the contingent that Yeshua would be the One whom he would kiss, mockingly calling Him "Rabbi" (Mark 14:44-45; Matthew 26:48-49; Luke 22:47-48a). Matthew's testimony records how the Lord told him, "Friend, *do* what you have come for" (Matthew 26:50a), Luke's testimony has the Lord asking Judas the question, "Judas, are you betraying the Son of Man with a kiss?" (Luke 22:48b), and John's record is the most dynamic of them all, as Yeshua has known all the time what was going to happen:

"So Yeshua, knowing all the things that were coming upon Him, went forth and said to them, 'Whom do you seek?' They answered Him, 'Yeshua the Nazarene.' He said to them, 'I am He.' And Judas also, who was betraying Him, was standing with them. So when He said to them, 'I am He,' they drew back and fell to the ground. Therefore He again asked them, 'Whom do you seek?' And they said, 'Yeshua the Nazarene.' Yeshua answered, 'I told you that I am He; so if you seek Me, let these go their way,' to fulfill the word which He spoke, 'Of those whom You have given Me I lost not one'" (John 18:4-9).

Of notable interest is how the Fourth Gospel specifies Yeshua saying *egō eimi* (ἐγώ εἰμι), the Septuagint rendering for the Hebrew *ehyeh asher ehyeh* (אֲשֶׁר אֶהְיֶה אֶהְיֶה) or "I AM WHO I AM," as first heard from the burning bush to Moses with God describing Himself (Exodus 3:14). Yeshua did not simply say "I am He," but "I AM" (John 18:5, 6, 8). At the declaration of Him being the "I AM," some supernatural power is manifested as the mob preparing to seize Him falls back (John 18:6). While Yeshua knows that He has an important destiny to fulfill, and He does not assert or claim His God privileges (cf. Philippians 2:6), His declaration as "I AM" nevertheless serves notice to those present that something greater than themselves is afoot.[55]

It is sometimes thought that the surname Iscariot is derivative of him being from Keriot, reflected in the Salkinson-Ginsburg Hebrew New Testament as *Yehudah ish-Q'riot* (יהודה איש־קריות), followed by the CJB with "Y'hudah from K'riot." Another thought is that "Iscariot could be derived either from *šqr*, 'lie,' 'liar,' or *sicarius*, 'dagger bearer'" (G.W. Buchanan, "Judas Iscariot," in *ISBE*, 3:1151).

[53] Mark 3:19; Matthew 10:4; 26:25; 27:3; Luke 6:16; John 6:71; 12:4; 13:2; 18:2, 5.

[54] "I said to them, 'If it is good in your sight, give *me* my wages; but if not, never mind!' So they weighed out thirty *shekels* of silver as my wages" (Zechariah 11:12).

[55] For a further discussion, consult G.M. Burge, "'I Am' Sayings," in *Dictionary of Jesus and the Gospels*, pp 354-356.

Yeshua is seized by the band of soldiers (Mark 14:46; Matthew 26:50b), but then one of His Disciples takes some rash action by drawing a sword, and severs the ear of the high priest's slave (Mark 14:47; Matthew 26:51; Luke 22:49-50), Malchus (John 18:10). It is, in fact, Peter who commits this act (John 18:10). If Yeshua is to be arrested and later tried, then His Disciples committing these violent deeds will certainly not help His testimony—and their attempts to try to defend Him are quite foolish considering He has angels at His command (Matthew 26:53). So Yeshua actually heals the poor slave's ear right there (Luke 22:51). Yeshua inquires of His captors why they had not tried to seize Him before, as He has been in the Temple complex many times where they could have done it in the daylight (Mark 14:48-49a; Matthew 26:55; Luke 22:52-53). Yeshua is direct in telling them, "While I was with you daily in the temple, you did not lay hands on Me; but this hour and the power of darkness are yours" (Luke 22:53). Yeshua intends to fulfill the Scriptures by His being captured (Mark 14:49b; Matthew 26:56), as He asks Peter, "the cup which the Father has given Me, shall I not drink it?" (John 18:11). And after being seized, "Then all the disciples left Him and fled" (Matthew 26:56b).

The next day, for some reason or another, the Judas who has betrayed his Rabbi comes to his senses (Matthew 27:1-3). It is possible that Judas did not know Yeshua was going to be condemned to death, as opposed to just being indefinitely imprisoned. "[W]hen Judas, who had betrayed Him, saw that He had been condemned, he felt remorse and returned the thirty pieces of silver to the chief priests and elders, saying, 'I have sinned by betraying innocent blood.' But they said, 'What is that to us? See *to that* yourself!'" (Matthew 26:3-4). Matthew's record is short in that Judas throws the betrayal money away, and then he hangs himself (Matthew 26:5). This money was apparently used by the priests to purchase a field for the burial of strangers (Matthew 26:6-10).

Luke's record in Acts about the death of Judas Iscariot is sometimes thought to be contradictory to Matthew's. Luke says how, "falling headlong, he burst open in the middle and all his intestines gushed out" (Acts 1:18). Obviously, whether Judas hanged himself, or he threw himself off a high point, neither record depicts an honorable or pleasant death. Yet there might not be a contradiction at all between either Matthew or Acts. It may very well have been that Judas hanged himself, but that his innards later burst open as his body decomposed. David G. Peterson describes how in Acts 1:18, "There is...a possibility that the Greek expression *prēnēs genomenos* [πρηνὴς γενόμενος] in v. 18 means 'swelling up' instead of 'falling headlong', in which case we can imagine his corpse becoming bloated in the heat and bursting open while still hanging."[56] Easier still, if the rope Judas used broke as his body decomposed, once hitting the ground his bowels could have ripped open as a result of the heavy fall.

The specific reason, that Judas Iscariot betrayed the Lord Yeshua, is one that will probably allude us for a long time. There are various proposals made, ranging from Judas just being a greedy man, to him being a political Zealot who wanted to overthrow the Romans. When Yeshua clearly did not intend to oust Rome from Judea, Judas might have then turned on Him in revenge.[57] At most, though, this is informed speculation. What the text tells us for certain, beyond any of the personal

---

[56] David G. Peterson, *Pillar New Testament Commentary: The Acts of the Apostles* (Grand Rapids: Eerdmans, 2009), 124.

[57] Cf. Buchanan, "Judas Iscariot," in *ISBE*, 3:1153.

motives that made Judas a vessel responsible for Yeshua's death, is that He was controlled by Satan (Luke 22:3; John 13:2). Even those from an Arminian theological framework, who largely emphasize the freewill of human beings, have to concede the likelihood of how Judas Iscariot may very well have been predestined by God to do what he did (Luke 22:22).

The Trial and Humiliation of Yeshua

The next scene which transpires before Yeshua's execution can be divided into two main segments: (1) He appears before the Sanhedrin and Pontius Pilate, and then (2) the Lord is mocked and beaten by Roman soldiers. It is important that we evaluate what took place in the sentencing of Yeshua, and how the Lord did little in terms of defending Himself. As He already acknowledged at His arrest, He could command legions of angels to deliver Him, but the Scriptures had to be fulfilled by Him being sacrificed.

When Yeshua is brought before the Council (Luke 22:66), as witnessed in the Synoptics, we see Peter trailing Him, somehow trying to sit on the outside looking in to what is taking place. The intention of the Sanhedrin was to find a testimony that could be used to execute Yeshua. Even though false witnesses are noted to be brought forward, their testimonies were inconsistent so as to merit anything (Mark 14:53-60; Matthew 26:57-60). A little traction against Yeshua is made with the claim that He would have seen the Temple torn down in three days (Matthew 26:60-61).

The Sanhedrin apparently gets frustrated with witnesses who do not produce what they were probably paid to do, and with questioning that goes nowhere. Yeshua largely stays silent to the fools who have made claims against Him (Matthew 26:62-63a). So the high priest gets direct with Yeshua, asking Him point blank, "Are You the Messiah, the Son of the Blessed One?" (Mark 14:61; cf. Matthew 26:63; Luke 22:66-68). The answer of Yeshua to the high priest is also quite direct: "I am; and you shall see THE SON OF MAN SITTING AT THE RIGHT HAND OF POWER, and COMING WITH THE CLOUDS OF HEAVEN" (Mark 14:62; cf. Matthew 26:64; Luke 22:69). Mark's transcription includes the usage of the theologically significant *egō eimi*, and Mark and Matthew both include quotations from Psalm 110:1 and Daniel 7:13:[58]

"The LORD says to my Lord: 'Sit at My right hand until I make Your enemies a footstool for Your feet'" (Psalm 110:1).

"I kept looking in the night visions, and behold, with the clouds of heaven One like a Son of Man was coming, and He came up to the Ancient of Days and was presented before Him" (Daniel 7:13).

These were both significantly loaded pieces of the Tanach from which Yeshua could quote. When the Sanhedrin asks the Lord, "Are You the Son of God, then?" He responds with "Yes, I am" (Luke 22:70), transcribed as *egō eimi*. With Yeshua saying "I AM" He has directly stated that He is a part of the Divine Identity, and is far more than just some agent sent by God. Even with sordid motives involved, and holding to a theology that would largely deny the relevance of the Prophets and Writings, the Saddusaical high priest could still rip his clothes and say to the rest of

---

[58] Aland, *GNT*, pp 182, 106.
Luke 22:69 only quotes from Psalm 110:1 (Ibid., pp 299-300).

the Sanhedrin that in considering Himself I AM, Yeshua was guilty of blasphemy (Mark 14:63; Matthew 26:64-65; Luke 22:71). Because they all considered **Yeshua's claim to God status** and application of Tanach passages to Himself to be blasphemy, the Sanhedrin condemned Yeshua to death. Then they blindfold and mock and spit on Him to see whether or not He was truly omnipotent, able to say who did it (Mark 14:64-65; Matthew 26:66-68). Yeshua just endures this humiliation, as this will only be a small part of what is to come.

While Yeshua has been tried and condemned as a blasphemer, Peter is outside waiting, standing near a fire to keep warm. Some of those present recognize who he is as a follower of Yeshua, although He strongly denies it. As Yeshua had told Him earlier during their *seder* meal, when confronted three separate times as to whether He knew Yeshua, Peter denies it before the crowing of the morning rooster (Mark 14:66-72; Matthew 26:69-75; Luke 22:54-65). The Fourth Gospel focuses on how Yeshua was taken before Annas, father-in-law of the high priest, first, before being taken before the Sanhedrin (John 18:13). After being arrested, Peter and another disciple (probably John) follow Yeshua into the court of the high priest (John 18:13-14), with this disciple allowed to go in, but with Peter having to wait outside (John 18:15). Peter is recognized as a Yeshua-follower, but denies it (John 18:16-17), although he continued to wait outside (John 18:18). John's record of what occurred emphasizes how Yeshua asks the high priest to legitimately bring forth those who have heard His teachings, which have been spoken out in the open, challenging the truthfulness of their claims against Him (John 18:19-23). Yeshua is then taken to Caiaphas (John 18:24) and before the whole Sanhedrin, the scene witnessed in the three Synoptics (cf. Matthew 26:57).

At this point in the narrative, Judas Iscariot hangs himself (Matthew 27:1-10).

Because of the Roman occupation of Judea, while the Sanhedrin had the power to condemn various criminals to death—even on the charge of blasphemy—the Sanhedrin lacked the significant power to then go and execute them. This power ultimately rested with the Romans, and so Yeshua's sentence would have to be approved by the governor, Pontius Pilate (Mark 15:1; Luke 23:1). When Yeshua stands before Pilate, the Synoptics record how he asks the Lord, "Are You the King of the Jews?", and Yeshua simply responds with "*It is as* you say" (Mark 15:2; Matthew 27:11; Luke 22:3). The chief priests are present there to press their case, and Pilate is amazed, witnessing how Yeshua does not answer a single one of their charges (Mark 15:3-5; Matthew 27:12-14). One can certainly think that in Pilate's experience in government he had seen many criminals hurrily defend themselves. There is a serenity in this *Iēsous* that he had never seen before.[59]

Luke adds that the specific allegation presented before Pilate was, "We found this man misleading our nation and forbidding to pay taxes to Caesar, and saying that He Himself is Messiah, a King" (Luke 23:2). This kind of claim, if proven true, would demonstrate Yeshua to be a revolutionary against Rome. For some reason or another, Pilate concludes before the priests and others gathered, "I find no guilt in this man" (Luke 23:4). Yet the desire on the part of the religious leaders, to see

---

[59] It should go without saying that while the spoken dialogue between Yeshua and those in the Sanhedrin was likely in Hebrew or Aramaic, the spoken dialogue between Yeshua, the priests, and Pontius Pilate was in Greek, as well as the dialogue between Pilate and the crowds demanding Yeshua to be crucified. (Even though the Romans used Latin, Greek was employed as the main language of their eastern Empire.)

Yeshua executed, is pressing. They insist to Pilate, "He stirs up the people, teaching all over Judea, starting from Galilee even as far as this place" (Luke 23:5). Pilate discovers that Yeshua is actually not from Judea, but instead Galilee, a realm which sits just outside his jurisdiction. So, Pilate has Yeshua sent to meet with Herod, whose jurisdiction did include Galilee, who is in Jerusalem for the Passover (Luke 23:6-7).

One of the most elusive aspects of Yeshua, before the Roman governor, is why Pontius Pilate seems so eager to just let Him go. Given common Roman prejudices against Jews, one would think that Pilate would not really care about another Jew being executed—for blasphemy against some "absurd" Jewish law no less. Did Pilate just send Yeshua off to Herod because he did not want to be bothered, and having a strong dislike for the Jewish religious leaders, letting Yeshua go would annoy them? Josephus' works do record some things about Pilate,[60] and the complicated relationship he had with those in Judea. He is known for three major incidents in Judea: (1) sending a garrison into Jerusalem with idolatrous images of the emperor, (2) funding a water project for Jerusalem with seized Temple funds (cf. Luke 13:1), and later (3) suppressing some fanatics in Samaria. As summarized by *ISBE*,

"Josephus portrayed Pilate as a governor who was determined to maintain Roman supremacy and to secure its recognition. Although given to unwise initiatives and quick to act against manifest dissidence, Pilate was ready to investigate and yield to the unfamiliar prejudices of his subjects."[61]

While Pilate seems favorably disposed toward Yeshua at this point in the narrative, as a Roman governor his job was to be a good politician, and maintain Caesar's dominion over Judea. He might have been impressed about Yeshua's composure before His accusers, but it was his responsibility to make sure that Roman interests were served first—and frequently that meant making sure that the people were placated, and not rebellious. Because Pilate could be recalled to Rome if Judea got out of control or riotous, by sending Yeshua to Herod whatever would happen with Him might be able to be pawned off on another official. Luke records how Herod was actually a bit pleased by seeing Yeshua, "for he had wanted to see Him for a long time, because he had been hearing about Him and was hoping to see some sign performed by Him" (Luke 23:8). Yeshua does not entertain Herod, and the chief priests and scribes there get their wishes answered. Herod's soldiers mock Yeshua, putting a robe on Him, and He is sent back to Pilate (Luke 23:10-11), because while Yeshua might mainly teach in Galilee, He was arrested in Judea. Herod and Pilate became friends over this, perhaps only because Pilate showed a political gesture of cooperation (Luke 23:12).

With Yeshua as the definite responsibility of Pontius Pilate, the Roman governor now has to face the priests and religious leaders who want Yeshua executed (Luke 23:13). He informs them, "You brought this man to me as one who incites the people to rebellion, and behold, having examined Him before you, I have found no guilt in this man regarding the charges which you make against Him. No, nor has Herod, for he sent Him back to us; and behold, nothing deserving death has been done by Him" (Luke 23:14-15). Pilate would just assume to punish

---

[60] *Antiquities of the Jews* 18.35, 55-62, 85-89; *Jewish War* 2.169-177.
Also see Philo *Embassy to Gaius* 299-305.
[61] A.N. Sherwin-White, "Pilate, Pontius," in *ISBE*, 3:868.

Him for the inconvenience—perhaps just by a beating—and then let Him go (Luke 23:16).

Precedents established during the Roman administration instead required that during the season of Passover, he release a Jewish prisoner held by his garrison (Mark 15:6; Matthew 27:15-16; Luke 23:18). The Jewish man "Barabbas had been imprisoned with the insurrectionists who had committed murder in the insurrection" (Mark 15:7; cf. Matthew 27:16; Luke 23:19). A crowd was assembled near the governor's office, and was expecting him to release someone (Mark 15:8). Pilate asks them, "Do you want me to release for you the King of the Jews?" (Mark 15:9), a description of Yeshua which would cause the chief priests to clearly be irritated (Mark 15:10; Matthew 27:18), in addition to Him simply being referred to as "Messiah" (Matthew 27:17). While Pilate may have wanted to embarrass the Jewish religious leaders, establishing his Roman hegemony, "the chief priests stirred up the crowd *to ask* him to release Barabbas for them instead" (Mark 15:11), and "they cried out all together, saying, 'Away with this man, and release for us Barabbas!'" (Luke 23:18).

Even if Pontius Pilate recognized that Yeshua the Messiah was really innocent of the claims against Him, the record that we read in the Synoptics should not make us think that Pilate was that distressed over seeing any Jew put to death. *Pilate's job was to keep Roman order in place.* Pilate is less concerned about Yeshua's actual innocence, as much as he is concerned about the future—and the kind of reputation Rome will have if his governorship makes a habit of executing proven-to-be-innocent Jews.

As he deliberates what to do with Yeshua, Pilate's own wife sends him a message: "Have nothing to do with that righteous Man; for last night I suffered greatly in a dream because of Him" (Matthew 27:19). *More than just political forces want Yeshua put away*, but this pagan woman has had a dream that her husband is to stay out of this. But this does not seem to have really affected Pilate. The crowds still have to be stirred by the chief priests and Sanhedrin members for them to demand Barabbas be released (Matthew 27:20-21).

What is to be done if Barabbas is released? The mob demands that Yeshua be crucified, in spite of Pilate not seeing that Yeshua is guilty of death (Mark 15:12-14; Matthew 27:22-23). Luke 23:20-22 records how, "Pilate, wanting to release Yeshua, addressed them again, but they kept on calling out, saying, 'Crucify, crucify Him!' And he said to them the third time, 'Why, what evil has this man done? I have found in Him no guilt *demanding* death; therefore I will punish Him and release Him.'" The mob was getting riotous (Luke 23:23; Matthew 27:24a), and so Pilate himself can claim deniability in the future, "he took water and washed his hands in front of the crowd, saying, 'I am innocent of this Man's blood; see *to that* yourselves'" (Matthew 27:24b). If Pilate's superiors might want to know in the future why it is claimed that he saw to the execution of an innocent Jew, Pilate can say that it was because it was to prevent an uprising.

Matthew's record includes a very significant statement by the crowd: "His blood shall be on us and on our children!" (Matthew 27:25). It is thought sometimes that this is a purposeful remark to portray the Jews as Messiah-killers, who will bear the responsibility for seeing Yeshua unjustly executed for all time. Yet, it is clear that not all Jews in the First Century world are present at the event—many are still out in the Diaspora knowing nothing about Yeshua or events in Judea—

and many are readying themselves at various domiciles in Jerusalem to commemorate the Passover, likewise ignorant of what is happening in the city. Those of the crowd, stirred and purposefully agitated by the priests and religious leaders, bear the responsibility. At the very most, as M. Eugene Boring describes, "The people in Matthew's story do not invoke guilt on all future generations, but on themselves and their children—i.e., the generation that experienced the devastation of Jerusalem and the destruction of the Temple."[62] Still, I am inclined for any kind of Divine retribution for Yeshua's death to only be issued upon those who made up the mob—being manipulated for sure, and some probably even bribed—who failed to understand what they were really demanding. This could also be extended to those who mocked Yeshua as He was dying on the cross later.

Pilate himself bears some of the responsibility for Yeshua's death, giving in to the demands of the mob (Mark 15:15a; Matthew 27:26). Luke 23:24-25 specifies, "Pilate pronounced sentence that their demand be granted. And he released the man they were asking for who had been thrown into prison for insurrection and murder, but he delivered Yeshua to their will." At this point, Pilate could have worried that if he did not do something, he could be removed from his position, or at least censured in some way by Rome. (Pilate's later suppression of the Samaritans did merit his having to return to face the Emperor.)

The record is clear, "Wishing to satisfy the crowd, Pilate released Barabbas for them, and after having Yeshua scourged, he handed Him over to be crucified" (Mark 15:15; cf. Matthew 26:26). Before being led to His execution, though, Yeshua is taken into the Praetorium to be mocked and flogged by the Roman battalion (Mark 15:16; Matthew 26:27). While there is speculation that a Roman flogging alone could have killed Yeshua,[63] what is recorded in both Mark and Matthew is more concerned with how Yeshua is mocked by the Romans as the so-called "King of the Jews." Keep in mind, while a Jewish mob has said that they will take responsibility for Yeshua's death, the Roman soldiers who mock Him certainly do enjoy their handiwork.

The Lord was dressed as a player in a dirty little game, in which these Romans wanted Him to participate. The purple or scarlet robe He was made to wear, was likely some kind of faded, second-hand soldier's garment, with the crown of thorns they twisted was put together from some nearby shrub, probably like acanthus, turned inward so He would bleed (Mark 15:17; Matthew 27:28-29a). The reed Yeshua is given was probably used for military floggings, itself having seen better days (Matthew 27:29b).[64] These Roman soldiers, hearing about the claims made of Yeshua, kneel before Him and mockingly declare "Hail, King of the Jews!" (Mark 15:18; Matthew 27:29c), to a leader who is portrayed as utterly defeated and helpless. Yeshua is spit upon, beaten with the reed that is to depict a fake scepter, and He is sufficiently humiliated by pagans (Mark 15:20; Matthew 27:30). *Certainly,*

---

[62] M. Eugene Boring, "The Gospel of Matthew," in Leander E. Keck, ed. et. al., *New Interpreter's Bible* (Nashville: Abingdon, 1995), 8:487.

[63] The verb *phragelloō* (φραγελλόω), employed in Mark 15:15 and Matthew 27:26, often related to a very serious and painful kind of scourging:

"Slaves, aliens, and criminals condemned to death might be beaten with a whip of knotted cord or leather straps, often weighted with pieces of metal or bone to aggravate the torture...[It] was administered upon the naked back, and was at times fatal" (M. Greenberg, "Scourging," in George Buttrick, ed. et. al., *Interpreter's Dictionary of the Bible*, 4 vols. [Nashville: Abingdon, 1962], 4:245-246).

[64] Cf. Keener, 386.

more humiliating acts could have been performed, but there was insufficient time. When the soldiers finish, the costume is taken off, and Yeshua is led away to be executed (Mark 15:21; Matthew 27:31). Yeshua does not possess enough strength to carry His cross, and so a certain Simon of Cyrene is pressed into service to do it for Him (Mark 15:21; Matthew 27:32; Luke 23:26).

The Messiah's humiliation by the Romans is something that He Himself said was going to happen: "the Son of Man will be delivered to the chief priests and scribes, and they will condemn Him to death, and will hand Him over to the Gentiles to mock and scourge and crucify *Him*" (Matthew 20:18-19; cf. Mark 10:33-34). While there is some responsibility placed upon the Jewish religious leaders for the death of the Messiah, the Romans without question played a very important part in it as well. Pontius Pilate's claim that Yeshua was "King of the Jews"—when in fact Pilate himself had final authority in Judea—could have been used to assert Roman hegemony by discrediting a traveling rabbi. It was by no means Pilate making a personal recognition of Yeshua's Messiahship or Divinity. Furthermore, the scene of the Lord's humiliation, with a faded soldier's cape, a torturous crown of thorns, and a reed as a scepter that they used to beat Him—**makes the Romans just as directly responsible** as anyone else for the events involving Yeshua's death.

The Fourth Gospel interjects many details into what transpired between Yeshua and Pontius Pilate. That Yeshua is crucified before the official Passover is clear, as most of the Jewish officials leading Him to meet with Pilate did not enter into the Praetorium so as to possibly be ritually defiled among pagans (John 18:28). Pilate comes out and asks what accusations they have to bring (John 18:29), and is simply told, "If this Man were not an evildoer, we would not have delivered Him to you" (John 18:30). Pilate says that Yeshua needs to be judged according to Jewish law, but is then informed that He cannot be executed by the Jews (John 18:31). Most likely, this regards how the authority for executing criminals ultimately had to be approved by Rome, although executing someone so close to the Passover and risking defilement could also be a factor.

Pilate himself has to see that the situation with Yeshua is handled. He asks the Lord whether He really is King of the Jews, and we see that Pilate is only acting on the information that he has been given by the Jewish religious leaders (John 18:33-35). Yeshua makes some rather poignant statements to Pilate, telling him "My kingdom is not of this world. If My kingdom were of this world, then My servants would be fighting so that I would not be handed over to the Jews; but as it is, My kingdom is not of this realm" (John 18:36). Yeshua affirms that Pilate's acknowledgement of His kingship is correct, and that He is a teacher of truth (John 18:37). Pilate can see that Yeshua is not someone worthy of death, even if he really does not understand Him and might think His sayings are a bit odd. All Pilate can conclude is "I find no guilt in Him" (John 18:38), but realizing how the Jewish religious leaders want Him executed, he allows the Passover tradition of releasing a prisoner to decide whether Yeshua or Barabbas is released (John 18:39-40).

With Barabbas released, Pilate has Yeshua flogged by his troops (John 19:1-3). Is there a serious contradiction between what we see in the Synoptics and the Fourth Gospel—with one set of witnesses having Yeshua flogged and then led to crucifixion, but here with Yeshua flogged and then led before the crowd? Probably not. It was Pilate's hope to not have to execute Yeshua at all, but a thorough beating (Luke 23:15) might be just enough to pacify the growing mob. Looking at the witnesses we have in the four Gospels, Barabbas was probably released at the insistence of the crowd, Pilate announced his intention to condemn Yeshua, the Lord was taken into the Praetorium to be mocked and beaten (John 19:4-5), and with the crowds still there—there was one final chance for Him to not have to be crucified (John 19:4-5).

The scene of a brutally beaten Yeshua does not placate the mob's desire for His life (John 19:6). The Fourth Gospel's witness is clear on why Yeshua was condemned to death: "We have a law, and by that law He ought to die because He made Himself out *to be* the Son of God" (John 19:7). Pilate was even more concerned because of this, and was clear to tell Yeshua that he had the authority to release Him or execute Him (John 19:8-10). Yeshua's words are direct to Pilate in how, "You would have no authority over Me, unless it had been given you from above; for this reason he who delivered Me to you has *the* greater sin" (John 19:11). Perhaps this statement was so direct, Pilate could recognize the supernatural nature of it (John 19:12a). But the Jewish mob outside gets the better of him, crying, "If you release this Man, you are no friend of Caesar; everyone who makes himself out *to be* a king opposes Caesar" (John 19:12b). On the Day of Preparation before the Passover, Pontius Pilate sat down and condemned Yeshua to death, for the specific reason of the Jews demanding that their only king be Caesar (John 19:13-15). The Fourth Gospel confirms how Pilate was still ultimately concerned in asserting Roman authority in Judea, and he was looking out for his own political self-interest.

The Crucifixion and Death of Yeshua

Yeshua the Messiah is taken to be executed at a place called Golgotha, derived from either the Hebrew *Gulgolet* (גֻּלְגֹּלֶת) or Aramaic *Gulgulta* (גֻּלְגַּלְתָּא), both meaning Place of a Skull. It is also commonly referred to as Calvary, derived from the Latin Vulgate. When Yeshua is hoisted up to die, He is given a wine beverage that He is unwilling to drink (cf. Psalm 69:21; Proverbs 31:6), while His clothes are divided up by the soldiers by lots (Mark 15:22-24; Matthew 27:33-35; Luke 23:32-33; cf. Psalm 22:18). Luke records how when on His way to the execution site, there was a large number of people, including women, mourning. Yeshua directs their attention not to the present, but to the future when terrible things will happen (Luke 23:27-30; cf. Hosea 10:8). The Lord is executed along with two other criminals (Mark 15:27-28; Matthew 27:38; cf. Isaiah 52:12), and Luke is clear to point out how "Yeshua was saying, 'Father, forgive them; for they do not know what they are doing'" (Luke 23:34). The site of Golgotha was probably a common place outside of Jerusalem where the Romans had executed criminals before, as Yeshua is notably not alone among those executed.

For some reason or another, when terms like "cross" or "crucifixion" are sometimes spoken in a Messianic environment, there can be some negativity witnessed. Much of this is due to Christian anti-Semitic acts performed in the sign of the cross stemming from the Middle Ages. Frequently, an alternative such as hearing that Yeshua died on "the tree," with the Greek *xulon* (ξύλον) also simply meaning "wood," is offered.[65] While it is perfectly legitimate to employ an alternative such as "tree" in one's speech, or also refer to Yeshua being "executed"

---

[65] Cf. Acts 5:30; 10:39; 13:29; Galatians 3:13; 1 Peter 2:24.

or "put to death," and not just "crucified"—it is not appropriate to deliberately skew how the Messiah was, in fact, crucified by the Romans. The cross or *stauros* (σταυρός) was certainly not something elaborate or ornate, as might be found in some churches today. It was, rather, an upright pole, onto which a crossbeam carried by the condemned was hoisted into a T shape, forcing one to endure a long and painful suffocation. In spite of some terrible things committed in later history to the Jewish people, with the sign of the cross involved, the events as they transpired in the First Century have to be understood on their own terms.

Enemies of the Roman Empire were often crucified so that they could be made a public example. It was intended to be quite brutal and humiliating, with the dead frequently prohibited burial, instead being left to decompose as carrion.[66] The Roman Senator Cicero would write, "To bind a Roman citizen is a crime; to flog him is an abomination; to slay him is almost an act of murder; to crucify him is—what? There is no fitting word that can possibly describe so horrible a deed."[67] To Jews of the First Century, to be crucified would probably mean that one fell subject to the curse of Deuteronomy 21:22-23.[68] During Titus' siege of Jerusalem in 70 C.E., Josephus records how he gave his soldiers great freedom to crucify: "So the soldiers, out of the wrath and hatred they bore the Jews, nailed those they caught, one after one way, and another after another, to the crosses, by way of jest; when their number was so great, that room was lacking for the crosses, and crosses lacking for the bodies" (*Jewish War* 5.451).[69] He also gives an extra-Biblical testimony to the crucifixion of Yeshua: "Pilate, at the suggestion of the principal men among us, had condemned him to the cross" (*Antiquities of the Jews* 18.64).[70] In the estimation of J.B. Green, "the historicity of the death of Jesus on the cross is beyond doubt."[71] In describing how crucifixion was commonly used by Rome for its political prisoners, he points out how "in the province of Judea it proved to be a generally effective weapon against resistance."[72]

Vassilios Tzaferis offers a rather long, but excellent summary, about some of the history, usage, and agony involved with crucifixion:

> "...Many people erroneously assume that crucifixion was a Roman intention. In fact, Assyrians, Phoenicians and Persians all practiced crucifixion during the first millennium B.C. Crucifixion was introduced in the west from these eastern cultures; it was used only rarely on the Greek mainland, but Greeks in Sicily and southern Italy used it more frequently, probably as a result of their closer contact with Phoenicians and Carthaginians.

---

[66] Consult J.B. Green, "Death of Jesus: Crucifixion: A Cruel Practice," in *Dictionary of Jesus and the Gospels*, pp 144-148.

[67] Cited in Gordon D. Fee, *New International Commentary on the New Testament: Paul's Letter to the Philippians* (Grand Rapids: Eerdmans, 1995), 217, fn#13.

[68] "If a man has committed a sin worthy of death and he is put to death, and you hang him on a tree, his corpse shall not hang all night on the tree, but you shall surely bury him on the same day (for he who is hanged is accursed of God), so that you do not defile your land which the LORD your God gives you as an inheritance" (Deuteronomy 21:22-23).

[69] *The Works of Josephus: Complete and Unabridged*, 720.

[70] Ibid., 480.

[71] Green, "Death of Jesus," in *Dictionary of Jesus and the Gospels*, 148.

[72] Ibid.

"During the Hellenistic period, crucifixion became more popular among the Hellenized population of the east. After Alexander died in 323 B.C., crucifixion was frequently employed both by the Seleucids (the rulers of the Syrian half of Alexander's kingdom) and by the Ptolemies (the rulers of the Egyptian half).

".....

"The traditional method of execution among Jews was stoning. Nevertheless, crucifixion was occasionally employed by Jewish tyrants during that Hasmonean period. Alexander Jannaeus crucified 800 Jews on a single day in 88 B.C.

"At the end of the first century B.C., the Romans employed crucifixion as an official punishment for non-Romans for certain legally limited transgressions. Initially, it was employed not as a method of execution, but only as a punishment. Moreover, only slaves convicted of certain crimes were punished by crucifixion. During this early period, a wooden beam, known as a *furca* or *patibulum* was placed on the slave's neck and bound to his arms. The slave was then required to march through the neighborhood proclaiming his offense. This march was intended as expiation and humiliation. Later, the slave was also stripped and scourged, increasing both the punishment and humiliation. Still later, instead of walking with his arms tied to the wooden beam, the slave was tied to a vertical stake.

"Because the main purpose of this practice was to punish, humiliate and frighten disobedient slaves, the practice did not necessarily result in death. Only in later times, probably in the first century B.C., did crucifixion evolve into a method of execution for those convicted of certain crimes.

"Initially, crucifixion was known as the punishment of slaves. Later, it was used to punish foreign captives, rebels and fugitives, especially during times of war and rebellion. Captured enemies and rebels were crucified *en masse*. Accounts of the suppression of the revolt of Spartacus in 71 B.C. tell how the Roman army lined the road from Capua to Rome with 6,000 crucified rebels and 6,000 crosses. After King Herod's death triggered a minor rebellion in Judea in 7 A.D., Quintilius Varus, the Roman Legate of Syria, crucified 2,000 Jews in Jerusalem. During Titus's siege of Jerusalem in 70 A.D., Roman troops crucified as many as 500 Jews a day for several months.

"In times of war and rebellion, when hundreds and even thousands of people were crucified within a short period, little if any attention was paid to the way crucifixion was carried out. Crosses were haphazardly constructed, and executioners were impressed from the ranks of Roman legionaries.

"In peacetime, crucifixions were carried out according to certain rules, by special persons authorized by the Roman courts. Crucifixions took place at specific locations, for examples, in particular fields in Rome and on the Golgotha in Jerusalem. Outside of Italy, the Roman procurators alone possessed authority to impose the death penalty. Thus, when a local provincial court prescribed the death penalty, the consent of the Roman procurator had to be obtained to carry out the sentence.

"Once a defendant was found guilty and was condemned to be crucified, the execution was supervised by an official known as the *Carnifix Serarum*. From the tribunal hall, the victim was taken outside, stripped, bound to a column and scourged. The scourging was done with either a stick or a *flagellum*, a Roman instrument with a short handle to which several long, thick thongs had been attached. On the ends of the leather thongs were lead or bone tips. Although the number of strokes imposed was not fixed, care was taken not to kill the victim. Following the beating, the horizontal beam was placed upon the condemned man's shoulders, and he began the long, grueling march to the execution site, usually outside the city walls. A soldier at the head of the procession carried the *titulus*, an inscription written on wood, which stated the defendant's name and the crime for which he had been condemned. Later, this *titulus* was fastened to the victim's cross. When the procession arrived at the execution site, a vertical stake was fixed into the ground. Sometimes the victim was attached to the cross only with ropes. In such a case, the *patibulum* or crossbeam, to which the victim's arms were already bound, was simply affixed to the vertical beam; the victim's feet were then bound to the stake with a few turns of the rope.

"If the victim was attached by nails, he was laid on the ground, with his shoulders on the crossbeam, which was then raised and fixed on top of the vertical beam. The victim's feet were then nailed down against this vertical stake.

"Without any supplementary body support, the victim would die from muscular spasms and asphyxia in a very short time, certainly within two or three hours. Shortly after being raised on the cross, breathing would become difficult; to get his breath, the victim would attempt to draw himself up on his arms. Initially he would be able to hold himself up for 30 to 60 seconds, but this movement would quickly become increasingly difficult. As he became weaker, the victim would be unable to pull himself up and death would ensue within a few hours.

"In order to prolong the agony, Roman executioners devised two instruments that would keep the victim alive on the cross for extended periods of time. One, known as a *sedile*, was a small seat attached to the front of the cross, about halfway down. This device provided some support for the victim's body and may explain the phrase used by the Romans 'to sit on the cross.' Both Irenaeus and Justin Martyr describe the cross of Jesus as having five extremities rather than four; the fifth was probably the *sedile*. To increase the victim's suffering, the *sedile* was pointed, thus inflicting horrible pain. The second device added to the cross was the *suppedaneum*, or foot support. It was less painful than the *sedile*, but it also prolonged the victim's agony. Ancient historians record many cases in which the victim stayed alive on the cross for two or three more days with the use of a *suppedaneum*. The church father Origen writes of having seen a crucified man who survived the whole night and the following day. Josephus refers to a case in which three crucified Jews survived on the cross for three days. During the mass crucifixions following the repression of the revolt of Spartacus in Rome, some of the crucified rebels talked to the soldiers for three days."[73]

Yeshua's execution was approved by Pontius Pilate, and it was carried out by Romans in a Roman style—so once again, any claim that the Jewish people are "Messiah killers," and that the Romans somehow are not, is quite absurd and without support. **All of sinful humanity is responsible for Yeshua's death.** Crucifixion was a principal way of dying, so that the Messiah's own word about His mission might be fulfilled:

"As Moses lifted up the serpent in the wilderness, even so must the Son of Man be lifted up; so that whoever believes will in Him have eternal life" (John 3:14-15; cf. Numbers 21:9).

The three Synoptic Gospels focus their attention on the main event of the crucifixion. Yeshua is crucified at the third hour, or around 9:00 AM,[74] and above His cross bore the inscription "THIS IS YESHUA KING OF THE JEWS" (Matthew 27:36; cf. Mark 15:25; Luke 23:38), just as would be seen on the Roman *titulus*. The charge against Yeshua was that He claimed to be some sort of King. In the Sanhedrin's eyes, Yeshua would be discredited to His followers or those who took interest in His teachings—and in Rome's eyes the Jews would have to look on Yeshua, seeing that Rome had the authority to execute one of their might-be liberators.

It must be interjected that in the Apostle Paul's writing to the Colossians, he does affirm that *something* was nailed to the cross of Yeshua, as he asserts that His sacrifice has "canceled out the certificate of debt consisting of decrees against us, which was hostile to us; and He has taken it out of the way, having nailed it to the cross" (Colossians 2:14). Many of today's Christians have actually taken this as being the Torah of Moses, yet does this at all fit the context of what occurs at Golgotha? Not at all. There is **no hint** that Yeshua considered His crucifixion to render the Torah completely inoperative. The term *cheirographon* (χειρόγραφον), used in Colossians 2:14, means "**a hand-written document, specif. a certificate of indebtedness,** *account, record of debts*" (*BDAG*).[75] Traditional views of Colossians 2:14 dating back to the Protestant Reformation often associated the certificate of debt as either the record of human sin, or the guilt of human sin incurred before God.[76] Another common view of Colossians 2:14, sees this certificate of debt as connected to the pronouncement of condemnation that hung over Yeshua as He was dying on the cross. Douglas J. Moo, who is not necessarily favorable to the Law

---

[73] Vassilios Tzaferis, "The Archaeological Evidence for Crucifixion," in Meinhardt, pp 95-100.

[74] Spiros Zodhiates, ed., *Hebrew-Greek Key Study Bible*, NASB (Chattanooga: AMG Publishers, 1994), 1341.

[75] *BDAG*, 1083.

[76] For one example, see John Wesley, *Explanatory Notes Upon the New Testament*, reprint (Peterborough, UK: Epworth Press, 2000), 747.

Many Protestant churches today hold services on Good Friday where people can write their sins or transgressions on small pieces of paper, and then actually nail them to a cross in the sanctuary, representative of how the record of human sin has been taken care of by Jesus' sacrifice. This concurs with Colossians 2:14 representing the condemnation upon human sin.

of Moses having any continual effect in the post-resurrection era, does, however, correctly describe,

"In causing him to be nailed to the cross, God (the subject of the verb) has provided for the full cancellation of the debt of obedience that we had incurred. Christ took upon himself the penalty that we were under because of our disobedience, and his death fully satisfied God's necessary demand for due punishment of that disobedience."[77]

Indeed, we should rightfully conclude that it was the record of human sin nailed to Yeshua's cross caused by disobedience, its penalty absorbed in His sacrifice—not the standard in the Law that defines sin. That which stood against us was not God's holy Torah delivered to His people by Moses, but rather the capital penalties within the Torah which condemn sin.[78]

Returning to the scene at Golgotha, if Yeshua had been executed by the Jewish religious leaders, then He would have been stoned. While it would have made for a painful and public death—it would not allow for the people to take a good look at what was happening for several hours. Yeshua is mocked as He is steadily suffocating up on the cross (cf. Psalm 22:7; 42:10; 70:3)—something that both the Jews and Romans present do, religious leaders and soldiers alike: "And the people stood by, looking on. And even the rulers were sneering at Him, saying, 'He saved others; let Him save Himself if this is the Messiah of God, His Chosen One [cf. Isaiah 53:11].' The soldiers also mocked Him, coming up to Him, offering Him sour wine, and saying, 'If You are the King of the Jews, save Yourself!'" (Luke 23:35-37; cf. Mark 15:29-31; Matthew 27:39-42). Matthew's record makes a reference to the people actually quoting from the Tanach, making fun of the Lord with, "'HE TRUSTS IN GOD; LET GOD RESCUE *Him* now, IF HE DELIGHTS IN HIM; for He said, 'I am the Son of God'" (Matthew 27:43; cf. Psalm 22:8).

As bad as it is for those looking on to taunt Yeshua to come down from off of the cross and save Himself, the two criminals being executed along with Him are also found insulting Him (Mark 15:32; Matthew 27:44). One of the two mockingly asks Yeshua to save them from execution (Luke 23:39), but the other actually comes to his senses, asking him, "Do you not even fear God, since you are under the same sentence of condemnation?", and then recognizes, "we indeed *are suffering* justly, for we are receiving what we deserve for our deeds; but this man has done nothing wrong" (Luke 23:40, 41). The thief is actually repentant for what sentenced him to death, acknowledging Yeshua as the Savior, perhaps knowing just enough of the Messianic expectation to see how the One who was entirely innocent is being unjustly slain. He asks Him, "Yeshua, remember me when You come in Your kingdom!" (Luke 23:42), and Yeshua tells him something even better than a future promise of the thief being a part of the Messianic Age: "Truly I say to you, today[79]

---

[77] Douglas J. Moo, *Pillar New Testament Commentary: The Letters to the Colossians and to Philemon* (Grand Rapids: Eerdmans, 2008), pp 211-212.

Commenting on Colossians 2:14, James D.G. Dunn rightly thinks "we should note that it is not the law which is thought of as thus destroyed, but rather its particular condemnation (χειρόγραφον) of transgressions, absorbed in the sacrificial death of the Christ (cf. Rom. 8:3)" (*New International Greek Testament Commentary: The Epistles to the Colossians and to Philemon* [Grand Rapids: Eerdmans, 1996], 166).

[78] For further discussion, consult the commentary *Colossians and Philemon for the Practical Messianic* by J.K. McKee.

[79] Grk. *sēmeron* (σήμερον); "*today, this very day*" (BDAG, 921).

you shall be with Me in Paradise" (Luke 23:43). The two of them, dying that day, would be ushered into Abraham's Bosom, or the Paradise side of Sheol (cf. Luke 16:23ff).

There is certainly drama that occurs as Yeshua's death draws closer between the sixth and ninth hours, or about 12:00 noon to 3:00 PM,[80] because darkness falls over the vicinity of Jerusalem (Mark 15:33; Matthew 27:45; Luke 23:44). In what can appear to be a rather cryptic expression, "At the ninth hour Yeshua cried out with a loud voice, 'ELOI, ELOI, LAMA SABACHTHANI?' which is translated, 'MY GOD, MY GOD, WHY HAVE YOU FORSAKEN ME?'" (Mark 15:34; cf. Matthew 27:46). This is a quotation from Psalm 22:1, expressing an alienation from the Father—no doubt caused by Yeshua's having to be sacrificed for *all* human sin. Yet, the Psalm ends with a message of triumph and praise for God, something we can assume is intended by how we know Yeshua would be resurrected from the dead:

"I will tell of Your name to my brethren; in the midst of the assembly I will praise You. You who fear the LORD, praise Him; all you descendants of Jacob, glorify Him, and stand in awe of Him, all you descendants of Israel. For He has not despised nor abhorred the affliction of the afflicted; nor has He hidden His face from him; but when he cried to Him for help, He heard" (Psalm 22:22-24).

When Yeshua speaks forth the Psalm, bystanders there thought He was calling out to Elijah (Mark 15:35; Matthew 27:47, 49), something that some Rabbis of the period apparently did when they were in distress (b.*Avodah Zara* 17b). The sour wine or vinegar offered to Yeshua was apparently done so to try to revive Him (Mark 15:36; Matthew 27:48).

The death of Yeshua triggers some rather significant phenomenon, as the sky has grown dark in the middle of the afternoon (Luke 23:45a). The Lord issues a loud cry with His final breath, "Father, INTO YOUR HANDS I COMMIT MY SPIRIT [Psalm 31:5][81]" (Luke 23:46; cf. Mark 15:37; Matthew 27:50). At this moment, two groups of people have something communicated to them. The veil in the Temple, separating out the Holy of Holies, rips in two (Mark 15:38; Matthew 27:51a; Luke 23:45b), something that any of the priests present would have noticed, and probably anyone else present. Likewise, the Roman centurion attending to Yeshua's crucifixion recognizes, at the earthquake which ensues, "Truly this was the Son of God![82]" (Matthew 27:54; cf. Mark 15:39) and how "Certainly this man was innocent," actually issuing some praise to God (Luke 23:47). Matthew also records a later sign, of how "many bodies of the saints who had fallen asleep were raised; and coming out of the tombs after His resurrection they entered the holy city and appeared to many" (Matthew 27:52-53). While certainly a mystery to be pondered, I think we can safely speculate that those who were raised to life here were some of the recently deceased.

While Yeshua could have been sacrificed at any time during the general Passover season to adequately suffice as having prophetically fulfilled the typology

---

"Truly I tell you, this day you will be with me in paradise" (Luke 23:43, Lattimore).

[80] Zodhiates, *Hebrew-Greek Key Study Bible*, NASB, 1341.

[81] Aland, *GNT*, 305.

[82] Grk. *legontes alēthōs Theou huios ēn houtos* (λέγοντες· ἀληθῶς θεοῦ υἱὸς ἦν οὗτος).

Note how *Theou* is in the singular. It would be quite impossible to render this with "Truly this was a son of the *gods*," as the Roman centurion would in some way have to be acknowledging the One God of the Jews as operating here.

of Passover lamb, we should think it most appropriate that Yeshua died at the same time as the main lamb was offered in the Temple on the 14th of Nisan. The Mishnah specifies, "The daily whole offering [of the afternoon] [generally] was slaughtered at half after the eighth hour [after dawn, about 2:30 P.M.] and offered up at half after the ninth hour [about 3:30 P.M.]" (m.*Pesachim* 5:1).[83] Keener indicates, "By expiring at 3:00 p.m., Jesus died about the official time of the evening lamb in the temple."[84] So when there was a high amount of activity in the Temple precincts—with the most amount of people present preparing for the Passover *seder* that evening—the Temple's interior curtain split. The pagans present would have noticed the dark sky and earthquake, but the Jews would have most especially noticed the curtain torn. The Talmud further records how in the forty years or so before the destruction of the Second Temple (starting around this time), the doors of the Temple would open and close themselves, likely connected to this:

"Forty years before the destruction of the sanctuary, the lot did not come up in the right hand, and the thread of crimson never turned white, and the westernmost light never shone, and the doors of the courtyard would open by themselves" (b.*Yoma* 39b).[85]

Some of those closest to Yeshua are recognized as having been present at the crucifixion site. Notably, almost all of Yeshua's followers present at His death are women, including: Mary Magdalene, Mary the mother of James and Joseph, the mother of John and James (sons of Zebedee), and well as various other acquaintances who had followed Him from Galilee (Mark 15:40-41; Matthew 27:55-56; Luke 23:48-49). Because of the low status of women in the First Century, their presence adjacent to the cross would not have been viewed as some kind of political threat—even if they were known followers of Yeshua—as they would just be dismissed. But, their presence at the death of the Lord does indicate, as Keener observes, "These women had followed Jesus as disciples in whatever ways they could, even ways that would have appeared scandalous in that culture."[86] Just as the *cheirographon* or indictment of capital penalties would be nailed to Yeshua's cross, the contingent of female Messiah followers present should also be a major clue to us as to the kind of other changes His death will inaugurate—reversing the curse of Genesis 3:16!

It was necessary that the body of Yeshua be taken down before day's end. A certain Joseph of Arimathea, who was a member of the Sanhedrin and a righteous man, received permission from Pontius Pilate to take Yeshua's body and place it in his own stone tomb (Mark 15:43-47; Matthew 27:57-61; Luke 23:51-56). Yeshua's body is wrapped in linen, and placed in the grave. Luke makes the point of recognizing how this Joseph "had not consented to...[the] plan and action" (Luke 23:51) of the Sanhedrin in wanting to condemn Yeshua, and his generosity is shown in that he will allow Him to rest in a tomb that had been hewn for himself. Some of the women from Galilee made notice of where Yeshua's body was placed, as

---

[83] Neusner, *Mishnah*, 236.
[84] Keener, 390.
[85] *The Babylonian Talmud: A Translation and Commentary.*
Cf. France, *NICNT: Matthew*, 1079, fn#27.
[86] Keener, 392.

they will use various spices and perfumes for anointing it, being customary to retard the smell of decay (Luke 23:55-56a).

Mark 15:42 tells us that Yeshua had to be interred quickly "because it was the preparation day, that is, the day before the Sabbath," and Luke 23:54 similarly states, "It was the preparation day, and the Sabbath was about to begin." Most naturally, readers take this to be the day before the weekly *Shabbat*, Friday evening. Jewish law did prohibit burial on the Sabbath (m.*Shabbat* 23:5), but Sabbath restrictions likely applied to festival days as well, given the dictum "There is no difference between a festival day and the Sabbath day except for preparing food alone" (m.*Megillah* 1:5).[87] Rest would be required on the High Sabbath associated with the Passover, the first day of Unleavened Bread (Leviticus 23:7) occurring on the 15th of Nisan. This should be a very good indication pointing to Yeshua being crucified before the Passover on the 14th of Nisan.

We can all agree that the women prepared for their anointing of Yeshua's corpse before a Sabbath period (cf. Luke 23:56), but was this period only 24 hours, following a Good Friday crucifixion, as is traditionally held? Or, was it possibly a bit longer? Obviously, as soon as the women could go attend to Yeshua's body, they would do so.

We see a good clue that the Day of Preparation on which Yeshua was crucified was not a Friday, because "on the next day, the day after the preparation, the chief priests and the Pharisees gathered together with Pilate" (Matthew 27:62), not being called the Sabbath. France points out, "Matthew surprisingly does not draw attention to that embarrassing fact by mentioning the sabbath by name."[88] Whether the day after the preparation is intended to be the weekly Sabbath or a High Sabbath, these religious officials have been caught violating the Torah, a result of their plot against the Lord and His followers. France, even though holding to a Good Friday crucifixion, thinks that "day of preparation" is used in Matthew 27:62 because it involves "not an ordinary sabbath but also the day of the Passover meal."[89]

A Wednesday crucifixion would allow for the Marys to go to the tomb as soon as Thursday evening, after a Thursday High Sabbath of Passover, but this runs contrary to how they are actually said to go to the tomb on the first day of the week.[90] The traditional Friday crucifixion *or* a Thursday crucifixion would allow for the Marys to be at the tomb as soon as Saturday evening or Sunday morning. With the latter two options, either the High Sabbath of Passover occurred on the same day as the weekly Sabbath, Saturday—or a High Sabbath occurred on Friday followed by the weekly Sabbath on Saturday, a Sabbath period of 48 hours. France is probably correct in that "the phrase 'the Preparation' does double duty."[91] But, whether Yeshua was crucified on a Wednesday, Thursday, or Friday also has to consider the Lord's claim that He will be raised after "three days and three nights" (Matthew 12:40), and the minimum length this time has to be (discussed further).

The narrative of Matthew's Gospel is most concerned, however, with the fact that the Jewish religious leaders broke protocol on a Sabbath day, and went to

---

[87] Neusner, *Mishnah*, 317.
[88] France, *NICNT: Matthew*, 1093.
[89] Ibid.
[90] Cf. Mark 16:2; Matthew 28:1; Luke 24:1.
[91] France, *NICNT: Matthew*, 1093.

meet with Pontius Pilate. For some reason or another, they are not satisfied that the Messiah is now dead. They remember how He has said He will resurrect after three days, and they want to make sure that when that third day after He is dead arrives—that there is a Roman guard at the entombment site. They do not want the Disciples to somehow "fake" Yeshua's resurrection by stealing His body. Having given in to the demand to execute Him, Pilate simply grants the request to set a guard at the tomb, along with an official seal (Matthew 27:63-66).

The record we see of Yeshua's death in the Fourth Gospel expands what we see in the Synoptics, adding more details. It specifically intends to connect Yeshua's death to more Tanach passages, adding some more depth to what took place. Yeshua is taken to Golgotha to be crucified, having to carry His cross at least some of the way, and being executed between two others His cross does bear the transcription "YESHUA THE NAZARENE, THE KING OF THE JEWS" (John 19:16-19). John makes the point of recognizing that this was actually "written in Hebrew, Latin *and* in Greek" (John 19:20), meaning that just about anyone seeing this—whether a native of Judea, a Diaspora Jew, one of the Roman soldiers, or a foreign traveler—could clearly see who this Yeshua or Iēsous or Iesus was. The chief priests object to what Pilate writes, as they only want it to say "I am King of the Jews" (John 19:21-22), so Yeshua could be discredited as a messianic figure.

Having hoisted Yeshua onto the cross, the soldiers agree to cast lots for His garments, as they might have some use for them. John makes an appeal to Psalm 22:18 being fulfilled (John 19:23-25a). The same women who the Synoptics indicate were present at the cross are also seen in the Fourth Gospel, with the addition of Mary the wife of Clopas and "the disciple whom He loved," presumably a very young John (John 19:25b-26a). Yeshua's own mother, Mary, is present as well, and He tells her from the cross that this disciple John is now her "son" and she is his "mother," with the indication that such a disciple began to take care of her (John 19:26b-27). With none of the other half-siblings or other Disciples of the Lord present, John must have been the only one who could see to Mary's needs. Furthermore, this could have communicated that Yeshua was no longer her "son," given the salvation history events in play.

More references to Yeshua fulfilling Scripture are made in terms of the sour wine vinegar given to Him, because it is placed on a branch of hyssop, an elemental connection to the Passover lamb's blood (John 19:28-29; cf. Exodus 12:22). After this occurs, all the Lord can say is "It is finished!" and He dies (John 19:30). The verb *teleō* (τελέω), employed here, can mean "*to complete, fulfil, accomplish*, and, generally, *to execute, perform*" (LS),[92] being related to the noun *telos* (τέλος), which itself often means "**the goal toward which a movement is being directed, *end, goal, outcome***" (*BDAG*; cf. Romans 10:4, Grk.).[93] Within the realm of lexical possibilities, John 19:30 can be rendered with "It is accomplished!" (CJB) or "It has been brought to the goal!" (my translation), speaking of the final atonement for human sin being offered, and full reconciliation between humankind and its Creator now provided for.[94]

---

[92] *LS*, 798.

[93] *BDAG*, 998.

[94] George R. Beasley-Murray adds,

"After drinking the wine [or vinegar], Jesus uttered his last word known to the Evangelist, τετέλεσται [*tetelestai*]. The rendering, 'It is finished!' conveys only half the meaning. For the verb τελέω

The Fourth Gospel asserts that the crucifixion of Yeshua occurred on the Day of Preparation, and not just for the Sabbath, but one that can be viewed as a High Sabbath independent of the normal weekly Sabbath (John 19:31)[95]—supported by the previous assertion of Yeshua dying on "the day of preparation for the Passover" (John 19:14) or "the eve of Passover" (NEB).[96] The legs of those being crucified would have to be broken to accelerate death, but Yeshua was already dead (John 19:32-33); instead He is pierced with a spear, and blood and water pour out (John 19:34), with the author of John confirming that he saw it himself (John 19:35). A direct appeal is made to Yeshua's sacrifice and the instructions of the Passover lamb (John 19:36; cf. Exodus 12:46; Numbers 9:12). Such an explicit connection between Yeshua's sacrifice and the Passover lamb slain in the Torah, in my estimation, makes it quite unlikely that He was offered at any time other than the 14th of Nisan, as the Passover lambs themselves were being killed. Another Tanach passage is referenced in Zechariah 12:10, in that deliverance is found in someone who is pierced (John 19:37).

Joseph of Arimathea receives permission to take Yeshua's body, being considered a secret disciple out of fear (John 19:38). Nicodemus, who had originally met Yeshua at night, brings about a hundred pounds worth of spices for the body (John 19:39). Yeshua's body is wrapped in linen, and John actually states that the tomb where He is placed is in a garden adjacent to the crucifixion site (John 19:40-41). Yeshua is laid there rather quickly because of the Day of Preparation (John 19:42). Whether this is before the weekly Sabbath also serving as a High Sabbath, or a High Sabbath, does not matter as far as the entombment was concerned; it simply had to be done quickly, with the final burial matters to be attended to later.

Three Days and Three Nights

In today's Messianic community, no part of the death of Yeshua is more controversial than His assertion, "for just as JONAH WAS THREE DAYS AND THREE NIGHTS IN THE BELLY OF THE SEA MONSTER, so will the Son of Man be three days and three nights in the heart of the earth" (Matthew 12:40; cf. Jonah 1:17). Even when it is emphasized that our attention as Believers during the Passover season needs to be focused more on what actually happened, than the exact timing of the events, there are often quite a few discussions and debates over the length of time Yeshua's body was actually interred in Joseph of Arimathea's tomb. The traditional view of Yeshua having died on Good Friday and resurrected on Easter Sunday morning is frequently thought to not suffice for His claim to be dead "three days and three nights." And this is not only something that many of today's Messianics question, but many Christians as well. Author Dave Hunt expresses his opinion,

"Obviously, had Christ been crucified on Friday, He couldn't possibly have spent three days and three nights in the grave by Sunday morning. The verification

---

fundamentally denotes 'to carry out' the will of somebody, whether of oneself or another, and so to fulfill obligations or carry out religious act" (*Word Biblical Commentary: John*, Vol 36 [Waco, TX: Word Books, 1987], 352).

To argue that "It is finished!" somehow pertains to a declaration made nullifying the Mosaic Torah, is quite out of place, as Yeshua's words concern atonement of sins.

[95] "There is nothing, as far as I know...that parallels this expression in the rabbinic literature, i.e., that when a Festival Shabbat falls on a weekly Shabbat, that day is referred to as the 'great Shabbat' or 'high Shabbat'" (Hegg, "The Chronology of the Crucifixion").

[96] A footnote in the NEB does include the alternative rendering, "It was Friday in Passover."

of that fact is simple. What was left of Friday afternoon can be counted as day one. All Saturday is day two. Friday and Saturday nights until dawn Sunday total two nights. The period comes up short by one day and one night."[97]

The traditional Good Friday-Easter Sunday scenario leaves Yeshua dead for only 36 hours or so, and so given the Lord's own reference to His being dead "three days and three nights," it is not surprising why many have insisted that He be interred for a full 72 hours. Yeshua dying on a Wednesday, and then being resurrected sometime between the Saturday evening and Sunday morning following, does seem to make sense, and it has become what is frequently heard among those who have questioned the traditional view. Yet, insisting that Yeshua remain interred for a full 72 hours has to be counterbalanced with the Apostolic Scriptures' own consistent affirmation that Yeshua would resurrect "on the third day" (Matthew 16:21; 17:23; 20:19; Luke 9:22; 24:7, 46; Acts 10:40), *te trite hemera* (τῇ τρίτῃ ἡμέρᾳ). The Jewish religious leaders insisted that Joseph of Arimathea's tomb remain secured with a Roman guard "until the third day" (Matthew 12:40).

From a textual standpoint, one has to weigh the "three days and three nights" sign of Jonah, together with the understanding that Yeshua was expected to resurrect sometime on the third day after His execution. Recognizing that Yeshua was to be resurrected sometime on the third day, those who hold to the traditional Good Friday-Easter Sunday reckoning feel that they have support. They do rightly point out that in the Tanach, any part of a day is considered as being a whole day:

- **Joseph's brothers were put in prison for three days, but were actually released on the third day:** "So he put them all together in prison for three days. Now Joseph said to them on the third day, 'Do this and live, for I fear God: if you are honest men, let one of your brothers be confined in your prison; but as for *the rest of* you, go, carry grain for the famine of your households, and bring your youngest brother to me, so your words may be verified, and you will not die.' And they did so" (Genesis 42:17-20).

- **Queen Esther told the Jews in Susa to fast for three days, either day or night, but then on the third day she readied herself to see the king:** "Go, assemble all the Jews who are found in Susa, and fast for me; do not eat or drink for three days, night or day. I and my maidens also will fast in the same way. And thus I will go in to the king, which is not according to the law; and if I perish, I perish.'...Now it came about on the third day that Esther put on her royal robes and stood in the inner court of the king's palace in front of the king's rooms, and the king was sitting on his royal throne in the throne room, opposite the entrance to the palace" (Esther 4:16; 5:1).

- **David feeds an Egyptian who had not eaten for three days and three nights, having been left behind three days prior:** "They gave him a piece of fig cake and two clusters of raisins, and he ate; then his spirit revived. For he had not eaten bread or drunk water for three days and three nights. David said to him, 'To whom do you belong? And where are you from?' And he said, 'I am a young man

---

[97] Dave Hunt, *How Close Are We?* (Eugene, OR: Harvest House, 1993), 170.

of Egypt, a servant of an Amalekite; and my master left me behind when I fell sick three days ago'" (1 Samuel 30:12-13).

After Yeshua was resurrected, the Lord disguised Himself and overheard two of His followers talking about what has transpired in Jerusalem, on their walk to Emmaus. They tell Him about the crucifixion scene, how "it is the third day since these things happened" (Luke 24:21), and how they had heard that some women encountered Him alive (Luke 24:22-24). The resurrected Yeshua reveals Himself to these followers (Luke 24:25-35), and Luke makes the point that "beginning with Moses and with all the prophets, He explained to them the things concerning Himself in all the Scriptures" (Luke 24:27). It had been less than 72 hours following Yeshua's death, and He was now resurrected. But had He been executed only one-and-a-half actual days prior?

It does seem that the common alternative to the traditional Good Friday-Eastern Sunday scenario—a Wednesday crucifixion with Yeshua resurrected by Sunday—comes up short because of the testimony of Him being resurrected on the third day, rather than after the third day. Among Messianics, Tim Hegg once advocated a 72 hour Wednesday-Saturday evening/Sunday morning scenario, but then changed to now adhering to the traditional Good Friday-Easter Sunday scenario—and he is notably not alone. Various other Messianic ministries, when seeing the evidence that any part of a day can constitute a full day, have gone from advocating a full 72 hour chronology for Yeshua's death, to now advocating the traditional Good Friday-Easter Sunday scenario as is taught during Holy Week in most churches.

I want you to understand that Yeshua the Messiah can surely fulfill His own words by being executed on Friday, and then being resurrected by Sunday morning. I attended church for many years, going to a special Good Friday service, and later an Easter Sunday service (something mind you that was almost completely devoid of references to the Easter bunny or various other side traditions) and found them to be quite spiritually edifying. Beyond the chronology issues, I understand the pull of some Messianic teachers who want to make Christians examining their Hebraic Roots easily understand Yeshua's commemoration of the Passover, followed by His death and resurrection, in terms that they already can relate to: the chronology of Good Friday-Easter Sunday. From this perspective:

1. Yeshua kept the Passover with His Disciples on the 14th of Nisan, the official date of the feast, with all of those in Jerusalem, a Thursday evening.
2. Yeshua was executed on the 15th of Nisan, the Preparation Day for the weekly Sabbath, a Friday (the High Sabbath of Passover).
3. Yeshua was resurrected either as the 16th of Nisan closed, a Saturday, or on the morning of the 17th of Nisan, a Sunday.

A Christian Believer who has held to the traditional Good Friday-Easter Sunday chronology, devoid of any Passover connection, only has to modify a few things here, and can be enriched with some Hebraic connections.

While I think that Yeshua could fulfill prophecy via this scenario, Messianics who adhere to it are most concerned with insisting that the Day of Preparation on which Yeshua was crucified (John 19:31) precede the weekly Sabbath, and not the Passover feast itself. Hegg asserts, "If there is any conclusion to which I have come, it is this: the crucifixion did take place on a Friday."[98] In contrast, if Yeshua were crucified on the Day of Preparation for the High Sabbath of Passover and not a weekly Sabbath exclusively, occurring on the 14th of Nisan, then this means that the Last Supper had to be held on the 13th of Nisan. The Last Supper then is either not a *seder* meal, contrary to the witness of the three Synoptics, is a *seder* meal held according to a competing sectarian calendar, **or** as we have proposed was a *seder* meal deliberately held a day early because of emergency circumstances.

Sadly, it has been my experience that there are various Messianics out there who are more concerned with Yeshua's adherence to the strict letter of the Law, rather than acknowledging how the year of His execution was something exceptional, with less-than-normal circumstances present. More significance is probably placed upon *seder* specifics, than the sacrifice Yeshua would offer up of Himself. The reason why the Good Friday-Easter Sunday scenario is being adopted by some Messianics, is simply because they require Yeshua to demonstrate a strict and rigid level of Torah keeping—without any exceptions—to guide their exegesis. I do not disagree with the possibility that an execution of the Lord on the 15th of Nisan, could suffice for prophetic fulfillment (although it would have been an execution occurring on a High Sabbath). But, it is far better to see Him executed on the 14th of Nisan, given the Fourth Gospel's explicit references to the Passover instructions from the Pentateuch (John 19:36; cf. Exodus 12:46; Numbers 9:12), and not any other prescribed offerings during the season.

If Yeshua had claimed that He would be entombed for "three days and nights," then the traditional Good Friday-Easter Sunday chronology would seem to have some support. Only touching on three actual days would then be necessary to fulfill the Lord's word. However, Yeshua claimed that He would be dead for "three days **and** three nights" (Matthew 12:40),[99] which many Bible readers, myself included, think implies something a little longer than Good Friday-Easter Sunday. At present among Messianic interpreters, the two main options which are proposed are Yeshua being dead a full 72 hours, and half this length at 36 hours. I would suggest a third option, where we consider "three days and three nights" to involve Yeshua being dead with three instances of daylight and three instances of dusk—where they are touched upon, but the actual length of time was likely around 52-54 hours.

One of the most cryptic words that some people encounter in the Apostolic Scriptures, is the Apostle Paul's claim that Yeshua the Messiah "was raised on the third day according to the Scriptures" (1 Corinthians 15:4).[100] I have encountered Messianic Believers who have actually had their faith shaken a little, because in their minds they have failed to find any specific prophecy that speaks of Yeshua being raised from the dead on the third day.

From a general perspective, there are, in fact various instances in the Tanach where some important event is associated with the third day (Hosea 6:1-2; Genesis 22:4; 2 Kings 20:5; Jonah 2:1-9; cf. Exodus 19:10; Esther 5:1; Ezra 6:15; Genesis 40:1-23; Leviticus 7:17-18; Judges 20; Joshua 1:11; 3:2).[101] Looking at these patterns,

---

[98] Hegg, "The Chronology of the Crucifixion."

[99] Grk. *treis hēmeras kai treis nuktas* (τρεῖς ἡμέρας καὶ τρεῖς νύκτας).

[100] Or, "in accordance with what the *Tanakh* says" (CJB).

[101] Cf. Michael L. Brown, *Answering Jewish Objections to Jesus, Volume 3: Messianic Prophecy Objections* (Grand Rapids: Baker Books, 2003), pp 182-183.

Michael L. Brown concludes that "Paul [has] the right to say that the Messiah rose from the dead on the third day according to the Scriptures."[102] Yet among the Tanach passages of redemptive or spiritual activity occurring on the third day, one should immediately jump out at us as relating to the resurrection of the Messiah:

"Come, let us return to the LORD. For He has torn *us*, but He will heal us; He has wounded *us*, but He will bandage us. He will revive us after two days; He will raise us up on the third day [*b'yom ha'sh'lishi yeqimeinu*, בַּיּוֹם הַשְּׁלִישִׁי יְקִמֵנוּ],[103] that we may live before Him."

Most frequently in today's Messianic world, and even among many Christians, Hosea 6:1-2 is viewed as relating to some future end-time scenario. It is concluded, in connection with words like Psalm 90:4, that this is describing the last two thousand years since the First Coming of Yeshua, and that in the third thousand year period the Second Coming will take place. While this is a popular view to be sure, it really does not do justice to the surrounding text.[104] The issue at hand is *the means* by which God will restore Israel, both of Ephraim and Judah, who have committed sins before Him (Hosea 6:3-5). Of important notice is the Prophet's assertion, "For I delight in loyalty rather than sacrifice, and in the knowledge of God rather than burnt offerings" (Hosea 6:6). But most important to understanding the being raised up on the third day, the Prophet says, "like Adam they have transgressed the covenant; there they have dealt treacherously against Me" (Hosea 6:7). It would be one thing if Israel, Ephraim addressed first and Judah addressed second, were compared to those who came out of Egypt, or those who entered into the Promised Land led by Joshua. But here, Israel is compared *k'adam* (כְּאָדָם), "like men" (KJV), meaning of course "like humanity." The raising up that is expected to occur on the third day, while immediately affecting Israel, has to take place because of a problem that affects all of humankind.

I do not believe it is difficult at all to see how Hosea 6:1-2 is indeed a prophecy referring to the death and resurrection of Messiah Yeshua, as the Lord was resurrected on the third day. Yeshua's death and resurrection, while immediately affecting Israel, is offered on behalf of all sinful humanity. It is quite notable that the Septuagint renders the Hebrew verb *qum* (קוּם) as *anistēmi* (ἀνίστημι), which can mean "to raise up by bringing back to life, *raise, raise up*" (BDAG), used in a number of places for the resurrection of the Messiah.[105] Here, we see how Israel stands as a proxy for all of sinful humankind, and how Israel's restoration is to come in its identification with something that is to last for two days, with them able to be standing by the third day. An appropriate parallel with Hosea 6:1-2 in the Apostolic Scriptures would be in recognizing how Believers are to be "buried with Him through baptism into death, so that as Messiah was raised from the dead through the glory of the Father, so we too might walk in newness of life" (Romans 6:4; cf. Colossians 2:12).

The Wednesday crucifixion chronology, while rightly recognizing that Yeshua entombed for only a day-and-a-half is insufficient, oversteps the expectation of Him being resurrected on the third day by insisting that three days and three nights be a full 72 hours. The traditional Good Friday-Easter Sunday chronology, while

---

[102] Ibid., 183; cf. Thiselton, pp 1195-1197.
[103] Grk. LXX *en tē hēmera tē tritē* (ἐν τῇ ἡμέρᾳ τῇ τρίτῃ); cf. Thiselton, 1195.
[104] Consult the FAQ entry on the Messianic Apologetics website, "6,000 Year Teaching."
[105] BDAG, 83; cf. John 6:39, 44; Acts 2:24, 32; 3:26; 13:44.

rightly recognizing that any part of a day can count for a day, typically has the Lord executed after the Passover itself has been commemorated, and not during the offering of the Passover lambs. The traditional scenario also does not do total justice to Yeshua's claim that He would be dead "three days and three nights," even if this does not have to be a full 72 hours. It is notable, that in reverting to the traditional chronology for Yeshua's death, Hegg now admits that he does not really know how to interpret the sign of Jonah given by the Lord:

"We are left...with wondering exactly how to interpret the 'sign of Jonah' in our Matthew text and if an alternative interpretation might fit with the chronology we have outlined....Is it possible that Yeshua's comparison of His own entombment with that of Jonah's time in the fish was not given as a chronological statement but has a different import?"[106]

The Thursday crucifixion scenario does, in fact, do justice to facts that Yeshua would be entombed for three days and three nights according to the sign of Jonah, but at the same time resurrected by the third day. It accounts for Hosea 6:1-2, in that Yeshua would be dead for a full two days, but by the third day would be raised. It also involves three daylight periods and three dusk periods:

1. Yeshua and His Disciples have their Last Supper as a *seder* meal on the 13th of Nisan, a Wednesday night. They deliberately held their *seder* early because of the Lord's impending death. However, due to the tens of thousands of lambs being slaughtered it the Temple, they probably had all the proper elements they needed for their meal.

2. Yeshua the Messiah is executed at Golgotha and dies around 3:00 PM on the 14th of Nisan, the same time when the main lamb is being slaughtered in the Temple, a Thursday. Yeshua's body is taken down before sunset, as it was the Day of Preparation for the Passover, affecting both the High Sabbath and weekly Sabbath that would follow.

3. Yeshua the Messiah has been dead for a period involving part of Thursday day and all night Thursday (day/night 1), all day Friday and all night Friday (day/night 2), and all day Saturday and into dusk or night on Saturday (day/night 3). Yeshua was resurrected by the third day, even though it was neither a full 72 hours nor the traditional 36 hours.

A Thursday crucifixion chronology is actually the most commonly proposed among interpreters, after the traditional Good Friday-Easter Sunday chronology.[107] A Thursday scenario, unlike the Good Friday-Easter Sunday scenario, does have the advantage of having Yeshua's death involve three days and three nights, but also allows Him to be resurrected on the third day. It simply extends the view that any part of a day *or* night accounts for a full day or night. A Thursday crucifixion chronology also factors in Hosea 6:1-2 as a death and resurrection prophecy of the Messiah, where by the third day an Israel identified with Him would be raised. **The Thursday crucifixion chronology is one we favor.**

---

[106] Hegg, "The Chronology of the Crucifixion."
[107] Cf. Longenecker, "Preparation, Day of," in *ISBE*, 3:953-954.

The Resurrection of the Messiah

It is sad to say this, but what is probably the most important part of the narrative beginning at Yeshua's crucifixion and death—**His resurrection** on the third day—is the most under-discussed aspect of all of the events among today's Messianics. While our faith community tends to have a good handle with wanting to make connections between the Last Supper and Passover *seder*, and also the Passover lamb and sacrifice of the Messiah—we often do not know what to do with the resurrection of the Lord or what it means. Is this just the result of a general avoidance of discussing the aspects of "death" altogether? Or is it because, once again, there are some issues we might have with the Lord's resurrection that we do not really know how to handle? Do we so not want to have any association with the questionable traditions of Easter Sunday, that we go overboard and fail to discuss the Messiah's resurrection itself?

In today's mainstream Christian thought, it is simply assumed that Yeshua the Messiah resurrected on Sunday morning, and so it should be no surprise why the Lord's resurrection is honored on Resurrection Sunday (many churches do make an honest effort to not use the term "Easter"). Yet, whether or not Yeshua was actually raised from the dead on Sunday morning can be challenged from the Greek text of the Synoptics:

"When the Sabbath was over [*Kai diagenomenou tou Sabbatou*, Καὶ διαγενομένου τοῦ σαββάτου], Mary Magdalene, and Mary the *mother* of James, and Salome, bought spices, so that they might come and anoint Him. Very early on the first day of the week, they came to the tomb when the sun had risen" (Mark 16:1-2).

"Now after the Sabbath [*Opse de sabbatōn*, Ὀψὲ δὲ σαββάτων], as it began to dawn toward the first *day* of the week, Mary Magdalene and the other Mary came to look at the grave" (Matthew 28:1).

"But on the first day of the week [*Tē de mia tōn sabbatōn*, Τῇ δὲ μιᾷ τῶν σαββάτων], at early dawn, they came to the tomb bringing the spices which they had prepared" (Luke 24:1).

All three of these witnesses indicate the Marys' intent to go and anoint the body of Yeshua with various spices and ointments, as it would retard the smell of decay. (Obviously following the death of Yeshua, there was no morgue available, where the body could be refrigerated until internment.) We can safely assume that they did make it to the gravesite, as early as they could be there, on Sunday morning. The Marys' intention to be at the tomb as soon as they could, by Sunday morning, should immediately cause us to see a critical problem in the Wednesday crucifixion scenario: as after the High Sabbath of Passover on Thursday they could have been at the gravesite by Thursday evening or Friday morning. Only a Thursday crucifixion or Friday crucifixion fits the evidence of the Marys being at the tomb by Sunday morning (discussed previously).

Both Mark and Luke indicate that the Marys had arrived at Yeshua's gravesite by Sunday morning, but Matthew's witness interjects something that we need not overlook. The clause which begins Matthew 28:1 is *Opse de sabbatōn* (Ὀψὲ δὲ σαββάτων), with the preposition *opse* (ὀψὲ) notably able to mean "*late in the day, at even"* (*LS*).[108] The 1901 American Standard Version opens Matthew 28:1 with "Now late on the sabbath day," followed by Lattimore's rendering, "Late on the sabbath." While some may think that the inclusion of "...as it began to dawn toward..." in Matthew 28:1 settles the fact that this was actually in the morning hours, the verb *epiphōskō* (ἐπιφώσκω) fully means "*to draw towards dawn*" (*LS*),[109] something which in Hebraic time reckoning begins in the evening. While some are inclined to think that Matthew is just using Jewish-specific language to describe what is entirely a Sunday morning event,[110] I would suggest that Matthew's witness interjects something additional into the record, especially given the occurrence of the earthquake (Matthew 28:2). In its entry for *epiphōskō*, AMG explains,

"In the evening of the Sabbath when the Jewish day was drawing on towards the first day of the week, Mary Magdalene and the other Mary went (or better, set out). It does not appear that they actually came at this time to visit the sepulcher, perhaps being delayed by the great earthquake (Matt. 28:2) which preceded our Lord's resurrection."[111]

Matthew's interjection of *Opse de sabbatōn*, more correctly regarding "Late on the Sabbath," indicates that the Marys' intention was to go to the gravesite of Yeshua as soon as the weekly Sabbath was over—in our estimation, having been preceded by the Passover High Sabbath on Friday, and now the weekly Sabbath on Saturday. They were stopped from proceeding, because as the Sabbath day closed, in the dusk moments, the earthquake signaling Yeshua's resurrection occurred. While the Marys would try again on Sunday morning, discovering the empty tomb, **this would mean that Yeshua did not actually resurrect from the dead on Sunday morning—but actually Saturday evening.** The witness of the Synoptics that follows only states that the empty tomb was discovered on Sunday morning.

There can be a great deal of unnecessary discussion that occurs among some Messianics, specifically as it concerns the Gospels' usage of "first day of the week," appearing in the Greek as *mian sabbatōn* (μίαν σαββάτων, Matthew 28:1) or *mia tōn sabbatōn* (μιᾷ τῶν σαββάτων, Mark 16:2; Luke 24:1). Confusion has been caused because a version like Young's Literal Translation renders these clauses as "the first of [the] sabbaths." Some people, seeing the term *sabbaton* (σάββατον) multiple times in a single verse, assume that something is up when in one place it is rendered as "Sabbath," and in another place it is rendered as "week." This has led to all sorts of proposals, one being that "first of [the] sabbaths" is not really the Marys arriving at the tomb on Sunday morning, but instead them arriving at the tomb on the first Sabbath of the counting of the *omer* toward *Shavuot*. While this might sound good at first glance, it fails to take into consideration the flexibility of uses that not only the Greek *sabbaton* possesses, but also its Hebrew progenitor *Shabbat* (שַׁבָּת).

Within the instructions about the counting of the *omer*, Leviticus 23:15 says that it is to involve "seven complete sabbaths" or *sheva Shabbatot temimot* (תְּמִימֹת שֶׁבַע שַׁבָּתוֹת). Later in Leviticus 25, though, we see that Jubilee years are determined by a count of "seven sabbaths of years" (Leviticus 25:8) or *sheva shabbatot shanim*

---

[108] *LS*, 582.
[109] Ibid., 306.
[110] Cf. Nolland, pp 1244-1245.
[111] Spiros Zodhiates, ed., *Complete Word Study Dictionary: New Testament* (Chattanooga: AMG Publishers, 1993), 645.

(שָׁנִים שַׁבַּע שַׁבְּתֹת שֶׁבַע). This latter usage of "sabbath" very clearly means "seven weeks of years" (RSV, NRSV, NJPS, ESV), just as the actual counting of the *omer* toward *Shavuot* is not determined by the weekly Sabbath, but actually periods of seven-day weeks (cf. Deuteronomy 16:9).[112] Lexically speaking, one finds how the term *Shabbat*, while frequently meaning "**day of rest, sabbath**," can also as the plural *Shabbatot* mean "**weeks**" (*CHALOT*).[113]

When the Hebrew Tanach was translated into Greek, the only term really available at the translators' disposal for the concept of "week" for the Septuagint was *hebdomas* (ἑβδομάς), simply meaning "*the number seven* or *a number of seven*" (*LS*, Leviticus 23:15 and 25:8, LXX).[114] By the First Century, though, the Hebrew loan word *sabbaton* (σάββατον) was used in the Greek-speaking Jewish community, with very much the same flexibility as *Shabbat*. "[T]he Greek term *sábbaton*…[was used] in the diaspora. The plural *tá sábbata* may mean one sabbath, several sabbaths, or the whole week (like the Hebrew term)" (*TDNT*).[115]

While it may seem odd to us today, the term "Sabbath" to a First Century Jew could mean "week," and it is in various places used in precisely this way. In Luke 18:12, for example, we see a Jewish person say "I fast twice a week," *nēsteuō dis tou sabbatou* (νηστεύω δὶς τοῦ σαββάτου), which would literally be "I fast twice on the sabbath" (LITV)—but this really makes no sense as fasting typically lasts an entire day or longer (a period of not eating between breakfast and supper can hardly be regarded as a "fast"), and so the translation of *sabbatou* as "week" is justified. In the *Didache*, from the late First Century C.E., it is said that the Jews "fast on the second and the fifth day of the week" (8:1), *deutera sabbatōn kai pemptē* (δευτέρᾳ σαββάτων καὶ πέμπτῃ), meaning twice a week.[116] Here, the plural *sabbatōn* or "sabbaths" is used. It here likewise has to represent the "week," as it would again make no sense for one to fast two times on the Sabbath day or Saturday.

What would have been the highlight for the ancient Jewish week? *The Sabbath occurring every seven days.* So, should we be too surprised that the "Sabbath" also affects the terminology "week"? As Nolland accounts, the dual usage of *sabbaton* in Matthew 28:1 is not irregular: "there can be no doubt about the sense—[as it] uses σάββατα for 'sabbath'…in its first use and for 'week' in its second use."[117] It stands justified to recognize that the Marys did arrive at Yeshua's tomb on Sunday morning. But, simply because they arrived at the tomb on Sunday morning by no means indicates that the seventh-day Sabbath has somehow been Divinely transferred to Sunday or invalidated, *and* neither does it mean that Yeshua's resurrection has somehow validated the Saddusaical reckoning of the counting of the *omer* which began on a Sunday (discussed further). All this means is that the Marys arrived at the gravesite to anoint Yeshua's body as soon as they could, and Sunday morning—following the delaying earthquake when everything was safe— was the earliest time.

---

[112] Note how most versions render *sheva Shabbatot temimot* in Leviticus 23:15 as "seven full weeks" or something close (RSV, NIV, NRSV, ATS, NJPS, ESV, HCSB, CJB, et. al.).

[113] William L. Holladay, ed., *A Concise Hebrew and Aramaic Lexicon of the Old Testament* (Leiden, the Netherlands: E.J. Brill, 1988), 360.

[114] *LS*, 220.

[115] E. Lohse, "*sábbaton*," in Geoffrey W. Bromiley, ed., *Theological Dictionary of the New Testament*, abridged (Grand Rapids: Eerdmans, 1985), 989.

[116] Cf. *BDAG*, 910.

[117] Nolland, 1244 fn#3.

When the women arrive at the tomb, they do ask who will roll the stone away that has sealed it, but they see that it has already been moved. They enter in, and rather than seeing a shrouded corpse, they see two angels sitting (Mark 16:3-5; Matthew 28:2-3; Luke 24:2-3). **The Lord Yeshua has already resurrected from the dead**, as He told them He would, and the Roman guard has been scared away (Matthew 28:4). They are told by the angels that Yeshua has been raised just as He said He would, and that the women are to tell His Disciples, in particular Peter, so that He can meet them in Galilee (Mark 16:6-8; Matthew 28:5-8; Luke 24:5-7). As the women leave the tomb, they actually encounter the risen Yeshua, they worship Him, and He tells them to go tell the Disciples to meet Him in Galilee (Mark 16:9-10; Matthew 28:9-10; Luke 24:8-10). When they hear what has transpired, the main Disciples largely refuse to believe the report (Mark 16:11; Luke 24:11), but Peter goes to the tomb and only sees the linen shroud that the Lord's body had been wrapped in, being amazed (Luke 24:12). We should think that the other Disciples were mostly concerned about their own welfare, given the tenuous circumstances of recent days. With the Sabbath period now over, they will be free to leave Jerusalem, but a mob might be looking for them.

Matthew interjects how the Roman guard reports to the chief priests how Yeshua's body is now missing. I am not sure that the Romans told them that Yeshua was raised from the dead, but all they knew is that there was an earthquake and then some kind of supernatural events. The chief priests give the Roman soldiers money for them to only say that the Disciples stole the body, and they promise that should they get into any trouble with their superiors, they will take care of it. The intention, for sure, was to quell any word that Yeshua might have been resurrected from the dead (Matthew 28:11-14). Matthew's narrative word is, "they took the money and did as they had been instructed; and this story was widely spread among the Jews, *and is* to this day" (Matthew 28:15), which would have likely been a few decades after the actual resurrection at the composition of Matthew's Gospel.

We have to remember that Yeshua's resurrection did not only affect the Eleven main Disciples of the Lord (minus Judas), but also other people who followed Him. Mark 16:12 indicates that Yeshua appeared to two who were walking to the country, something expanded upon by Luke in Yeshua's encounter with the two on the road to Emmaus, a town adjacent to Jerusalem (Luke 24:13). While walking, the risen Yeshua walks alongside them, although they do not recognize who He is (Luke 24:14-16). The Lord asks the two what they are talking about (Luke 24:17), and Cleopas answers Him, "Are You the only one visiting Jerusalem and unaware of the things which have happened here in these days?" (Luke 24:18). The two tell Him about how Yeshua was crucified, and how they had both seen the empty tomb. But, they express doubts as they had not seen the resurrected Yeshua themselves (Luke 24:19-24).

Hearing this, Yeshua asks the two, "O foolish men and slow of heart to believe in all that the prophets have spoken! Was it not necessary for the Messiah to suffer these things and to enter into His glory?" (Luke 24:25-26). The Lord then explains the Messianic expectation from the Torah and the Prophets (Luke 24:27). The two disciples, approaching the village, ask Him to join them because it was evening (Luke 24:29-29). They recline to eat, and taking the bread and blessing it—the *matzah* for the week of Unleavened Bread (Luke 24:30)—they immediately recognize who this man is as the Messiah, and so Yeshua vanishes away (Luke 24:31). They ask themselves, "Were not our hearts burning within us while He was speaking to us on the road, while He was explaining the Scriptures to us?" (Luke 24:32). They return to Jerusalem at that moment to meet with the Eleven Disciples, reporting how they have seen the resurrected Yeshua (Luke 24:33-34). Luke narrates, "They *began* to relate their experiences on the road and how He was recognized by them in the breaking of the bread" (Luke 24:35).

The Eleven Disciples have not followed Yeshua's instruction to meet Him in Galilee; they are still in Jerusalem huddled down and afraid. The other Messiah followers, who encountered Him on the road to Emmaus, have quickly gone back to Jerusalem—but their report is dismissed (Mark 16:13). Presumably, sometime late on Sunday evening while the Eleven are eating, Yeshua then simply appears to them, and "He reproached them for their unbelief and hardness of heart, because they had not believed those who had seen Him after He had risen" (Mark 16:14; cf. Luke 24:36).

Luke records how "they were startled and frightened and thought that they were seeing a spirit" (Luke 24:37). Yeshua confirms to them that He is no ghost, but that He has real hands, feet, and a body (Luke 24:38-40). The Disciples are noticeably excited, and to show them that He really was resurrected and is no apparition or specter, Yeshua asks them for something to eat, being handed some broiled fish (Luke 24:41-42). While Yeshua in His resurrected state possess the power to transport Himself at will from place to place, He can still eat food. Just as He did to those on the road to Emmaus, Yeshua explained to them His fulfillment of the Scriptures about suffering, dying, and resurrecting on the third day (Luke 24:43-46). Yeshua announces His intention that the Disciples be able witnesses of these events, being sent forth with power from Jerusalem, to proclaim the good news of repentance and forgiveness to all (Luke 24:47-49).

While it is easy to think that the remaining narrative of the Synoptics (Mark 16:15-20; Matthew 28:16-20; Luke 24:50-53) deals with only the few days or so following Yeshua's resurrection, He was actually present with His followers an additional forty days until His ascension into Heaven (Acts 1:3)—just under six of the seven total weeks of the counting of the *omer* to *Shavuot*/Pentecost. At Pentecost, the Holy Spirit would be poured out on the Believers so that they could now accomplish the mission and tasks that Yeshua had left for them, with His sacrificial work now completed.

The Fourth Gospel adds important details to what the Synoptics record of what takes place in the moments following Yeshua's resurrection. Mary Magdalene arrives at the gravesite when it was still dark, very early in the morning, and sees the stone removed (John 20:1). She runs to Simon Peter and John, announcing that the Lord is gone (John 20:2). Peter and John go to the tomb, enter in, and they see the various linen wrappings (John 20:3-7). John, who had arrived just ahead of Peter to the scene, believes that Yeshua is resurrected (John 20:8), but the other disciples present did not fully understand and they go away (John 20:9-10). Yet, hearing and seeing that the body of Yeshua was gone, what would they have actually thought? Did some of Yeshua's detractors steal His remains? The body could not have decomposed in such a short time. All John 20:9 says is, "they did not understand the Scripture, that He must rise again from the dead."

Some disciples leave the scene of the gravesite—not believing that He has been resurrected, even though Yeshua's body is gone. *Stupidly, they just leave.* Mary Magdalene steps into the tomb (John 20:11). She sees two angels sitting where Yeshua's body had rested, and they ask her why she is crying (John 20:12). She simply responds with, "Because they have taken away my Lord, and I do not know where they have laid Him" (John 20:13). At this moment, she turns around and sees a man standing, who also asks her why she is crying—not knowing that this was actually Yeshua (John 20:14-15a). She thinks it is actually the gardener, and asks this "gardener" where Yeshua's body is so she can take it away (John 20:15b). All Yeshua has to say to her is "Mary!" and she recognizes that it is her Rabbi (John 20:16). Yeshua instructs her not to grab Him, an indication that she cannot prevent Him from His eventual departure to the Father in Heaven (John 20:17). Even though Yeshua has been resurrected from the dead, He will soon leave for Heaven.

Mary Magdalene tells the Disciples that she has encountered the risen Yeshua (John 20:18). On that Sunday evening, for fear of their lives, the Disciples have locked themselves away. This does not matter for their risen Lord, as He simply appears to them (John 20:19), showing them the wounds on His hands and side—with the Disciples rejoicing (John 20:20). Yeshua issues peace to them, and breathes on them so that they can receive of the Holy Spirit (John 20:21-22), including some specific power regarding sins (John 20:23).

The disciple Thomas was not present to witness the appearance of Yeshua, and how He was resurrected from the dead (John 20:24). Even though the others tell him that they have seen the Lord, Thomas will not believe, asserting, "Unless I see in His hands the imprint of the nails, and put my finger into the place of the nails, and put my hand into His side, I will not believe" (John 20:25). John says that eight days actually pass, and then Yeshua appears again, *with* Thomas now present (John 20:26). He simply says to Him, "Reach here with your finger, and see My hands; and reach here your hand and put it into My side; and do not be unbelieving, but believing" (John 20:27). Thomas' skepticism totally vanishes, and the narrative actually records that he recognizes Yeshua's Divinity in the declaration "My Lord and my God!" (John 20:28).[118] While Thomas believes Yeshua because he has seen Him, the Lord says nonetheless, "Blessed *are* they who did not see, and *yet* believed" (John 20:29). And Thomas did believe, because according to early Church history, he made his way proclaiming the good news into Parthia (Eusebius *Ecclesiastical History* 3.1.1), and according to local tradition down into India as well—one of the largest geographical areas of any of the original Disciples of the Messiah.

The witness of the Apostle Paul, in his writing to the Corinthians, adds even more details than what in seen in the Gospels regarding Yeshua's post-resurrection appearances. He says, "He appeared to Cephas, then to the twelve. After that He appeared to more than five hundred brethren at one time, most of whom remain until now, but some have fallen asleep; then He appeared to James, then to all the apostles" (1 Corinthians 15:5-7). After His ascension into Heaven, Yeshua also

---

[118] To claim that this is simply Thomas using the First Century equivalent of "Good Lord!" or "Oh my God!" fails to take into consideration that only up until the late Twentieth Century, such sayings were often considered to be some kind of violation of the Third Commandment.

appeared several years later to Paul himself, on the road to Damascus (1 Corinthians 15:8).[119]

Yeshua as the Firstfruits of the Resurrection

The resurrection of Yeshua the Messiah is **the most important event** for our Biblical faith—even more important than the theophany of Mount Sinai, as important as that is. The Apostle Paul is clear to assert, "if there is no resurrection of the dead, not even Messiah has been raised; and if Messiah has not been raised, then our preaching is vain, your faith also is vain" (1 Corinthians 15:13-14). Without an historically sustainable resurrection of Messiah Yeshua, then not only is the gospel message of His salvation untrue, but we have no final victory over the power of sin. Those who have testified of His resurrection have led us astray, and full communion between humanity and its Creator cannot be restored via acceptance of the gospel. Yet, if Yeshua is resurrected, then it assures us not only of such final victory, but also guarantees us the future resurrection of deceased saints, and the *complete unfolding* of the Father's plan of salvation history in future time.

Within evangelical Christianity, the resurrection of Yeshua is certainly a major centerpiece of not only Holy Week, but also teaching and preaching and spiritual reflection throughout the year. Quoted in many churches throughout the world, the Apostles' Creed rightly emphasizes the centrality of the resurrection for people of faith—not only the resurrection of Yeshua—but of His Second Coming to judge the world and the future resurrection of the dead:

> "I also believe in Jesus Christ his only son, our Lord, conceived of the Holy Spirit, born of the Virgin Mary, suffered under Pontius Pilate, crucified, dead and buried; he descended into hell, rose again the third day, ascended into heaven, sat down at the right hand of the Father, thence he is to come to judge the living and the dead."[120]

The doctrine of resurrection *significantly* separates the Bible from pagan religion. Whereas both the Bible and paganism (Ancient Near Eastern and classical Greco-Roman religion for our purposes) largely affirm some kind of a disembodied afterlife—and Yeshua Himself was in Sheol or the netherworld for a short time (Luke 23:42-43; 1 Peter 3:18-20)—the Biblical message runs quite contrary to the pagan message **as the entire person** of both body and consciousness are to be restored to wholeness (cf. 1 Thessalonians 5:23), and in paganism the body is often discarded as some kind of garbage.[121] *In Scripture, any kind of a disembodied afterlife*

---

[119] For a further discussion about the post-resurrection events, and the differences we see among the four Gospels, consult the relevant sections of Walter C. Kaiser, Peter H. Davids, F.F. Bruce, and Manfred T. Brauch, *Hard Sayings of the Bible* (Downers Grove, IL: InterVarsity, 1996), especially pp 506-508.

[120] Henry Bettenson and Chris Maunder, eds., *Documents of the Christian Church* (Oxford: Oxford University Press, 1999), 26.

[121] For a description of what might be termed "holistic dualism," meaning that while the body and consciousness of a person can be separated—this is by no means an ideal or permanent condition, consult John W. Cooper, *Body, Soul & Life Everlasting: Biblical Anthropology and the Monism-Dualism Debate* (Grand Rapids: Eerdmans, 1989); J.K. Chamblin, "Psychology," in Gerald F. Hawthorne, Ralph P. Martin, and Daniel G. Reid, eds., *Dictionary of Paul and His Letters* (Downers Grove, IL: InterVarsity, 1993), pp 766-767.

is something only intermediate, and is not at all permanent. In the Biblical sense, salvation is not to be exclusively understood in terms of "going to Heaven" when you die, but salvation is consummated in receiving a resurrected and restored body similar to Yeshua's when He was resurrected, then being ushered into the Messianic Kingdom (cf. Hebrews 9:28). While the good Jewish Pharisee Paul did affirm that after death he would depart to be with the Messiah in Heaven (Philippians 1:21-23), he also rightly emphasized the reality of the resurrection for the saints:

"For our citizenship is in heaven, from which also we eagerly wait for a Savior, the Lord Yeshua the Messiah; who will transform the body of our humble state into conformity with the body of His glory, by the exertion of the power that He has even to subject all things to Himself."

N.T. Wright explains how "the early Christian belief in hope beyond death belongs demonstrably on the Jewish, not the pagan, map....the early Christian future hope centered firmly on resurrection. The first Christians did not simply believe in life after death; they virtually never spoke of simply going to heaven when they died...When they did speak of heaven as a postmortem destination, they seemed to regard this heavenly life as a temporary stage on the way to the eventual resurrection of the body."[122] And indeed, too many of us forget that our material bodies are very much a part of our beings, every bit as much as an immaterial consciousness. So even if we are multi-dimensional creatures made in God's image (Genesis 1:26), it is not His intention that our body be in one location, and our consciousness in another location, permanently after death—as any period of separation of the two is appropriately described as being "naked" (2 Corinthians 5:3). Wright has done us all a good service in emphasizing how the Bible is more concerned with the "life *after* the afterlife," or the future Messianic Kingdom to come.[123]

The resurrection of Yeshua itself, and His conquering of physical death, certainly did signal some major transitions within the spiritual order. The resurrection of Yeshua ensures us that we ourselves will one day be resurrected. Yet at the same time, if we are to be resurrected from the dead—and the Bible places a significant emphasis on the Kingdom to come—should this not also affect how we accomplish the Lord's purposes now in the present age? **As citizens of the Kingdom to come, are we not to demonstrate its qualities and characteristics today?** This not only involves declaring the message of Yeshua's salvation to the lost perishing in sin—but also involves caring for the poor, destitute, homeless, sick, hungry, imprisoned, and all others who are abused and suffering. If Yeshua sacrificed Himself to atone for our sins, then being transformed by the message of the cross, Messiah's followers should truly try to give of themselves in some way by serving Him and demonstrating His love.

Today's evangelical Christianity tends to rightly emphasize the gravity of the cross, how the Messiah has been sacrificed for our sins and resurrected from the dead, and how this reality is to change people both in their relationship to God and one another. Today's Messianic community, for a variety of reasons, tends to not often discuss the death and resurrection of the Lord—either during the Passover

---

[122] N.T. Wright, *Surprised by Hope: Rethinking Heaven, the Resurrection, and the Mission of the Church* (New York: HarperCollins, 2008), pp 40, 41.
[123] For a further discussion, consult the article "To Be Absent From the Body" by J.K. McKee.

season or outside of it. While some of it might be due to the fact that Messianic thanatology (study of death) is underdeveloped, it probably has more to do with an aversion to some of the traditions of Easter Sunday than anything else. The resurrection of Yeshua is frequently associated with that word "Easter," and so various Messianic Believers feel content with really not discussing His resurrection at any time during the season of Passover and Unleavened Bread, much less during the rest of the year.

There are Messianic Believers who have honestly tried to help evangelical Christians who remember Easter Sunday, to what they believe is a more Biblical remembrance: what they call the "Festival of First Fruits." Adhering to the Saddusaical reckoning of counting the *omer* toward *Shavuot*/Pentecost (cf. Leviticus 23:11), which would begin on the first Sunday during the week of Unleavened Bread, various Messianics assume that the early Church got this "Festival of First Fruits" mixed up with what would later become Easter Sunday. Today's Messianic community, it is believed, has a responsibility on the first Sunday during the week of Unleavened Bread to honor Yeshua's resurrection. Frequently, but not always, this will align with Easter Sunday.

No one can deny the Biblical reality that Yeshua is "the first fruits of those who are asleep," being the first in the order of those who are to be resurrected (1 Corinthians 15:20, 23). There is a typological connection to be made between Yeshua's resurrection and the offering of the *omer reisheet* (עֹמֶר רֵאשִׁית) or sheaf of firstfruits (Leviticus 23:10).[124] As David H. Stern has rightly noted, "Sha'ul probably wrote this letter between *Pesach* (5:6-8) and *Shavu'ot* (16:8), during the season for presenting the **firstfruits** of the harvest at the Temple (Leviticus 23:9-15)."[125] But even while there can be no doubting the connection between the sheaf offering and Yeshua's resurrection, the Torah does not specify that this is to occur in conjunction with any holiday known as "*Chag HaBikkurim*" or the "Festival of First Fruits." The Torah knows of a *Chag haKatzir* (חַג הַקָּצִיר), a synonym for *Shavuot* (Exodus 23:16), and also how *Shavuot* is known as *yom ha'bikkurim* (יוֹם הַבִּכּוּרִים).[126] In contrast, the offering up of the sheaf or *omer* of firstfruits at Unleavened Bread, while being a distinct and special ceremony associated with the Passover season, is not viewed as being any kind of separate holiday.

While I can surely empathize with Messianics who want their Christian brethren to be able to easily understand Yeshua's resurrection—simply transferring an Easter Sunday remembrance now into a "First Fruits" Sunday remembrance—things are really not as simplistic as this. The Biblical data for the counting of the *omer* (Leviticus 23:11, MT compare LXX; Deuteronomy 16:9) really does not lend strong support for the Saddusaical method of starting on the first Sunday of the week of Unleavened Bread. The historical data we have recognizes that most of the Jews in the Second Temple period began the counting of the *omer* on the 16th of Nisan, according to the Pharisaical method of starting on the day after the High Sabbath (Josephus *Antiquities of the Jews* 3.250-251; Philo *Special Laws* 2.162). And, the Apostle Paul—who affirmed that Yeshua was firstfruits of the resurrection—was a Pharisee by virtue of belief in the resurrection (Acts 23:6), something which

---

[124] Cf. Leon Morris, *Tyndale New Testament Commentaries: 1 Corinthians* (Grand Rapids: Eerdmans, 1987), 209.

[125] Stern, *Jewish New Testament Commentary*, 488.

[126] Cf. "firstfruits," in *Dictionary of Judaism in the Biblical Period*, 228.

the Sadducees fully denied (Matthew 22:23; Mark 12:18; Luke 20:27; Acts 23:8). Given Yeshua's endorsement of Pharisaic authority in many matters of *halachah* (Matthew 23:2-3), it seems quite improbable that either the Lord or His Apostles would have followed the Saddusaical reckoning of counting the *omer*.

So how does Yeshua fulfill the offering of firstfruits? As we have previously noted, the Fourth Gospel makes explicit reference to Yeshua's death being associated with the Passover lamb, with Torah instructions referred to (John 19:36; cf. Exodus 12:46; Numbers 9:12)—which gives strong support to Him being executed in conjunction with the Passover lambs killed on the 14th of Nisan. Paul's passing references in 1 Corinthians 15:20, 23 to Yeshua's resurrection being firstfruits, is all we see in the Apostolic Scriptures, so we cannot similarly insist upon Yeshua resurrecting from the dead on the actual day the sheaf of firstfruits would be offered. And, when this was offered depends very much on the chronology one posits for the Passover the year of Yeshua's death, and whether the Saddusaical or Pharisaical method was followed in the Temple precincts— something likely determined by the politics of the Sanhedrin.

Messianics who hold to the traditional Good Friday-Easter Sunday chronology, or those such as ourselves who hold to a Thursday crucifixion, both recognize that the 16th of Nisan would have been Saturday. The major difference between these two views is that the first posits a 15th of Nisan death for the Lord, as a festal offering, and the second posits a 14th of Nisan death for the Lord, as a Passover offering. The Pharisaic counting of the *omer* would have officially started on the 16th of Nisan, a weekly Sabbath, occurring after the High Sabbath on the 15th of Nisan. The Saddusaical counting of the *omer*, beginning on the Sunday after the weekly Sabbath, would have started on the 17th of Nisan.

The difference between the Pharisaical and Saddusaical reckonings for counting the *omer*, the year of Yeshua's death, would have only been one day. As we have concluded that Yeshua was probably resurrected as the Sabbath closed on the 16th of Nisan, this places Yeshua's resurrection right after the official start of the Pharisaical count and right before the official start of the Saddusaical count. Obviously, Yeshua can easily fulfill the typology of firstfruits if He were resurrected immediately before *or* immediately after the offering up of the sheaf in the Temple—regardless of which method is followed. However, we are justified to acknowledge that the Pharisaic method was probably followed in the Temple, as the Pharisees had the people at large on their side, and the Sadducees did not, in spite of any objection by the Sadducees.[127]

Things get a little complicated, though, when we see that in the Second Temple period, the Pharisaical Sages were debating whether or not it was actually work to gather the barley for the sheaf of the firstfruits offering on a Sabbath day. The Talmud records this debate:

"Said R. Hiyya bar Abba said R. Yohanan, 'Not for all purposes did R. Eliezer say, "What is required to make it possible to carry out a religious duty overrides the restrictions of the Sabbath," for lo, the two loaves represent the obligation of the day, and R. Eliezer derives the rule [that baking them overrides the restrictions of the Sabbath] only from an argument based on a verbal analogy

[127] Cf. Alfred Edersheim, *Sketches of Jewish Social Life* (Peabody, MA: Hendrickson, 1994), 220. See Edersheim's further remarks in *The Temple*, pp 203-204.

[rather than holding that just as the duty is to put them out as an offering to the Lord, so baking them, necessary to carry out that duty, is permitted on the Sabbath as well]. *For it has been taught on Tannaite authority:* R. Eliezer says, 'How do we know that what is needed for the preparation of the two loaves of bread [as well as the actual rite itself] overrides the Sabbath? We find a reference to "bringing" in connection with the presentation of the first sheaf of barley, and we find the same word in connection with the two loaves of bread. Just as the use of the word "bringing" in connection with the presentation of the first sheaf of barley indicates that preparation for the rite, not only the rite itself, overrides the restrictions of the Sabbath, so the presence of the word "bringing" stated with respect to the two loaves of bread indicates that the same rule applies, so that preparing for the rite overrides the restrictions of the Sabbath'" (b.*Shabbat* 131a).[128]

"Said Rabbah bar Hannah said R. Yohanan, 'R. Eleazar b. R. Simeon follows the principle of R. Aqiba, his father's master. *For we have learned in the Mishnah:* An operative principle did R. Aqiba state, "Any sort of labor [in connection with circumcision] which it is possible to do on the eve of the Sabbath does not override [the restrictions of] the Sabbath, and that which it is not possible to do on the eve of the Sabbath does override [the prohibitions of] the Sabbath" [M. Shab. 19:1]. *And he furthermore takes the position of R. Ishmael, who has said that reaping the barley for the sheaf of first barley is a religious duty. For we have learned in the Mishnah:* R. Ishmael says, "[Rather the verse teaches us that] just as ploughing, [which] is a voluntary act, [is prohibited on the Sabbath] so [only] harvesting [which likewise] is voluntary [is prohibited on the Sabbath]. This excludes harvesting the first sheaf [and is therefore permitted even on the Sabbath]" [M. Shebiit 1:4K-L]. *Now if you were to imagine that if the barley for the sheaf of first barley that has not been reaped in accord with the religious duty that pertains to it is valid, why in the world should it override the Sabbath? Do it the eve of the Sabbath. And since it does override the restrictions of the Sabbath, it must follow that he holds that if it was reaped not in accordance with its prescribed rite, it is invalid*" (b.*Menachot* 72a).[129]

Keep in mind that the discussion seen above took place several centuries after the time of Yeshua. By this time, the Rabbis clearly ruled that "*Doesn't he also know that the act of slaughtering the animal always has overridden the prohibitions of the Sabbath? So it must follow that Rabbi takes the view that reaping the barley for the first sheaf of grain does not override the prohibitions of the Sabbath*" (b.*Menachot* 72a).[130] By the Third-Fifth Centuries C.E., the Rabbis considered gathering the barley to offer before the Lord on the weekly Sabbath to not be "work." Yet, in the First Century the discussion was still probably going on and had not been finalized.

The fact that the question "Is offering the barley sheaf before God work if performed on the Sabbath?" was asked does leave us the distinct possibility that in the First Century, **it may have been considered work.** The Rabbis are reflecting centuries later, and leave us a unique window whereby Yeshua can fulfill the firstfruits expectations of **both** the Sadducees and Pharisees for the specific year of His death. It is possible, however infrequent, that the Pharisees could have started their *omer* count on a Sunday, should their actual first day occur on a weekly

---

[128] *The Babylonian Talmud: A Translation and Commentary.*
[129] Ibid.
[130] Ibid.

Sabbath after a High Sabbath on Friday. Note that this would have occurred during a time when the Sadducees controlled the Temple, with constant friction occurring between the two parties in the Sanhedrin. Even with the people on their side, the Pharisees had to make concessions just as the Sadducees—probably when their respective *omer* counts began so close together.

In this case, on the year of Yeshua's death, the Pharisaic *omer* count could have begun on the 17th of Nisan. The reason is simply that enough Pharisees might have considered it work to gather the sheaf for the offering on a weekly Sabbath, something needing to be postponed until the following day. With the Pharisees and Sadducees following the same *omer* count for this year, a level of civility could be maintained between these two rival factions.

The Gospels depict that although the Sadducees had the most to gain by Yeshua's death, that there were Pharisees involved in the conspiracy as well (Matthew 27:62; John 18:3). If the *omer* count for both the Sadducees and Pharisees began on the Sunday following Yeshua's resurrection—then both parties would have had something communicated to them. If the Roman soldier at the foot of the cross could recognize that something supernatural was afoot (Mark 15:39; Matthew 27:54; Luke 23:47), then it is not difficult to extrapolate how unique circumstances on the year of Yeshua's death and resurrection could have communicated something to both the Sadducees and Pharisees as they began the counting of the *omer* together.

If the counting of the *omer* for both the Sadducees and Pharisees began on the Sunday after Yeshua's resurrection, it would only have been because of unique circumstances that one year. We do not have grounds to disregard both the Biblical and historical evidence that points to the Pharisaical method actually being the best interpretive option for the counting of the *omer*. The Messiah would not have endorsed the Torah views of an utterly corrupt sect of Judaism that categorically denied the doctrine of resurrection,[131] and Paul's claim before the Sanhedrin of what we see transcribed as *egō Pharisaios eimi* (ἐγὼ Φαρισαῖός εἰμι)—"I am a Pharisee" (Acts 23:6)—is a strong indication that he would have followed the 16th of Nisan start of the *omer* count (cf. Acts 20:16) in normal years. Today's broad Messianic movement will have to learn how to properly balance the unique circumstances of the year Yeshua died and was resurrected, and how to observe the counting of the *omer* and *Shavuot* on the same traditional dates as the worldwide Jewish community, which today follows the Pharisaical reckoning.[132]

Arriving at a Consensus?

There is a great deal of data and perspectives that have to be weighed in determining a proper chronology for Yeshua's death, burial, and resurrection. What we can all agree on for certain is that by Sunday morning Joseph of Arimathea's tomb had been vacated, and by Sunday evening the risen Lord appeared to His Disciples. Other than this, the Wednesday, Thursday, and Friday crucifixion

---

[131] Ancient Jewish theology actually held that the Sadducees' denial of the resurrection would exclude them from a place in the Kingdom to come (m.*Sanhedrin* 10:1).

[132] Consult the FAQ entry on the Messianic Apologetics website, "*Omer* Count" (reproduced in this publication's section on "FAQs on the Spring Holiday Season"). Also consult the article "Sadducees, Pharisees, and the Controversy of Counting the Omer" by J.K. McKee.

scenarios each have their own pros and cons that you have to be aware of, in considering which you think best fits:

A Wednesday Crucifixion

PROS: guided by doing justice to Yeshua's reference to being dead "three days and three nights" (Matthew 12:40)

CONS: the Marys should have gone to the empty tomb on Thursday evening or Friday morning to anoint Yeshua's body, as the High Sabbath of Passover would be over, and not Sunday morning as is testified in all four Gospels (Mark 16:2; Matthew 28:1-2; Luke 24:1; John 20:1)

A Thursday Crucifixion

PROS: a chronology between Thursday afternoon and Saturday evening involves three daylight periods and three dusk periods, even though it is not a full 72 hours, in recognition that the Lord would be resurrected by the third day (cf. Hosea 6:1-2);[133] Yeshua is executed before the High Sabbath of Passover and the weekly Sabbath; the resurrection occurs after the official *omer* count for the Pharisees has started, and before the official *omer* count of the Sadducees begins

CONS: posits that the Day of Preparation and the Sabbath affects both a High Sabbath for the week of Passover on Friday, and then a normal weekly Sabbath on Saturday—a two day "Sabbath period" so to speak

A Friday Crucifixion

PROS: the traditional view adhered to in most of today's Christianity, and Messianic teachers can simply help enrich Christians' Hebraic Roots without having to go into many specifics; points out how that "three days and three nights" does not necessarily have to be a full 72 hours

CONS: unless Yeshua celebrated His Passover *seder* earlier than most everyone else, on the 13th of Nisan, then Yeshua's Passover offering of Himself is probably not on the afternoon of the 14th of Nisan leading into Passover (John 19:36), but on the 15th of Nisan as a festal offering; "the day of preparation for the Passover" (John 19:14) is not the eve of the 14th of Nisan, but is rather a complicated way of saying "the day of preparation for the weekly Sabbath during the Passover season"; Yeshua's execution on the 15th of Nisan can raise some questions, as it would have been the High Sabbath of Passover

---

[133] Matthew 16:21; 17:23; 20:19; 27:64; Luke 9:22; 18:33; 24:7, 21, 46; Acts 10:40.

Evaluating the different points of view, I have concluded that the **Thursday crucifixion scenario** does the most amount of justice to the information. If this needs adjusting in the future, because of new data or perspectives to be considered, then I am certainly open to revising my conclusions. But this article has tried to focus on the events surrounding the death, burial, and resurrection of Messiah Yeshua *more than anything else*. As I noted at the beginning, affirming that our Messiah and Savior died and rose again is a salvation issue; how this all actually happened in a day-to-day sequence is not. I will certainly not look at those Messianics who are sincerely convicted that a Wednesday or Friday crucifixion scenario is best, as though they somehow deny Yeshua's prophetic fulfillment of the Passover.

In favoring the Thursday scenario, while the Biblical and historical data does affect my deliberations, I am also very much guided by a missional ethos surrounding the sacrifice and resurrection of the Lord. **I am most inclined to favor the chronology where the most amount of people are going to take notice of what is happening.** This means that when the Temple curtain is ripped in two, the time it can make the most sizeable impact is during the sacrifice of the main Passover lamb between 2:30-3:30 on the 14th of Nisan, and not a festal offering later. Similarly, if because of circumstance the Pharisaical and Saddusaical *omer* counts had to begin on the same day, both of these two sects that played some role in the Lord's death would have something communicated to them, as word would get back to them about the empty tomb as the firstfruits ceremony commenced. Surely, if the sky blackening and the ground shaking communicated something to the pagan Romans present—then there are specific, Biblically-rooted signs that would communicate important things to the Jews present.

I know that the information and perspectives I have provided in this article will not at all be the end of this discussion. But, I do hope that we will all learn **not** to approach Yeshua's prophetic fulfillment of the Passover season—by His Last Supper, His atoning sacrifice for us, and His resurrection—in a simplistic manner. *We cannot allow ourselves to think that Yeshua's Passover chronology of fulfillment can be presented in a nice, clean-cut package with a big bow on it any more.* There are pieces of information that have been left out of our deliberations for far too long. Any binary thinking we have adopted of prophetic fulfillment in os and 1s needs to now be jettisoned.

It is my hope that when we discuss this subject in the future, we will approach it in an honest and constructive spirit of inquiry, where we are all respectful to one another and **we really can focus on the substance of what happened.** I would especially like to see all of the rigidity witnessed in recent years to be retired to the past, and for more moderate voices to control the conversation, in order to bring honor and glory to the Lord.

What Really Matters!

How is today's Messianic community to properly proceed during the season of Passover? We will certainly hear a great number of teachings about the original Passover, and the deliverance of Ancient Israel from Egypt. Will this be mirrored with an emphasis on the Lamb of God, Messiah Yeshua, and how final redemption has been secured by His death? Will anyone hear about the events surrounding His resurrection? What will your Passover *seder* look like? If you are a Messianic congregational or fellowship leader, you are responsible for conveying to those you serve an adequate and appropriate understanding of **all the relevant Biblical events** regarding this sacred season of the year.

Admittedly, unlike our Christian brethren who have a somewhat packaged weekend from Good Friday to Easter Sunday, our remembrance of Messiah Yeshua in the Passover *seder*, and our retelling of the events, might not have such a day-to-day sequence. We will have to speak more in terms of the "Passover season," and not overlook the various elements of either the *seder* or Yeshua's suffering for us which affect us as people of faith. We have the awesome opportunity to really plow into the Scriptures, and significantly focus on why the Lord died for us, on many different levels. We really get to understand how the capital punishments of the Torah have been absorbed in His sacrifice (Colossians 2:14), and memorialize what took place with far more elements than just bread and wine. We get to consider Yeshua in the scope of the Exodus message, and realize that without His blood covering us, we all stand as unregenerate and condemned sinners.

Will we heed the call, and learn to proclaim that simple, yet quite profound message of deliverance available to all people?

> "[I]f you confess with your mouth Yeshua *as* Lord, and believe in your heart that God raised Him from the dead, you will be saved; for with the heart a person believes, resulting in righteousness, and with the mouth he confesses, resulting in salvation. For the Scripture says, 'WHOEVER BELIEVES IN HIM WILL NOT BE DISAPPOINTED' [Isaiah 28:16]. For there is no distinction between Jew and Greek; for the same *Lord* is Lord of all, abounding in riches for all who call on Him; for 'WHOEVER WILL CALL ON THE NAME OF THE LORD WILL BE SAVED' [Joel 2:32]" (Romans 10:9-13).

~10~

Some Features of the Ancient Passover Seder

Mishnah Pesachim 10:1-9

Chapter 3 and the previous chapter both make specific reference to various elements present in the traditional Jewish seder, as well as during Yeshua's Last Supper meal. As Messianic Believers, our ministry affirms how Yeshua's Last Supper was actually a traditional Passover seder. The Mishnah tractate **Pesachim** *10:1-9 summarizes some of the significant traditions developing in First Century Judaism in relation to Passover. We have reproduced it here for your perusal.*[1]

10:1 A. On the eve of Passover from just before afternoon's daily whole offering, a person should not eat, until it gets dark.

B. And even the poorest Israelite should not eat until he reclines at his table.

C. And they should provide him with no fewer than four cups of wine,

D. and even if [the funds] come from public charity.

10:2 I A. When they have mixed the first cup of wine—

B. the House of Shammai say, "He says a blessing over the day, and afterward he says a blessing over the wine."

C. And the House of Hillel say, "He says a blessing over the wine, and afterward he says a blessing over the day."

10:3 A. [When] they bring him [the food], he dips the lettuce [in vinegar]

B. before he comes to the breaking of the bread.

C. They brought him unleavened bread, lettuce, and *haroset* and two dishes—

D. even though *haroset* is not a religious obligation.

---

[1] Reproduced from Neusner, *Mishnah*, pp 249-251.
Cf. t.*Pesachim* 10:1-13.

E. R. Eleazar b. R. Sadoq says, "It is a religious obligation."

F. And in the time of the Temple they would bring before him the carcass of the Passover offering.

10:4 II A. They mixed for him a second cup of wine.

B. And here the son asks his father [questions].

C. But if the son has not got the intelligence to do so, the father teaches him to ask by pointing out:]

D. "How different is this night from all other nights!

E. "For on all other nights we eat leavened or unleavened bread. But this night all of the bread is unleavened.

F. "For on all other nights we eat diverse vegetables, but on this night, only bitter herbs.

G. "For on all other nights we eat meat which is roasted, stewed, or boiled. But this night all of the meat is roasted.

H. "For on all other nights we dip our food one time, but on this night, two times."

I. In accord with the intelligence of the son the father instructs him.

H. He begins [answering the questions] with disgrace and concludes with glory, and explains [the Scriptures from], *A wandering Aramean was my father...* [Dt. 26:5ff] until he completes the entire section.

10:5 A. Rabban Gamaliel did state, "Whoever has not referred to these three matters connected to the Passover has not fulfilled his obligation, and these are they: Passover, unleavened bread, and bitter herbs.

B. "*Passover*—because the Omnipresent passover over the houses of our forefathers in Egypt.

C. "*Unleavened bread*—because our forefathers were redeemed in Egypt.

D. "*Bitter herbs*—because the Egyptians embittered the lives of our forefathers in Egypt."

E. In every generation a person is duty-bound to regard himself as if he personally has gone forth from Egypt, since it is said, *And you shall tell your son in that day saying, It is because of that which the Lord did for me when I came forth out of Egypt* (Ex. 13:8). Therefore we are duty-bound to thank, praise, glorify, honor, extol, and bless him who did for our forefathers and for us all these miracles. He brought us forth from slavery to freedom, anguish to joy, mourning to festival, darkness to great light, subjugation to redemption, so we should say before him, Hallelujah.

10:6 A. To what point does one say [Hallel]?

B. The House of Shammai say, "To *A joyful mother of children* (Ps. 113:9)."

C. And the House of Hillel say, "To *A flintstone into a springing well* (Ps. 114:8)."

D. And he concludes with [a formula of] Redemption.

E. R. Tarfon says, "'...who redeemed us and redeemed our forefathers from Egypt.'

F. "And he did not say a concluding benediction.'"

G. R. Aqiba says, "'...So, Lord, our God, and God of our fathers, bring us in peace to our other appointed times and festivals, rejoicing in the rebuilding of your city and joyful in your Temple worship, where may we eat of the animal sacrifices and Passover offerings,' etc., up to 'Blessed are you, Lord, who has redeemed Israel.'"

10:7 III A. They mixed the third cup for him.

B. He says a blessing for his food.

IV. C. [And at] the fourth, he completes the *Hallel* and says after it the grace of song.

D. Between these several cups of wine, if he wants to drink, he may drink wine.

E. But between the third and the fourth cup of wine, he may not drink.

10:8 A. And after the Passover meal they do not conclude with dainties

B. [If] some of those present fell asleep, they may eat [again].

C. But if all [fell asleep], they may not eat again.

D. R. Yose says, "[If they merely] droused, they may eat again. But if they fell into a deep sleep, they may not eat again."

10:9 A. The Passover offering after midnight [at which point it may no longer be eaten] imparts uncleanness to hands.

B. That which is made of refuse and remnant impart uncleanness to the hands.

C. "[If] one has said the blessing for the Passover offering, he renders unnecessary a blessing over [any other] animal sacrifice [which he may eat].

D. "[If] he said a blessing over [another] animal sacrifice which he ate, he has not made unnecessary a blessing over the Passover offering," the words of R. Ishmael.

E. R. Aqiba says, "This one does not render that unnecessary, and that one does not render this unnecessary."

Messianic Spring Holiday Helper

~11~

What is the Problem With Easter?

J.K. McKee

It comes every Spring, usually sometime in March or April.[1] You know it because in stores you see the baskets, candy, rabbits, eggs, and the annoying fake grass that goes in those baskets. You see the Cadbury cream egg commercials on television with the rabbits gobbling like chickens. Its name is Easter.

Most sincere Christians celebrate the season of Easter not as a time to fawn over rabbits or eat candy, but as a serious time to remember the resurrection of Messiah Yeshua (Christ Jesus). They commemorate His death on Good Friday and His resurrection on Easter Sunday. Certainly, of all the events in our faith, the resurrection of our Lord is the most important. The Apostle Paul validly writes, "But if there is no resurrection of the dead, not even Messiah has been raised; and if Messiah has not been raised, then our preaching is vain, your faith also is vain" (1 Corinthians 15:13-14). However, when we consider the pre-Messianic and pre-Christian origins of "Easter," we do need to reevaluate it.

It comes as a shock to many Christians, but Messianic Believers do not celebrate Easter. We do not see this holiday mandated in Scripture as one of the Lord's *moedim* or "appointed times." We believe it to be a *substitute* holiday in place of what God has asked His people to do in the Spring. By celebrating Good Friday and Easter Sunday, we think that can communicate a view of Yeshua coming to die as a random man or a common criminal on the cross at Golgotha (Calvary), in a "generic" manner for the sins of humanity. He does not necessarily come as the Messiah of Israel, in fulfillment of our Heavenly Father's appointed times. The common celebration of Easter today often downplays how Yeshua is the blameless Passover Lamb slain for our sin, and the unleavened, sinless Bread of Life who was scourged for our iniquities.

There are certainly Christians today who criticize Messianics, without mercy, for not celebrating Easter. Yet as it has sadly been the case, many Messianics usually respond to these Christians without mercy as well. They accuse Christians of participating in pagan "fertility rites" or that they are worshipping the Babylonian goddess Ishtar or the sun god. Likewise, because Messiah Yeshua's death, burial, and resurrection are not emphasized at many "Messianic" Passover *seders*, such

---

[1] This article was originally written for the *Torah In the Balance, Volume I* (Kissimmee, FL: TNN Press, 2003).

Christians may feel that we have lost hold of this monumental event, and perhaps can rightfully say of some people that they treat Yeshua's resurrection with disgust (cf. Hebrews 10:29).

How are we as fair-minded Messianic Believers to handle Easter? How are we to be mature, Spirit-filled, Torah obedient Believers who follow the example of Yeshua the Messiah? At what time are we to appropriately remember what He did for us on the cross 2,000 years ago? Easter or Passover?

What did God tell us to do in the Spring?

It is only natural that Believers should want to do something to honor God in the Springtime. Spring is a wonderful time of year when we see new leaves on trees, flowers blooming, grass becoming green again, and things are warming in preparation for Summer. It is indeed a time for the remembrance of "new life." In the Springtime, in the Hebrew month of *Aviv* or *Nisan*, the Passover is to be celebrated: "Speak to all the congregation of Israel, saying, 'On the tenth of this month they are each one to take a lamb for themselves, according to their fathers' households, a lamb for each household'" (Exodus 12:3). Exodus 12:6 further instructs, "You shall keep it until the fourteenth day of the same month, then the whole assembly of the congregation of Israel is to kill it at twilight."

Detailed instruction is given in Exodus 12:1-13 about how the Passover was originally to be observed in commemoration of the Ancient Israelites' flight from Egypt. Further details are given regarding the Festival of Unleavened Bread in Exodus 12:14-20, and how "In the first *month*, on the fourteenth day of the month at evening, you shall eat unleavened bread, until the twenty-first day of the month at evening" (v. 18), establishing that this special time is to last seven days. Concerning Unleavened Bread, the Lord states that "you shall observe this day throughout your generations as a permanent ordinance" (v. 17). "Permanent ordinance" in Hebrew is *chuqat olam* (חֻקַּת עוֹלָם), or as the NIV renders this command, "Celebrate this day as a lasting ordinance for the generations to come." These things are not to be easily forgotten.

The two holidays of Passover and Unleavened Bread were codified among the appointed times in Leviticus 23:5-14:

"'In the first month, on the fourteenth day of the month at twilight is the LORD's Passover. Then on the fifteenth day of the same month there is the Feast of Unleavened Bread to the LORD; for seven days you shall eat unleavened bread. On the first day you shall have a holy convocation; you shall not do any laborious work. But for seven days you shall present an offering by fire to the LORD. On the seventh day is a holy convocation; you shall not do any laborious work.' Then the LORD spoke to Moses, saying, 'Speak to the sons of Israel and say to them, "When you enter the land which I am going to give to you and reap its harvest, then you shall bring in the sheaf of the first fruits of your harvest to the priest. He shall wave the sheaf before the LORD for you to be accepted; on the day after the sabbath the priest shall wave it. Now on the day when you wave the sheaf, you shall offer a male lamb one year old without defect for a burnt offering to the LORD. Its grain offering shall then be two-tenths *of an ephah* of fine flour mixed with oil, an offering by fire to the LORD *for* a soothing aroma, with its drink offering, a fourth of a hin of wine. Until this same day, until you have brought in the offering of your

God, you shall eat neither bread nor roasted grain nor new growth. It is to be a perpetual statute throughout your generations in all your dwelling places.""

It is only natural for us to want to celebrate new life and commemorate something in the Spring. This is why our Heavenly Father has instructed His people to celebrate Passover and Unleavened Bread. We as Messianic Believers observe these holidays not only in remembrance of the Ancient Israelites' Exodus from Egypt, but also for the prophetic fulfillment in Messiah that these festivals demonstrate. Partaking of Yeshua's salvation, we experience an exodus from slavery to sin to freedom and new life in Him. He has been slain as the Passover Lamb for us, and was bruised like the unleavened *matzah* (מַצָּה) bread. We get to consider these spiritual truths in a very real and tangible way during the Passover season, as we observe the *seder* meal.

What does the New Testament say?

In the Apostolic Scriptures, the Apostle Paul makes a strong parallel between Passover and Unleavened Bread and the salvation that we have in Messiah Yeshua. He writes, "Clean out the old leaven so that you may be a new lump, just as you are *in fact* unleavened. For Messiah our Passover also has been sacrificed" (1 Corinthians 5:7). "Leaven"[2] here is representative of sin, and as Believers in Messiah we are told to clean it out, as the verb *ekkathairō* (ἐκκαθαίρω) means "**to remove as unclean, clean out**" (BDAG),[3] and "*to cleanse out, clean thoroughly*" (*Thayer*).[4] This demonstrates how serious it is for us to get the sin out of our lives. Why are Believers told to do this? The answer may startle many Christians:

"Therefore let us celebrate the feast, not with old leaven, nor with the leaven of malice and wickedness, but with the unleavened bread of sincerity and truth" (1 Corinthians 5:8).

Why are people of faith instructed to clean out the leaven in their lives? So we can all properly celebrate *the feast*. What feast would Paul be referring to here? Obviously, he would be referring to the Passover! 1 Corinthians 5:8 states quite plainly that born again Believers are to "celebrate the festival," the verb *heortazō* (ἑορτάζω) meaning "*to celebrate as* or *by a festival*" (*LS*).[5] These verses take on some key dynamics with the Hebrew terms used in the Complete Jewish Bible:

"Get rid of the old *hametz* [leavened dough], so that you can be a new batch of dough, because in reality you are unleavened. For our *Pesach* lamb, the Messiah, has been sacrificed. So let us celebrate the *Seder* not with leftover *hametz, the hametz* of wickedness and evil, but with the *matzah* of purity and truth."

1 Corinthians 5:7-8 establishes how important it is that born again Believers remember Passover, and likewise the Feast of Unleavened Bread. These appointed times were established by God long before the Messiah's First Coming, and give us the pattern of the Messiah being our blameless Passover Lamb atoning for our iniquities, and then being the scourged, sinless, leavenless Bread of Life as was prophesied in Isaiah 53:5:

---

[2] Heb. *seor* (שְׂאֹר), *chametz* (חָמֵץ); Grk. *zumē* (ζύμη).

[3] *BDAG*, 303.

[4] Joseph H. Thayer, *Thayer's Greek-English Lexicon of the New Testament* (Peabody, MA: Hendrickson, 2003), 195.

[5] *LS*, 277.

"But He was pierced through for our transgressions, He was crushed for our iniquities; the chastening for our well-being *fell* upon Him, and by His scourging we are healed."

This prophecy speaks of Messiah the Suffering Servant. Those of you who have seen unleavened bread or *matzah* know that it has lines with small holes in it, a visible and tangible reminder of Yeshua's suffering for us. A "scourge," or *chaburah* (חַבּוּרָה) in Hebrew, is defined as *"stripe, blow, stroke,"* and *"blows that cut in"* (*BDB*).[6] Eating *matzah* for a week should cause us to pause and seriously consider how He was mocked and beaten—especially as the sinless Son of God (Mark 15:16-20; John 19:1-5).

Paul asserts in Colossians 2:17 that the Biblical festivals specified by God in the Torah "are a shadow of the things to come, but the substance belongs to Christ" (ESV). In understanding these times to be shadows, we know that they give an outline of the prophetic fulfillment of Yeshua's First and Second Comings, as the ultimate *sōma* (σῶμα) or "substance" is to be found in His redemptive work. By understanding times like Passover, we can better comprehend God's plan of salvation history.

We as Messianic Believers are of the strong position that the Lord gave His people the appointed times for a reason. He gave them to us to show us the reality of Messiah Yeshua, giving testimony about His plan for order in Creation. Yeshua's First and future Second Coming are not "random events" on the calendar, as many Christians may perceive them. They are rather ordered events that occur in a set pattern according to the Father's "appointed times" or *moedim*.

What was "the Last Supper"?

We have to recognize, of course, that many Christians today believe in the prophetic significance of the Biblical festivals, including Passover, and many churches regularly do hold Passover *seders*. (My late father himself conducted Passover *seders* in our evangelical, United Methodist church, in the late 1980s and early 1990s.) A Passover *seder* conducted in an evangelical church will open the eyes of many to the Hebraic and Jewish Roots of our faith. It will stimulate many evangelical Believers to really sit down and consider how Yeshua's Last Supper—as it is commonly called—was actually a traditional, First Century *seder* meal. This has been one of the best ways that the Messianic movement has grown in recent years, as evangelical Believers have considered the salvation history themes of Passover and the Exodus, and how these things all relate to our faith in Jesus the Messiah.

As important as this is, though, when reading the different accounts in the Gospels, one cannot help but notice that there appears to be some differences between what the Synoptics (Mark, Matthew, Luke) say about the Last Supper, and what John says. The Synoptics indicate that the Last Supper was a Passover meal:

"Now on the first *day* of Unleavened Bread the disciples came to Yeshua and asked, 'Where do You want us to prepare for You to eat the Passover?' And He said, 'Go into the city to a certain man, and say to him, "The Teacher says, 'My time is near; I *am to* keep the Passover at your house with My disciples.'"' The

---

[6] *BDB*, 289.

disciples did as Yeshua had directed them; and they prepared the Passover" (Matthew 26:17-19; cf. Mark 14:12-16; Luke 22:8-15).

Some waver as to whether or not the Last Supper was actually "Passover" (although some editions of the NASB have Matthew 26:20-25 titled as "The Last Passover").[7] This is based on John 19:14, which states that Yeshua was crucified on "the day of preparation for the Passover," meaning that the Passover actually began the evening of His crucifixion. The previous evening, when the Lord and His Disciples partook of the Last Supper, would thus not have been the Passover. Is it possible that the Last Supper was just a regular meal?

Various solutions have been proposed for this. Did Yeshua follow one of the competing sectarian calendars, and not the mainline Jewish calendar of the time, making the "real" Passover a day early? I have heard the opinion that "practice Passovers" were common in the First Century, prior to the actual *seder* beginning. Rabbis could do this with their students to train them to conduct their own Passover meals, or for those entering to Jerusalem from afar to become accustomed to Passover in the Judean tradition. But whether there is really evidence to prove that this was common is difficult to tell, even though if they did take place, it is not impossible for Yeshua to have held such a meal with His Disciples.

The answer might be staring right at us, but quite easy to overlook. The Greek clause *prōtē tōn azumōn* (πρώτῃ τῶν ἀζύμων) actually lacks the term *hēmera* (ἡμέρα) or "day" (Matthew 26:17), so "first of unleavened bread" might actually refer to the general time immediately preceding Passover and Unleavened Bread. If this were the case, would it be inappropriate for the Last Supper meal Yeshua and the Apostles shared to be a Passover *seder* held a bit early? Those holding to a rigid, inflexible reading of the instructions in the Torah would say "yes." Yet I can very much appreciate the perspective of R.T. France, who in his commentary on Matthew, summarizes,

> "[T]he Gospel of John (see esp. Jn. 13:1; 18:28; 19:14) plainly dates the Last Supper on the night which began Nisan 14 (*i.e.* the night *before* the regular Passover meal), so that Jesus in fact died on the afternoon at the end of Nisan 14, the time when the Passover lambs were killed....Is Matthew (following Mark) then wrong in describing this as a Passover meal and dating its preparation on Nisan 14? The matter is too complex for full discussion here, and has given rise to innumerable theories...The simplest solution, and the one assumed in this commentary, is that Jesus, knowing that he would be dead before the regular time for the meal, deliberately held it in secret one day early...Of course it was strictly incorrect to hold a 'Passover' at any time other than the evening of Nisan 14/15, **but Jesus was not one to be bound to formal regulations in an emergency situation!**" (emphasis mine).[8]

France finds his support in the fact that Yeshua had a strong desire to commemorate the Passover with His Disciples one more time before His death.

---

[7] Zodhiates, *Hebrew-Greek Key Study Bible*, NASB, 1305.

[8] France, *TNTC: Matthew*, 365.

France is also author of a much larger work on Matthew in the *New International Commentary on the New Testament* series (Grand Rapids: Eerdmans, 2007).

The Messiah certainly says, "I have eagerly desired to eat this Passover with you before I suffer" (Luke 22:15, NRSV). Translated "earnestly desired" (NASU, NIV, RSV),[9] *epithumia* (ἐπιθυμία) means "*a longing after* a thing, *desire of* or *for* it" (LS).[10] **Yeshua strongly desired to celebrate Passover with His Disciples.** If it were a day early, then certainly the One who was Lord of the Sabbath[11] can surely also be allowed to be the Lord of the Passover. Yeshua's Disciples who ate with Him at this time definitely had an education! I find no significant problems with the suggestion of Yeshua's Passover *seder* held a little early.

Just as Yeshua earnestly desired to remember the Passover with His Disciples before He died, so should we also desire to come together every year, and consider what new lessons the Lord might teach us during this time. Yeshua was preparing to inaugurate the era of the New Covenant with His own blood, and commission His Disciples to continue His work:

"While they were eating, Yeshua took *some* bread, and after a blessing, He broke *it* and gave *it* to the disciples, and said, 'Take, eat; this is My body.' And when He had taken a cup and given thanks, He gave *it* to them, saying, 'Drink from it, all of you; for this is My blood of the covenant, which is poured out for many for forgiveness of sins'" (Matthew 26:26-28; cf. Mark 14:22-24; Luke 22:19-20).

The common practice of communion or "the Lord's Supper," as the tradition is often observed today in various denominations, is derived from the Passover. In Luke 22:19 Yeshua says "do this in remembrance of Me." Today, multitudes of Believers are learning more about the intricacies of the Last Supper, beyond just the symbols of the bread and wine.[12]

A Brief History of Easter

Following Yeshua's final Passover meal He was arrested in the Garden of Gethsemane, taken before Pontius Pilate, scourged and beaten by the Roman soldiers, and then crucified, atoning for humanity's sin. Three days later He arose from the dead, and forty days following He ascended to the right hand of the Father in Heaven. The story sounds all too familiar, but it can take on a completely new light, and many different dimensions, when viewed with the significance of God's appointed times in mind.

So how did we get Easter Sunday, observed in Christianity today, a holiday that by many accounts seems to be divorced from Passover? At Passover time we are told to eat unleavened bread and focus on the lamb, whereas on Easter Sunday yeast rolls and hams are commonplace. Yeast or leaven represents sin in relation to Passover and the Festival of Unleavened Bread. Swine is an unclean animal, the consumption of which God says is "an abomination unto you" (Leviticus 11:10, 11, 12, 20, 23).

One of the things that we have to understand is that the Apostles and early Believers never celebrated what we today call "Easter." They observed the Passover and the Festival of Unleavened Bread as they always had, and remembered the Messiah in all. "Easter" as its own holiday was not formalized and mandated until centuries later at the Council of Nicea. While establishing many critical doctrines

---

[9] "I have earnestly and intensely desired" (Amplified Bible).
[10] LS, 292.
[11] Matthew 12:8; Mark 2:28; Luke 6:5.
[12] For a further discussion, consult Chapter 9, "The Last Seder and Yeshua's Passover Chronology."

of our faith, including the Messiah's Divinity,[13] later Church councils such as the Council of Antioch (341 C.E.) and the Council of Laodicea (363 C.E.) made it illegal for Christians to participate in the Sabbath or Passover. Susan E. Richardson's comments from *Holidays & Holy Days* confirm this:

> "...In A.D. 325, the Council of Nicea set aside a special day just to celebrate the Resurrection. The problem with an official day was deciding whether or not the Resurrection should be celebrated on a weekday or...on a Sunday.
> "Many felt that the date should continue to be based on the timing of the Resurrection during Passover. Once Jewish leaders determined the date of Passover each year, Christian leaders could set the date for Easter by figuring three days after Passover...
> "...As Christianity drew away from Judaism, some were reluctant to base the Christian celebration on the Jewish calendar."[14]

This should essentially confirm the fact that the Church of the Fourth Century wanted to establish a holiday largely separate from anything "Jewish." Commemorating the resurrection of Yeshua three days after the Passover—on any day of the week other than Sunday—was just unthinkable. Like Jeroboam of old, many of the bishops wanted to dismiss the Lord's appointed times with their own replacement holidays. Richardson continues,

> "Since Easter is a celebration of Jesus' Resurrection, you would think there wouldn't be room for paganism. However, Easter is one of the holidays most intertwined with pagan symbolism and ritual.
> "The origin of the word *easter* isn't certain. The Venerable Bede, an eighth-century monk and scholar, suggested that the word may have come from the Anglo-Saxon *Eostre* or *Eastre*—a Teutonic goddess of spring and fertility..."[15]

We do point out, however, that Richardson does state, "Recent scholars haven't been able to find any reference to the goddess Bede mentioned and consider the theory discredited."[16] There may be, nor may not be, a similarity and connection between the name "Easter" and the Babylonian fertility goddess Ishtar But, Richardson does admit that "*easter* would be linked to the changing of the season"[17] and hence be connected to Spring fertility and growing. Either way, the fact that "Easter" Sunday is connected to paganism should raise some eyebrows among those wanting to follow Scripture.[18]

Whether "Easter" is a name of pagan origin or not in this case is *unimportant*. The fact that there are strong pagan connections to it as Richardson, a Christian author, readily attests, should be shocking to those endeavoring to be Bible

---

[13] Bettenson and Maunder, pp 27-29; consult also "The Ecumenical Creeds," in Hugh T. Kerr, ed., *Readings in Christian Thought* (Nashville: Abingdon, 1990), pp 74-77.
[14] Susan E. Richardson, *Holidays & Holy Days* (Ann Arbor, MI: Vine Books, 2001), 58.
[15] Ibid., 58-59.
[16] Ibid., 59.
[17] Ibid.
[18] For a further summary, consult D. Larry Gregg, "Easter," in *EDB*, pp 362-363.

Believers who follow Scripture. The fact that later generations of Christians would form a holiday honoring the Messiah's resurrection originally based in paganism, and not celebrate Passover and the Festival of Unleavened Bread, casts a shadow upon Good Friday and Easter Sunday. People have largely decided to ignore what God asks us to do in Leviticus 23, reemphasized by Paul in 1 Corinthians 5:7-8, and instead feel it prudent to assert their own holidays. The typology of the ancient Passover and Exodus, foretelling the sacrifice of Yeshua at Golgotha, has been too summarily disregarded by many Christians over the centuries. **Yet today this is changing!** Today, many Messianic Jewish Believers are invited into evangelical churches to not only testify of their faith in Jesus the Messiah, but also of the great significance of Yeshua as the Passover Lamb.

We should not be so dense so as to think that all Christians over the centuries have been participating in "fertility rites." ***They haven't.*** I do believe that God has honored those who have celebrated Easter Sunday in ignorance, truly wanting to serve Him. They have surely been blessed for wanting to remember the resurrection of Jesus Christ (even by attending various sunrise services), an event that we should remember and consider every year. However, the Father is leading us into a time when the fuller truth is being restored. Christians today can be blessed and spiritually enriched in their faith *even more*, if they learn to partake of the Passover and are truly able to grasp the significance of the Exodus in light of the cross.

Fairy Tale Reasoning

Of course, there are some specific traditions associated with Easter that are supposed to "commemorate" the resurrection of Yeshua. What about the venerable "Easter bunny"? Where did it come from? Did the Apostles truly consider remembering the resurrection of the Messiah by thinking of a white rabbit wearing a pastel suit? I do not think so. The only place rabbits are mentioned in Scripture is in Leviticus 11:6 and Deuteronomy 14:7, where the Lord declares them to be unclean animals that we are forbidden to eat. We once again turn to Richardson's commentary from *Holidays & Holy Days*:

> "There are several reasons for the rabbit, or hare, to be associated with Easter, all of which come through pagan celebrations or beliefs. The most obvious is the hare's fertility. Easter comes during spring and celebrates new life."[19]

This statement is disturbing because rabbits are commonly associated with sex. A popular expression in relation to young people is that they "have sex like rabbits." (And I would point out that *this sex* is usually always outside the bounds of marriage.) God did not tell us to associate new life with rabbits in the Spring. Richardson also states, "The hare or rabbit's burrow helped the animal's adoption as part of Easter celebrations. Believers saw the rabbit coming out of its underground home as a symbol of Jesus coming out of the tomb. Perhaps this was another case of taking a pre-existing symbol and giving it Christian meaning."[20]

---

[19] Ibid.
[20] Ibid., 60.

Adopting a rabbit's coming out of its underground burrow and comparing it to Yeshua's resurrection is complete *fairy tale reasoning* in my assessment—and makes little or no sense whatsoever! This really is about as factual as the White Rabbit we all think of from Alice in Wonderland.

Is "Easter" mentioned in Scripture?

There is, however, one instance where some Christians may tell us that "Easter" is mentioned in the Bible—not necessarily referring to the resurrection of the Lord. "Easter" appears in the King James Version rendering of Acts 12:4:

"And when he [Herod] had apprehended him [Peter], he put *him* in prison, and delivered *him* to four quaternions of soldiers to keep him; intending after Easter to bring him forth to the people."

This is not an accurate translation of the Greek text at all. The Greek does not have "Easter" but *Pascha* (πάσχα), the transliteration of the Hebrew *Pesach* (פֶּסַח) or "Passover." The New King James Version has corrected this error:

"So when he had arrested him, he put *him* in prison, and delivered *him* to four squads of soldiers to keep him, intending to bring him before the people after Passover" (Acts 12:4, NKJV).

King James Only advocates, who believe that the KJV is perfect and without error, superior to the original Hebrew or Greek, have argued that this rendering of "Easter" for *Pascha* is accurate. Why is this the case? Because King Herod, they say, the one who took Peter captive, was a pagan and celebrated Easter. While this is unsupported by the text, notably because Acts 12:3 tells us that "Then were the days of unleavened bread" (KJV), connecting *Pascha* to Passover—it is interesting that they must admit that "Easter" is a holiday of non-Biblical, rather than Biblical, origins.

Easter in Perspective

Many Christians will not understand why Messianic Believers do not celebrate Easter Sunday, and instead honor Passover and the Festival of Unleavened Bread. Some, in their ignorance, could look at us with disdain, and will claim that we deny the resurrection of Messiah Yeshua. But this is truly **not the case** as Messiah is our Passover Lamb slain for the forgiveness of sin, and "is the firstfruits of those who have died" (1 Corinthians 15:20, CJB). We do not deny Yeshua's death or His resurrection; we just believe that Christians are commemorating it inappropriately. They are honoring it outside of the bounds God has given us, and have given credence to a holiday that has some questionable origins. We advocate that Yeshua's atoning work and resurrection are best remembered in the context of Passover, and various teachings during the week of Unleavened Bread.

But potential problems that exist, just as during the Christmas season, are compounded by Messianics who condemn Christians mercilessly and claim that they are worshipping Ishtar or the sun god on Easter Sunday. **I do not believe that Christians worship the sun god on Easter Sunday,** and would consider such criticism to be unwarranted and unjustified. Many of the Messianics who vehemently protest "Easter," do not really seek to honor or remember Yeshua's death, burial, and resurrection that much at their Passover meals. Yeshua Himself says, "For in the way you judge, you will be judged; and by your standard of measure, it will be measured to you" (Matthew 7:2). Many of these same people will readily claim that when *they* celebrated Easter *they* were not celebrating pagan fertility rites, yet somehow most Christians today are celebrating fertility rites when Easter comes. This kind of unbalanced scale will not help the Messianic cause.

Messianic Believers need to set the higher standard when Easter comes. It is only one day out of the year, and fortunately it is not given the same type of commercialization as Christmas is. Let us be the ones who lead by our example of loving others who are ignorant of the truth of Easter's origins and who celebrate it because they do not know any better, believing the Biblical appointed times of the Lord to be unimportant. They, in ignorance, do not really know the origins of the holiday and are often unaware of the greater blessings and significance of celebrating Passover. We should invite them to a Passover *seder* in our homes, or at our Messianic congregations and fellowships, enabling them to see Yeshua the Messiah for who He was at the Last Supper—as the Lord preparing Himself to be crucified for our sins. Let them partake of the good things of the *Pesach* season that we have partaken of!

For many of today's Christians, "Easter" may be described as a somewhat neutered celebration from God's larger plan and purpose. **It is our responsibility as the emerging Messianic movement to encourage all Believers to take a hold of the Passover,** and do so in a very edifying way that brings glory to Him and what He has accomplished for us.

What is the problem with Easter?

While as Messianics we do not celebrate Good Friday or Easter Sunday, because they were adapted by Roman Catholicism to replace Passover, I do not condemn those who celebrate it in ignorance, and neither do I condemn those who defiantly celebrate it and are opposed to us celebrating the Lord's appointed times. (God will handle them). But I would ask Christians to reconsider what they are doing, and really consider whether or not "the Church" has the right to replace God's holidays with its own holidays.

Today's Messianics find no Biblical justification for the historical Church completely abandoning the Passover and replacing it with something else. We choose to commemorate the Messiah's resurrection at its appropriate time connected to the Spring appointments—not a holiday that historically has connections to pagan fertility rites. We consider it to be quite important to view Yeshua's sacrifice for us as a part of God's orderly plan, rather than a part of the unorderly and unsanctified days of the nations.

What is the problem with Easter? Easter was not established by God. It was established to be a substitute of some of the most important events on the Biblical calendar: Passover and the Festival of Unleavened Bread. Just as the Ancient Israelites were delivered via Exodus from Egypt and brought into the Promised Land, so too have we as born again Believers received Messiah Yeshua into our hearts and have experienced our own exodus from sin into new life—including the promise of remembering the Passover with Him in His Kingdom on Earth (Matthew 26:29; Mark 14:25)! We have the confidence of knowing that He came in a preordained order, not as part of a random, unordered day of revelry.

~12~

Passover: Paradox or Outreach?

Mark Huey

The return of temperate sun soaked days, coupled with drenching Spring rains to the Northern Hemisphere, rekindles growth in the dormant flora while igniting the migratory patterns of the reinvigorated fauna—ranging from insects to crawling creatures to birds.[1] Of course, the majority of humanity birthed in the "cradle of civilization" that has remained north of the equator is not overlooked. Certain "rites of spring" and/or other seasonal traditions, celebrating what appears to be the tangible rebirth of life, are repeated around the globe. The multifaceted cultures of the world are replete with various ways to acknowledge that human life, as it is known and appreciated, continues to enjoy another day of existence. Lamentably for many, living for the moment by eating, drinking, and indulging in the desires of the flesh is all that matters, because adherence to the ancient pagan philosophy that "tomorrow we die" (cf. Isaiah 22:13), predominates many of these heathen activities.

Yet for those influenced by the Holy Scriptures in the Judeo-Christian world, there are other choices for annual celebrations occurring in the Spring season—depending on your perspective—for observation or participation. These commemorations are not inspired by new growth in the vegetation, the lengthening of days, or the smells of flower blossoms or budding trees (although each of these are evident). Without getting into all of the calendar debates that often manifest themselves, the Bible admonishes, "Observe the month of Abib and celebrate the Passover to the LORD your God, for in the month of Abib the LORD your God brought you out of Egypt by night" (Deuteronomy 16:1). The development of the Hillel II lunisolar calendar, used by mainline Judaism and Messianic Judaism today, unites the worldwide Jewish community as to when the month of Aviv/Nisan begins and when faithful Jews are to celebrate Passover every year.[2]

For those involved in a Messianic expression of faith, who consider themselves to be the Israel of God (Galatians 6:16), the requirement to remember and celebrate the Passover has brought great joy! The Scriptures detail that the Passover or *Pesach* (פֶּסַח), a special time of appointment and remembrance, is to be observed

---

[1] This article originally appeared in the March 2009 issue of Outreach Israel News.

[2] The calendar controversy will be addressed in the forthcoming book *Torah In the Balance, Volume II* by J.K. McKee.

forever in perpetuity. It is to be something that children ask their parents about for critical spiritual and life lessons:

"'For the LORD will pass through to smite the Egyptians; and when He sees the blood on the lintel and on the two doorposts, the LORD will pass over the door and will not allow the destroyer to come in to your houses to smite *you*. **And you shall observe this event as an ordinance for you and your children forever** [*l'choq-lekha u'l'baneykha ad-olam*, לְחׇק־לְךָ וּלְבָנֶיךָ עַד־עוֹלָם]. When you enter the land which the LORD will give you, as He has promised, you shall observe this rite. **And when your children say to you, "What does this rite mean to you?" you shall say, "It is a Passover sacrifice to the LORD who passed over the houses of the sons of Israel in Egypt when He smote the Egyptians, but spared our homes."'** And the people bowed low and worshiped" (Exodus 12:23-27).

When the *moedim* (מוֹעֲדִים) are listed for the first time, all together in Leviticus 23—detailing the appointed times when the Lord will meet with His people—after the weekly Sabbath is recognized, the specifics for the Passover and Festival of Unleavened Bread are articulated. It includes the admonition to remember the days as a perpetual statute:

"'These are the appointed times of the LORD, holy convocations which you shall proclaim at the times appointed for them. In the first month, on the fourteenth day of the month at twilight is the LORD's Passover. Then on the fifteenth day of the same month there is the Feast of Unleavened Bread to the LORD; for seven days you shall eat unleavened bread. On the first day you shall have a holy convocation; you shall not do any laborious work. But for seven days you shall present an offering by fire to the LORD. On the seventh day is a holy convocation; you shall not do any laborious work.' Then the LORD spoke to Moses, saying, 'Speak to the sons of Israel and say to them, "When you enter the land which I am going to give to you and reap its harvest, then you shall bring in the sheaf of the first fruits of your harvest to the priest. He shall wave the sheaf before the LORD for you to be accepted; on the day after the sabbath the priest shall wave it. Now on the day when you wave the sheaf, you shall offer a male lamb one year old without defect for a burnt offering to the LORD. Its grain offering shall then be two-tenths *of an ephah* of fine flour mixed with oil, an offering by fire to the LORD *for* a soothing aroma, with its drink offering, a fourth of a hin of wine. Until this same day, until you have brought in the offering of your God, you shall eat neither bread nor roasted grain nor new growth. **It is to be a perpetual statute** [*chuqat olam*, חֻקַּת עוֹלָם] **throughout your generations in all your dwelling places"''** (Leviticus 23:4-14).

The Lord instructed Ancient Israel, "This is to be a lasting ordinance for the generations to come, wherever you live" (NIV), not indicating that remembering Passover and Unleavened Bread were to only be temporary observances (cf. Leviticus 23:21, 31, 41). *They have important things to teach us about the plan of redemption* (Colossians 2:17). Despite various alterations in celebration that have occurred down through the centuries, either by the Jewish Synagogue adding many dogmas that can take one's attention away from the basic remembrance of the Passover and Exodus, or by the Christian Church which has largely ignored it altogether[3]—I would say that **it is not principally a matter of why, or even when, one remembers these commands.** Instead, the challenge for modern-day Messianic Believers scattered abroad, is often *how* we honor these commands in a way that is pleasing to the Holy One of Israel. How do we recall the substance of what they teach us about God's plan of deliverance?

Setting aside the somewhat frivolous discussions (often leading to contentious debates) about the calendar that have surfaced in recent years—by those who self-righteously attempt to usurp the authority bestowed upon the Jewish people in this area (Matthew 23:2-3; Romans 3:2; 11:29), who have been faithfully observing these appointed times for millennia—we **still have to answer the question of how Passover is to be celebrated.** Not only are we remembering Passover on the other side of the Exodus and Golgotha, but most of us live in a Twenty-First Century Western environment. If not raised in the Jewish Synagogue, we may have to overcome various prejudices and social hurdles during this time of year.

Some might refer to this annual dilemma as a *Passover paradox*, because of all the controversy that tends to bubble to the surface, especially as the independent Messianic community struggles for identity and cohesion. Our ministry simply considers it to be a manifestation of how the Messianic community has developed (positively *or* negatively) as each congregation, fellowship, or even observant family essentially does "its own thing" based on whatever the leadership decides is appropriate. Some of the decisions people have made are very wise, and they have helped people grow spiritually and understand the important themes of both Passover and Yeshua's offering as the Lamb of God. Yet, some of the other decisions people have made are very poor, and they have made this season into one where God's people often divide over minor details, forgetting the larger aspects that are to unite us. (And even if the details on Passover and Unleavened Bread are largely agreed upon, there is still the issue of how to treat our Christian brethren who just observe Easter Sunday.) **How do we learn to look at the bigger picture this time of year?**

Disciple and Love

What has prompted me to write this—utilizing the annual Passover paradox as a framework for discussion—is somewhat of a reaction to the larger cultural battles we are all currently witnessing in the world where we live. Two age-old challenges, to (1) make disciples of Yeshua and (2) love one another, have dominated my thoughts. In order to win the war for our culture, individual lives must be won and redeemed a single heart at a time. Yeshua's departing command to His followers was to go forth and make disciples of those who believed in Him, instructing them in His teachings and the example that He left to emulate:

"And Yeshua came up and spoke to them, saying, 'All authority has been given to Me in heaven and on earth. Go therefore and make disciples of all the nations, baptizing them in the name of the Father and the Son and the Holy Spirit, teaching

---

[3] This is not to say that all Christians have ignored the significance of the Passover and Exodus. Even while clouded in non-Biblical traditions surrounding "Easter," the Great Vigil of Easter practiced in many Anglican and Episcopalian churches on the Saturday night before Easter Sunday directly connects the resurrection of Yeshua to the symbolism and deliverance of the Exodus (*The Book of Common Prayer*, pp 285-287).

them to observe all that I commanded you; and lo, I am with you always, even to the end of the age'" (Matthew 28:18-20; cf. Acts 1:8).

At Yeshua's Last Seder meal, Yeshua commanded His Disciples to love one another—something that should certainly be second nature to any of us who are regenerated by the Holy Spirit! We often find, though, that loving others is a "new" commandment because it too frequently goes *unused:*

"A new commandment I give to you, that you love one another, even as I have loved you, that you also love one another. **By this all men will know that you are My disciples, if you have love for one another**" (John 13:34-35; cf. Leviticus 19:18).

Lamentably, a lack of love for one another often seems to manifest itself every year around Passover in various sectors of the broad Messianic community. *Among those who claim to be disciples of the Messiah Yeshua, this is very disturbing!* Is something missing among us? Is this not a time when we are to testify via our actions and remembrance of the Passover that we truly love a God who delivered Ancient Israel—and who also loved us by sending His Son to die for us (John 3:16)?

The fact that Yeshua's followers will be known via their love for one another should be a positive testimony to the world that there is something distinctively different about us. It should be an obvious sign that the Spirit of God is indeed working within those who call themselves disciples of Yeshua or Messianic Believers, whether they be Jewish or not. The message of Passover and the Exodus is something that while having affected Ancient Israel, is a powerful theme that various religious and political movements have appropriated for centuries (even without considering the prophetic message of Yeshua's sacrifice as Passover Lamb).[4] **It is not something exclusive**, because it is a universal message of release from oppression.

We should not be using this season as a time to divide, but rather unite God's people. The Apostle Paul recognized this in his writing to the Corinthians, telling a broad audience of Jewish and non-Jewish Believers,

"For I do not want you to be unaware, brethren, that our fathers were all under the cloud and all passed through the sea; and all were baptized into Moses in the cloud and in the sea; and all ate the same spiritual food; and all drank the same spiritual drink, for they were drinking from a spiritual rock which followed them; and the rock was Messiah" (1 Corinthians 10:1-4).

Paul says *hoi pateres hēmōn pantes* (οἱ πατέρες ἡμῶν πάντες), "all our ancestors" (NRSV), participated in the Passover and Exodus. This is true whether one knows his Jewish ancestors were present in Egypt, or whether one becomes a part of Israel via faith in Messiah Yeshua (Ephesians 3:6). **This is a special season of the year that affects all of us who place our trust in the Holy One of Israel,** and the last thing any of us should be doing is trying to skew the unity in His Son that our Father wants us to be united around (cf. Galatians 3:28).

Remembering Yeshua's instruction to make disciples and love others, how should Messianic Believers approach and observe the celebration of the Passover? Should we not approach our commemoration with an objective of instructing not only those among us, but *also* those who might be drawn to us during this time, because of our testimony of faithful obedience (Deuteronomy 4:6)?

---

[4] For a discussion of this, consult Michael Walzer, *Exodus and Revolution* (New York: Daniel Doron, 1979); Wright, "God's Model of Redemption," in *The Mission of God*, pp 265-323.

Salt and Light

When I look outward to the lost and perverted generation that is increasingly imposing its will upon the world, rather than inward to some of the petty battles that take place within the confines of the Messianic community, I think about Yeshua's requirement that we be salt and light to all those we encounter:

"You are the salt of the earth; but if the salt has become tasteless, how can it be made salty *again*? It is no longer good for anything, except to be thrown out and trampled under foot by men. You are the light of the world. A city set on a hill cannot be hidden; nor does *anyone* light a lamp and put it under a basket, but on the lampstand, and it gives light to all who are in the house. **Let your light shine before men in such a way that they may see your good works, and glorify your Father who is in heaven**" (Matthew 5:13-16).

How do we let our light shine before others? *We properly follow God's Torah* (Matthew 5:17-19) *as Yeshua did!* Followers of the Holy One of Israel have the paramount responsibility to be salt and light to the world, being required to share the hope of salvation that is within us (1 Peter 3:15). How are today's Messianic Believers going to make a sizeable impact on our contemporary culture unless we allow God to use each of us in His work to share the good news? *This primarily takes place by others witnessing our obedience to Him.* And the gospel being witnessed is by no means a "New Testament" concept, exclusively. Isaiah understood the need to share the good message of salvation coming forth from Zion:

"'Therefore My people shall know My name; therefore in that day I am the one who is speaking, "Here I am."' How lovely on the mountains are the feet of him who brings good news, who announces peace and brings good news of happiness, **who announces salvation,** *and* says to Zion, 'Your God reigns!'" (Isaiah 52:6-7).

The Apostle Paul appropriates Isaiah's message in his treatise to the Romans, not only detailing how the good news is for all people, but more specifically how non-Jewish Believers are to provoke the Jewish people at large—who do not know Messiah Yeshua—to jealousy for faith in Him:

"For the Scripture says, 'WHOEVER BELIEVES IN HIM WILL NOT BE DISAPPOINTED' [Isaiah 28:16]. For there is no distinction between Jew and Greek; for the same *Lord* is Lord of all, abounding in riches for all who call on Him; for 'WHOEVER WILL CALL ON THE NAME OF THE LORD WILL BE SAVED' [Joel 2:32]. **How then will they call on Him in whom they have not believed? How will they believe in Him whom they have not heard? And how will they hear without a preacher? How will they preach unless they are sent?** Just as it is written, 'HOW BEAUTIFUL ARE THE FEET OF THOSE WHO BRING GOOD NEWS OF GOOD THINGS!' [Isaiah 52:7]. However, they did not all heed the good news; for Isaiah says, 'LORD, WHO HAS BELIEVED OUR REPORT?' [Isaiah 53:1]. So faith *comes* from hearing, and hearing by the word of Messiah. But I say, surely they have never heard, have they? Indeed they have; 'THEIR VOICE HAS GONE OUT INTO ALL THE EARTH, AND THEIR WORDS TO THE ENDS OF THE WORLD' [Psalm 19:4]. But I say, surely Israel did not know, did they? First Moses says, 'I WILL MAKE YOU JEALOUS BY THAT WHICH IS NOT A NATION, BY A NATION WITHOUT UNDERSTANDING WILL I ANGER YOU' [Deuteronomy 32:21]. And Isaiah is very bold and says, 'I WAS FOUND BY THOSE

WHO DID NOT SEEK ME, I BECAME MANIFEST TO THOSE WHO DID NOT ASK FOR ME'
[Isaiah 65:1]. But as for Israel He says, 'ALL THE DAY LONG I HAVE STRETCHED OUT
MY HANDS TO A DISOBEDIENT AND OBSTINATE PEOPLE' [Isaiah 65:2]" (Romans 10:11-
12).

Paul instructs the non-Jewish Believers in Rome that one of the reasons
salvation has come to them is "to make Israel jealous" (Romans 11:11, RSV). Our
family has been convicted for quite some time that an excellent way non-Jewish
Believers can fulfill this mandate is by following God's Torah *and certainly* by
celebrating the Passover! If more non-Jewish Believers would take hold of their
spiritual inheritance in Israel, faithfully observing the Passover and the Festival of
Unleavened Bread, do you think we would make a difference? *What kind of a
testimony would we have to the Jewish community?*

Obviously, we commemorate Passover because "Messiah, our Passover lamb,
has been sacrificed" (1 Corinthians 5:7, ESV). Many of the Jewish traditions
associated with the Passover meal eloquently give substance to us understanding
the greater fullness of Yeshua's Last Supper. If you are a non-Jewish Believer, can
you imagine the positive witness you could have to Jewish people—who do not
know Messiah Yeshua—by observing Passover along with them every year?
Furthermore, for a Christian community that desires to know more about why
Jesus had to come and die for them, what does celebrating Passover communicate
to them? When you can put aside ancient, ungodly prejudices that have divided
God's people for far too long, can you really recognize the power that comes by
sitting down at the *seder* table?

Being "salty" Believers in the Messiah Yeshua, sharing His salvation, is what is
expected for His followers. Salt was often used as an ancient preservative, and
remembering Passover each year helps us to persevere in faith, as we are reminded
of God's great acts of salvation. We can also be reminded of how we are to use the
wisdom God has granted us to bring His truth into various situations, most
especially during this season as we commemorate the Exodus and the sacrifice and
resurrection of God's Son. The Apostle Paul instructed the Colossians,

"Devote yourselves to prayer, keeping alert in it with *an attitude of*
thanksgiving; praying at the same time for us as well, that God will open up to us a
door for the word, so that we may speak forth the mystery of Messiah, for which I
have also been imprisoned; that I may make it clear in the way I ought to speak.
**Conduct yourselves with wisdom toward outsiders, making the most of the
opportunity. Let your speech always be with grace,** *as though* **seasoned with salt,
so that you will know how you should respond to each person**" (Colossians 4:2-6).

Passover Seders

Over the years, we have met scores of people who have a testimony of coming
into the Messianic movement as a *direct result* of attending some kind of Passover
seder. When one's eyes are opened to the richness of our Hebraic Roots via the
Passover, and how they illuminate our understanding of Yeshua's ministry and
work for us, it is not difficult to see how additional questions and inquiries lead one
into a pursuit of Messianic things. Once someone is confronted with the basic truth
that the appointed times are to be celebrated forever—as an instructional witness
to posterity—Believers often wonder why today's Christianity seldom speaks about
them. This prompts many to dig a little deeper into the Hebraic and Jewish Roots

of their faith. If they are truly seekers of the Most High, we have witnessed that a voracious appetite for more understanding is often initiated, and within a short time such people will often leave their Church settings and join a Messianic congregation.[5]

On the other hand, we have witnessed Messianic assemblies that unfairly restrict the attendance to their Passover *seder*s, under the influence of believing that only circumcised men can be in the audience. While it is true that originally within Ancient Israel only the physically circumcised could participate in the Passover (Exodus 12:47-49), it is also true that it is impossible for anyone today to follow all of the instructions of Passover down to the letter. There is no Temple in Jerusalem where one can offer the prescribed sacrifices, and most people—including Jews—who remember Passover are remembering it in some kind of a Diaspora setting where a creative *halachah* has had to be enacted, compensating for the different circumstances. *At best, all any of us can do is observe a Passover memorial.* And certainly with the sacrifice and resurrection of Yeshua to consider, Messianic remembrance of Passover will have more to consider than just the Exodus from Egypt.[6]

Passover is the best time of the year for you to reach out to others and testify of your Messianic walk of faith. Your family needs to have a home *seder* meal where you can invite your extended family and close friends to participate. A hands on experience of breaking *matzah*, eating bitter herbs, and drinking the cups of wine will focus both your and their attention on what these things mean to us as people of faith. Within the intimacy of your home, each person at the *seder* table will learn something new. People will be refamiliarized with the deliverance of Ancient Israel at the Exodus, and they will have more to consider regarding Yeshua's sacrifice for their sins.

Yet we know that Passover should not only be remembered by individuals or individual families. The corporate setting of a congregational *seder* meal gives all within the assembly the opportunity to invite and include friends, relatives, seekers, or others to be presented to the celebration and message of the Passover. This is an opportune time for your associates to discover that you believe that Yeshua is the Messiah and that He is the Passover Lamb, as depicted via the deliverance of Israel from Egypt. **Passover is *the* time of year when Messianic congregations receive the largest number of visitors and new members.** Do not let this opportunity go to waste!

Passover is a very special time when we get to flex our spiritual muscles and be diligent in making disciples of Messiah Yeshua. We have the privilege of displaying His love for one another, demonstrating that we have been supernaturally changed. We most especially have the opportunity to testify of Messiah Yeshua to the Jewish community, even if all we do is purchase *matzah* and various other Kosher for Passover items—wishing a Jewish merchant, or a Jewish person in line at the supermarket, a blessed Passover. And if you are non-Jewish, by having a traditional *seder* meal in your home, you may even force a Messianic Jew (currently wondering why so many non-Jewish Believers are being

---

[5] For our family's testimony of becoming Messianic, consult the Introduction section of *Hebraic Roots: An Introductory Study.*

[6] The issue of circumcision is addressed more fully in the article "Is Circumcision for Everyone?" by J.K. McKee.

led into Messianic things), to possibly reconsider his or her approach toward those "other people" who are fellow citizens within the Commonwealth of Israel (Ephesians 2:11-12, 19; 3:6).

Are you starting to see the benefits? You can actually turn the Passover paradox—where God's people have often been divided and do not know what to do—into a Passover outreach. This Passover outreach will serve as a positive testimony to not only your congregational members, but also those who are invited to the celebration. You will have a great opportunity to be salt and light to those in attendance. You might just have the privilege of leading some of the lost to the reality that Yeshua was sacrificed for their sins and resurrected from the dead.

The benefits of using the season of Passover as an outreach toward others far outweigh the possible negatives. People exposed to this annual activity will have an entirely new understanding of what this season means for those who have experienced the deliverance available in the Messiah of Israel. Not only will they understand more clearly the availability of deliverance from the clutches of sin, but they will be presented with the eternal solution that is only found in Him. Being reminded every year of Yeshua's prophetic fulfillment as Passover Lamb, the sinless unleavened Bread of Life, and the firstfruits of those resurrected—will instruct God's people more and more about His ongoing plan of salvation history, as this season conveys timeless messages that need not be forgotten any more.

Be encouraged in your making Passover an opportunity for outreach to those beyond the walls of your congregation or fellowship. Give those with whom you assemble the privilege of exercising love for one another, which will confirm to those in the wider world that you are loving disciples of the Messiah. Be a blessing to others! Our constant prayer should be that as we look ahead to the years before us, the Spring festivals of the Lord will be met with great joy and anticipation as the work of His Kingdom continues in our midst. Let us always take advantage of the opportunities that we have during this special season!

~13~

Celebrating Passover Today

Margaret McKee Huey

"These are the appointed times of the LORD, holy convocations which you shall proclaim at the times appointed for them. In the first month, on the fourteenth day of the month at twilight is the LORD's Passover. Then on the fifteenth day of the same month there is the Feast of Unleavened Bread to the LORD; for seven days you shall eat unleavened bread. On the first day you shall have a holy convocation; you shall not do any laborious work. But for seven days you shall present an offering by fire to the LORD. On the seventh day is a holy convocation; you shall not do any laborious work. Then the LORD spoke to Moses saying, 'Speak to the sons of Israel, and say to them, "When you enter the land which I am going to give to you and reap its harvest, then you shall bring in the sheaf of the first fruits of your harvest to the priest. And he shall wave the sheaf before the LORD for you to be accepted; on the day after the Sabbath the priest shall wave it...It is to be a perpetual statue throughout your generations in all your dwelling places"'" (Leviticus 23: 4-11, 14b).

Since 1995, our entire family has been in a state of transition concerning the Spring holiday celebrations. As evangelical Christians, we were originally raised to celebrate and observe Easter, thinking that it was indeed a Biblical holy day. The account of the resurrection of the Messiah was recorded for us in the Gospels, after all. Were not the events so profound that the sky darkened, an earthquake occurred, the curtain in the Temple was torn in two, and the Messiah was raised from the dead?[1]

But how many of our past Easter celebrations have only had the simplicity of the wonderful message of "He is risen!"? Most of us who celebrated Easter did not hold to this simplicity of observance. Instead, the Easter we remember is full of traditional practices that have little or nothing to do with the event that happened in Jerusalem at the Feast of Passover and Unleavened Bread in the Land of Israel two millennia ago, when our Lord was crucified and resurrected. And, it is safe to say that it is **these traditional practices** that so many of us have been challenged to stop. So then, how did the Biblical Passover change to Easter in the Church?

In 325 C.E., the first ecumenical council in which the Eastern and Western Churches came together was the Council of Nicea. The Emperor Constantine headed this Council, which had its purpose to settle the Arian controversy so that

---

[1] Cf. Matthew 27:33-28:1-10; Mark 15:22-16:6; Luke 23:33-24:12.

the Church could be united and at peace. Although this Council had many goods points that it embraced, it also was the first time state authority involved itself in theological affairs. It set a precedent where later church councils, at state insistence, officially pulled away from the Hebraic understanding of the Biblical practices.

Various pockets of Christians had been celebrating the Passover (or a kind of Passover) with the Jews on the 14th of Nisan until this time. Many of the Eastern churches, claiming to follow a tradition delivered to them by Polycarp, a disciple of the Apostle John, were remembering the resurrection of Yeshua ("Easter") three days after the Jewish Passover on any day of the week.[2] The Western Church strongly believed that this practice had to be stopped, and determined that Easter should be calculated on the Sunday that came next after the full moon of the vernal equinox. In 341 C.E. the Council of Antioch forbade Christians from celebrating the Jewish Passover at all, and ordered them to only celebrate Easter:

> "But if any one of those who preside in the Church, whether he be bishop, presbyter, or deacon, shall presume, after this decree, to exercise his own private judgment to the subversion of the people and to the disturbance of the churches, by observing Easter [at the same time] with the Jews, the holy Synod decrees that he shall thenceforth be an alien from the Church, as one who not only heaps sins upon himself, but who is also the cause of destruction and subversion to many; and it deposes not only such persons themselves from their ministry, but those also who after their deposition shall presume to communicate with them" (Canon 1).[3]

We are not to continue to embrace non-Biblical practices that have been handed down to us in ignorance by our forbearers. While the historical circumstances of the early centuries of Christianity are undoubtedly complicated, there were some things that took place which were not good. Why were some traditional practices, handed down to us over the centuries, never really fully evaluated? Why do Christians today follow some traditions that were rooted in ancient anti-Semitism? Were many of our ancestors just ignorant, not knowing what to do? In some ways, yes. Too many were not fully grounded in the ways of God's Torah, and many did not know any better. They did not know that we were not to mix the holy with the profane, and that it was inappropriate for the institutional Church to divorce the commemoration of the Messiah's resurrection from the season of Passover.

Even the godly Protestant Reformers, who saw many of Catholicism's errors four to five centuries ago, did not have the benefit of the Jewish-Christian dialogue and relations that we have today—which has led more modern Bible teachers to search out the Hebraic Roots and Jewish origins of our faith. It has forced them to consider Jewish literature and perspectives on the New Testament, that previous generations were unable to do. For those of us who have now been awakened and have embraced a Messianic walk with Yeshua, we have the benefit of historical information that people in the past did not have. We need to learn to obey the

---

[2] Cf. "Quartodecimans," in Bercot, 547.

[3] *The Post-Nicene Fathers*, P. Schaff, ed.; <u>Libronix Digital Library System 1.od: Church History Collection</u>. MS Windows XP. Garland, TX: Galaxie Software. 2002.

Lord in a more comprehensive way, which will not only cause us to obey Him more fully, but also be enriched spiritually!

Personal Family Testimony

For our family, the walk of faith that has led us to become Messianic has caused us to actively change three areas in our faith observance that are different from our Church upbringing. First, we now observe the *Shabbat* rest, instead of Sunday Church. Second, we now eat Biblically kosher, instead of anything that our palate desires. And third, we now observe the Biblical appointed times that are given to us in the Torah, instead of the Church holidays that were passed down from the Catholic Church to the Protestant ones.

Has this transition been an easy one? No! Family traditions are hard to change. Yet, I am happy to say that within our own small family, we have been able to adopt the Biblical practices and drop the un-Biblical ones "fairly" easily. The main reasons that the changes have not been too hard are two-fold. First, we earnestly desire to be as Biblical as possible, and to continue down the path that our Reforming and Protesting ancestors did before us. Not all of them, unfortunately, were able to see the larger picture of the Torah, holidays, *Shabbat*, food, etc. that we see today. Yet as we have changed our habits and lifestyle, we have tried to do so in a way that is honoring and respectful to those who have preceded us in the faith. And second, we desire as a family to walk and to be like our Messiah Yeshua in all things, as much as possible. We use the Spring holiday season as a time to reflect on some extremely important themes of God's plan of salvation history.

I can say that in the continual transformation that our family has been through to become as Biblical as possible, we have been able to put away our Easter observance with few difficulties. Instead, we now celebrate Passover, the Festival of Unleavened Bread, and we remember Yeshua as the First Fruits of the resurrection. We look forward to the season of Counting the Omer to *Shavuot*, and how the Passover season itself is preceded a month earlier by *Purim*. Our family has come to the conclusion that to observe these things is to emulate what Yeshua did. That alone is reason enough to remember them!

Yeshua's Last Supper was the Passover meal or *seder*, in which He spoke to His Disciples concerning His atoning death that was shortly to come. He was crucified as our Passover Lamb when priests were killing Passover lambs in Jerusalem. Yeshua was raised from the dead after three days and nights, being resurrected as firstfruits unto the Father. Needless to say, we no longer have any desire to color Easter eggs, have Easter baskets, or go on Easter egg hunts! The season of Passover has brought a significant and deep richness to our faith that we dare not ignore any more.

Family Observance

Our family has come to that place in our lives where memories of Easter are just that—memories. Yes, we have extended family and friends who do not understand why we no longer have Easter baskets, Easter eggs, egg hunts, sunrise services, and Easter ham dinners with yeast rolls. In fact, they never understood **why we did not have the Easter Bunny when we still celebrated Easter!** And as much as I love my extended family and friends, I love my Savior more. It is He whom I wish to please! So, with that in mind, I want to share with you just a bit of our family celebration of the Passover season.

The wonderful thing about the Biblical holidays it that our Heavenly Father wants us to remember these great events by celebrating them! Passover has so many wonderful truths that we can commemorate. When Yeshua observed Passover during His life, He did so in Jerusalem, with the ultimate fulfillment seeing Him sacrificed as the Passover Lamb of God. We can delight in rejoining with our Jewish brethren by celebrating Passover with them, and we consider how without the original Exodus, we would not be able to be fully delivered from our sins in salvation that Yeshua now brings to us.

Our family observes these festivities very practically. First, we take the time after *Purim* (one month before Passover) to start our Spring cleaning. This cleaning culminates in getting all of the leaven or yeast out of our house before the first night of Passover. Second, we prepare to have our own family Passover *seder* meal with all of our best china and the traditional elements to remember the first Passover, and Yeshua's Last Seder, as we are instructed to do in the Torah. (See **Liturgical Resources** section for **Passover**.) And third, we often attend a much larger congregational *seder* the next night. During the Festival of Unleavened Bread, we continue to remember the story of the Exodus, as well as what transpired after the Messiah's crucifixion. We do not eat any leavened bread, just like the Israelites who came out of Egypt.

We also remember the resurrection of our Messiah Yeshua, and how His Disciples found the tomb empty. We remember the two who walked to the town of Emmaus with Yeshua after the resurrection, and how they did not recognize Him until they broke *matzah* with Him. We also remember how they said He had opened up the Scriptures to them as they walked on the road and that their hearts burned within them (Luke 24:13-35).

The whole Passover season is a wonderful time for our family to truly reflect on what the Lord has done for us as His blood has been put on the doorposts of our hearts, so that we too will be passed over by the death angel and walk in resurrected life. A general feeling of family and fellowship should permeate each day. The love of the Messiah should be strongly felt in each home, and what His sacrificial work has accomplished should cause us each to be highly reflective on our spirituality. Our family can truly say that it is not missing out on anything during the Spring holiday season!

Loving Each Other

If our extended family or friends question why we do not celebrate Easter any more, we make sure to let them know that even though we have stopped practicing non-Biblical traditions that Easter now represents—**we still very much believe in the Biblical account of the resurrection of Yeshua as it is recorded in the Gospels.** We believe that He is the Passover Lamb of God. We believe that His Last Supper was His Last Seder. We believe that He was crucified, just as a blameless Passover lamb would be killed. We believe that He rose from the dead on the third day. Although our family and friends sometimes do not understand why we are doing all these "Jewish" things, they still very much see that we have not stopped believing in the Messiah. *Many are sincerely intrigued,* and are provoked to some kind of thought.

Yet many of today's Messianics take a different approach when explaining why Easter is no longer a part of their yearly celebrations. Many have been taught, and we believe wrongly, to announce to Christian family and friends that: "We don't celebrate Easter any more, because it is pagan!" If this has been something that you have ever done before, then your Christian family and friends will often think you do not believe in the crucifixion or resurrection of Jesus—or even *in Him* anymore! Your problem is actually not with these Biblical events, but rather with traditional observances that have become associated with them. I would encourage you to **not** let "Easter is pagan!" be your testimony to others during this special and holy time of year. Instead, invite people to your home to be made a part of your Passover table. Let your family and friends partake of the richness that you have partaken of.

How do we deal with our extended family and friends who still do not understand why we are not celebrating Easter like they are? Our family believes that the restoration of the Spring holidays is a blessing to us! We, who are to walk as Messiah Yeshua walked, must reach out to others in love at this time, when the Father is restoring His appointed times to His people. We are to show others that we believe in the Messiah *even more than we ever have*, during the time of Passover.

Yeshua told us that people would know that we are His disciples by the love that we have for one another (John 13:35). So, let us love our family and friends in such a way concerning these feasts that they will be drawn to us, and not repelled. It is only through our unconditional love for them that one day they will want to know what we know about walking like the Messiah. One day they will want to know why we have become thoroughly Messianic. This can happen when we learn to be a blessing to others, during this special season.

~14~

A Summarization
of Shavuot Traditions

Margaret McKee Huey and J.K. McKee

Shavuot (שָׁבֻעוֹת)[1] is one of three pilgrimage festivals that is commanded in the Torah (Exodus 23:14-17; Deuteronomy 16:16). In Hebrew, its name means "weeks," derived from the command in Deuteronomy 16:19, "You shall count seven weeks for yourself; you shall begin to count seven weeks from the time you begin to put the sickle to the standing grain." Many Christians know *Shavuot* from its Greek-derived name "Pentecost," as *Pentēkostē* (πεντηκοστή) means "fiftieth," indicative of the fifty days that are to be counted between Passover and this time.

In Biblical times, *Shavuot* was originally celebrated as a harvest festival. The Torah calls it "the Festival of the Harvest, first fruits of your labor that you sow in the field" (Exodus 23:16, Alter). It would occur at the end of the barley crop and the beginning of the wheat crop, also known as *Chag haKatzir* or Harvest Festival. In Rabbinical literature it is commonly referred to as *Yom haBikkurim* or the Day of First Fruits to commemorate the new wheat crop. The Mishnah records that this was a time of great rejoicing:

"Those [who come] from nearby bring figs and grapes, but those [who come] from afar bring dried figs and raisins. And an ox walks before them, its horns overlaid with gold, and a wreath of olive [leaves] on its head. A flutist plays before them until they arrive near Jerusalem. [Once] they arrived near Jerusalem, they sent [a messenger] ahead of them [to announce their arrival], and they decorated their firstfruits. The high officers, chiefs, and treasurer [of the Temple] come out to meet them. According to the rank of the entrants, they would [determine which of these officials would] go out. And all the craftsmen of Jerusalem stand before them and greet them, [saying], 'Brothers, men of such and such a place, you have come in peace'" (m.*Bikkurim* 3:3).[2]

Surely, when we come to celebrate *Shavuot* as one of the Lord's appointed times as Messianic Believers today, we are to remember how it was commemorated in ancient times. Wherever we may be from, we are to open our

---

[1] Pronounced as *Shavuos* in the Ashkenazic Jewish tradition.
[2] Margaret Wenig Rubenstein and David Weiner, trans., in Neusner, *Mishnah*, pp 172-173.

arms to our fellow brothers and sisters and tell them "*Shalom*, you have come in peace!" and be hospitable in the Spirit of the Lord.

Going Before the Lord

"You shall bring in from your dwelling places two *loaves* of bread for a wave offering, made of two-tenths *of an ephah*; they shall be of a fine flour, baked with leaven as first fruits to the LORD. Along with the bread you shall present seven one year old male lambs without defect, and a bull of the herd and two rams; they are to be a burnt offering to the LORD, with their grain offering and their drink offerings, an offering by fire of a soothing aroma to the LORD. You shall also offer one male goat for a sin offering and two male lambs one year old for a sacrifice of peace offerings. The priest shall then wave them with the bread of the first fruits for a wave offering with two lambs before the LORD; they are to be holy to the LORD for the priest" (Leviticus 23:17-20).

When celebrating *Shavuot*, it is clear that the Torah itself does not offer that many instructions concerning its observance. The first command is to bring "two loaves made of two-tenths of an ephah of fine flour, baked with yeast, as a wave offering of firstfruits to the LORD" (NIV). Also to be offered before God are "seven yearling lambs without blemish, one bull of the herd, and two rams, with their meal offerings and libations, an offering by fire of pleasing odor to the LORD" (NJPS). The third set of offerings to be delivered up are "one he-goat as a sin-offering, and two lambs in their first year as feast peace-offerings" (ATS). All of the offerings are to be, as the Hebrew states, *qodesh yih'yu l'ADONAI l'kohen* (לַכֹּהֵן קֹדֶשׁ יִהְיוּ לַיהוָה), "holy to the LORD for the priest."

The challenge when considering *Shavuot* today, either as Messianic Believers, or simply as a member of the Jewish community, is that much of it is focused around being a harvest festival with animal sacrifices. Without a doubt, *Shavuot* is intended to be a time when we are **to go before God and rejoice**. Simply being alive and healthy are adequate reasons enough for us to go before the Lord. But, much of this was intended to be done in Jerusalem at the Temple. How are we to celebrate *Shavuot* today?

Shavuot and the Word of God

The most significant Jewish tradition associated with *Shavuot* is the connection between the Feast of Weeks and the giving of the Torah. This belief was extant sometime during the Second Temple era, as the Talmud refers to "*Pentecost: it is the day on which the Torah was given*" (b.*Pesachim* 68b).[3] Consequently, most celebrations of *Shavuot* following the destruction of the Temple are focused as an anniversary of commemorating the giving of the Ten Commandments to Moses. The Torah portion associated with *Shavuot* is the reading of the Ten Commandments (Exodus 19:1-20:26), and apparently "This section was read daily in the Temple."[4]

Much of our celebration surrounding *Shavuot* should be focused around the Word of God as a great gift that our Father has given us. Of course, the Word of God was not *exclusively given* at Mount Sinai, but the scene of Sinai covered in fire

---

[3] *The Babylonian Talmud: A Translation and Commentary.*
[4] Eisenberg, 299.

and smoke and surrounded by the very presence of the Almighty is something awesome to contemplate, and *Shavuot* is a worthy time for us to remember it. When we all enter into fellowship with one another and focus on the goodness of what He has done for us, we need to remember that the easiest way to focus on our Creator is to examine the Scriptures He has given us for our life's instruction.

It is interesting that just as during Passover we are commanded to eat unleavened bread before the Lord, that on *Shavuot* the priest was to offer two leavened loaves. Many Jewish commentators have connected the offering of leavened loaves to the giving of the Torah on Mount Sinai. Ronald L. Eisenberg summarizes this view in *The JPS Guide to Jewish Traditions*:

"Bringing the leavened loaves on Shavuot may indicate that the giving of the Torah at Mount Sinai on that date should be understood as the culmination of the process of redemption from slavery that began on Passover, when only matzah could be consumed. Just as the two loaves marked the staple of our physical existence, so the historical process that began with the Exodus from Egypt and culminated with the giving of the Torah reflected the essence of our spiritual existence."[5]

The teachings of Yeshua the Messiah mirror the fact that bread alone is not sufficient for our well-being. Yeshua refuted Satan in the wilderness, "It is written, 'MAN SHALL NOT LIVE ON BREAD ALONE, BUT ON EVERY WORD THAT PROCEEDS OUT OF THE MOUTH OF GOD'" (Matthew 4:4; cf. Luke 4:4). Of course, Yeshua was quoting directly from Deuteronomy 8:3, where Moses reminded the Ancient Israelites, "He humbled you and let you be hungry, and fed you with manna which you did not know, nor did your fathers know, that He might make you understand that man does not live by bread alone, but man lives by everything that proceeds out of the mouth of the LORD." When we celebrate *Shavuot*, how many of us stop to consider the importance of the Word of God in our lives, and how important it is to not only know the Scriptures—but actually be able to *live them out*?

Miscellaneous Jewish Traditions

Some Jewish traditions have developed since Second Temple times that can be edifying to the Messianic community. However, it is important to note that since *Shavuot* is so innately connected to the Temple service, that not all of the traditions intended to augment the absence of the Temple are necessarily good. Obviously, the study of God's Word *at any time*, including *Shavuot*, **is something to be encouraged.**

A major custom that is observed in many segments of the Orthodox Jewish community is *Tikkun leil Shavuot*, meaning "the Prepared [texts] of the night of Shavuot." This is an all-night vigil that was actually developed by Jewish Kabbalists, and the tradition became "devoted to the study of passages from the Bible, Talmud, and Zohar. The popular explanation is that staying up all night on the eve of Shavuot atones for the behavior of the Israelites at Sinai, who according to tradition slept late that morning and had to be awakened by Moses...an opposite view is that this practice is based on the legend that thunder and lightning kept the

---

[5] Ibid., 298.

Israelites awake and trembling all night while Moses was on Mount Sinai receiving the Torah."[6]

Some in Messianic congregations choose to observe a kind of all-night vigil during *Shavuot*, studying the Scriptures or focusing on some kind of Biblical topic. This should not be discouraged, but it should be noted that this custom gained popularity by Kabbalists who believed the study would help atone for them. As Believers in Messiah Yeshua, He alone provides our atonement, and any kind of study should be to uplift Him and thus edify one another. It is interesting that "In some communities, the Shavuot eve study session concludes with the only sunrise service of the Jewish year, a symbol either of the light of the Torah or of the Jews as a 'light to the nations' (Isa. 49:6)."[7] Certainly, if you choose to stay up all night on the eve of *Shavuot*, do so with the intention of the Lord using you as a light to others.

Common Scriptures that are examined by the Jewish community may include an all-night reading of the entire Book of Psalms during the eve of *Shavuot*. This is influenced by a belief that David, author of many of the psalms, was born and died on *Shavuot*. In certain Sephardic Jewish communities, a *ketubah* or marriage contract is read before the ark containing the Torah scroll in the synagogue, per the opinion that God was "married" to Israel at Mount Sinai. Another common text read at *Shavuot* is the Book of Ruth, as Ruth is connected closely to David as his great-grandmother, and because the story occurs at harvest time (Ruth 2:23).[8]

During *Shavuot* as a harvest time, it is also not uncommon for Jewish synagogues to be elaborately decorated in plants and flowers. This is frequently based on Proverbs 3:18, which says that the Torah "is a tree of life to those who take hold of her, and happy are all who hold her fast." Rabbinic exegesis on Exodus 34:3 connects Mount Sinai to originally being a great green mountain with trees and shrubs, and so by decorating one's place of worship, we are connected back to that idyllic setting.

Dairy foods and honey are traditionally eaten during *Shavuot* for a number of important reasons. One reason is the Jewish view that Song of Songs 4:11, "honey and milk are under your tongue," pertains to the Torah. Another view is that the prohibition of boiling a kid in its mother's milk is given right after the offerings for *Shavuot* are detailed: "You shall bring the choice first fruits of your soil into the house of the LORD your God. You are not to boil a young goat in the milk of its mother" (Exodus 23:19). Yet another opinion is "that the Israelites [were] exposed for the first time to the wondrous world of Torah…like newborns…[and] just as babies drink only milk, so Jews commemorate the moment at Sinai by drinking and eating only dairy foods."[9]

A traditional food eaten among Ashkenazic Jews during *Shavuot* are cheese blintzes. These are thin crepes filled with various sweet cheeses, and often topped with fruits or jams. In some other communities triangular dumplings are eaten stuffed with three types of cheese, because the Bible consists of three parts (Law, Prophets, Writings), the Torah was given by God in the third month, through

---

[6] Ibid., 299.
[7] Ibid.
[8] Ibid.
[9] Ibid., 300.

Moses who was the third child born to his parents, to a people divided into three groups (priest, Levite, and Israelite).[10]

Another important feature among non-Orthodox Jews is a ceremony of confirmation, where teenagers are acknowledged as having completed a formal course of study on the Torah and commit themselves to its teachings. Sometimes these are *bar/bat mitzvah* proceedings, but not always.[11]

Shavuot for Messianics

"Pentecost" in Christian tradition has some equal theological significance as does *Shavuot* for Judaism. The Day of Pentecost is most commonly associated as being the time when the Holy Spirit was poured out upon those gathered at the Upper Room. Yeshua the Messiah had promised His Disciples, "you will receive power when the Holy Spirit has come upon you; and you shall be My witnesses both in Jerusalem, and in all Judea and Samaria, and even to the remotest part of the earth" (Acts 1:8). This was the time when the 120 Believers gathered were miraculously empowered to speak foreign languages or "tongues" (Acts 2:6), and three thousand new converts were evangelized and saved (Acts 2:41). From this point onward the Book of Acts records a massive evangelistic campaign throughout the Mediterranean world. In fact, many of the first Messianic congregations outside of the Land of Israel were likely started by those who had traveled great distances to come observe *Shavuot* at the Temple.[12]

In Christianity, though, Pentecost is commonly viewed as "mark[ing] the shifting of God's redemptive purpose from a particular people (the descendants of Abraham via Isaac and Jacob) to all peoples. On that day the Church was formed and empowered for its worldwide mission; the event thus marks the resumption of universal history, with which the Bible begins (Gen. 1-11)" (*ISBE*).[13] As Messianic Believers, who understand ourselves to all be a part of the Commonwealth of Israel (Ephesians 2:11-12), how are we to understand *Shavuot*? Even though *Shavuot*, as a Biblical festival, was not the "birth of the Church,"[14] the *Shavuot* when the Spirit was poured out did signal the beginning of a worldwide expansion of the good news of the God of Israel and His Messiah Yeshua. How many of us as Messianic Believers, because of the high focus on "Israel," often forget that Israel is to be a light to the whole world?

Consider the fact that there are two loaves of bread commanded to be offered by the high priest before God at *Shavuot*. Why is this the case? What do these two loaves represent? These two loaves represent Israel *and* the nations—because the high priest did not *serve Israel exclusively*. The author of Hebrews writes that "every high priest taken from among men is appointed on behalf of men in things pertaining to God, in order to offer both gifts and sacrifices for sins" (Hebrews 5:1). Every priest of Israel that served before God serves "mortals" (NRSV) or "humans"

---

[10] Ibid., pp 300-301.

[11] Ibid., 302.

[12] This notably includes the mixed congregation(s) of Jewish and non-Jewish Believers in Rome, to whom Paul wrote in his Epistle to the Romans, and who many expositors (ourselves included) believe could have possibly been the primary audience of the anonymous Epistle to the Hebrews.

[13] A.F. Glasser, "Pentecost," in *ISBE*, 3:757.

[14] Consult the article "When Did 'the Church' Begin?" by J.K. McKee.

(Grk. *anthrōpōn*, ἀνθρώπων).[15] Those who came to the *Shavuot* event when the Spirit was poured out came from all over the Jewish Diaspora, and this included proselytes. They did not just come from among Jews living in Israel:

"Parthians, Medes and Elamites; residents of Mesopotamia, Judea and Cappadocia, Pontus and Asia, Phrygia and Pamphylia, Egypt and the parts of Libya near Cyrene; visitors from Rome (both Jews and converts to Judaism); Cretans and Arabs—we hear them declaring the wonders of God in our own tongues!" (Acts 2:9-11, NIV).

Shavuot is a time when we as Messianic Believers certainly need to focus on the regenerative work of the Holy Spirit in our lives. But *Shavuot*, perhaps more than anything else, is a time when **we need to understand the global vision of God.** According to some Rabbinical opinions on Deuteronomy 1:5, when God delivered His commandments to Moses on Mount Sinai, they were delivered in the seventy languages of humanity that existed at the time—*meaning that they were not for Israel exclusively.* Israel just happened to be the vessel God would use to convey His good news to others.

That has still not changed. As Believers in Yeshua, we are all a part of Israel via our faith. The responsibility is still the same, but the means are much easier. The Torah was given by God to Israel at the first *Shavuot*, and many years later the Holy Spirit was poured out on another *Shavuot*. We now have to take God's two most powerful evangelistic tools: His Law and His Spirit, and be empowered to change the world. *Shavuot* is one of the most significant displays of our Heavenly Father's *salvation history* plan for the world.

When we celebrate *Shavuot*, we need to be committed to do the work of the evangelist—making sure that all know Yeshua as their Lord and Savior. We as Messianics can do this by not only knowing Yeshua for who He is in the writings of the Apostles, but also in the Scriptures that precede Him. It begins by us knowing that the Torah is to reveal the sin in our lives, and why we desperately need Him. At each *Shavuot*, let us celebrate the festival with a fullness that only those who have both the Torah *and* the Holy Spirit can experience!

---

[15] We do note that the priesthood of Melchizedek, which supersedes the Levitical priesthood, with much further clarity serves all people. For a further discussion of this subject, consult *Hebrews for the Practical Messianic* by J.K. McKee.

~15~

The Message of Ruth

J.K. McKee

The Book of Ruth is a text that people turn to when they need to be reminded of the goodness and kindness of God's chosen toward strangers, and how He demonstrates His faithfulness through the actions of normal people. Elements common to the human condition, including: life, death, hardness, sustenance, love, and happiness are all the things that make the story of Ruth so important to the Biblical narrative. We consider Ruth when we want to be reminded about the acceptance that God displays toward us, and how He desires us to all be redeemed and be one with Him.

The account of Ruth begins during the time of the judges in Israel, when there was a famine in the land (1:1). Because the famine was so significant, Elimelech, his wife Naomi, and their two sons had to move to Moab to live in order to survive (1:2). While living in Moab, Elimelech dies (1:3). The two sons marry Moabite women, one of them being Ruth (1:4), but after a period of ten years both of the sons die, "and Naomi was left without her two sons and her husband" (1:5). A dilemma arises for Naomi, as to what to do next with her life.

The good news is that Naomi hears "that the LORD had come to the aid of his people by providing food for them" (1:6). As she prepares to return to the Land of Israel, she tells her two daughters-in-law, "go back, each of you, to your mother's home. May the LORD show kindness to you, as you have shown to your dead and to me. May the LORD grant that each of you will find rest in the home of another husband" (1:8-9a). The two daughters-in-law are distraught, declaring, "We will go back with you to your people" (1:9b). But Naomi tells them that she is unlikely to remarry, much less have any more sons for them to marry (1:12-13). The first daughter-in-law, Orpah, kisses her goodbye, "but Ruth clung to her" (1:14). As she leaves, Naomi encourages Ruth to do the same, but Ruth tells her very clearly: "Don't urge me to leave you or to turn back from you. Where you go I will go, and where you stay I will stay. Your people will be my people and your God my God" (1:16). Ruth commits to staying beside Naomi, and that only "death separates you and me" (1:17). "When Naomi realized that Ruth was determined to go with her, she stopped urging her" (1:18).

Both Naomi and Ruth make their way to Bethlehem, whose inhabitants somehow recognize that Naomi has returned. Yet, Naomi is clear to tell the people, "Don't call me Naomi...Call me Mara, because the Almighty has made my life very bitter. I went away full, but the LORD has brought me back empty…the Almighty has brought misfortune upon me" (1:20-21). The reason she says this to her old neighbors is quite clear: it was greatly bitter to be a widow in the Ancient Near East—one with no husband, sons, or any significant others to support her. Both Naomi and Ruth, while having come to Bethlehem in Israel, still find themselves destitute.

Naomi is not without any hope. She does have "a relative on her husband's side, from the clan of Elimelech, a man of standing, whose name was Boaz" (2:1). Ruth goes to glean from the fields, so that the two of them might have food to eat (2:2), and as she does so, "she found herself working in a field belonging to Boaz" (2:3). While she is gleaning, Boaz arrives, greets the harvesters, and asks "Whose young woman is that?" (2:5). A foreman explains to Boaz that she is a Moabitess, having recently arrived in Bethlehem with Naomi (2:6). Boaz decides to be quite generous to her, saying, "My daughter, listen to me. Don't go and glean in another field and don't go away from here. Stay here with my servant girls. Watch the field where the men are harvesting, and follow along after the girls. I have told the men not to touch you. And whenever you are thirsty, go and get a drink from the water jars the men have filled" (2:8-9).

Ruth is surprised at Boaz' graciousness, and asks him, "Why have I found such favor in your eyes that you notice me—a foreigner? "(2:10). Boaz simply says, "I've been told all about what you have done for your mother-in-law since the death of your husband—how…you left your homeland and came to live with a people you did not know before. May the LORD repay you for what you have done. May you be richly rewarded by the LORD, the God of Israel, under whose wings you have come to take refuge" (2:11-12). Boaz then invites her to come and eat all that she wants (2:14), and he instructs his men to show her some special treatment when she comes to glean again (2:15-16). When Ruth returns to Naomi that evening, all she can ask her is, "Where did you glean today?...Blessed be the man who took notice of you!" (2:19a). Ruth then tells Naomi that it was Boaz (2:19b).

Naomi explains to Ruth how important Boaz has been for her family: "He has not stopped showing kindness to the living and the dead…That man is our close relative; he is one of our kinsman-redeemers" (2:20). A kinsman-redeemer[1] was one whose responsibility it was to redeem family lands and pay outstanding debts, to make sure that family members were not reduced to complete servitude (Numbers 27:8-11). Naomi, with little doubt, considered herself to be of "the dead," having lost her husband and sons. Naomi advises her to stay close to Boaz' estate, as he will allow her to glean (2:22-23).

Naomi has the wisdom to wait and see what will become of Ruth and Boaz' new acquaintanceship. One day she tells Ruth, "My daughter, should I not try to find a home for you, where you will be well provided for? Is not Boaz…a kinsman of ours?" (3:1-2). Naomi instructs her to go to Boaz' threshing floor, wait until he eats and lies down, and then uncover his feet and lie down. She is to wear "perfume…and put on [her] best clothes" (3:3). Lying down next to one's feet was a customary, nonverbal way of requesting marriage in those days.[2]

Ruth follows Naomi's instructions. "When Boaz had finished eating and drinking and was in good spirits, he went over to lie down at the far end of the

---

[1] Heb. *go'elenu*; "one of our closest relatives" (NASU).
[2] *NIV Archaeological Study Bible*, 391.

grain pile. Ruth approached quietly, uncovered his feet and lay down. In the middle of the night something startled the man, and he turned and discovered a woman lying at his feet" (3:7-8). Awakening, Ruth tells Boaz, "Spread the corner of your garment over me, since you are a kinsman-redeemer" (3:9). Boaz cannot help but be impressed with her, as he has showed her kindness and beneficence since he first saw her. He responds with the words, "This kindness is greater than that which you showed earlier: You have not run after the younger men, whether rich or poor. And now, my daughter, don't be afraid. I will do for you all you ask. All my fellow townsmen know that you are a woman of noble character" (3:10-11).

Boaz then tells Ruth, "there is a kinsman-redeemer nearer than I. Stay here for the night, and in the morning if he wants to redeem, good; let him redeem. But if he is not willing, as surely as the LORD lives I will do it" (3:12-13). While Boaz was a close family member to Naomi, there was apparently another kinsman-redeemer who was much closer in relation. Because he was closer, he got the first choice of Ruth—but Boaz is clear to say that if he declines he will gladly take her. Boaz lets her return the next morning to Naomi, with "six measures of barley" (3:15) not wanting her to be empty-handed (3:16-17). Naomi is pleased with what has transpired, and is clear to tell Ruth: "Wait, my daughter, until you find out what happens. For the man will not rest until the matter is settled today" (3:18).

Boaz goes to the gate of the town, waiting for the closer kinsman-redeemer to arrive (4:1). Explaining the situation in front of the town elders, he tells the man, "Naomi, who has come back from Moab, is selling the piece of land that belonged to our brother Elimelech. I thought I should bring the matter to your attention and suggest that you buy it in the presence of the elders of my people. If you will redeem it, do so. But if you will not, tell me, so I will know. For no one has the right to do it except you, and I am next in line" (4:3-4). The man agrees, but then Boaz is keen to tell him, "On the day you buy the land from Naomi and from Ruth the Moabitess, you acquire the dead man's widow, in order to maintain the name of the dead with his property" (4:5). It is then that this kinsman-redeemer does not wish to acquire Naomi's land, as it may endanger his own estate (4:6). Boaz now has the right to acquire this property himself (4:8). Boaz then assertively declares to those gathered around him:

"Today you are witnesses that I have bought from Naomi all the property of Elimelech, Kilion and Mahlon. I have also acquired Ruth the Moabitess, Mahlon's widow, as my wife, in order to maintain the name of the dead with his property, so that his name will not disappear from among his family or from the town records. Today you are witnesses!" (4:9-10).

Those at the gate of the city express their desire that God would bless him, and that "the LORD make the woman who is coming into your home like Rachel and Leah, who together built up the house of Israel" (4:11). "So Boaz took Ruth and she became his wife" (4:12), and Ruth has a son. Naomi is restored to a place of having her needs taken care of, and God is clearly credited with sending her a kinsman-redeemer (4:14-15). Naomi helps to raise Boaz and Ruth's son, Obed. As the book closes, Obed "was the father of Jesse, the father of David" (4:16ff).

The Book of Ruth has a timeless message for every person who reads it, who needs to be reminded that when one joins to God's people, He is sure to provide. For some reason or another, the Moabitess Ruth knew there was something significant about Naomi's people and the God of Israel, and she did desire to join with them leaving Moab behind. Destitute and without a means of provision, Boaz takes a liking to Ruth, and is not only willing to purchase Naomi's land, but also take Ruth as his own wife. Boaz steps in as the kinsman-redeemer, when the closer kinsman-redeemer did not desire to take the required action. As idealistic as it may sound, the Book of Ruth concludes with a happy ending, and the reader is told that from the line of Boaz and Ruth would come King David.

While Ruth can surely be read and considered at any time of year, in the Jewish tradition Ruth is often contemplated during the festival of *Shavuot*. Why is this the case? It is because the giving of God's Torah on Mount Sinai to Israel is not to be an Israel-only affair. It is to be something that involves Israel reaching out beyond itself and serving the nations. Moab was one of the most rightly-hated nations by Israel, due to its great idolatry, abominations, and the child sacrifices it would offer to Molech. Yet in Ruth, a Moabite woman is nevertheless attracted to Israel's God, welcomed among Israel's people, and is shown true love by Boaz.

What does the Book of Ruth teach us as today's Messianics? It asks us to make sure that we are accomplishing that mission—of seeing that even those of some of the most hated people can be welcomed into the fold, and be shown all of the goodness and grace that God offers. Fulfilling this task is only intensified for those of us who believe in Yeshua, who has provided final atonement for all sin, and in emulating the example of His Apostles who accomplished this call to the max.[3]

---

[3] Consult the entry for the Book of Ruth in *A Survey of the Tanach for the Practical Messianic* for a summary of its date, composition, etc.

~16~

The Gospel According to Torah: It Happened at Shavuot!

Margaret McKee Huey

delivered live at Shavuot 2006, Orlando

As we approach the End of the Age, many people are being restored back to the Hebraic Roots of the faith. It is an exciting time to watch, as scales fall off of the eyes of many brothers and sisters in the Lord, as Jewish people come to faith in Messiah Yeshua, and non-Jewish Believers embrace a return to the First Century ways of the early Believers! People are returning to the ancient paths! People are starting to fully walk the way Yeshua walked!

We who are embracing a Messianic expression of faith are honoring the seventh-day *Shabbat* again. We have been encouraged to obey the words of Moses:

"Remember the Sabbath day, to keep it holy. Six days you shall labor and do all your work, but the seventh day is a Sabbath of the LORD your God; in it you shall not do any work, you or your son or your daughter, your male or your female servant or your cattle or your sojourner who stays with you. For in six days the LORD made the heavens and the earth, the sea and all that is in them, and rested on the seventh day; therefore the LORD blessed the Sabbath day and made it holy" (Exodus 20:8-10).[1]

We are studying the Torah on a weekly basis. In the Book of Acts, James the brother of Yeshua states the following about those who were coming into the faith in the First Century, who were not raised in the Synagogue, much like us today:

"For Moses [meaning, the first 5 books of the Bible called the Torah] from ancient generations has in every city those who preach him, since he is read in the synagogues every Sabbath" (Acts 15:21).[2]

We Messianics are observing the appointed times of the Lord:

"These are the appointed times of the LORD, holy convocations which you shall proclaim at the time appointed for them" (Leviticus 23:4-5, 6-44).

---

[1] For more information, consult the *Messianic Sabbath Helper* by Messianic Apologetics.

[2] For more information, consult the chapter "What Happened at the Jerusalem Council?" in *Torah In the Balance, Volume I* by J.K. McKee.

Moses goes on to teach about Passover, Unleavened Bread, the Feast of Weeks/Pentecost, the Feast of Trumpets, the Day of Atonement, and the Feast of Tabernacles.

We Messianics are practicing a set-apart, sanctified lifestyle by following commandments that will instruct us how to be purified from the things of the world, things like the dietary laws which teach us how to separate the holy from the profane. These are the words of James the Just, to the new followers of Yeshua who came from the nations, about their eating habits:

"But that we write to them that they abstain from things polluted by idols and from fornication and from *meats* strangled and from blood" (Acts 15:20).[3]

All of these things that we do as Messianic Believers compose what we often call being "Torah observant"—indicating that we "follow the commandments." In fact, in Revelation 12:17, it reads that the end-time saints are those "who keep the commandments of God and hold to the testimony of Yeshua."

I have just mentioned some of the different ways in which we are now actively keeping the commandments of God as never before, as we are striving to live like the First Century Believers—**but what about having the testimony of Yeshua?** Obeying God must be joined by knowing that we have been redeemed by the work of His Son. Let us look at what happened to Peter and the other Apostles on that first *Shavuot* fifty days after the resurrection of Yeshua—and only ten days after He had ascended into Heaven!

"And when the day of Pentecost had come, they were all together in one place. And suddenly there came from heaven a noise like a violent wind, and it filled the whole house where they were sitting. And there appeared to them tongues as of fire distributing themselves, and they rested on each of them. And they were all filled with the Holy Spirit and began to speak with other tongues, as the Spirit was giving them utterance. Now there were Jews living in Jerusalem, devout men, from every nation under heaven. And when this sound occurred, the multitude came together, and were bewildered, because they were each hearing them speak in his own language" (Acts 2:1-6).

On that first *Shavuot*, after the resurrection of Yeshua, Peter preaches to those who are gathered in Jerusalem. He says,

"Men of Israel, listen to these words: Yeshua the Nazarene, a man attested to you by God with miracles and wonders and signs which God performed through Him in your midst, just as you yourselves know" (Acts 2:22).

Peter then reviews the events of the life, death, and resurrection of Yeshua of Nazareth. Many had been in Jerusalem during these events, but others had come a long way, as they lived in the Diaspora, and had not been in Jerusalem to hear about the events surrounding Yeshua's execution. Peter recites a prophecy of the resurrection from Psalm 16, where David speaks of the Messiah who was to come and who was to be raised from the dead. Peter proclaims that he, the Apostles, and others have been witnesses to all of these events, and that it was the promise of the Holy Spirit being poured forth—that these people who were assembled had all just seen and heard on this *Shavuot*. But this next Scripture is the most important of all when they respond to Peter and the others:

---

[3] For more information, consult the article "To Eat or Not to Eat?" by J.K. McKee.

"Now when they heard this, they were **pierced to the heart**, and said to Peter, and the rest of the apostles. 'Brethren, what shall we do?' And Peter said to them, 'Repent, and let each of you be baptized in the name of Messiah Yeshua for the forgiveness of sins; and you shall receive the gift of the Holy Spirit. For the promise is for you and your children, and for all who are far off, as many as the Lord our God shall call to Himself'" (Acts 2:37-39).

It is recorded in the Book of Acts that three thousand were saved that day:

"And day by day continuing with one mind in the temple, and braking bread from house to house, they were taking their meals together with gladness and sincerity of heart, praising God, and having favor with all the people. And the Lord was adding to their number day by day those who were being saved" (Acts 2:46-47).

And as further recorded by Luke in Acts, Peter and the others continue to proclaim the gospel of salvation to all they interacted with, as they testified about the restoration of all things:

"Repent therefore and return, that your sins may be blotted out, in order that seasons of refreshing may come from the presence of the Lord; and that He may send Yeshua, the Messiah appointed for you, whom Heaven must receive until the time of restoration of all things, about which God spoke by the mouth of His holy prophets from antiquity" (Acts 3:19-21).

So, as part of this end-time move of the Lord today, while Believers are being restored back to the things of the First Century, and we learn to be a mixed assembly of Jewish and non-Jewish Believers in Yeshua—we have to be both keeping the commandments of God *and* sharing the testimony of Yeshua that we have. It is the testimony of Yeshua and truly being born again ourselves, and then the sharing of this gospel from Scripture, as Peter did, that we need to really emphasize! This is because whenever a wonderful move of God is at hand, the enemy always works overtime to see who he can deceive and devour. How much more so should we be on guard now, during this amazing time of restoration, when the Father is drawing people into a Messianic walk of faith from very diverse backgrounds?

We have to return to the spiritual experiences of that day of *Shavuot* and share salvation that comes from Yeshua. Righteousness does not come from trying to keep the commandments. Righteousness comes from the blood of Yeshua covering our sins, because we really can never completely keep the Torah. *This is why Yeshua died in our place.* This is why we have to repent of our sin nature and receive Him, be baptized or immersed in His name, and be filled with the Holy Spirit. And if we really are in the end-times (or at least getting closer), then we need to be very aware of the major end-time lie that Paul warns us about:

"[A]nd with all the deceivableness of unrighteousness in them that perish, because they received not the love of the truth, that they might be saved. And for this cause God shall send them strong delusion, that they should believe a lie" (2 Thessalonians 2:10-12).

Here is the question of this age: How can a person, who is coming back to the Hebraic Roots of the faith and being obedient to God's commandments, ever be swept away by the end-time strong delusion that appears to be for only the unrighteous people who are perishing? Could such a person be practicing a form of righteous living, yet really be unrighteous? Remember that on that day of *Shavuot* or Pentecost, those who heard Peter preach were people who followed the commandments—yet they were "pierced to the heart"—and said to Peter and the other Apostles, "Brethren, what shall we do?" Peter knew that they had been convicted about their sinful hearts, and that they had been pierced, so he was then able to tell them **to repent!**

Those gathered at Shavuot were "cut" (RSV, NIV) or "pierced to the heart" (NASB). Richmond Lattimore's translation renders it as "they were stricken to the heart." The verb used by Luke to describe this deep emotion is *katanussomai* (κατανύσσομαι), meaning to "be *pierced, stabbed* fig., of the feeling of sharp pain connected w. anxiety, remorse" (*BDAG*).[4] It is interesting to note that this verb is used in the Septuagint, in Genesis 34:7, to describe the intense pain of the Shechemites after they had circumcised themselves. Is not then this "pierced heart" the same as the circumcision of the heart that is required at the new birth?

So again, how can a person be unrighteous who is practicing righteous living?

The answer is very simple and yet so profound that it usually escapes even the most serious so-called "Believers." The answer is simply that "**they received not the love of the truth, that they might be saved**" (2 Thessalonians 2:10, KJV). *Might be saved?* Isn't that easy? Don't you just ask Yeshua or Jesus into your heart because you believe He is the Messiah? Those present with Peter at *Shavuot* found out that it was a heart issue.

The Answer

To find the answer to the question, we must determine what the "love of the truth" is. It is simply, yet profoundly, receiving the Divine *agapē* love that the Father uses by His Holy Spirit to bring us to the point of desiring, above all else, to find out the truth concerning ourselves so that we can repent and be saved. We have to earnestly, with our whole hearts, come to the point of being broken before a holy and righteous God to such a degree—that we finally realize that nothing we can do in or by ourselves will ever make us righteous. Our heart has to be pierced! We have to recognize that we, although made in the image of God, have also inherited the nature of our fallen ancestor, Adam. We have to come to the point of realizing just how much of a sinner we are!

Unfortunately, this gospel of salvation is rarely preached from many Christian or Messianic platforms today. The key, to understanding what the "love of the truth" is, is to come to grips with who we are ourselves. As Yeshua, so directly, told Nicodemus,

"Truly, truly, I say to you, unless one is born again he cannot see the kingdom of God…Are you the teacher of Israel and do not understand these things?" (John 3:3, 10).

The Lord further warns His listeners, who may study the Bible faithfully, that they are yet falling short:

"You search the Scriptures because you think that in them you have eternal life; it is these that testify about Me; and you are unwilling to come to Me so that you may have life" (John 5:39-40).

What is the key ingredient that so many of us overlook? **We have to truly understand why we need to be saved!** We have to have truly come to terms with

---

[4] *BDAG*, 523.

the hard fact that we are sinners and that we deserve to be forever separated from God. We have to have come to the realization that we do not have the power to even see the Kingdom of God in our natural, unregenerated state. We have to have come to terms with the fact that we could keep the commandments of the Torah perfectly, but still miss something.

We must realize that the vast majority of us have always been commandment breakers, and we are predisposed to always function in our flesh. We have to have truly come to the end of ourselves, and to have had our hearts broken concerning ourselves, so that we can honestly proclaim ourselves to be the sinners that we are! We have to have come to the end of ourselves with godly sorrow and have repented of our sin, which means to turn from those ways of sin, that we do indeed know we have committed. Listen to the following words of Yeshua concerning repentance for the sinner:

"I tell you, no, but unless you repent, you will all likewise perish" (Luke 13:3).

"I tell you that in the same way, there will be *more* joy in heaven over one sinner who repents than over ninety-nine righteous persons who need no repentance" (Luke 15:7).

Take important notice of these words that Yeshua spoke to His followers, just following His resurrection:

"Then He opened their minds to understand the Scriptures, and He said to them, 'Thus it is written, that the Messiah would suffer and rise again from the dead the third day, and that repentance for forgiveness of sins would be proclaimed in His name to all the nations, beginning from Jerusalem'" (Luke 24:45-47).

The Apostle Paul teaches us the difference between the sorrow that is prompted by God and the sorrow that comes from the world:

"For the sorrow that is according to the will of God produces repentance without regret, leading to salvation; but the sorrow of the world produces death" (2 Corinthians 7:10).

In order to be saved, we need to have grasped hold of the reality that Messiah Yeshua died in our place to cover us with His atoning sacrifice for our sin—but we have to have died to ourselves before we can lay claim to this sin covering. In Hebrews 9:22 we read,

"This is the blood of the covenant which God has commanded you…and according to the Law, one may almost say, all things are cleansed with blood, and without shedding of blood these is no forgiveness" (Hebrews 9:20, 22).

We have to have died to our pride, our independence, our self-justification, our self-righteousness, or self-esteem—in essence, **we have to have died to ourselves.** In the fallen state of people, God Himself moves on them through the words in His Torah and brings to their mind and soul that they are sinners and not keeping the commandments out of cleansed hearts, *if at all.* He moves them to be real with themselves and admit that they have fallen far from His glory. It is the sorrow that He works in them that allows them to be real with themselves and want to repent with their whole hearts. The sorrow that is from the world is that which makes us sorry that we were caught doing something; it does not cause us to really want to change and turn—to repent. This worldly sorrow will only led to our spiritual death in the long run. We will never be saved if we only have worldly sorrow.

My friends, this message of salvation is rarely preached or taught anymore. It is not a popular message, but it is the message of the **pierced heart.** It is the message that was first delivered to the saints by Yeshua and was proclaimed by all of the Apostles. It is called the gospel of salvation! It is the salvation that saves us from the penalties of not keeping Torah fully. Let's repeat again the words of Peter right after that first *Shavuot* when the Holy Spirit was poured out on those who believed and repented:

"Repent therefore and return, that your sins may be blotted out, in order that seasons of refreshing may come from the presence of the Lord; and that He may send Yeshua, the Messiah appointed for you, whom Heaven must receive until the time of restoration of all things, about which God spoke by the mouth of His holy prophets from antiquity" (Acts 3:19-21).

Personal Testimony

I was raised in a fairly typical American Christian home in the 1950s and 1960s. I went to Church and Sunday School on Sunday. I sang in the Church Youth Choir from the ages of 10 through 17. I was active in the Youth Group in high school, even being its president for two years. I believed Jesus (Yeshua) was the Messiah. I believed everything that I had been taught about Him that was contained in the Apostles' Creed that we repeated every Sunday. I had asked Him into my heart at a young age. **I had even said "the sinner's prayer."** Good Heavens, my grandfather was even a minister! Yet I was completely and hopelessly lost. I was perishing. I was not born again—and I didn't even know it. I, myself, was under the strong delusion!

I was under the delusion that I did not have to deal with being a sinner, specifically. I was too young to do that when I had been led in the sinner's prayer. I was under the delusion that I could believe in Jesus, but not have to repent. I was under the delusion that as a young child I could make a "decision" that dealt with sin, yet I was too young to understand what sin was. I stayed in this state of delusion until I was 30 years old.

You see, as a child I knew the difference between right and wrong, and good and bad, for I had inherited that trait from my ancestor Adam when he ate from the Tree of the Knowledge of Good and Evil. In fact, I was a very good child! I was very careful to do all that I was told, but I did not have a handle on what sin was. For knowing that you are a sinner with a black sinful heart, especially when you are a "good person," really does not happen until you leave your childhood years. It is then when we arrive at the time that we go from childhood to young adulthood that our black heart starts to get exposed to ourselves. Rebellion is the first area where sin usually manifests itself, because it so often just stays in the heart and grows in the darkness of it. We no longer really wish to please our parents or our teachers as we did when we were younger. We want to experience life for ourselves and try the things that we know are "bad." We, who still appear outwardly "good," are now hiding secret sins of rebellion, lust and covetousness, even though we may know better than to actually act upon these new desires. We know we shouldn't be thinking these things, but we can't help ourselves.

When I came to this new reality about my heart and its dark secrets around the age of 13-14, it never occurred to me that I needed to turn to God with sorrow that only He could cause me to understand, and then to repent of my sins and receive the atoning sacrifice of Yeshua to give me the blood covering that was required by the Torah. **It never occurred to me, because I had been told that I was already covered!** Do you realize that nowhere in the Bible does it tell us to ask "Jesus into our hearts" or to recite a sinner's prayer by rote or to "make a decision for Christ?"

So there I was, lost in my sin, yet being deceived myself that I was "okay." Yet I knew that I had lost my childhood innocence. **Deep in my sinner's heart, I knew I was not saved!** *My heart had not been pierced!*

I can remember, as a teenager, reading 1 Corinthians 13 over and over again hoping that I would somehow get peace. You recognize that chapter! It is the one that goes on and on about love, but I did not have the foggiest idea what point Paul was trying to make. You see he was sharing about that *agapē* love that only can be understood by one who has been supernaturally changed from above, and has the Holy Spirit resident inside.

I would read Psalm 100 in the same way. That is the wonderful Psalm of thanksgiving to the Lord. I even had that one memorized, yet I did not really feel thankful to Him.

I would read the "red words" of Yeshua from my Bible, hoping that I would feel like I did as a child again. I knew instinctively that I wasn't clean, yet the Christians around me told me I was a fine Christian girl.

I am sorry to report that I stayed in such a dreadful state of delusion until I turned 30 years of age. My problem was that, even though I knew I was a sinner, I could not admit it to God. I did not want the relationship with Him that would make me so transparent that I would have to come to the end of Margaret. I did not want Him first in my life, because I was first.

Then I read these verses that cut me to my very unsaved soul from 2 Corinthians 13:5:

"Test yourselves to see if you are in the faith; examine yourselves! Or do you not recognize this about yourselves, that Yeshua the Messiah is in you–unless indeed you fail the test?"

These verses caused me to feel so sick inside, because I knew that somehow I failed the test that I was in the faith. But God in His infinite mercy, goodness, and grace, intervened with a problem that would shake up my life—and give me the help I needed to repent of my sins and come to Him the way He requires. He had a wonderful plan for my life that would allow me to see that, no matter what I did, I was now going to have to come to terms with being a failure and a sinner. My late husband, Kim McKee, and I went through the loss of the family business that resulted in us losing everything except our house. I was finally faced with the reality that nothing I could do could fix the problem. I had to finally face the fact that I had put myself first in my life, but I was a failure. I had to face the fact that I had spent my whole life daily breaking the First Commandment: "I am the LORD your God, who brought you out of the land of Egypt, out of the house of slavery. **Your shall have no other gods before Me**" (Exodus 20:2-3).

I was devastated with the reality of this sinner called Margaret who had never truly understood who her God was! All I wanted was to disparately get right with Him! I fell on my face before God and cried out for mercy. I finally realized why I was separated from Him. I didn't know Him and I didn't love Him, even though I thought I knew and believed everything about Him. I got real about Margaret with the God of Israel. I confessed and repented of every secret sin I could think of. *My heart was finally pierced.* I begged Him to cover me with the blood of Yeshua. And finally and miraculously, I knew I had gotten through to my Heavenly Father after all of those years of knowing that we were estranged. His overwhelming presence was felt all over me in such a supernatural way that I would no longer question if I were forgiven or not. *I knew I was forgiven, cleansed, and restored back to God.* I was filled with such love for Him and my brethren that I didn't know existed. I was never to be the same again. I finally understood what grace was. I was finally born again! The love chapter in 1 Corinthians now made sense!

The most amazing part of finally having this assurance of my salvation is that I truly was a changed person. I no longer would walk in self-justification, but I would walk in Divine *agapē* love. I loved others because He first loved me—and I expected nothing in return for loving others. I knew, that in and of myself, I was nothing. It was only He in me that was anything. These words of Paul literally sang to me:

"The mystery which has been hidden from the *past* ages and generations, but has now been manifested to His saints, to whom God willed to make known what is the riches of the glory of this mystery among the Gentiles, which is Messiah in you, the hope of glory" (Colossians 1:26-27).

The Solution

So how do we make sure that we do not fall under the "strong delusion" that God Himself will send to those who did not receive the love of the truth that they might be saved? That even though they think they serve Him, their pride and egos give them away.

We go to Him and make sure that we truly have put Him first in our lives— and we get honest about ourselves and our sins! If we are truly born again and walking in the power of His Holy Spirit, than the deception at the End of the Age will not overpower us. We will not believe the lies that will come from the antimessiah and his system. We will thank the Father daily for choosing us to be part of His end-time restoration of all things. We will cling to Yeshua the Messiah and His atonement for our sins—the good news.

So let us now repeat the verses that warn us about the strong delusion, and then listen to how the Apostle Paul ends this warning with encouragement:

"[A]nd with all the deceivableness of unrighteousness in them that perish, because they received not the love of the truth, that they might be saved. And for this cause God shall send them strong delusion, that they should believe a lie...But we should always give thanks to God for you, brethren beloved by the Lord, because God has chosen you from the beginning for salvation through sanctification by the Spirit and faith in the truth. It was for this He called you through our gospel, that you may gain the glory of our Lord Yeshua the Messiah" (2 Thessalonians 2:10-12, 13-14).

I want to end my testimony with this Scripture that has truly given me that assurance of my own salvation:

"Let us draw near with a sincere heart in full assurance of faith, having our hearts sprinkled clean from an evil conscience and our bodies washed with pure water. Let us hold fast the confession of our hope without wavering, for He who promised is faithful; and let us consider how to stimulate one another to love and good deeds, not forsaking our own assembling together, as is the habit of some, but encouraging one another, and all the more, as you see the day drawing near" (Hebrews 10:22-25).

The day that is being spoken of is the end-times that are steadily approaching us. But right after the author of Hebrews encourages us that we can have the assurance of our salvation, he goes right into warning us that we can still be deceived by the strong delusion in the end, if we do not hold on tight to the truth of salvation:

"For if we go on sinning willfully after receiving the knowledge of the truth, there no longer remains a sacrifice for sins, but a certain terrifying expectation of judgment and the fury of a fire which will consume the adversaries" (Hebrews 10:26-27).

So, are we to fall under the strong delusion that God Himself sends in the end-times, because we really have not received salvation and its truth? Are we so often consumed with sharing the Messianic lifestyle, that we have forgotten to share the saving faith that can come only through the Messiah Himself? Or are we to walk in the assurance of our salvation, because we love the truth and have repented Biblically of our sins? And in so doing, are we now sharing faithfully the gospel of salvation through the commandments that we now keep as Messianic Believers? Let us be those people who "keep the commandments of God and have the testimony of Yeshua" (Revelation 12:17; 14:12).

And let us share both of these critical truths with others. These are the signs of the true end-time Messianic Believer. This is the gospel according to Torah! It is truly good news that can change your life!

Let's pray.

Father, help us to test ourselves that we may be sure that we are in the faith. Help us be real with ourselves, so that we can recognize that we either do or do not exhibit the evidence that we are saved through the fruit of the Holy Spirit—which is love, joy, peace, patience, kindness, goodness, faithfulness, gentleness, and self-control (Galatians 5:22-23). Help us test ourselves to make sure that we have gotten right with You in truly confessing our sins and turning from them. Help us abide in You as You help us live that separated life from the world by keeping Your commandments daily in our hearts and in our deeds. Help us love our neighbors with that supernatural *agapē* love that comes only through You, and in the way in which we pray that they will love us in return. Help us put You first, Father, in all that we do through the power of Your Holy Spirit. And let us do all of these things in the name of our Messiah Yeshua, who is indeed our Rock and our Salvation. Amen.

~17~

The Work of the Holy Spirit: Perfection of the Heart

J.K. McKee

delivered live at Shavuot 2006, Orlando

In the past year-and-a-half (2004-2006), more or less, the emerging Messianic movement has experienced some major upheavals. This is to be expected in any reforming movement, as the history of our faith has demonstrated that when lost theological ideas or forgotten concepts of how we are to relate to God are restored, certain people will "run with it" to promote themselves or a particular agenda. Consider all of the various groups that arose out of the Radical Reformation in the late Sixteenth Century thinking that they could raise people from the dead or establish a New Jerusalem here on Earth. We should not be surprised that with a movement as important as restoring our faith to its First Century Hebraic and Jewish foundations that we would have people going too far. In the past year-and-a-half, many have challenged and denied the Divinity of Yeshua the Messiah, questioned the canonicity and inspiration of key Biblical books, have promoted mysticism and/or beliefs that are not substantiated by Biblical history, but more than anything else have gotten many people confused and off track from performing the work of the Kingdom. What are we to do?

I would like to tell you about an incident that took place several years ago at one of the local churches here in the Orlando area.[1] This was a rather new and budding church, appealing largely to younger families and college students. It was multi-cultural, and was able to attract a diverse group of people. This church had a large facility and staff, and it appeared that it was performing a critical function in the community. But then some sin crept in. One woman, who was being counseled by the senior pastor for a divorce she was going through, fell into having an affair with him. The senior pastor, knowing that this forbidden relationship must end stopped the "counseling sessions," and transferred her case to the assistant pastor. Shockingly, the assistant pastor also fell into an adulterous relationship while counseling the woman. Not too much time passed until the story got out, and the

---

[1] This story was relayed to me by Prof. Burrell Dinkins of Asbury Theological Seminary, in my Fall 2005 class Vocation of Ministry.

district superintendent of the denomination was brought in to take care of it. Both the assistant pastor and senior pastor were relieved of their positions, and on one Sunday morning the congregation got to hear that their senior pastor had fallen into sin. Then, if that hadn't been enough, in the next moment they got to hear that their assistant pastor had likewise fallen into sin. As the church members came up for communion that Sunday, one of my seminary professors, who attended this church, was asked to help distribute it. As he gave the bread to each person, and they dipped it in the cup, he repeated a part of the old liturgy which was that "this is for the healing of your souls."

Of course, the healing process was not over. Both the senior and assistant pastors were removed from their positions, and the church had a huge mortgage hanging over it. At least half of the church members did not show up the following Sunday. What do you do when something like this happens? Obviously, disciplinary action was taken against the offenders—but do you know who has the biggest responsibility? **The new pastor!** He has to minister to sheep who have been gravely wounded and whose spiritual confidence may be at an all time low. He has to get them focused on the future and what they need to be doing in order to grow spiritually and be walking closer with the Lord.

Some of the things that we have faced in the Messianic community as of late are no different than the story that I have just described. We have had sin, arrogance, insolence, gross unbiblical behavior, and even some perditious heresy enter into the camp. Some have been disciplined, and some sin continues. As a teacher and as a Messianic apologist I feel that it is my responsibility to you, the hungry sheep—or even the hurt sheep—to give you a message of encouragement. It is my hope that my two messages delivered this afternoon, and later tomorrow afternoon, are delivered in that spirit of working for the "healing of your soul." Each one of us as Messianic Believers needs to focus on the future, and we need to know how we should be transformed by the power of the Holy Spirit, and thus be a witness so others around us can likewise be transformed.

Every year, we as Messianic Believers read through the weekly Torah portions. We begin each cycle with *Bereisheet*, the Book of Genesis. While everyone has a distinct way of studying the Torah, and indeed the Bible, every year it seems—at least to me—that a substantial amount of the weekly Torah portions is overlooked. Much of this is unintentional, as a teacher can only exposit upon so much in a teaching, and because of the fact that our minds can only handle so much to consider. But in the first Torah portion, the one that sets the stage for the entire story of God revealing Himself to His Creation, one important concept often gets overlooked. Perhaps it is because it is so profound and complicated that many choose to just jump over it, deciding not to "go there." Perhaps because of what it means not only to us as individuals, but also to those we interact with, it is overlooked:

"Then God said, 'Let Us make man in Our image, according to Our likeness; and let them rule over the fish of the sea and over the birds of the sky and over the cattle and over all the earth, and over every creeping thing that creeps on the earth.' God created man in His own image, in the image of God He created him; male and female He created them" (Genesis 1:26-27).

We as human beings have been created in the *tzelem Elohim* (צֶלֶם אֱלֹהִים) or the image of God. Being made in God's image, we possess qualities that none of the animals possess. We have the ability to communicate in verbal language, the ability to reason complex situations or issues in our minds, as well as the ability to choose how we treat one another. These are abilities that we do not inherit via instinct, but have been imparted to us because we have been created by God for His special Divine purposes. Psalm 8:4-6 says that humans were made just a little lower than God (the Greek Septuagint says "angels"), indicating that they indeed have a connection to the supernatural. Jewish commentator Nahum Sarna well summarizes some of what it means for us to be made in God's image:

"A human being is the pinnacle of Creation. This unique status is communicated in a variety of ways, not least by the simple fact that humankind is last in a manifestly ascending, gradual order. The creation of human life is an exception to the rule of creation by divine fiat…Human beings are to enjoy a unique relationship to God, who communicates with them alone and who shares with them the custody and administration of the world."[2]

Because of the sin of Adam, however, each one of us has inherited a fallen sin nature. Every fiber of our being is prone to sin. Each one of us has the potential to be perpetually on the wrong side of God, violating His mandates for the world, and going against what He originally intended to be good. Things got so bad in early history that save Noah and his family, God had to basically "wipe the Earth clean" and repopulate it all over again with a new batch of humans. But in spite of this, and in spite of the fact that we are prone to sin, each one of us is still made in the image of God. Genesis 9:6 says, "Whoever sheds man's blood, by man his blood shall be shed, for in the image of God He made man." People who are killed by sinful people are still considered by God to be made in His image.

As Believers in Yeshua we know that we need not take a knife and plunge it into someone's chest, take a rope and choke the esophagus, or pull a trigger on a gun to murder someone. The Messiah says to us in Matthew 5:22, "I say to you that everyone who is angry with his brother shall be guilty before the court; and whoever says to his brother, 'You good-for-nothing,' shall be guilty before the supreme court; and whoever says, 'You fool,' shall be guilty *enough to go* into the fiery hell." We can commit character assassination through what we say about someone. When delivering His Sermon on the Mount, Yeshua actually tells His audience not to call anyone "raca" (NIV), likely some kind of Aramaic curse word unique to First Century Galilee.[3] I do not think it necessary to list all of the potential curse words that we have the capacity to unleash today. But I do think it is necessary that we control our tongues and what we say to one another. James the Just, the half-brother of Yeshua, puts it this way:

"For every species of beasts and birds, of reptiles and creatures of the sea, is tamed and has been tamed by the human race. But no one can tame the tongue; *it is* a restless evil *and* full of deadly poison. With it we bless *our* Lord and Father, and with it we curse men, who have been made in the likeness of God" (James 3:7-9).

With our tongues, we have the capacity to bring life or death, order or chaos to a situation. We have the capacity to edify others, to testify to them of who the Lord is in our lives and what He has done for us. Or, we have the capacity to cause

---

[2] Nahum M. Sarna, *JPS Torah Commentary: Genesis* (Philadelphia: Jewish Publication Society, 1989), 11.

[3] *BDAG*, 903.

problems. According to James, while every species has been tamed by humankind, the tongue has yet to be tamed. The tongue can only be tamed through the power of God's Holy Spirit and a transformation of our hearts and attitudes. As those who hopefully have had a spiritual encounter with the God of the Universe through His Son, Yeshua the Messiah, we have the responsibility of recognizing that all men and women on Earth, whether they know Him or not, have been made in God's image—*and they all deserve our respect*. John Wesley once put it this way, "there remains from thence an indelible nobleness, which we ought to reverence both in ourselves and others."[4]

The severe challenge with being able to do this is that each one of us not only needs to know Yeshua the Messiah as our Personal Savior, but have a true transformation of the heart. This includes a complete purging of all ungodly attitudes, ideas, concepts, and ways of acting—and having them replaced by godly attitudes and ways of acting that will bring glory to our Heavenly Father and accomplish His Kingdom's work here on Earth. Admittedly, the process of sanctification or "being perfected," if you will, is lifelong. If we are not continually being sanctified and transformed by the power of the Holy Spirit, what are we preparing ourselves for? Are we preparing ourselves for glory, or for condemnation? The Prophet Jeremiah gives us a very bleak picture of a heart that does not seek after God or His ways:

"The heart is more deceitful than all else and is desperately sick; who can understand it? I, the LORD, search the heart, I test the mind, even to give to each man according to his ways, according to the results of his deeds" (Jeremiah 17:9-10).

The idea being communicated is that the heart is "desperately corrupt" (RSV), "beyond cure" (NIV), or "perverse" (NRSV). However it appears in your Bible, this is not a good description. The unregenerated, untransformed, ungodly, and wicked human heart is something that we need not have within us. Have you ever truly sat down and considered what it means to have a wicked heart? This is something that Rabbis, theologians, Sages, Bible teachers, pastors, and many others have had a very, very long time to think about. Consider the following words on the tendencies of the human heart and what sins can come forth:

"gnawing cares, disquiet, griefs, fears, wild joys, quarrels, law-suits, wars, treasons, angers, hatreds, deceit, flattery, fraud, theft, robbery, perfidy, pride, ambition, envy, murders, parricides, cruelty, ferocity, wickedness, luxury, insolence, impudence, shamelessness, fornications, adulteries, incests, and the numberless uncleanness and unnatural acts of both sexes, which it is shameful so much as to mention; sacrileges, heresies, blasphemies, perjuries, oppression of the innocent, calumnies, plots, falsehoods, false witnessings, unrighteous judgments, violent deeds, plunderings, and innumerable other crimes that do not easily come to mind, but that never absent themselves from the actuality of human existence."[5]

---

[4] John Wesley, *Explanatory Notes Upon the New Testament*, reprint (Peterborough, UK: Epworth Press, 2000), 864.

[5] St. Augustine, "City of God," in Mitchell Cohen and Nicole Fermon, eds., *Princeton Readings in Political Thought* (Princeton, NJ: Princeton University Press, 1996), pp 133-134.

If this list of gross immoralities has not upset you in some way, perhaps you need a graphic description...

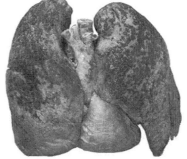

This picture may be disgusting and gross to some of you. This is an image of a smoker's heart and lungs. For perhaps thirty, forty, or fifty years this person inhaled tobacco smoke into the lungs and infections steadily were spread to the heart and probably other areas of the body. While many of us know the dangers of smoking, consider what this is like on a spiritual level. When the center of our being, our heart, is black, sin has the tendency to spread to the other parts of our being. It will not just stay in the heart, but penetrate into our minds and how we think, to our words and what we say, and quite probably into our actions. Today, you can wreak absolute havoc by typing a few keystrokes on a computer. Sometimes this might be by ruining a person financially—and more often it may be by defaming someone's character. Do you know how easy it is to setup a personal blog web page now? Do you know how flippantly people can write every day how they are feeling and who has offended them and caused them harm—and how they want to get back?

When our heart thinks that it is better than everyone else, that no one else but ourselves actually understands what is going on, *or* that no one but us has the "truth," is it a sign that we have an unregenerated heart?

These are sins that, sadly, much of the Messianic community today falls into all the time. We think ourselves better than everyone else. We think that we are the only ones who have any kind of understanding—and certainly the only ones who have had the truth the past 2,000 years. On the whole, we largely fail to recognize that we have a shared theological heritage with both the Jewish Synagogue *and* the Christian Church. Oftentimes, only one is recognized at the expense of the other, yet in some circles it is becoming more en vogue to oppose both. My friends, if we have these kinds of attitudes present in ourselves, we have a long way to go before Yeshua can return for a renewed and transformed people. Individually, we have a long way to go before God can use us to minister to others, and accomplish His tasks on Earth.

Consider the sins that I listed for you a moment ago. Were you offended by them? Did any kind of godly indignation rise up in you when thinking about the fallen world we live in? Did any of you think about how important it is for others to hear about the good news of salvation in Yeshua, and how we need to be living holy and separated lives? **I sincerely hope so.**

But I have one question for you: Does more indignation rise up in you when I tell you that the one who listed these gross immoralities was Augustine, Bishop of Hippo, otherwise known as St. Augustine? I would dare say that many Messianics are *more upset* at the mention of Augustine than at the sins that he listed in his book *City of God.* I do not agree with every single point of Augustine's theology; but I recognize that without the work that he performed for his time, we would be in a much worse condition. How many of us as Messianics treat people like this—who are long since dead and buried—as being part of "the problem," when the real problem is our fallen humanity? Each generation of God's followers has a specific task to perform, as He has sovereignly decreed. The task of those who have gone before us was different than the tasks that we should be performing as today's Messianic movement. Each of us as individuals has the capacity to be sinners or saints, be we Messianic, Christian, or Jewish. How many of us still need to be transformed—or at least have a serious heart check—because we are more offended by people than by sin? Did not Yeshua die for all members of the human race? Is not Israel to serve the world, by testifying to the world who the One True God is?

While things may seem to be bleak at times, there is always a message of hope. Jeremiah 17:7-8 gives us the promise, "Blessed is the man who trusts in the LORD and whose trust is the LORD. For he will be like a tree planted by the water, that extends its roots by a stream and will not fear when the heat comes; but its leaves will be green, and it will not be anxious in a year of drought nor cease to yield fruit." Ezekiel prophesies that when Israel is restored that the Lord says, "I will give you a new heart and put a new spirit within you; and I will remove the heart of stone from your flesh and give you a heart of flesh" (Ezekiel 36:26). The promise of the New Covenant of Jeremiah 31 is that the Lord, by the power of His Holy Spirit, will write the commandments of the Torah onto our hearts, not only so we might keep them—but that we might keep them properly to His glory! The promise is that we might keep them as we perform His Kingdom's work in the world. Each one of us is to be transformed so that we reflect God's character, holiness, love, and compassion to a world that desperately needs to change.

In the Messianic community today, many of us claim to be Torah observant. We do this by remembering the seventh-day Sabbath or *Shabbat*, the appointed times of Leviticus 23 (of which *Shavuot* is one), and the kosher dietary laws. These are three areas that distinctly separate us from our Christian brothers and sisters. While these aspects are important to follow, they by no means make up all of the elements of "Torah observance." A true Torah observance is very much to be reflected by us having ethical and moral lives, and treating others with love, mercy, and respect. James admonishes us, "Therefore, putting aside all filthiness and *all* that remains of wickedness, in humility receive the word implanted, which is able to save your souls" (James 1:21). How many of us understand the fact that if we are to live out God's Word in our lives, the implanted Word, we have to have all of the evil filth put away? Unless we have experienced redemption in Yeshua, we cannot be used to perform good works.

I have heard the words following this in James 1:22 quoted many times in the Messianic community: "But prove yourselves doers of the word, and not merely hearers who delude themselves." I have heard this quoted in the context of the fact that when we hear what the Torah says, we need to do it. *I agree.* But far too frequently James is hijacked as saying something that he is not. History proves that James himself was very, very Torah observant, hence his being called "James the Just." He maintained ritual purity at all times, was a vegetarian, and seldom missed prayers in the Temple. But James also spent more time on his knees before God in prayer for the salvation of others.[6] When James talks about us being doers of God's Word, it is *primarily* in the context of us performing works of grace and mercy

---

[6] Eusebius *Ecclesiastical History* 2.23.4-5.

toward others—just as he did. The challenge for us is how we can maintain a proper balance in our ethics and morality, coupled with the days we remember, how we eat, and how we function as distinct members of the Commonwealth of Israel. Remember that James' Torah observance was always coupled with his constant intercession. While James is an excellent example of a Torah observant Jew who believed in Yeshua, He is also an excellent example of one who loved and served others.[7]

We face some challenges in our quest to become Torah observant because many of us were raised in theological traditions where it was taught that the Torah or Law of Moses is to be subdivided between the "moral law" and "ceremonial law." The moral law was believed to include commandments and regulations regarding human relations, how we are to treat others, how we are to care for others, not lie, not cheat, not steal, and be honest people who are hard working. The ceremonial law, in contrast, was believed to include those commandments relating to, among other things, the seventh-day Sabbath, the appointed times, distinctions between clean and unclean meats, male circumcision, and many other things that were viewed as making Israel distinct among the nations. In this hour of restoration, the Lord is restoring these things to us as His people. I fully believe that these things should be followed by all Believers, but too many are embracing what were viewed as "ceremonial commandments" at the expense of the "moral commandments." There is no such distinction in the Scripture itself. Your celebration of *Shavuot*, for example, does not negate the need to love others or treat others with respect. On the contrary, when you understand the symbolism of *Shavuot*, your responsibility to love others and spread the gospel is enhanced—and it is even more severe if you fail to do it.

I would like to briefly discuss a Scripture passage that I am frequently asked about as a Messianic teacher: Mark 7. In this scene, we see some Pharisees come toward Yeshua and they have some criticisms for His students. These Pharisees were likely of the School of Shammai, a very strict sect that held to rather rigid interpretations, unlike the School of Hillel—which the Apostle Paul was a part of, having been trained by Gamaliel (Acts 22:3)—that was more understanding and tolerant. Their criticism of Yeshua was "Why do Your disciples not walk according to the tradition of the elders, but eat their bread with impure hands?" (Mark 7:6). They issued this negative word, because they believed that one must rigorously wash hands before eating, in what is today known as *n'tilat yadayim* in Orthodox Judaism.

I do not believe that Yeshua was against washing our hands, but He did say to these people, "You are experts at setting aside the commandment of God in order to keep your tradition" (Mark 7:9). The reason He says this is not because Yeshua was necessarily against tradition, either. Yeshua Himself followed many, if not most, of the mainline Jewish traditions extant in the First Century. But when anything takes us away from the right attitude we are to be exhibiting in our hearts toward others—it becomes a problem. Yeshua makes it perfectly clear that what comes forth from us defiles us more than what we ingest:

"That which proceeds out of the man, that is what defiles the man. For from within, out of the heart of men, proceed the evil thoughts, fornications, thefts,

---

[7] For further consideration, consult the commentary *James for the Practical Messianic* by J.K. McKee.

murders, adulteries, deeds of coveting *and* wickedness, *as well as* deceit, sensuality, envy, slander, pride *and* foolishness. All these evil things proceed from within and defile the man" (Mark 7:20-23).

If we have transformed hearts, these things should not be prone to coming out of our mouths. When we speak, we should be speaking words of life, encouragement, mercy, and always be about to share the good news of salvation in Messiah Yeshua. The challenge when it comes to Mark 7 is that it is often interpreted as though Yeshua is negating the kosher dietary laws of the Torah, and so much of our discussion is focused on this part of the text rather than on the definite spiritual principles He wishes to communicate. Mark 7:18-19, in particular, is often a cause of much confusion for Messianics:

"And He said to them, 'Are you so lacking in understanding also? Do you not understand that whatever goes into the man from outside cannot defile him, because it does not go into his heart, but into his stomach, and is eliminated?' (*Thus He* declared all foods clean.)"

What we must take important note of here are Yeshua's words, as rendered in *The Message*, "Are you being willfully stupid? Don't you see that what you swallow can't contaminate you?" What the Lord is telling us is that eating food—note, Biblically defined food (Leviticus 11 & Deuteronomy 14)—with unwashed hands does not matter. This is because if you have a little dirt on your hands, the human body is powerful enough to kill germs and bacteria. What happens to this food is that it goes "into [the] stomach, and then out of [the] body" (NIV). Then we read the little phrase "*Thus He* declared all foods clean," which is actually very easy to understand if we look at Mark's underlying Greek.

The Greek phrase that is commonly rendered "*Thus He* declared all foods clean" is *katharizōn panta ta brōmata* (καθαρίζων πάντα τὰ βρώματα). What is missing from this phrase is the verb *legō* (λέγω), meaning "to say" or "to speak." Literally what this means is "purging all the foods" (LITV). There has always been the long-standing minority opinion in Bible translation that "purging all the foods" is the more accurate rendering. Robert A. Guelich attests to this in the *Word Biblical Commentary*, "Others view this as a possible anacoluthon drawing an obvious, if sarcastic, conclusion that the digestive process 'cleanses all foods.'"[8] Food eaten with dirty hands goes into the stomach and out of the body, because the body is able to "purify" it via excretion.

Which is more important: eating kosher or not demonstrating malice toward others? Please understand that I *fully believe* that the kosher dietary laws are to be followed today. In fact, I am of the opinion that there might even be a legitimate Biblical basis for (at least partially) separating meat and dairy. But I know that the Apostles in their journeys were sometimes served things that were unkosher. I know they just looked beyond what was on their plate, and prayed that God would give them an unbelievable amount of grace and mercy for those who they were ministering to. Sometimes it was difficult, but they asked Him for that extra part of His Spirit so they would recognize that person as being made in His image

---

[8] Robert A. Guelich, *Word Biblical Commentary: Mark 1-8:26*, Vol. 34a (Dallas: Word Books, 1989), 378.

For a further analysis of Mark 7:19, including the connection/non-connection between the Greek participles *legei* (λέγει) and *katharizōn* (καθαρίζων), consult the article "A Short Note on Mark 7:19" by Tim Hegg, available for access at <www.torahresource.com>.

just as they were, knowing that Yeshua died for all. How are we as Messianic Believers to maintain the proper balance between something as key to our Torah observance as *kashrut*, while recognizing that what comes out of our hearts is more important?

My friends, let me be honest with you for a moment: I respect and have received a great amount of spiritual instruction from people over the years who eat bacon on a regular basis and do not know any better. Those who first instructed me in my faith in Yeshua the Messiah, who loved Jesus with all of their hearts, still eat sausage. I have actually received *less instruction* from those who abstain from bacon on how to love others and demonstrate the Messiah's compassion to the world. How does that reflect on the current state of the Messianic community? I hope we can experience some changes where we can show that one's heart attitude and eating kosher—among other commandments—do not have to negate one another. Both can be maintained and be used as witnessing tools to show others what God is doing in our lives.

One of the reasons that we celebrate *Shavuot* is to remember the outpouring of the Holy Spirit that took place after the ascension of Yeshua. At this time, we see the first major explosion of evangelism taking place, as the responsibility of spreading the good news was given to the Apostles, who then had to go out to the rest of the world. Is this one of the reasons why you celebrate *Shavuot*? Is the work of God's Kingdom in the world something important to you?

My all-time favorite theological term is not something that is Hebrew, Aramaic, Greek, Latin, or even English. Some of you who have gone through our Wednesday Night Bible Studies on the Internet have heard me use it. It is the word *Heilsgeschichte*, meaning "salvation history." *Das ist ein gute deutsche Wort.* **This is a good German word.** Many of the German Reformers of the Sixteenth and Seventeenth Centuries used it to describe the Bible as presenting an unfolding plan of God's salvation for the world. In theological study, God's redemptive purpose for humanity becomes the controlling factor. When we read Scripture, we are to understand that all of the events that occur are designed for us to be brought closer to God and for us to understand His redemptive work.

God's unfolding "salvation history" is one of the major reasons why we celebrate the appointed times. They commemorate events in the world where the Divine has interrupted the lives of people in order to radically change things. We see this at *Shavuot* in the scene of fire and smoke with the Ten Commandments being given to Moses. And we definitely see it with the giving of the Holy Spirit to the Believers assembled in Jerusalem. *Shavuot* is a major example of *Heilsgeschichte*—as the salvation of the world is its major theme. The outpouring of the Holy Spirit in the First Century led us to seeing men and women enlivened to go out into the world, and proclaim the good news that the Savior had come. Synagogues in Antioch, Alexandria, Corinth, and even as far as Rome itself got to hear some amazing stories when congregants returned home from Jerusalem. *Shavuot* began the first major *worldwide* evangelistic campaign in the history of Israel.

We come to celebrate *Shavuot* this weekend so we can remember the unfolding plan of the Lord, and how He wishes to have a redeemed people. **We come to focus on Yeshua who is salvation.** But I would ask you, do you, personally, have an event that you commemorate, where God's salvation has been present in your own life? Do you remember the time when you received Yeshua and were spiritually regenerated? Do you remember any trials or difficulties that you were able to overcome because the Lord delivered you through them? Are there any seasons of the year that you have a fondness for, because of past experiences when you have had to rely on the Lord like never before? Do you have a testimony of "salvation history" in your own life? Corporately, we celebrate the appointed times of Leviticus 23, but individually, what do we remember? May it be our hope and prayer that every day be an unfolding of His salvation to us!

We face some challenges in the coming years as the Messianic movement grows and matures. We have a great responsibility before us. If we are to properly complete the work that God has assigned to us, we need to have some serious one-on-one time with Him. We need to recognize that what happens to the Jewish community affects us. We also need to recognize that what happens to the Christian community affects us. Atrocities that happen to Christians in the third world should sicken us, and we should pray for our brothers and sisters every day. Most of these people will never know about the Sabbath, the appointed times, or what it means to eat kosher. They just know that they love Jesus and that He brought them out of bondage and into freedom. They look forward to the day when they can see Him face to face in glory. Do we look forward to that day? Is our heart warmed when we think about Yeshua exalted in Heaven? Do we tear up at all? Do we think about all those who have gone before us, and how we get to complete the reforming work that they began?

Shavuot was the time when God poured out His Holy Spirit upon all men and women who had received the good news of Messiah Yeshua. It was the time when many people became "charismatic," so to speak. But being charismatic does not necessarily mean having a dominant personality, speaking in unintelligible or intelligible tongues, raising hands in worship, or jumping and dancing for joy. The term charismatic is derived from the Greek word *charis* (χάρις), a secondary meaning of which is "gift." But its primary meaning is "grace."

Someone who is truly "charismatic" is one who has been transformed by the power of the Holy Spirit and is able to be used as a means of grace in the world. Any servant of the Most High should be charismatic. We should all be full of God's love, His grace, mercy, and compassion to others. Do you pray for this every day? I know I do. It is not always easy, and some things I have to leave totally to Him, but that is part of the sanctification process. I would dare say that none of us will be "totally perfect" until about one minute before we die and enter into eternity. At this *Shavuot*, it is my hope that we can be used as a means of grace for our Father's Kingdom work. But the only way that we can be used as a means of grace is for us to have a transformed heart that is being continually transformed into the character of the Lord Yeshua. It is my prayer that you have this transformed heart. Let's pray...

~18~

The Work of the Holy Spirit: Perfection of the Mind

J.K. McKee

delivered live at Shavuot 2006, Orlando

In my first teaching, which dealt with the perfection of the heart (Chapter 17), I began to speak about our need to have the center of our beings transformed into the character of our Messiah Yeshua. A transformed heart brings forth love, compassion, and mercy toward others, and is concerned about the salvation of the world. When we as individuals experience salvation we are to have a heart that orients itself toward God, and then every other aspect of our being begins to be changed. After the heart, **the first area of ourselves that must experience transformation is the mind.**

One of the challenges that we all face as a part of the fallen condition of humanity is that none of us will ever reach complete perfection. Even if we are redeemed souls who believe that Yeshua is the Savior, we will by-and-large be looking for that day when we wake up and we will be "entirely perfect." Whether one is Jewish, Christian, or even Messianic, we largely adhere to an Aristotelian idea of perfection. The classical definition of perfection as given by Aristotle is that something is perfect when it "lacks nothing in respect of goodness or excellence" and "cannot be surpassed in its kind" (*IDB*).[1] The problem with this definition is that total goodness or excellence cannot exist in the fallen world in which we live. Even as Believers in Messiah Yeshua, we will not ever be "perfect" in this context because we live in a fallen world and will often slip up at times.

Of course, this does not mean that we are to not seek perfection, or be striving to overcome sin. Yeshua Himself taught, "Therefore you are to be perfect, as your heavenly Father is perfect" (Matthew 5:48). But this is something that we are to *strive for* in our daily walk of faith, as opposed to having it simply imparted to us. Notice that Yeshua issues this as a command. Perfection is something that must be sought out.

---

[1] J.Y. Campbell, "Perfection," in *IDB*, 3:730.

In the Scriptures themselves, we see a somewhat different portrayal of perfection than Aristotle's definition. In the Hebrew Tanach, the term commonly indicating "perfection" is *tamim* (תָּמִים). This can mean "**whole, entire**," "**intact**," "**free of blemish**," and "**blameless**" (*CHALOT*).[2] In relation to human character, it is most often rendered as "upright" or "blameless." In the Greek Septuagint and Apostolic Scriptures the term *teleios* (τέλειος) is used, primarily "**pert. to being mature, *full-grown, mature, adult***" or quite possibly even "**to being fully developed in a moral sense**" (*BDAG*).[3] What all of these concepts indicate is that one who is striving to be "perfect" wants sinful behavior removed from his or her life, wants to be mature, and wants to be developing as an adult in the faith, able to deal with complicated ideas.

In Yeshua's repetition of the *Shema* of Deuteronomy 6, He says that the greatest command is to "LOVE THE LORD YOUR GOD WITH ALL YOUR HEART, AND WITH ALL YOUR SOUL, AND WITH ALL YOUR MIND" (Matthew 22:37; cf. Mark 12:30; Luke 10:27). One aspect of our faith that I think is frequently overlooked and downplayed is the need for us to worship God with our minds. When we come to gatherings such as this and assemble in worship, many of us are singing loudly, we are raising our hands, some are even dancing in the aisles, but do we ever seriously consider what it means to worship God with our minds? Do we know what it means to have a transformation of our minds?

After our heart, the mind is clearly the first part of our beings that is to experience transformation. If one examines Yeshua's Sermon on the Mount and His sayings about one being angry with a neighbor, one having lustful inclinations, or simple hate for others, you can be rest assured that the Lord does place a high priority on our thoughts. It is not solely enough for us to commit a sinful act to be guilty; it is sufficient for us to have thoughts of committing a sin for us to be guilty. While some of us may watch science fiction shows where human telepaths are used to probe the thoughts and feelings of criminals or potential criminals, and we might shake our heads about how ludicrous and subjective it might be, God probes our minds all the time. He knows what each one of us is thinking right now. He knows if our thoughts are focused on Him, His Word, and the work that He has assigned us to do—or if we are thinking things that will take us away from Him and damage the relationship that He desires with us.

I hope that every day you wake up and you spend several moments in one-on-one time with the Lord. I hope that you pray for Him to give you a heart toward other people, and that you can properly represent Him in our sin-cursed world. But how many of you pray that He gives you a mind that can focus on Him?

I do not think enough people realize this, but when you enter into the Messianic movement you will not only be spiritually challenged, but also mentally challenged. Not only does the enemy not want you to succeed in changing your lifestyles so that you can fully live like Yeshua lived, he does not want you to progress beyond the essentials of the faith. The enemy wants you to remain as a simplistic child *not able* to handle complicated ideas or concepts. The very word "theology," meaning the study of God, summarizes it all quite well. Having a transformed heart should lead us to having a wonderful relationship with God and

---

[2] *CHALOT*, 391.
[3] *BDAG*, 995.

with other Believers, but having a transformed mind **should enable us to have a theology**, allowing us to understand who God is from His Word and in His Creation. I am readily reminded of the Apostle Paul's words which speak to much of our situation. He says in 1 Corinthians 13:11, "When I was a child, I used to speak like a child, think like a child, reason like a child; when I became a man, I did away with childish things."

As a Reforming movement, we have a long way to go before a more definite Messianic "theology" can be established. While I am not a Calvinist—in fact, I am a strong Arminian—I nevertheless admire the work of John Calvin and how in the early decades of the Reformation he spent most of his life in Geneva writing commentaries on books of the Bible in an early Protestant movement that desperately needed some systematic view of the Scriptures. I believe that the Messianic movement is only now beginning to enter into that stage when we can begin to systematize our theology, and take into consideration a vast amount of Jewish literature and commentary that five-hundred years ago the early Reformers did not have access to, and only in the past fifty years or so have English speakers really been able to examine. Did you know that the Mishnah and Talmud were translated into French and German before English? That can seriously limit the amount of people who can access it.

A further challenge has been caused by the so-called Jesus Seminar of the past twenty or so years. This was largely a liberal compendium of theologians assembled to determine which parts of the Gospels are authentic and which are inauthentic. In their findings, they concluded that most of the Gospels were inauthentic, and evangelical Christians found themselves at a loss of knowing how to respond. When liberals say that it is not in Yeshua's character to call Pharisees "vipers," for example, because it does not seem to be loving, how do conservatives respond? The only way that one can respond is by understanding the distinct Jewish character and world in which Yeshua lived.

The mistake that is largely made is that we see Yeshua on the outside, criticizing others on the inside. This is not an historically valid way of looking at the Messiah. Evangelicals are now having to engage with the contemporary Jewish literature of Yeshua's time, and they are beginning to see that Pharisees called other Pharisees "vipers" quite frequently. Yeshua's criticism of them is largely done on an intra-mural level as though He were one of them. It is no different than me saying that my sister Jane is "something," and getting away with it because we're family. I would not be able to go to your family and easily call you "something." But these theological ideas not only require that we have hearts open to change, but that we also have open minds and that we can comprehend new, and controversial ideas. Certainly, having entered into the Messianic movement, none of you should be strangers to controversy. But too many are strangers to dealing with complex ideas.

The key to having a transformed mind more than anything else is that we need to have our thoughts focused on God. As we pray that the Holy Spirit renews us each day, we must focus our thoughts off of ourselves and onto Him. This is one of the reasons why education is so highly valued in the Jewish community. In all things a Jew is to bring glory to God. One need not be a rabbi to do this, but can be the best Jewish scientist, mathematician, soldier, and yes, even banker. But in the Messianic community too much has been said of the so-called Hebrew vs. Greek mind, when all the Bible itself tells us is to "have the mind of Messiah" (1

Corinthians 2:16). The mind of Messiah is focused upon our Heavenly Father and performing His tasks well in the world. What is ironic about some who promote the idea of a Hebrew versus Greek mind, is that what is often considered to be Hellenistic or Greek is actually not Greek, but is Twenty-First Century European-American and has nothing to do with classical Greek philosophy.

To demonstrate this point, I have prepared the following chart of four cities. These four cities represent power centers on Earth that have each affected us either religiously, socially, or economically:

Jerusalem	New York London Frankfurt
Athens	Geneva

I would like to briefly compare these four cities with a concept that each one of us has to deal with on a daily basis: **work.** Whether we like it or not, each of us has to work in some capacity. Each one of these cities has historically had a distinct position on "work." Some of this you will be able to identify with, and other parts will seem somewhat strange.

What Jerusalem represents should be obvious. In Exodus 20:9 God commands us, "Six days you shall labor and do all your work." The Hebrew verb *ta'avod* (תַּעֲבֹד) appears in the Qal imperfect tense, meaning that an absolute literal translation would appear as "You work" (context determines what English helping verbs should be added).[4] Whether we realize it or not, the Bible tells us that we should be working, *at least in some capacity*, for six days of the week. (Note: I do not think that the Bible is against us having a vacation from time to time.) In Jewish theology, work is viewed as a command from God, because the one who does not work has the propensity to sin.

The Athenian view of work sits in stark contrast to this. R. Paul Stevens writes in his book *The Six Other Days*, "Work was a curse, unmitigated evil; and to be out of work was a piece of singularly good fortune. Unemployment allowed for one to participate in the political domain and to enjoy the contemplative life...Not surprisingly, 80 per cent of the Greek city-states were comprised of slaves, which Aristotle defined as instruments endowed with life. Work was called 'unleisure'."[5] Many of the Athenians were, in no misuse of the term, "bums" who did not work. What I think is very important for us to note is that *ta'avod* was rendered in the Septuagint as *erga* (ἔργα) appearing in the future middle indicative tense. *Erga* would definitely be translated into English as "you will work," and that you are involved in the work as though it is unavoidable. This is because work is a part of the human condition that each one of us must experience, and the Rabbis who rendered it knew exactly what they were communicating to Greeks who would hear it. Many of them, upon entering into the Synagogue as Jewish converts, may have had to "work" for the first time.

---

[4] In most cases, the Qal imperfect tense in Hebrew is rendered as the future tense in English.
Cf. C.L. Seow, *A Grammar for Biblical Hebrew*, revised edition (Nashville: Abingdon, 1995), 207.
[5] R. Paul Stevens, *The Other Six Days* (Grand Rapids: Eerdmans, 1999), 110.

The New Yorker view of work is distinct from these previous two. New York, along with London and Frankfurt, is one of the world's principal business centers. The whole focus of Wall Street is one acquiring wealth as quickly and cheaply as possible. Profit margins and the 24/7 ability to make money is the philosophy of this dog-eat-dog world. This is the primary view of work that saturates the industrialized world that we live in today, and sits in opposition first to the Athenian view of work, and then to the Jerusalemite view of work which at least recognizes that one day must be totally devoted to God.

The view of work represented by Geneva is actually the closest that we see connected to Jerusalem. The Protestant work ethic, which largely came from the teachings of John Calvin and others, was birthed out of the belief that if one is a member of God's elect, then a person will demonstrate it through faithful labors during the six days designated for work. This even led to some of the Reformers preaching that if an individual does not work during the designated time, that he or she is actually sinning! Of course, the Protestant Reformers were limited by their inability to see the validity of *Shabbat*, as opposed to the Christian Sunday, but to many of them a "Sunday sabbath" was rigidly enforced, and no work of any kind was permitted.

I mention these examples to point out that there are worldly philosophies beyond that of the Hebrew versus Greek mindset. There is an entire Oriental way of thinking espoused in the Far East that many of us likewise do not consider, because it is so foreign to us. The overwhelming fact of our lives is that the mind of Messiah is not focused on self-pleasure, or wanton acquisition of things, but on doing good works and in obeying the Lord. This is what we see modeled in the Jerusalem view of work, and surprisingly to some of you, what we also see represented by Geneva as well.

Every day we have to ask the Lord to transform our minds so that we can adequately perform the tasks and assignments that He has for each of us. We need to pray that our thoughts and contemplations are focused on Him and His Word, because His thoughts are certainly centered toward His Creation, and to us as humans, the pinnacle of that Creation. As we are continually sanctified and perfected, we have a responsibility to God and to ourselves, and even to fellow members of the community of faith, to move beyond some of the basic essentials of our faith. As we each progress toward adulthood in our faith, we need to ask the Lord to give us the capacity to deal with complicated thoughts and ideas that require the ability for us to use our brains.

An excellent example I can give you from the Bible is seen in the Epistle to the Hebrews. Anyone who has read Hebrews should be able to tell you that this is a letter that deeply ministers to the spirit. We see Yeshua exalted in Heaven, worshipped by angels. We see the humanity of Yeshua, as He suffered and died for us. We see Yeshua functioning in the priesthood of Melchizedek before the Father in Heaven, interceding for us. We see Yeshua's priesthood inaugurating the New Covenant with the Spirit writing the Law onto our hearts. And perhaps most importantly, we see Yeshua as being superior to all things. But when you go and read Hebrews a second time, your mind is deeply challenged. While on the first read, your spirit is to be enlivened and quickened, the second read requires us to use our brains because the author uses a very sophisticated and complex methodology in communicating to his audience.

What makes Hebrews unique among the texts of the Apostolic Scriptures, is that we do not know for sure who the author is, or for that matter the specific target audience. We can rightfully assume, for example, that the author was not the Apostle Paul, because he identifies himself in Hebrews 2:3 as having heard the gospel from "those who heard" it from the Lord Yeshua. This identifies him as being a second-generation Believer, excluding any of the Apostles or Paul because they had first-hand encounters with the Messiah. The theology of the letter does have some Pauline character to it, but the writing style does not. The author is more succinct, he does not go on extensive diatribes, and his vocabulary is much more advanced than Paul's. The author is direct and to the point, more than anything else. Most theologians are agreed that someone in Paul's inner circle probably wrote the letter, perhaps either Barnabas or Apollos, accounting for the elements of Pauline teaching. But Paul writing it is a sheer impossibility.[6]

When it comes to the audience of the Epistle to the Hebrews, a Jewish audience is rightly assumed. The challenge with this is the fact that while most in the Messianic community would assume that it was written to Jews living in Israel, almost two-thirds of the Jewish population of the First Century lived outside of Israel in the Diaspora. If you take a look at this map, we see a large Jewish dispersion from as far east as Babylon, in modern-day Iraq, to as far West in what is today Belgium and southeastern England (even though some of the further reaching Jewish settlement may have come after the destruction of the Second Temple):

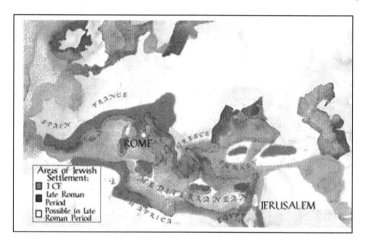

We certainly see the Jewish Diaspora presented to us in the Book of Acts, as significant pockets of Jews lived in Antioch, Cyprus, Corinth, Crete, Macedonia, North Africa, and possibly even Spain. Alexandria boasted a Jewish population of over 300,000, and Rome itself had a population of 40,000-60,000 Jews. These people cannot be ignored when it comes to our understanding of the New Testament. They have to be recognized as viable members of the Jewish community, and when we examine the letter to the Hebrews, it is more likely that it was penned for these Jews, than Jews living in the Holy Land.

---

[6] For further consideration, consult the commentary *Hebrews for the Practical Messianic* by J.K. McKee.

Of course, since we do not know the exact audience, we cannot discount anyone. Jews living in the Holy Land, those living in the Diaspora, and even the sectarian Qumran community that gave us the Dead Sea Scrolls must all be considered. For that same matter, we cannot exclude non-Jewish Believers as being among the intended audience. The letter was written to address the impending destruction of the Temple in the late 60s C.E. and how Yeshua's sacrifice and priesthood supersede the Levitical priesthood. Many Jewish Believers in the First Century did not know what do to about this, and were questioning their faith as a result. The author had to assure them of the grave consequences of considering denying the Messiah. The most significant of those consequences, elaborated in Hebrews 4, would be that dissenters would never experience God's eternal rest not only typified in the weekly Sabbath, but in the Messianic Kingdom on Earth. They would be giving up on the time when humanity would be restored to its original position as second only to God in His universe.

Many Bible teachers, myself included, believe that the primary audience of Hebrews was actually the Jewish community in Rome. This is partially because we see it quoted in the Epistle of 1 Clement as early as 95 C.E., written from Rome. We also see some interesting parallels between Paul's letter to the Romans, and statements in Hebrews that appear to be amplifying Paul's previous teaching to them. The author, being a contemporary of Paul, may be reflecting on things that this group of Believers has already heard.

Paul writes in Romans 12:2, for example, "do not be conformed to this world, but be transformed by the renewing of your mind, so that you may prove what the will of God is, that which is good and acceptable and perfect." The author of Hebrews parallels this by writing his audience, "For though by this time you ought to be teachers, you have need again for someone to teach you the elementary principles of the oracles of God, and you have come to need milk and not solid food. For everyone who partakes *only* of milk is not accustomed to the word of righteousness, for he is an infant. But solid food is for the mature, who because of practice have their senses trained to discern good and evil" (Hebrews 5:12-14).

Apparently, whomever this audience was, and we cannot disclude the Romans, and to a lesser extent probably also the Corinthians, they had been instructed by the Apostles adequately enough so that they could be teachers. But instead of being equipped in what the New English Bible renders as "the ABC of God's oracles," they must learn them all over again. They are still spiritually immature to be able to deal with "solid food." Note that our author does not say that his audience are "children"; he says that they are "infants." Paul issued similar words to the Corinthians in 1 Corinthians 3:2: "I gave you milk to drink, not solid food; for you were not yet able *to receive it*. Indeed, even now you are not yet able."

When one is new in the faith, we are to be trained in what the NIV says are "the first principles of God's Word." These are the basic essentials of learning how to relate to God, loving God, loving one another, serving one another, learning about the characters and people of the Bible. We learn about Adam and Eve, Noah and the Flood, Abraham, Jacob, Joseph, Moses, Joshua, Kings David and Solomon, Yeshua the Messiah, the Apostles, etc., etc. We learn how to pray. We learn how to demonstrate God's grace and His mercy to others in the world we live. We learn how to make sacrifices and give Him complete control over our lives. These are the essential things in the faith, and I pray that each one of us has a firm basis in them in our relationship with the Lord.

However, a critical part of growing in our faith is being able to move beyond these things. These things are certainly not to be negated by moving beyond them, but as we strive for spiritual adulthood the challenges that will be delivered to us will get increasingly more difficult. When we strive for adulthood we should not have to go through the essentials of faith over and over again, specifically because the Holy Spirit has supernaturally empowered us with discernment and reasoning abilities to handle complex situations. These complex situations require us to have a mind and thought life that are focused on the Lord and on performing His work ably in the world in which we live.

There are any number of situations that I could go into that require us to think with godly reasoning skills, but most of them pertain to ethical subjects. Whether you are a pastor or teacher or not does not matter here, because each of you at one point in your life either have had, or will have to deal with a complex situation. Every pastor or spiritual leader is guaranteed that at one point in a thirty-fifty year ministry that he or she will have to deal with an unmarried pregnant teenage girl, or a teenage boy who has impregnated someone. Some have even more difficult situations to deal with. How do I counsel someone going through a divorce? How do I counsel someone who has just gotten cancer? And God forbid, what do I tell someone whose loved one is on life support, and may never come out of a coma?

What if, God forbid, someone in your Messianic congregation or fellowship were to have a massive heart attack? What if the only treatment for that heart attack would be to have a pig valve installed in the heart? Do you know that there are Messianic Believers who would just as soon die than have a pig valve installed in their heart? What is ironic about this is that many Orthodox Jews would have the pig valve installed, because Judaism allows for any ritual commandment to be broken, save idolatry, for human life to be preserved.

Some of these are hypothetical examples, but they speak of the need for one to have a mind transformed by the Holy Spirit and focused on God and His Word. There will be situations that you face in life that are not directly, or even indirectly, addressed in the Bible. For that same matter, they may not even be addressed in extra-Biblical literature. Many of the controversial issues that we are going to face today, or will be facing in the next few decades—and this includes mainline Judaism and Christianity—deal with bio-ethics. You know, I have never heard a single Messianic teacher (as of 2006) ever talk about stem cell research. It is not addressed in the Bible, other than the fact that we are to respect life. I do not know what the answer is regarding cloning your organs should they fail on you. But I know that these are the kinds of issues that require us to move beyond the essentials of the faith. The great evangelical theologian F.F. Bruce observed, "It is ethically mature people…who have built up in the course of experience a principle or standard of righteousness by which they can pass discriminating judgment on moral situations as they arise."[7] Thus, my friends, we must not only have a relationship with God, but have a mind focused on God.

How do we experience a transformation of the mind in our own individual walks of faith? When each of you entered into the Messianic movement, you likely

---

[7] F.F. Bruce, *New International Commentary on the New Testament: The Epistle to the Hebrews* (Grand Rapids: Eerdmans, 1990), 136.

experienced—as I know I certainly did—a period of "information overload." Like some of the newer versions of Microsoft Windows, you likely froze up a few times, and felt like you needed a reboot. Some of your lifestyle practices and traditions that you had been raised with, more than anything else, were being challenged as non-Biblical. You got to hear about the significance of the weekly *Shabbat*, the appointed times, the kosher dietary laws, and got a taste of the Jewish character of Yeshua's teachings. For many of you, the introduction to the Messianic movement was an up and down roller coaster ride, or like being told by the pilot that the aircraft is about to experience some turbulence. But all roller coaster rides come to an end, and turbulence does not always last. We have to come to a point both individually and corporately where we can be comfortable, and above all stable, in this newfound walk.

I have been in the Messianic community for almost eleven years (since 1995). It is not an easy place to be, especially today. Our own ministry has dubbed 2006 "the transitional year out of the year of transition," as certain projects and teaching series have begun that I believe will help renew hearts, and yes, transform minds for the Lord's work that each of us must perform. Any of you who have spoken with me in private, or have corresponded with me in the past, **know that I am dead serious about studying the Bible.** I believe that a consistent study of the Bible is the only way for any person to experience a true transformation of the mind, because it is in a detailed study of Scripture where we can ask God to show us what the text meant "back then," and what it means for us today. In particular as a Messianic Believer, there should be three distinct things that you should be focusing on weekly as you open God's Word, and allow it to minister to your heart, as well as to your brain (keep in mind that this can be applied both congregationally and personally):

1. You should be reading through and examining the weekly Torah portions on *Shabbat.*

Much of this is accomplished in home fellowships or study groups. This is how many Messianic congregations get their start.

2. You should be examining some kind of other Biblical text throughout the week as a group, independent of the Torah.

Much of this can be done in some kind of mid-week study, where you go through a systematic examination of a text of the Apostolic Scriptures, or perhaps one of the Prophets or histories of the Tanach.

3. You should be examining a text of Scripture yourself, different from the first two.

The responsibility for teaching or examining the first two areas can rest entirely on a congregational or fellowship leader; you just need to make sure that you are engaged somehow in those two weekly studies. This third one you have to take the initiative on, and is entirely contingent on you and what the Holy Spirit is convicting you to examine in the Bible.

Now, with some of this said—and I believe that we have some important objectives to accomplish—I would like to briefly comment on some of the over-emphasis that has taken place in the Messianic community regarding the Torah. Over the past two to three years (2003-2006) I have personally witnessed a radical shift in the study habits of many Messianics, where it seems that the only Scriptures that matter to them, or have any relevance concerning their lives, are the

Torah or Pentateuch. In some extreme cases, it can appear that the relationship that is pursued is not with the Giver of the Torah, God Himself, but rather with the Torah. And what is ironic, is that having participated or being privy to some of these Torah studies, I really do not think that the Torah is being studied properly at all.

As a point of reference, many of you are aware that in the weekly audio studies that I have done, we have primarily focused on books of the Apostolic Scriptures. Going through a text verse-by-verse, we go through quite a bit of information that incorporates the Torah and Tanach, as well as some extra-Biblical literature. I do not believe it is enough for us to examine the Torah without seeing how it is embodied in the lifestyle and *halachah* of Yeshua and the Apostles. And, not knowing about this has caused some controversy when we see Yeshua and the Apostles living out the Torah *and* most of the contemporary Jewish traditions of their time. When we deal with the First Century, we actually have it quite easy. In an elongated sense, we are only dealing with a period of about 120 years. When we consider the large First Century world, we are, for the most part, dealing with about four language groups. Sadly, this is difficult for many Messianics to understand, because their focus can be on the tree called "Israel" so much, that the forest called "the world" is forgotten. The salvation of the world can likewise be forgotten, as well as God's desire to communicate His Word in tongues other than Hebrew or Aramaic.[8]

But this is only the tip of the iceberg, because as I believe that we, as a movement, are only now beginning to really see the need to examine the Apostolic Scriptures from a distinct Messianic point of view, I believe we also have quite a long way to go in our examinations of the Torah and Tanach. This is because when we deal with the Tanach, we are dealing with a period that begins with the creation of humankind and ends with the Jewish exiles having returned from Babylonian captivity. Conservatively, we are dealing with a composition period stretching anywhere from 3,000-4,000 years or longer. K.A. Kitchen, who is a professor emeritus at the University of Liverpool, summarizes it this way in his book *On the Reliability of the Old Testament*:

"Doing justice to the Old Testament meant a minimum span of two thousand years overall (three thousand for full background), ability to draw upon documents in vast quantity and variety in some ten ancient Near Eastern languages, and a whole patchwork quilt of cultures."[9]

Of course, thanks to people like Kitchen, and other commentators and theologians, most of us do not have to do primary research in fields like archaeology or have to sift through thousands upon thousands of pages of ancient texts to get a feel for the Ancient Near East. But we certainly need to incorporate available data into our Torah studies. After all, as I commonly say every Passover: "If you want to get the most out of Passover, we have to know a few things about Egypt." While some people have a fear that knowing about history may somehow

---

[8] For further examination, consult this writer's workbook *A Survey of the Apostolic Scriptures for the Practical Messianic*.

[9] K.A. Kitchen, *On the Reliability of the Old Testament* (Grand Rapids: Eerdmans, 2003), xiii.

subtract from the inspiration of a text, it actually enhances it and should make it more real to us.[10]

When we study the Bible, we have to understand that while it is the inspired Word of God, it was not written directly to us. We have to learn to examine texts of Scripture to the audience it was originally written to. We have to transport ourselves back in time and pray that the Lord is able to help us think in terms that can be foreign to us. When we can properly understand a text as it was originally given to an audience, and then when it comes to the Torah, see how it was lived out in the lives of Yeshua and the Apostles, then we can begin to make practical, real life applications for us today. This is the whole point of why we must study God's Word. Most of the time, the answer is there, we just have to dig for it and do a little work. I believe this bears witness with most of you here, and it would be my hope that in the years to come we can see more of an emphasis on examining the Bible, *realistically for what it originally meant*, than perhaps "fancifully" for what we think it might say. Yes, my friends, this might mean that we have to deal with some Biblical history, and even wade through some extra-Biblical literature. But who ever said our faith was easy? Are we being transformed so that we will be able to deal with increasingly more difficult concepts? Is not the Holy Spirit to give us critical reasoning abilities?

We live in a fallen world that is only getting worse and worse. Many of the challenges that the Messianic community faces have to be dealt with by those who have minds that have been transformed by the Holy Spirit. A transformed mind is constantly thinking about God, His Word, His Kingdom's work, and about contemplating solutions for life's ills. Each of us must have a mind that thinks about the needs of others, not uplifting ourselves. We have to pray each day, that the Lord extends His hand from Heaven, and just for a moment, massages our brain so that we might be focused on Him and His plan for the world. Remember Yeshua's admonition to us that we are to worship God not only with our whole heart, but also with our mind...

---

[10] For further examination, consult this writer's workbook *A Survey of the Tanach for the Practical Messianic.*

FAQs on the Spring Holiday Season

adapted from the Messianic Apologetics website[a]

Purim

Do you think that all Messianic Believers should celebrate Purim?

There are some in the independent Messianic community (as opposed to Messianic Judaism), who do not believe it is necessary to observe Purim. *Purim* is obviously not listed among the appointed times of Leviticus 23, because the events that it commemorates occurred after the giving of the Written Torah to Moses on Mount Sinai. *Purim* commemorates the events of the Book of Esther, where the Jews are threatened with annihilation at the hands of the evil Haman. Via the sovereignty of God, Esther is in the right place at the right time to thwart his evil plans.

While not one of the *moedim* in Leviticus 23, the Book of Esther does record that the commemoration of these events was to be honored by the Jews for centuries to come, and never to be forgotten:

"For Haman the son of Hammedatha, the Agagite, the adversary of all the Jews, had schemed against the Jews to destroy them and had cast Pur, that is the lot, to disturb them and destroy them. But when it came to the king's attention, he commanded by letter that his wicked scheme which he had devised against the Jews, should return on his own head and that he and his sons should be hanged on the gallows. Therefore they called these days Purim after the name of Pur [lot]. And because of the instructions in this letter, both what they had seen in this regard and what had happened to them, the Jews established and made a custom for themselves and for their descendants and for all those who allied themselves with them, so that they would not fail to celebrate these two days according to their regulation and according to their appointed time annually. **So these days were to be remembered and celebrated throughout every generation, every family, every province and every city; and these days of Purim were not to fail from among the Jews, or their memory fade from their descendants**" (Esther 9:24-28).

As Believers, we have the responsibility to remember these events as well, not only because the account of Esther is a significant part of the Biblical tradition—but most especially because if the Jewish people had been eliminated, then there would have been no people of Israel and thus no Messiah. It is not only the Jewish people who survived Haman's plan that were supposed to remember *Purim*, but it was also for "their descendants and all who joined them" (v. 27, RSV). This is strong Biblical evidence for the necessity for today's Messianics to remember *Purim*.

We should always be rejoicing in the triumphs of God's people over evil, and *Purim* is definitely an appropriate time for us to remember the mighty deeds that He has performed. It is also an excellent time for us to stand up to fight the evils of

---

a The complete FAQ section is available for access at <messianicapologetics.net/faq>.

anti-Semitism, as the spirit of Haman has never left us, embodying itself in anyone who wants to destroy the Jewish people.

The Exodus

Exodus 1:8 says that a Pharaoh came to power in Egypt who did not know Joseph. How is this possible when the final part of Genesis says that Joseph was made second only to Pharaoh? How did the Israelites find themselves enslaved by Egypt?

Genesis 41:40-43 neatly summarizes the position that the Pharaoh of Egypt gave to Joseph:

"'You shall be over my house, and according to your command all my people shall do homage; only in the throne I will be greater than you.' Pharaoh said to Joseph, 'See, I have set you over all the land of Egypt.' Then Pharaoh took off his signet ring from his hand and put it on Joseph's hand, and clothed him in garments of fine linen and put the gold necklace around his neck. He had him ride in his second chariot; and they proclaimed before him, 'Bow the knee!' And he set him over all the land of Egypt."

With Joseph being made viceroy of Egypt and saving Egypt from the terrible famine, one would expect that some kind of record would have been made about him. We would assume that successive Pharaohs would have at least known about Joseph, but this does not seem to be the case in the opening verses of Exodus, where a new Pharaoh comes to power and the Israelites in Egypt are enslaved:

"Now a new king arose over Egypt, who did not know Joseph. He said to his people, 'Behold, the people of the sons of Israel are more and mightier than we. Come, let us deal wisely with them, or else they will multiply and in the event of war, they will also join themselves to those who hate us, and fight against us and depart from the land'" (Exodus 1:8-10).

There are a variety of views as to why a Pharaoh came to power "who did not know about Joseph" (NIV). A proper view of this can allude many interpreters who are not equipped with an historical understanding of the Scriptures, which can generally be nursed by employing good commentaries. The *ArtScroll Chumash*, commonly used in today's Messianic community, indicates that "Either it was literally a new king, or an existing monarch with 'new' policies, who found it convenient to 'ignore' Joseph's monumental contributions to the country (*Sotah* 11a)."[b] While this gives us an important clue, and is indeed very possible, there are some more specific things that we need to consider.

Nahum Sarna indicates that "The most reasonable explanation for the change in fortune lies in the policies adopted by the pharaohs of the Nineteenth Dynasty (ca. 1306-1200 B.C.E.), and especially by Ramses II (ca. 1290-1224 B.C.E.), who shifted Egypt's administrative and strategic center of gravity to the eastern Delta of the Nile."[c] He gives a further clue on his commentary for vs. 9-10 as to why the Egyptians may have been fearful of the Ancient Hebrews:

---

[b] Nosson Scherman, ed., et. al., *The ArtScroll Chumash, Stone Edition*, 5th ed. (Brooklyn: Mesorah Publications, 2000), 293.

[c] Sarna, *Exodus*, 4.

"The eastern Delta of the Nile was vulnerable to penetration from Asia. In the middle of the eighteenth century B.C.E. it had been infiltrated by the Hyksos, an Egyptian term meaning 'rulers of foreign lands.' The Hyksos were a conglomeration of ethnic tribes among whom Semites predominated. They gradually took over Lower Egypt and ruled it until their expulsion in the second half of the sixteenth century B.C.E."[d]

When we consider some of these factors in our reading of Exodus 1, what is most likely to have happened is that the Ancient Israelites found themselves embroiled in a political conflict beyond their control. This would have been the general time that Jacob and his family migrated into Egypt to avoid the famine, if we accept the prophecy that Israel would be in Egypt four hundred years (Genesis 15:13). This would have occurred at about the same time of the Hyksos invasion of Egypt, who later took over Northern Egypt where the Israelites lived. The Egyptians, not making any distinctions between the Hyksos and the Hebrews—both being Semitic peoples, coupled with the possibility of a new dynasty coming to power, would have easily enslaved them as they took back control of their land.

A new Pharaoh of Egypt from a new dynasty could have easily not known of Joseph because the Israelites settled in Goshen, in the Nile Delta region of Lower Egypt, and as Pharaoh he would have been from Upper Egypt or Southern Egypt, moving back into previously conquered territories. Wanting to rebuild an empire that had been lost, the Israelites having multiplied would make a convenient workforce. Politically it would have been easy to enslave them, because as Semites they would remind many Egyptians of the Hyksos invasion.

What can you tell me about the controversy surrounding the numbers of the Exodus?

Whether one is aware of it or not, there has been considerable discussion over the past century regarding the numbers of the Exodus, and hence the population of Ancient Israel in the wilderness. This is not a liberal discussion or a conservative discussion, exclusively. Both liberals and conservatives, Jewish and Christian scholars, have expressed various opinions about the meanings of the population of Israel as seen in both Exodus 12 in Numbers 1. *NIDB* offers a summation of the traditional view:

"The Bible states that 600,000 men took part in the Exodus (Exod 12:37). A year later the number of male Israelites over the age of twenty was 603,550 (Num 1:46)."[e]

The Rabbinic tradition as seen in the Talmud likewise seems to confirm this:

"**R. Simeon b. Judah of Kefar Akko says in the name of R. Simeon, 'You have nothing whatsoever in the Torah for which six hundred three thousand five hundred and fifty covenants were not made, equivalent to the number of people who went forth from Egypt.' Said Rabbi, 'If matters are in accord with the view of R. Simeon of Judah of Kefar Akko which he said in the name of R. Simeon, then you have nothing whatsoever in the Torah on account of which sixteen covenants**

[d] Ibid., 5.
[e] Charles F. Pfeiffer, "Exodus," in Merrill C. Tenney, ed., *The New International Dictionary of the Bible* (Grand Rapids: Zondervan, 1987), 334.

were not made, and there is with each one of them six hundred three thousand five hundred and fifty'" (b.*Sotah* 37b).[f]

This discusses the opinion that 603,550 individual "covenants" were made at Mount Sinai.

Exodus 12:37 in most English versions appears: "the sons of Israel journeyed from Rameses to Succoth, about six hundred thousand men on foot, aside from children." This number is then often extrapolated as meaning that plus women, children, and others of the "mixed multitude" (Exodus 12:38), the total number of the Ancient Israelites must have been in the range of 2-3 million. Numbers 1:46 will later say, "all the numbered men were 603,550." Many in Orthodox Judaism and evangelical Christianity accept this without any further engagement, and almost no Messianics as of today (at least to our ministry's knowledge) have really engaged this subject further.

Doubts over the total numbers of the Exodus reaching 2-3 million have always existed in both liberal *and* conservative circles. As K.A. Kitchen summarizes, "For the last century or more, commentators have fought shy of the statement that 'about 600,000 went on foot, plus women and children' (Exod. 12:37), with its seeming implication of an exodus of two million people or so."[g] Far from this being only an academic discussion, untenable to your average layperson, the venerable *NIV Study Bible* notes (commenting on Numbers 1), "[V]arious speculations have arisen regarding the meaning of the Hebrew word for 'thousand.'"[h] The *New Oxford Annotated Bible* goes a step further, indicating:

"The census total of 603,550...is extremely high...It has been suggested that the Hebrew word translated 'thousand'...is an old term for a subsection of a tribe..., based on the procedures for military muster employed by other ancient peoples, and that the original number follows 'thousand' in each case, e.g. Reuben had forty-six tribal subsections with a total of five hundred men (v. 21). This reduces the total [of Reuben] to 5,550."[i]

Bible translations, whether produced by conservatives or liberals, generally do sit on the overly conservative side (often for market reasons). Thus, no Bible translation to date has really broken out of rendering "thousand" as something otherwise, even though there are plenty of commentaries on the Pentateuch that will discuss this issue.

There are good textual reasons to suggest that the total numbers of the Exodus were less than 2-3 million, and even less than 600,000. When one thinks that 2-3 million people were leaving Egypt, heading toward the Red Sea, he or she should be somewhat perplexed at how easily the Israelites were disturbed when only 600 Egyptian chariots chase them down (Exodus 14:7). As the people cry to Moses, "Is it because there were no graves in Egypt that you have taken us away to die in the wilderness? Why have you dealt with us in this way, bringing us out of Egypt?" (Exodus 14:11). More than a few people wonder if 2-3 million people could have been severely threatened by a mere 600 chariots. (These were not armored tanks!)

[f] *The Babylonian Talmud: A Translation and Commentary.*
[g] Kitchen, 264.
[h] Kenneth L. Barker, ed., et. al., *NIV Study Bible* (Grand Rapids: Zondervan, 2002), 189.
[i] Herbert G. May and Bruce M. Metzger, eds., *The New Oxford Annotated Bible With the Apocrypha*, RSV (New York: Oxford University Press, 1977), 161.

Either the Ancient Israelites were even more foolish than we commonly give them credit, or there is something that we might have missed.

The issue in question in both Exodus 12 and Numbers 1 concerns the Hebrew term *elef* (אֶלֶף), and what it might mean against its Semitic cognates. Nahum M. Sarna comments, "the logistics involved in moving two million people together with their cattle and herds across the Sea of Reeds with the Egyptian chariots in hot pursuit" begs many questions. "In response to these problems, it has been suggested that the Hebrew *'elef*, usually rendered 'thousand,' here means a 'clan' or that it signifies a small military unit—the number of fighting men levied from each tribe."[j] Kitchen goes on to explain,

"In the Biblical texts, the actual words for 'ten(s)' and 'hundred(s)' are not ambiguous, and present no problem on that score; the only question (usually) is whether they have been correctly recopied down the centuries. With *'eleph*, 'thousand,' the matter is very different, as is universally accepted. In Hebrew, as in English (and elsewhere), words that look alike can be confused when found without a clear context. On its own, 'bark' in English can mean the skin of a tree, the sound of a dog, and an early ship or an ancient ceremonial boat. Only the content tells us which meaning is intended. The same applies to the word(s) *'lp* in Hebrew. (1) We have *'eleph*, 'thousand,' which has clear contexts like Gen. 20:16 (price) or Num. 3:50 (amount). But (2) there is *'eleph* for a group—be it a clan/family, a (military) squad, a rota of Levites or priests, etc....It is plain that in other passages of the Hebrew Bible there are clear examples where *'eleph* makes no sense if translated 'thousand' but good sense if rendered otherwise, e.g., as 'leader' or the like."[k]

When this information is all considered, one is presented with a number of possibilities concerning the total numbers of the Exodus, which does reduce it from 603,500. Scholars have proposed various sums, ranging anywhere from 20,000-22,000 to often as high at 140,000.[l] When offering any alternatives to the traditional view of 2-3 million in both Exodus and Numbers, one has to ask whether 603 *elef* 550 are the total numbers of fighting men, or the total numbers of men. What about the priests, shepherds, and other men in Israel who formed the infrastructure of the camp? What about the women and children, and the average size of families? What about the men under twenty who could not fight? What about any others? When these factors are considered, one can certainly say *in general terms*, that several hundred thousand could very well have been involved in the Exodus.

In the future as Messianic Biblical scholarship becomes more engaged with contemporary opinion, there are likely to be more discussions regarding this issue. Many will still hold to the traditional view of 2-3 million in the Exodus. But many others are likely to just say that several hundred thousand were involved. Either way, both positions rightly advocate that there were scores of people involved, and to hold to only several hundred thousand being in the Exodus is by no means a liberal position. A liberal position would be suggesting that the Exodus and God's judgments on Egypt are only important *myths* that formed the basis of a group of

---

[j] Sarna, *Exodus*, 62.
[k] Kitchen, 264.
[l] Cf. Ibid., 265.

nomads called "Israel," and at the very most, 600 people were involved in some kind of wandering with the numbers exaggerated.

Can you summarize for me the debate over when the Exodus took place? Did it occur in the Fifteenth or Thirteenth Century B.C.E?

There is a long standing debate among conservative Biblical scholars—those who believe that a legitimate Exodus did take place in real history—as to whether or not the Israelites left Egypt in the Fifteenth Century or Thirteenth Century B.C.E. This is notably not a debate among those of the critical tradition, where the Exodus is often viewed as being some kind of historical fiction for a group of nomadic Semites (who became the Israelites) that steadily made their way into Canaan. As J.H. Walton is quite keen to note,

"In this day and age of biblical scholarship the debate no longer rages whether or not there was any exodus of biblical proportions. In fact, the consensus that there was not has become firmly entrenched in critical circles. In such a climate, the question concerning the date of the exodus might be lightly dismissed in some quarters as naive, presumptuous or quaint. Nevertheless, for those who take the biblical record seriously, debate continues concerning the most appropriate historical setting for this pivotal event in Israel's theology and self-understanding."[m]

Even though not all conservatives are agreed on the timing of the Exodus, **all are agreed that a large group of Israelites was freed from Egyptian servitude at some point in real live history.**

Both Fifteenth and Thirteenth Century B.C.E. advocates of the Exodus have to recognize that by 1209 B.C.E., the Egyptian Pharaoh Merneptah, successor to Ramses II, was responsible for subduing "four entities...in Canaan: Ascalon, Gezer, Yenoam, and Israel" (*ABD*).[n] The Merneptah Stela includes a victory poem, remarking how "Israel is laid waste; its seed is not."[o] So, sometime by the late Thirteenth Century B.C.E., the Israelites had established themselves to some decree or another in the Promised Land—numerous enough to have been attacked and defeated in battle by an invading Egyptian force.

The **Fifteenth Century B.C.E.** timing of the Exodus comes from a straightforward reading of the Biblical text. 1 Kings 6:1 states, "Now it came about in the four hundred and eightieth year after the sons of Israel came out of the land of Egypt, in the fourth year of Solomon's reign over Israel, in the month of Ziv which is the second month, that he began to build the house of the LORD." The Exodus is placed 480 years before Solomon's fourth year as king, which was 967 B.C.E. Counting 480 years back, then, yields a date of 1447 B.C.E. Even if some rounding off of numbers is considered, it is still thought that the Exodus occurred in the mid-to-early Fifteenth Century B.C.E.[p] This would mean that among the candidates of the Pharaoh for the Exodus would include either Thutmose III or Amenhotep I.[q] Around two centuries would have transpired to allow the Israelites

---

[m] J.H. Walton, "Exodus, Date of," in *Dictionary of the Old Testament Pentateuch*, 258.

[n] K.A. Kitchen, "Exodus, the," in *ABD*, 2:702.

[o] Walton, in *Dictionary of the Old Testament Pentateuch*, 262.

[p] Cf. Raymond B. Dillard and Tremper Longman III, *An Introduction to the Old Testament* (Grand Rapids: Zondervan, 1994), 59.

[q] Cf. Walton, in *Dictionary of the Old Testament Pentateuch*, 267.

time to settle in the Promised Land and establish themselves to a considerable degree, so much so that the later Pharaoh Merneptah would be able to attack an entrenched resident of Canaan.

Advocates of the **Thirteenth Century B.C.E.** timing of the Exodus consider it a bit lackadaisical to just take the 480 years of 1 Kings 6:1 at face value (K.A. Kitchen actually considers it the "lazy man's solution"),[r] and that it instead needs to be interpreted as a representative number, such as a holder for 12 generations of 40 years or something. Looking at events within Ancient Egypt, Exodus 1:11 records how the Israelites "built for Pharaoh storage cities, Pithom and Raamses." It is noted how the city of Pi-Ramesse (presumably named for the Pharaoh) was an east-delta city built by Ramses II (1272-1213 B.C.E.), and as Kitchen concludes, "the end of the oppression and the start of the Exodus could not precede the accession of this king at the earliest, i.e., not before 1279 B.C...That is only a little more than 300 years before Solomon" (*ABD*).[s] He also details how the Book of Judges probably also includes overlapping terms of various judges, which are not to be viewed in strict sequence.[t] From a theological perspective, Kitchen also thinks, "it must be emphasized that the formation of the Sinai/Moab covenant (Exodus-Leviticus; Deuteronomy) in its basic framework belongs squarely within the period 1380-1200 B.C." (*ABD*).[u]

In response to the Thirteenth Century B.C.E. Exodus view, Fifteenth Century Exodus B.C.E. advocates like to present a series of archaeological sites from Canaan, conquered by Joshua, that they feel date to a much earlier period than the 1200s B.C.E.[v] Of particular note is what city of Jericho was destroyed by Joshua during the Conquest, as there are various Jerichos to choose from. Walton indicates, "If Jericho city IV is the city conquered by Joshua...the exodus must have been in the fifteenth century," but then goes on to point out, "There is still much to be done before this perennial controversy can begin to find resolution."[w] Fifteenth Century B.C.E. advocates point to the presumed dates of archaeological locations in Israel, and move backward to the Exodus. Contrary to this, Thirteenth Century B.C.E. advocates try to place the Exodus within the history of Ancient Egypt, and then they move forward. There is no doubting that one's starting point is what determines what date of the Exodus is favored.

Even if conservative interpreters are not entirely agreed on the timing of the Exodus, this does not mean that they treat the Book of Exodus as an historical fiction. Raymond B. Dillard and Tremper Longman III note in their work *An Introduction to the Old Testament*, "it appears that the archaeological evidence may be harmonized with the most natural reading of biblical texts that describe a fifteenth-century Exodus and conquest. The text, however, does not permit certainty on the subject. There are arguments for a late date for the Exodus...that treat the text with integrity."[x] One will encounter conservative resources on Exodus, and the whole of the Pentateuch today, that include edifying and relevant

---

[r] Kitchen, in *ABD*, 2:702.
[s] Ibid.
[t] Ibid.
[u] Ibid., 2:703.
[v] Cf. Walton, in *Dictionary of the Old Testament Pentateuch*, pp 264-266.
[w] Ibid., 270.
[x] Dillard and Longman, 62.

commentary for Believers in Messiah compiled from both a Fifteenth and Thirteenth B.C.E. Exodus viewpoint.

Most of today's Messianics probably hold to a Fifteenth Century B.C.E. Exodus, thus making the Torah approximately 3,500 years old. There are various Messianic teachers, including Messianic Apologetics editor J.K. McKee, who lean toward a Thirteenth Century B.C.E. Exodus, making the Torah approximately 3,300 years old. He feels that it is best that we consider the role of the Ancient Israelites living under Egyptian servitude *first*, and that it is probably best for us to recognize that the later chronology of the Judges and Israelite monarchs is not at clear-cut as some may want it to be. However, the most important point is that we treat the Book of Exodus with integrity, affirming how God acted miraculously in delivering Ancient Israel out of bondage and into freedom, humiliating the Egyptian Empire. No Messianic teacher today, even those with some liberal theological leanings quite thankfully, has ever promoted that the Israelites' deliverance from Egypt was total fiction.[y]

What do you think is the correct route of the Exodus taken by the Ancient Israelites?

The challenge that Biblical scholars have had regarding the route of the Exodus has varied facets to it. While there are certainly some specific details given to us in the Torah of Ancient Israel's trek from Egypt to Mount Sinai (Exodus chs. 14-19; Numbers 33), too frequently this is more of a list of obscure place names that no longer exist than anything else. While everyone can be agreed that the Israelites moved in territory that today composes the countries of Egypt, Israel, and possibly also Jordan and Saudi Arabia, it is difficult to tell for certain what the exact route was that the Israelites took. Sadly, modern day politics and the volatility of the region, frequently prevent archaeologists from examining the different sites relevant to the Ancient Israelites' journeys.

There are three main views of the route of the Exodus, which Biblical scholars and students, do have available to them to consider, in their evaluations of the Israelites' journeys:

1. The **Northern Route Theory** argues that the Israelites crossed Lake Sirbonis, adjacent to the Mediterranean, and that Mount Sinai was located in the northern Sinai Peninsula. This view does not have a wide amount of support today. Notably against it is how God prohibited the Israelites from traveling via a route that would take them into Philistia (Exodus 13:17).

2. The **Southern Route Theory** is the most widely espoused today. It advocates that the Israelites probably crossed between the many marshy, water boundaries (now dry) in the isthmus between Egypt and the Sinai Peninsula, which moved northward from the Gulf of Suez. The Israelites headed south to a site in the Sinai Peninsula, the traditional location of Mount Sinai being Jebel Musa. While

---

[y] For further consideration, consult Kitchen's full article, in *ABD*, 2:700-708, and Walton's full article, in *Dictionary of the Old Testament Pentateuch*, pp 258-272.

You may also wish to consult the entries for Exodus and Numbers in *A Survey of the Tanach for the Practical Messianic* by J.K. McKee.

there are variations of this viewpoint, one of the main criticisms of it is that the Sinai Peninsula (or at least some of it) was controlled by the Egyptian Empire, and an escape from Egypt would surely have to constitute being completely removed from Pharaoh's jurisdiction.

3. The **Arabian Route Theory** is something that has only been recently suggested. It postulates that the traditional location of Mount Sinai is wrong, and that the Red Sea that the Israelites crossed is today's Gulf of Aqaba, sitting to the east of the modern-day Sinai Peninsula. Since the Sinai Peninsula was still controlled by Egypt, the Israelites could have escaped via the Darb el-Hajj, or a trade route connecting Egypt to Arabia. The volcanic Mount Bedr is proposed as a possible site for Mount Sinai. While there are compelling reasons in favor of this theory, not enough work or investigation has been undertaken at present to confirm it.

Given the three options proposed for the route of the Exodus, there are some good reasons for us to consider the suggestions made by the Arabian Route Theory. It does advocate that the Israelites would be completely out of Egyptian territory before arriving at Mount Sinai. What it lacks is enough scholarly research and support at present. But, given the great appreciation that evangelical Christians have for the Exodus, as well as the interests of Jewish academia, we can be guaranteed that more investigation into this third proposal will be available in the future.[z]

Passover

Where did the traditions from the *seder* meal employed during Passover come from?

Obviously, the Torah itself issues some specific commands concerning the observance of the Passover. There were some specific commandments relating to the first Passover, the deliverance from Egypt, which included slaughtering a lamb and spreading its blood upon the doorposts of the house, and eating the meal in haste, as the Ancient Israelites were preparing to leave (Exodus 12). Passover or *Pesach* (פֶּסַח) is codified as one of the appointed times in Leviticus 23, and regulations on how to observe it in the Promised Land are detailed in Numbers 9.

Between the first Passover in Egypt to the Passovers kept in the Land of Israel, coupled with the division and dispersion of Israel, and later with a vast Diaspora Jewish community by the time of Yeshua, the celebration of Passover developed substantially. By the time of Yeshua, the specific order of service for Passover became codified in the Haggadah of Passover, first referred to in the Mishnah. This was focused around a midrashic interpretation of Deuteronomy 26:5-9, which allowed for one to recline and remember the mighty deeds God performed before the Egyptians in delivering Israel:

---

[z] The information summarized here has been largely adapted from the *Archaeological Study Bible*, pp 108-109, 112.

"You shall answer and say before the LORD your God, 'My father was a wandering Aramean, and he went down to Egypt and sojourned there, few in number; but there he became a great, mighty and populous nation. And the Egyptians treated us harshly and afflicted us, and imposed hard labor on us. Then we cried to the LORD, the God of our fathers, and the LORD heard our voice and saw our affliction and our toil and our oppression; and the LORD brought us out of Egypt with a mighty hand and an outstretched arm and with great terror and with signs and wonders; and He has brought us to this place and has given us this land, a land flowing with milk and honey."

We see elements of the traditional Jewish Passover of the First Century included in Yeshua's Last Supper, and some slight deviations. The *Dictionary of Judaism in the Biblical Period* summarizes the central elements of Passover contained in the Haggadah:

"The ritual found in the Haggadah is first referred to in M. Pesaḥim, chapter 10, which describes a festival meal marked by a set order of foods and a required liturgy (seder). At the heart of the meal is an explanation of the significance of three foods (unleavened bread, bitter herbs, and the passover offering) and the recitation of the Hallel-psalms. In early Amoraic times, this basic ceremony was embellished through the addition of a discussion of Israelite history, leading up to and including captivity in Egypt. In later developments, continuing to the present, liturgical poems and other homilies have been added to the basic format set in talmudic times."[aa]

Today, we obviously see a wide variation of Passover customs and traditions present in the Jewish community and in Messianic Judaism. There are significant variations between Sephardic and Ashkenazic Jews, as well as between Orthodox, Conservative, and Reform (or Progressive) Judaism. The Passover *haggadah* (הַגָּדָה) is something that has been adapted and changed by each denomination of Judaism, as some *haggadah*s include an all-night service, where one stays awake and focuses on certain Scriptures, to those that are only focused around a meal at one's home with family and close friends. There are traditions present in Passover today that are unique to the lands where the Jewish people have been scattered.

Messianic Judaism has adapted many of these traditions to form its own Passover *haggadah*s, which demonstrate how we are to rejoice in God delivering Israel from Egypt, and Yeshua delivering us from the bondage of sin.

Should we eat lamb as Messianics during Passover? Is it true that the Jews do not eat lamb during Passover?

It is notable that there are divergent practices among the Sephardic and Ashkenazic Jewish communities as it relates to Passover and whether or not lamb is allowed to be eaten. Ashkenazic Jewry (Northern, Central, and Eastern European) does not eat lamb at Passover. This is based on the Biblical command, "You are not allowed to sacrifice the Passover in any of your towns which the LORD your God is giving you; but at the place where the LORD your God chooses to establish His name, you shall sacrifice the Passover in the evening at sunset, at the time that you came out of Egypt" (Deuteronomy 16:5-6). Because this is a clear

---

[aa] "Haggadah of Passover," in *Dictionary of Judaism in the Biblical Period*, pp 266-267.

reference to the Temple in Jerusalem, and since the Temple has been destroyed, Ashkenazic Jewish *halachah* prohibits the consumption of lamb at Passover, and instead allows for poultry. Sephardic Jewry (Spain, North Africa, and Arab lands) does permit lamb to be eaten at Passover, as a memorial to the Exodus.

Messianic Jewish practice is often divided as to whether or not someone was raised Ashkenazic or Sephardic. Some Messianic *seders* have lamb, and others frequently serve chicken. At Messianic congregations that have both Ashkenazic and Sephardic Jews, sometimes both lamb and chicken are served at the community's *seder* meal. A viable *halachah* for Messianic non-Jews is frequently debated, and we would encourage you to find the tradition that you are the most comfortable with.

Why do Jews have an egg on their *seder* plates? Does this not come from Easter?

The egg on the *seder* plate at Passover is a post-Second Temple Rabbinical addition. The roasted egg or *beitzah* in most Jewish traditions symbolizes the hardness of Pharaoh's heart. We would speculate that after the destruction of the Temple and the Dispersion of the Jewish people from the Land of Israel, new traditions were added to Passover to compensate for the loss of no longer observing it in the appointed place. New debates likely arose as Jews were spread abroad into many places where they had never lived before. As additions to the *seder* arose, eggs were probably an item that all Jewish communities could agree were "kosher for Passover," and the custom of having a roasted egg on the *seder* plate was instituted.

The inclusion of eggs at Easter time is a debated practice in Christianity. No one is entirely certain how they came about, but it is likely that they stem from some kind of Babylonian fertility rite. However, we do not stop eating eggs simply because pagans used them in their worship. Similarly, because the Jewish community employs an egg on the *seder* plate during Passover, we cannot all of a sudden make the judgment that they borrowed it "from Easter." There is always an alternative view that frequently eludes those who are out on an "egg witch hunt."

How can I determine what is, and what is not, kosher for the Passover season?

One of the major Biblical injunctions concerning Passover is to eat unleavened bread for seven days, remembering the bread of haste that the Ancient Israelites had to eat as they left Egypt (Deuteronomy 16:3). By extension, not only does the command pertain to eating unleavened bread, but it is a week-long prohibition against eating anything with leavening agents. This has been interpreted and applied in different ways, with some divergent *halachah*, in the Jewish community over the centuries.

The Talmud, for example, specifically rules that there are five types of grain that can be used for the production of *matzah* or unleavened bread: wheat, barley, oats, rye, and spelt (b.*Pesachim* 35a), and notably the list does not include rice and millet. Ashkenazic authorities would later extend the list of forbidden grains to include "legumes" such as beans, peas, corn, lentils, buckwheat, and sometimes peanuts. The prohibition exists because of the belief that flour made from these substances could be easily confused with leavened flour. It is notable that the addition of legumes comes largely from Medieval European Jewry, having made contact with the New World, and debates over what grains are "kosher for Passover" do not come from the First Century. In more modern times, various segments of Orthodox Ashkenazic Jewry have liberalized their stance on whether or not rice, beans, or corn can be eaten at Passover, as prohibitions against eating these things were largely given for a different time. Of course, this has not stopped many Ashkenazics from other branches of Judaism from eating "legumes" during the season of Passover.

Generally, Jewish *halachah* in both the Ashkenazic and Sephardic communities permits *matzah* to be mixed with grape juice, oil, or egg for the young and infirm. Egg *matzos* for Passover are *not intended* to be eaten by everyone during this time, although if one is confused, consulting one's rabbi is recommended.

Much of the confusion surrounding what is "kosher for Passover" in the Messianic community comes from Jewish Believers who were raised in nominally observant or relatively liberal homes. It also comes from non-Jewish Believers who were not raised in the Synagogue (or possibly even adjacent to any sizeable Jewish community), and hence are not familiar with many of the customs and traditions surrounding this holiday. In significant parts of the Jewish community, it is not uncommon for most homes to have a special set of dishes just to be used for Passover and Unleavened Bread. In some sects, kosher for Passover toothpaste, bottled drinking water, Coca-Cola, and even toilet paper are available. When some people see all of the Rabbinical injunctions, they easily get confused, even though they do not need to be.

The commandment regarding unleavened bread in the Scriptures pertains to eating and one's daily consumption. Obviously, any kind of bread or cereal that has yeast cannot be eaten. Various kinds of alcohol that have been produced with yeast (i.e., beer) cannot be consumed. This does not necessarily mean that one has to buy "kosher for Passover" cheese, because the cows who provided milk for the cheese ate corn for their diet. Most of the questionable items pertain to things that one would normally eat with bread, and you should check to see if there is a kosher for Passover section at your supermarket.

This should give you a good idea about what you can eat. You may also want to consult a Jewish cookbook that will have many kosher for Passover recipes. (Consult the **Kosher Your Plate** section for a variety of recipes.) More than anything else, we would urge you not to feel condemned if you make a few mistakes in an effort to be kosher during Passover. God's grace covers our sins, our "leaven," and when we find that we do make mistakes, we try to quickly rectify them.

Do you believe that males should be circumcised?

We are aware that the issue of circumcision is extremely controversial in the Messianic world. Most of Christianity has decided to largely ignore circumcision as an "Old Testament rite" entirely unimportant for Believers today.

Circumcision is the memorial sign of the Abrahamic Covenant (Genesis 17:11). The Patriarchs Abraham, Isaac, and Jacob were all circumcised. Yeshua the Messiah was circumcised (Luke 2:21). The Apostle Paul was circumcised

(Philippians 3:5). If we intend to appreciate the spiritual example and lives of these figures, and they could even be encouraged to be circumcised a matter of simple obedience. Yet, being circumcised as a male adult must always be tempered with knowing that Abraham was considered righteous while uncircumcised (Romans 4:9-10; cf. Genesis 15:6), later being circumcised (at the age of ninety-nine) as he advanced in faith (Romans 4:11; cf. Genesis 17:1, 10-11).

We do not consider circumcision to be a salvation issue at all, as the power of the gospel is blind in saving males who are either circumcised or uncircumcised (Colossians 3:11). We do, however, recognize the place of circumcision for the *appropriate* reasons (concurrent with the example of Abraham). The reason circumcision was such a controversial issue in the Apostolic Scriptures (New Testament) is that the non-Jewish males coming to faith were not circumcised as infants as the Scriptures prescribe. Had they been circumcised as infants, even as some kind of ancient medical procedure, then the controversy may not have really arisen. Among various groups, the foolish Galatians believed that circumcision of the flesh would assure them a place among the righteous, to which the Apostle Paul said, "Behold I, Paul, say to you that if you receive circumcision, Messiah will be of no benefit to you" (Galatians 5:2; cf. Acts 15:1). To these people he said that if you think circumcision will save you, do not even bother receiving it. (Note that circumcision was widely required of proselytes to Judaism, and there is good cause for us to believe that the phrase "receive circumcision" in Galatians, at least, was more concerned with being "converted to Judaism.")

Circumcision has become a common medical practice for many non-Jews in North America and in other parts of the Western world since the late 1800s. We do not believe this is by coincidence. As the Messianic movement has grown considerably in the past few decades, it is probably not by happenstance that many non-Jewish males in the United States and elsewhere have been circumcised as a simple medical practice not widely looked at as strange or taboo. (Please note that this is not to exclude those elsewhere who are not circumcised; we are only making an observation). Yet, in recent days in Western Europe, legislation has been proposed that would make infant circumcision illegal, via the guise of it being "genital mutilation." Sadly, various Christians are in support of making infant circumcision illegal.

We believe that Messianic families—either Jewish or non-Jewish—should be encouraged to circumcise their infant males. Although the practice of circumcision is not a salvation issue, it does have medical and health benefits, and it can be employed as a simple memorial of the Abrahamic Covenant. Circumcision for *all* Believers—male *and* female—should be of the heart (Deuteronomy 10:6; 30:6; Romans 2:29) more than anything else, but this in no way nullifies the benefits of a male being circumcised in the flesh. Being circumcised as an adult male should be an issue of maturity, as Believers are called to "abide" or "continue" (Grk. *menō*, μένω) in the faith (1 Corinthians 7:20). It may not be necessary to be physically circumcised in order to be saved, but going through the procedure as a simple act of obedience (not as some kind of proselyte procedure) should not be discouraged. This kind of obedience would be no different than a urologist advising a man that circumcision would be useful for his penile health.

The issue of circumcision is especially touchy during the Passover season, as the Torah clearly specifies that "no uncircumcised person may eat of it" (Exodus

12:48). Within the Messianic community, there are some groups that do not let uncircumcised males attend their Passover *seders*. Is this right or is it wrong? We do need to keep in mind the fact that a Messianic Passover *seder* conducted today is often just a memorial of the Passover, and there are many elements that are not observed because there is no Temple to go to where the sacrificial lamb can be offered. Because we are in the Diaspora, there are things that the Torah originally specified that cannot be followed. And in our Passover memorials, we have to not only weigh in the difference of venue, but also the reality of the post-resurrection era in which we live.

We do not believe that it is necessary for males to be circumcised to attend a Messianic Passover memorial. However, it might be encouraged that participation of individuals within the order of service or events at a Messianic *seder* could be limited to only those males who are physically circumcised. (And, by extension, it would be appropriate to require any males within the leadership structure of a Messianic congregation to be physically circumcised.)[bb]

Do you think that Messianic congregations should practice communion with bread and wine on a regular basis? I have noticed that some do, and some do not.

When Paul writes the Corinthians, "For as often as you eat this bread and drink the cup, you proclaim the Lord's death until He comes" (1 Corinthians 11:26), he delivers this instruction in the context of speaking to them about the yearly Passover meal (cf. 1 Corinthians 5:8-9). Many over the centuries, though, having been separated from the Hebraic Roots of our faith, have interpreted this as relating to the sacrament of communion. Certainly, while Christian communion has been a spiritually beneficial practice for many to remember the Last Supper, it is often removed from its First Century Jewish context, or its origins in the Passover. What we are to remember is the point in the *seder* meal where Yeshua lifted up the *afikoman* and said: "This is My body which is given for you; do this in remembrance of Me" (Luke 22:19; cf. Matthew 26:26; Mark 14:22).

It is our opinion that the Lord's Supper, our remembering of when He said "This is My body," should be observed once a year during Passover at **a very solemn point** in the *seder* meal. However, with this said we should understand why many Christians observe it more frequently. Remembering Yeshua's Last Supper is by no means something that is wrong or "evil." But, most Christians' understanding of this is separated from the Last Supper being a Passover meal, and that is why communion is often observed with leavened bread in many churches (even though various Christian traditions do use some kind of leavenless bread).

Some Messianic congregations observe a form of "communion" with *matzah* or unleavened bread. This would be more accurate than what many churches do, but it is still a definite holdover from Christian observance. It is not "wrong" to partake of a communion when it is offered, especially if you are visiting a church with a friend or relative. Yet, proper *halachah* for the Messianic community should more closely try to keep it in line with the season of *Pesach*. If Messianic congregations serve a communion with leavened bread, typically *challah*, and wine, it can only be taken as *kiddush* and not a true remembrance of Yeshua's Last Seder where *matzah*

[bb] For a further discussion of this issue, consult the chapter "Is Circumcision for Everyone?" in the book *Torah In the Balance, Volume II* by J.K. McKee (forthcoming).

was used. If you are in an environment that observes this kind of an observance weekly, then partake of it, but if not and you are leading a home fellowship or study group, then we recommend you keep it consigned to Passover.

The Last Supper, Crucifixion, and Resurrection

Is it true that there are some substantial objections to the Last Supper being a Passover meal? If there are any, how do you respond to these arguments?

There are some objections that are commonly made to the Last Supper being a Passover meal, but very few of them are made in light of Yeshua's words to His Disciples: "I have earnestly desired to eat this Passover with you before I suffer" (Luke 22:15). According to the Messiah, the meal that He *ate* with His Disciples was the Passover, and what may appear to be divergent accounts among the Gospel authors need to be theologically reconciled. The text does not say that He just *celebrated* the Passover, but specifically that He *ate* (Grk. *esthiō*, ἐσθίω) a *seder* meal. And while we commonly consider "Passover" to just be a holiday, in Scripture the *pesach* (פֶּסַח) can be the "sacrifice."[cc]

Some objections to the Last Supper being a Passover *seder* include the references to it occurring on the Day of Preparation (John 19:14), Passover eaten with solely a group of men as opposed to a family, the fact that there is no distinguishing between "bread" or "unleavened bread" in the accounts, and wine being consumed from a common cup. In contrast to this, the meal was eaten at night as the Passover should be, the obligatory drinking of wine was remembered, Yeshua and the Disciples customarily reclined for the meal, and a hymn was sung as was observed for Passover (Matthew 26:30). They do appear to have followed the prescribed protocol for a First Century Judean Jewish *Pesach*.

In total, it does seem that some modifications were made between Yeshua's *seder* meal and the main *seder* that would have been observed during His time. There have been various proposals made for this, including the thought that Yeshua's Last Seder was a "teaching *seder*" held between a Rabbi and students, or quite simply that the Lord held His Last Seder a day early as He was preparing to be sacrificed.[dd]

I have heard some Messianic teachers say that Yeshua was not crucified on a cross. Can you clarify this for me?

Many Messianics have been hesitant to use terms like "cross" or "crucifixion" for any number of reasons. The Complete Jewish Bible, for example, uses the term "execution stake" instead of cross, and it is not uncommon to also hear the term "tree" being used. While these are perfectly acceptable alternatives to the more common terms "cross" or "crucify," it by no means negates them. Much of the Messianic movement, sadly, has an immature attitude when it comes to the symbol of the cross. Many Messianic Jews, for whatever reason, are offended by it. Perhaps

---

[cc] *CHALOT*, 294.
[dd] For a brief examination of this issue, consult the article "The Last Supper and the Passover" in the *Archaeological Study Bible*, p 1611.

some of this is due to historical Christian abuses of the Jewish community done in the "sign of the cross," but the same can be said of just about any religious symbol. While we should be sensitive to those who may not always like the term "cross," the Apostle Paul himself writes that "we preach Messiah crucified, to Jews a stumbling block and to Gentiles foolishness" (1 Corinthians 1:23). For Believers in Yeshua, the cross is a bittersweet symbol of the pain and suffering that the Lord endured for us.

History fully attests that criminals in the Roman Empire were crucified upon some kind of a cross. It was an extremely brutal, humiliating, and painful way to suffer and die. It was intended to serve as a public warning to others not to infuriate the Roman state:

"Under the Roman Empire, crucifixion normally included a flogging beforehand. At times the cross was only one vertical stake. Frequently, however, there was a cross-piece attached either at the top to give the shape of a 'T' (*crux comissa*) or just below the top, as in the form most familiar in Christian symbolism (*crux immissa*). The victims carried the cross or at least a transverse beam (*patibulum*) to the place of the execution, where they were stripped and bound or nailed to the beam, raised up, and seated on a *sedile* or small wooden peg in the upright beam. Ropes bound the shoulders or torso to the cross. The feet or heels of the victims were bound or nailed to the upright stake. As crucifixion damaged no vital organs, death could come slowly, sometimes after several days of atrocious pain" (*ABD*).[ee]

When we consider this scholastic description of crucifixion, it portrays exactly what Yeshua did for us. Yeshua's crucifixion on a cross at Golgotha (Calvary) in the vicinity of Jerusalem was an historical fact. **You can stand rest-assured that the traditional view of Yeshua being executed on a Roman cross is generally accurate,** even though it was by no means something elaborate or glorified as some Christian portrayals may make it. Crucifixion was common in the First Century world. Any "alternative theories" that many Messianics may try to offer describing Yeshua's execution often try to make it something less brutal and horrific than it was. In fact, the Messianic immaturity concerning Yeshua's death can be so bad in some cases, that the book *Come Out of Her, My People* actually concludes that the cross could be the mark of the beast:

"What is the 'mark of the beast' of which we read in Rev[elation]…a mark on people's foreheads and on their right hands?….Different interpretations have been given to the 'mark of the beast,' and also the cross has been suggested."[ff]

If true, these are blasphemous statements designed to trivialize the sufferings that our Lord experienced for us. The fact that Yeshua was crucified on a cross does not necessarily make the cross a "holy symbol." The cross is, first and foremost, an instrument of death. When Yeshua says "take up your cross and follow Me" (Matthew 10:38; 16:24; Mark 8:34; Luke 9:23), He means that you must follow Him to the point of dying or being martyred—an unpopular subject in just about any religious venue.

It is also important to note that if Yeshua had been executed as solely a Jewish criminal, then He would have been stoned. But Yeshua was not stoned; He was executed by the Romans. This is because the sin of the *entire world*—and not just

---

[ee] Gerald G. O'Collins, "Crucifixion," in *ABD*, 1:1208-1209.
[ff] Koster, 34.

the Jewish people—was responsible for His death. **We are the ones responsible for Yeshua's crucifixion, and we should not try to trivialize His death.** Crucifixion is one of the most painful and humiliating forms of execution that humans have ever devised, and those who would try to make Yeshua's death something that it was not are on extremely dangerous ground.

I heard a Messianic teacher say that the Divine Name YHWH was spelled out on the writing above Yeshua's cross? Is this true?

The Scriptures that are often made light of concerning this belief include Matthew 27:37, "And above His head they put up the charge against Him which read, 'THIS IS YESHUA THE KING OF THE JEWS,'" and John 19:19, "Pilate also wrote an inscription and put it on the cross. It was written, 'YESHUA THE NAZARENE, THE KING OF THE JEWS'" (cf. Mark 15:26; Luke 23:38). What we know for certain from the Gospels is that Hebrew was not the only language in which this superscription was written. John 19:20 makes the important remark, "many of the Jews read this inscription, for the place where Yeshua was crucified was near the city; and it was written in Hebrew, Latin *and* in Greek." At the very least, this indicates that there were more than just Hebrew-speaking Jews present in Jerusalem at the time of Yeshua's crucifixion, but also probably indicates that the Greeks and Romans present at this event needed to know that Yeshua was indeed King of the Jews.

Some have made light of the record in John 19:21-22, where "the chief priests of the Jews were saying to Pilate, 'Do not write, "The King of the Jews"; but that He said, "I am King of the Jews."' Pilate answered, 'What I have written I have written.'" This claim is made to support the belief that the Divine Name YHWH was somehow spelled out in the Hebrew superscription above our Lord as He was dying. Some conclude that the Sadducees wanted the name YHWH pulled down and the words be re-written. But notice that this is not what the text tells us. They wanted it torn down because they wanted Pilate to write the mocking statement "I am King of the Jews." History reveals that Pontius Pilate was no friend of the Jewish people in Israel, and that he was censored by the authorities in Rome for how he treated them. Varied traditions indicate that he was either executed, committed suicide, or was exiled because of his poor administration.[88] If indeed antagonistic toward the Jews, Pilate would have wanted Yeshua's cross to say something to the effect that the king of the Jews was a "dead man," and that Rome had prevailed over them.

While our ministry *fully affirms* the Divinity of Messiah Yeshua, we can find no evidence to support the conclusion that the name YHWH was spelled above the cross in the words "Yeshua the Nazarene, the King of the Jews." Many who make this assumption claim that the Hebrew would have read *Yeshua haNatzri v'melech haYehudim*, beginning with the first four letters of God's Divine Name: YHVH or YHWH. The problem with this is that the statement actually translates as "Yeshua the Nazarene **and** king of the Jews," notably including the Hebrew conjunction *vav* (ו), generally meaning "and." If this were an accurate rendering it would be reflected in John's Greek transcription with the conjunction *kai* (καί), also generally meaning "and." But all John 19:19 reads with is *Iēsous ho Nazōraios ho*

---

[88] Cf. Lorman M. Petersen, "Pilate," in *NIDB*, pp 789-790.

basileus tōn Ioudaiōn (Ἰησοῦς ὁ Ναζωραῖος ὁ βασιλεὺς τῶν Ἰουδαίων), with no *kai* present in the text.

The conjuction *vav* (ו) or "and" is also not present in modern Hebrew translations of the Greek Apostolic Scriptures in John 19:19. The Salkinson-Ginsburg translation reads with *Yeshua haNatzri melech haYehudim* (מֶלֶךְ הַיְהוּדִים יֵשׁוּעַ הַנָּצְרִי), meaning "Yeshua the Nazarene, king of the Jews." The 1991 UBSHNT reads with *Yeshua m'Natzerat melech haYehudim* (יֵשׁוּעַ מִנְּצֶרֶת מֶלֶךְ הַיְהוּדִים), "Yeshua from Nazareth, king of the Jews." While it may sound interesting, and tickle some ears, the Hebrew that would have appeared above Yeshua's cross did not spell out the Divine Name YHWH. Author Douglas Hamp confirms these conclusions:

"In none of the texts above do we see the word *kai*, which, if the acrostic YHWH had been written in Hebrew, would have appeared in the Greek. If it appeared in at least one of the texts, then we might conclude that it was really there. However, since we don't see it in any of the texts, which are our *only* records of what was (or was not) on that sign, we must conclude that the acrostic YHWH was not on the cross. It is best to be silent where the Bible is silent. Regardless, however, of what it spelled out, the reason that the Jewish leaders were angry was not because the writing somehow spelled out *YHWH*, but because it said He was the king of Jews, an obvious declaration of messiahship, which they plainly rejected."[hh]

If Bible readers really want to see Yeshua the Messiah portrayed as YHWH, then it would be much more beneficial for them to investigate the many intertexual references from the Tanach, quoted in the Apostolic Scriptures—where passages directly applying to the LORD **are applied to Yeshua**, with Him integrated into the Divine Identity.[ii]

Is it really true that Yeshua was resurrected on Sunday?

Aside from all of the debates surrounding the chronology of Yeshua's frequently-called "Passion Week," which are present in both evangelical Christianity and the Messianic movement, it can be legitimately challenged from the Greek text of Matthew 28:1 whether or not the Messiah was resurrected on a Sunday morning. In most versions, the text reads as, "Now after the Sabbath, as it began to dawn toward the first *day* of the week, Mary Magdalene and the other Mary came to look at the grave" (NASU). Notably different from this is the 1901 American Standard Version, which has, "Now late on the sabbath day, as it began to dawn toward the first *day* of the week, came Mary Magdalene and the other Mary to see the sepulcher."

The difference between "after" or "late on" depends how one renders the Greek preposition *opse* (ὀψέ), which can mean "*after a long time, late,*" or applied as "*late in the day, at even.*"[jj] Did the Marys leave to go to Yeshua's tomb on Sunday

---

[hh] Douglas Hamp, *Discovering the Language of Jesus* (Santa Ana, CA: Calvary Chapel Publishing, 2005), 77.

[ii] For further consideration, consult Robert M. Bowman, Jr. and J. Ed Komoszewski, *Putting Jesus in His Place: The Case for the Deity of Christ* (Grand Rapids: Kregel, 2007), and Richard Bauckham, *Jesus and the God of Israel* (Grand Rapids: Eerdmans, 2008).

[jj] *LS*, 582.

morning, or late on the Sabbath day on what we would consider Saturday evening? This is a subject that will require further discussion and analysis.

Certainly, by the first day of the week, the Marys and many of the Disciples had discovered that Yeshua the Messiah had resurrected from the dead. Most in Christianity believe that because of Yeshua's so-called "Sunday morning resurrection" that it validates the transference of the Sabbath to Sunday, or the institution of "the Lord's Day" in place of the Sabbath. Yet, the Apostolic testimony that we see in the Book of Acts continues to indicate that they continued to observe the seventh-day Sabbath. The "first day" Biblically understood begins in the evening on Saturday, and would have been an appropriate time for the First Century Believers to handle the business and financial affairs of their assemblies, which they would have not done on the Sabbath.

Resurrection, Commemorating: How do you think that today's Messianics should commemorate the resurrection of Yeshua?

Honoring the resurrection of Yeshua the Messiah is something entirely appropriate for men and women of faith. The Apostle Paul's words in 1 Corinthians 15:13-14 testify, "if there is no resurrection of the dead, not even Messiah has been raised; and if Messiah has not been raised, then our preaching is vain, your faith also is vain." **Yeshua's resurrection is the most important event to our Biblical faith.** As the Messianic movement has grown, and many non-Jewish Believers have stopped celebrating Easter and instead started remembering Passover, there is still undeniably a desire to want to remember Yeshua's resurrection sometime during the week of Passover and Unleavened Bread. *There is nothing wrong or reprehensible about this.* How we learn to do this as a developing faith community, may be a bit of a challenge, though.

Those who follow the Saddusaical reckoning for the counting of the *omer* believe the answer is very straightforward. Interpreting "the day after the sabbath" (Leviticus 23:15) as being the weekly Sabbath on which the sheaf of firstfruits was to be waved before the Lord, it would seem pretty easy to connect this with Yeshua's Sunday morning resurrection, Yeshua being the firstfruits raised from the dead (1 Corinthians 15:20). The early Church must have mixed up this "firstfruits" commemoration with some errant practices that later became "Easter." Connecting a Sunday sheaf waving to Yeshua's resurrection is fairly easy for Christians, who currently celebrate Easter Sunday, to understand.[kk]

Not all Messianics are convinced, however, that the Biblical and historical data supports the Saddusaical reckoning of the counting of the *omer*, and believe that it would be more appropriate to honor Yeshua's resurrection not on a specific day of the week like Sunday—but instead closer to the actual date it would have taken place. Remembering Yeshua's resurrection on any day of the week adjacent to Passover may not be very palatable for some of today's Christians, but it has a significant precedent in the annals of early Church history. The Quartodecimans were a major sector of the Second-Fourth Century Church, present in Asia Minor, who commemorated the resurrection of Yeshua three days after the Jewish Passover, claiming to follow a tradition handed down to them by the Apostle John.

[kk] This point of view is explained more thoroughly by Zola Levitt, *The Seven Feasts of Israel* (Dallas: Zola Levitt Ministries, 1979), pp 6-8.

Once the Synagogue came out with the official date for the Passover, the Quartodecimans followed suit. **It was not irregular for them to commemorate Yeshua's resurrection on *any* day of the week,** versus the Roman Church that insisted on the first Sunday after the Spring equinox.[II]

Today's emerging Messianic movement, in the short term, is likely to see some variance in regard to how Yeshua's resurrection should be commemorated. Those following the Saddusaical reckoning of counting the *omer* are likely to hold some kind of firstfruits/Resurrection Sunday service. Those adhering to a Quartodeciman style approach could hold some kind of prayer service or other commemoration three days following 14 Nisan. A fair approach to whatever position one holds is to focus on the broad themes of Yeshua's Last Supper, His betrayal and arrest, His beating and humiliation, His crucifixion, and His resurrection in teaching and preaching during this season. We should maintain our attention on *these events* (cf. 1 Corinthians 2:2), and not try to pick apart on which days these events "must" have taken place, as though prophetic fulfillment is contingent on some kind of a Twenty-First Century binary thinking of os and 1s.

What the Messianic movement does in the long term is likely to be contingent on further studies that are conducted in the Gospels, and a renewed appreciation for a traditionally Jewish approach to the appointed times.

[II] Consult "Quartodecimans," in Bercot, 547; "Paschal Controversy," in Ibid., pp 500-501.

Shavuot

Do you follow the method of the Pharisees or Sadducees for the counting of the *omer* to determine *Shavuot?* It seems that most in the independent Messianic movement follow the counting method of the Sadducees.

The counting of the *omer* is commanded in Leviticus 23:11, "He shall wave the sheaf before the LORD for you to be accepted; on the day after the sabbath the priest shall wave it" (NASU). There were three distinct ways that this passage was interpreted among the Judaisms of the First Century:

1. The Sadducees interpreted "the day after the Sabbath" to be the weekly Sabbath that occurs during the week of the Festival of Unleavened Bread. The counting of the *omer* was thus to begin on a Sunday, and end on a Sunday fifty days later.[mm]

2. The Pharisees interpreted "the day after the Sabbath" to be the High Sabbath that occurred immediately after the first day of the Festival of Unleavened Bread, 16 Nisan. The counting of the *omer* would (usually) begin on any day of the week, and the day of the week that *Shavuot* would be commemorated would likewise fluctuate. Later Jewish tradition would set the 6th of Sivan as the specific day for *Shavuot.*

3. The Essenes (of which the Qumran community was a part) interpreted "the day after the Sabbath" to be the weekly Sabbath that occurred after the week of the Festival of Unleavened Bread was over. Thus, the Essenic community would observe *Shavuot* a week after the Sadducees.[nn]

Many in the independent Messianic community, outside of Messianic Judaism, prefer to follow the Saddusaical method for counting the *omer*—the same method followed by the Karaites—always remembering *Shavuot* or Pentecost on a Sunday. While some of these people do so because they are following a calendar different than the standard Rabbinical Jewish calendar used today, many others continue to follow the dates for the appointed times on the standard Jewish calendar with this being a notable exception.

There are likewise many in the independent Messianic community who believe that *Shavuot* should be observed on the traditional Jewish date of the 6th of Sivan, originally determined by the Pharisees, and that the Bible supports this viewpoint. **This includes Messianic Apologetics editor J.K. McKee**, although he does emphasize that we should respect those who hold to the Saddusaical view.

Making this disagreement about when to start counting the *omer*, into some kind of an issue about "Sunday," entirely misses the point. The discussion about when to count the *omer* is really about whether or not today's Messianic Bible

---

[mm] The entry for "Firstfruits" by R.O. Rigsby, in *Dictionary of the Old Testament Pentateuch*, simply states, "the wave sheaf of immature barley [was] offered during the Feast of Unleavened Bread on the first Sunday after Passover" (p 314).

It is notable though, that there is no engagement with the differing opinions in Second Temple Judaism in this article regarding *how* the command of Leviticus 23:9-14 was interpreted, and assumptions are made without any dialogue with external resources.

[nn] For another summation of all three views, consult Baruch J. Schwartz, "Leviticus," in Adele Berlin and Marc Zvi Brettler, eds., *The Jewish Study Bible* (Oxford: Oxford University Press, 2004), pp 263-264.

teachers have joined, or are at least beginning to join, into an interpretational conversation that involves more than just a single English version of the Scriptures and a Strong's Concordance.[oo] There are many people who get into a debate over this issue, and may argue quite strongly, but they are working from incomplete information.

The following has been compiled to present you both sides of the issue of how to count the *omer*, and thus when to commemorate *Shavuot*. The points presented for the Saddusaical view have been listed first, with a counterpoint response by the Pharisaical view. We would encourage you to make an informed decision for yourself based on what is provided below, should you have ever made any hasty conclusions about this in the past. We would also encourage you to not be unnecessarily divided with others who may share a different opinion at present.

Messianics who favor a Saddusaical determination of Shavuot

1. Leviticus 23:11 tells us that the counting of the *omer* is to begin on a weekly Sabbath:

"He shall wave the sheaf before the LORD for you to be accepted; on the day after the sabbath the priest shall wave it."

The day after the *Shabbat*, the weekly Sabbath during the Festival of Unleavened Bread (not the High Sabbath), is the day that the counting of the *omer* (עֹמֶר) or sheaf offering is to begin. After this, one is to count *sheva Shabbatot temimot* (שֶׁבַע שַׁבָּתוֹת תְּמִימֹת) or "seven complete sabbaths" (Leviticus 23:15). This means that *Shavuot* will always occur on the first day of the week or a Sunday. Its date is not fixed by a number date on the calendar, and can vary from year to year.

2. If the "Sabbath" referred to in Leviticus 23:11 were the High Sabbath of Unleavened Bread, then the Hebrew word *Shabaton* would have been used:

In Leviticus 16:31 *Yom Kippur* is referred to as a *Shabbat Shabaton* (שַׁבַּת שַׁבָּתוֹן) or "a sabbath of solemn rest," in other words, a High Sabbath. *Yom Teruah* is referred to as a special "rest" or *Shabaton* in Leviticus 23:24, a High Sabbath. *Yom Kippur* is again referred to as a *Shabbat Shabaton* in Leviticus 23:32, "a sabbath of complete rest." *Shabaton* is used twice in Leviticus 23:39 to refer to the first and last "rest" days of *Sukkot*.

Shabaton means "a **sabbath** that is markedly different from the usual שַׁבָּת inasmuch as it is to be observed strictly and to be celebrated in a special way" (*HALOT*),[pp] hence "a High Sabbath." If the counting of the *omer* were to begin after the High Sabbath of the Festival of Unleavened Bread, then this term should have been used in Leviticus 23:15, rather than the more normal *Shabbat*, which clearly designates the weekly Sabbath.

3. **Yeshua the Messiah is the firstfruits of the resurrection, thus we must always remember His Sunday resurrection in the counting of the *omer*.**

Yeshua the Messiah, according to the Apostle Paul, is the firstfruits of the resurrection (1 Corinthians 15:20, 23). The *omer* counting begins on the weekly Sabbath during the Festival of Unleavened Bread and allows us to commemorate

---

[oo] Consult the article "Getting Beyond Strong's Concordance" by J.K. McKee.
[pp] *HALOT*, 2:1412.

Yeshua's Sunday morning resurrection when the firstfruits would have been offered. The command in Leviticus 23:10-11 is, "**you shall bring in the sheaf of the first fruits of your harvest** to the priest. He shall wave the sheaf before the LORD for you to be accepted; on the day after the sabbath the priest shall wave it." As the Marys left to go to the tomb, "after the Sabbath, as it began to dawn toward the first *day* of the week" (Matthew 28:1), it is clear that this took place after the weekly Sabbath on the Day of First Fruits.

It is interesting that now in the Jewish community, the counting of the *omer* begins after the High Sabbath or the first day of Unleavened Bread, which does not occur on a Sunday. Why is this the case? Was this started to downplay Yeshua's prophetic fulfillment of the firstfuits and His resurrection? Did this happen so that His resurrection would be denied?

4. The Messianic community should observe *Shavuot* in a way that appeals to Christians' understanding of Pentecost.

The Christian Church recognizes what Pentecost Sunday is—fifty days after Resurrection Sunday—and has actually gotten this correct in spite of centuries of Jewish misinterpretation of Leviticus 23. Following the Saddusaical determination of counting the *omer*—from the Hebrew of Leviticus 23 alone—we can educate our Christian brothers and sisters on the prophetic fulfillment of Yeshua's firstfruits resurrection and the outpouring of the Holy Spirit at *Shavuot* without any major complications.

Messianics who favor a Pharisaical determination of *Shavuot*

1. *Shavuot* is the "Feast of Weeks," and not the "Feast of Sabbaths":

It is quite significant that the name of the holiday in question is *Shavuot* (שָׁבֻעוֹת), the plural of the Hebrew *shavua* (שָׁבוּעַ), meaning "week." Before examining any Scriptures, why would the designation of this festival be *Shavuot*, meaning "Weeks"—rather than *Shabbatot* (שַׁבָּתוֹת), meaning "Sabbaths"? Is this not an indication that the date of *Shavuot* is to be determined using the *week*, and not the Sabbath? What constitutes what one would consider to be an "incomplete Sabbath"? This can only be the case if the term *Shabbat* can be used to represent "week."

There is strong evidence in favor of the fact that the Hebrew term *Shabbat* (שַׁבָּת) need not always refer to the Sabbath day. While the primary usage of *Shabbat* is undoubtedly "the day of rest, the sabbath" (*HALOT*),[99] this does not disallow other possible usages—including "week" (*Jastrow*)[rr] as seen in other Scriptures and certainly throughout Rabbinical literature. This is why most Bibles actually render Leviticus 23:15 with the counting of the *omer* being determined by "seven weeks" (RSV, NIV, NRSV, ATS, NJPS, ESV, HCSB, CJB, et. al.). The only major versions that leave it as "sabbaths" are the KJV, NKJV, and NASU.

Shortly after the listing of the *moedim* in Leviticus 23, instruction about the Sabbatical year and year of jubilee are given in Leviticus 25, notably including the command, "You are also to count off seven sabbaths of years for yourself, seven times seven years, so that you have the time of the seven sabbaths of years, *namely,*

---

[99] Ibid., 2:1411.
[rr] Marcus Jastrow, *Dictionary of the Targumim, Talmud Bavli, Talmud Yerushalmi, and Midrashic Literature* (New York: Judaica Treasury, 2004), 1520.

forty-nine years" (Leviticus 25:8). Here, it is undeniable that *sheva shabbatot shanim* (שֶׁבַע שַׁבְּתֹת שָׁנִים) means "seven weeks of years" (RSV, NRSV, NJPS, ESV), and that the term "sabbath" is flexible enough to regard more than just the weekly Sabbath day.

Rabbinic literature itself indicates this flexibility. The Mishnah includes a usage of *Shabbat* used to represent "week":

"[He who says,] 'Qonam if I taste wine today,' is prohibited only to nightfall. [If he referred to] 'this week [*shabbat zo*],' he is prohibited the entire week [*b'kol ha'shabbat*], and the Sabbath [which is coming is included] in that past week" (m.*Nedarim* 18:1).[ss]

Even the Greek equivalent of *Shabbat*, the carryover term *sabbaton* (σάββατον) present in the Apostolic Scriptures, has a variance of usages. "The plural *tá sábbata* may mean one sabbath, several sabbaths, or the whole week (like the Hebrew term)" (*TDNT*).[tt] In the *Didache*, from the late First Century C.E., it is said that the Jews "fast on the second and the fifth day of the week" (8:1), *deutera sabbatōn kai pemptē* (δευτέρα σαββάτων καὶ πέμπτῃ), meaning twice a week.[uu] Here, the plural *sabbatōn* or "sabbaths" is used. It has to represent the "week," as it would make no sense for one to fast two times on the Sabbath day or Saturday.

The term "sabbath" having some variance of usages should not be that disturbing to us. Consider that in a similar vein, the Hebrew term *yom* (יוֹם) primarily means "day of twenty-four hours" (*HALOT*),[vv] but there are most certainly instances when *yom* means "a period of time" such as a "year" (*HALOT*),[ww] or simply "division of time" (*BDB*)[xx] that may or may not be specified.[yy] Will we allow God some variance in the vocabulary that He uses in His Word?

2. We cannot ignore the witness of Deuteronomy 16:9 and the Septuagint rendering of Leviticus 23:11:

Deuteronomy 16:9 gives us further clarification of how *Shavuot* is to be determined, stating, "You shall count seven weeks for yourself; you shall begin to count seven weeks from the time you begin to put the sickle to the standing grain." The command here is not to count using "Sabbaths," but rather to count *sheva shavuot* (שָׁבְעָה שָׁבֻעֹת) or "seven weeks." Are we to ignore this instruction to count via "weeks," and *only follow* what Leviticus 23:15 may be telling us?

Liberal theologians would actually conclude that there is a noticeable difference between the command delivered in Leviticus 23:15, to count "seven complete sabbaths," and the command in Deuteronomy 16:9 to count "seven weeks." Attributing these differences to the JEDP documentary hypothesis,[zz] they may claim that the command seen in Leviticus 23 is from P or the Priestly writer,

---

[ss] Neusner, *Mishnah*, 421.

[tt] E. Lohse, "*sábbaton*," in *TDNT*, 989.

[uu] Cf. BDAG, 910.

[vv] *HALOT*, 1:399.

[ww] Ibid., 1:400.

[xx] BDB, 398.

[yy] The most debated of these for certain would be how *yom* is used in Genesis 1.

[zz] Consult the entries for the Pentateuchal books (Genesis, Exodus, Leviticus, Numbers, Deuteronomy) in *A Survey of the Tanach for the Practical Messianic* for a conservative analysis and response to the JEDP documentary hypothesis.

and that the command seen in Deuteronomy 16 is from D or the Deuteronomist. Those of us who believe in unified authorship of the Mosaic Torah have the responsibility *to reconcile* these "differences," lest any of us be accused of following "P" or "D." When we reconcile these differences and synthesize the two passages, the Pharisaical view of starting the *omer* count on the High Sabbath of Unleavened Bread is validated.[aaa]

The Hebrew of Leviticus 23:11 is vague, indicating that the counting of the *omer* is to begin *m'mochorat ha'Shabbat* (מִמָּחֳרַת הַשַּׁבָּת), literally "from the morrow the Sabbath," understood to be "the day after the sabbath." With the Sabbath not specified, the Sadducees interpreted this as the weekly Sabbath—whereas the Pharisees interpreted this as the High Sabbath during the first day of Unleavened Bread (also based on similar language seen in Joshua 5:10-12). This is where a great deal of division took place, with the Hebrew unclear on this point. The exegesis of Messianics who advocate that the Saddusaical method is correct often stops here.

We should not be consigned to make a decision solely on the basis of what the Hebrew Masoretic Text of Leviticus 23:15 might say about "the day after the sabbath." Around three centuries before the coming of Yeshua, the Hebrew Tanach was translated into Greek resulting in what we now call the Septuagint. The LXX is the most significant complete textual witness to the Hebrew MT, and was frequently used by the Apostles in their quotations of the Tanach. **The Apostles' usage alone requires us to consider how the LXX renders Leviticus 23:11.**

The Greek LXX rendered the Hebrew *m'mochorat ha'Shabbat,* "the day after the sabbath," with *tē epaurion tēs prōtēs* (τῇ ἐπαύριον τῆς πρώτης), or "On the morrow of the first day" (LXE). Is this "first day" the weekly Sabbath? Obviously not. It is the first day of the Festival of Unleavened Bread. If we follow the Saddusaical argument using the LXX, then the counting of the *omer* would actually begin on a Monday, the day after "the first day." But this is an improper conclusion based on what "first" actually translates. Tim Hegg notes in his article "Counting the Omer: An Inquiry into the Divergent Methods of the 1st Century Judaisms," that "Here the Hebrew שַׁבָּת, *shabbat,* is translated by πρῶτος, *protos,* 'first,' meaning the 'first day of the Festival.' The Lxx, clearly an authoritative text in the 1st Century CE, gave direct substantiation for the Pharisaic reckoning."[bbb]

Furthermore, in Leviticus 23:15, the LXX rendered the Hebrew *sheva shabatot temimot,* "seven complete Sabbaths," with *hepta hebdomadas holoklērous* (ἑπτὰ ἑβδομάδας ὁλοκλήρους), meaning "seven full weeks" (LXE).[ccc] This is more

---

[aaa] No Messianic advocating the Saddusaical view would argue that the command to congregate "in the place which [God] chooses, at…the Feast of Weeks" (Deuteronomy 16:16) is unimportant, especially per the many Jews assembled from all over the known world as seen in Acts 2 following Yeshua's resurrection. Yet, as Schwartz indicates, "in P this festival [*Shavuot*] is not marked by a pilgrimage" (*Jewish Study Bible,* 264), as though Moses did not have anything to do with it and the command to commemorate is a later addition of the so-called Deuteronomist from the time of the Josianic reforms.

Certainly, the need to understand *additional* Scriptures and their relationship to Leviticus 23 should be apparent.

[bbb] Tim Hegg (2002). *Counting the Omer: An Inquiry into the Divergent Methods of the 1st Century Judaisms. Torah Resource.* Retrieved 12 March, 2007, from <http://www.torahresource.com>.

[ccc] The LXX was obviously compiled before the New Testament term *sabbaton,* a carryover from Hebrew and Aramaic, was used by Greek-speaking Jews. Leviticus 23:15 employs the more classical term *hebdomas* (ἑβδομάς), used by Aristotle to represent *"a period of seven days"* (LS, 220).

confirmation of how *shabbat* can be understood in a greater context beyond that of just the "Sabbath day," and can also include "week."

If we consider the Greek LXX to have any kind of relevance in our theological exegesis, then it supports the counting of the *omer* beginning immediately after the first day of Unleavened Bread on the 16th of Nisan, in conjunction with the Pharisaic method that is observed in mainline Judaism today. Furthermore, this is a textual indicator that the debate over determining *Shavuot* goes back several centuries before the time of Yeshua, and thus one cannot claim that there was a later "conspiracy" to downplay His resurrection by having the *omer* count begin on a day other than Sunday. This issue was present long before His Earthly ministry.

In today's Messianic movement, the Greek Septuagint is often casually dismissed among teachers as a valid resource to use for exegetical analysis. Its rendering of Leviticus 23:11 gives strong support for the Pharisaic reckoning of *Shavuot*. But in all honesty this is a rather minor issue on which to ignore the LXX. There are many more substantial issues pertaining to the Septuagint such as the quotation of Tanach Scriptures in the Apostolic Writings where the LXX differs from the Hebrew MT. If we get into the habit of ignoring the Septuagint on minor issues such as the determination of *Shavuot*, **then we may ignore it in more significant issues** such as the quotation of various Messianic prophecies used by the Apostles.[ddd] So should we remove the LXX from our conversation on when *Shavuot* is to be observed?

3. *Shabaton* can refer to the weekly Sabbath equally as much as a High Sabbath in the Torah:

Advocates of the Saddusaical view often claim that if the High Sabbath were being referred to in Leviticus 23:11, "on the day after the sabbath," then the Hebrew word *Shabaton* (שַׁבָּתוֹן) would be used instead of *Shabbat* (שַׁבָּת) or in conjunction with it. It is asserted that *Shabaton* is only used in the Torah to refer to High Sabbaths, and likewise that *Shabbat* is only used to refer to weekly Sabbaths, thus the beginning of the *omer* count starts after a weekly Sabbath.

What Saddusaical advocates have conveniently avoided is that *Shabaton* can be used in reference to the weekly Sabbath every bit as much as a High Sabbath:

"['T']hen he said to them, 'This is what the LORD meant: Tomorrow is a sabbath observance [*Shabaton*], a holy sabbath to the LORD. Bake what you will bake and boil what you will boil, and all that is left over put aside to be kept until morning'" (Exodus 16:23).

"Then Moses assembled all the congregation of the sons of Israel, and said to them, 'These are the things that the LORD has commanded *you* to do: For six days

---

[ddd] A widescale dismissal of the relevance of the Greek Septuagint for Messianics took place in 2005, with an incoherent teaching released on the canonicity of the Epistle to the Hebrews, a text which not only (almost) exclusively quotes from the LXX, but also makes distinct arguments about Yeshua from its unique renderings. Rather than considering the importance of the Septuagint for Biblical Studies, the accusation was made that the author of Hebrews misquoted from the Tanach, and did not know what he was talking about, meaning that Hebrews should not be considered authoritative Scripture for Messianic Believers today. Such misguided assertions bring gross discredit to the theological credibility of the emerging Messianic movement, in addition to planting seeds of doubt that the Apostolic Scriptures cannot be trusted. Hebrews is not the only book in the Apostolic Scriptures where the LXX is quoted proficiently.

Consult the commentary *Hebrews for the Practical Messianic* by J.K. McKee.

work may be done, but on the seventh day you shall have a holy *day*, a sabbath of complete rest [*Shabbat Shabaton*] to the LORD; whoever does any work on it shall be put to death" (Exodus 35:1-2).

"For six days work may be done, but on the seventh day there is a sabbath of complete rest [*Shabbat Shabaton*], a holy convocation. You shall not do any work; it is a sabbath to the LORD in all your dwellings" (Leviticus 23:3).

When we see that *Shabaton* is used equally to refer to the weekly Sabbath as well as High Sabbaths in the Hebrew Torah, no one can insist that the *Shabbat* for beginning the *omer* count must be a weekly Sabbath. No one would insist that the Sabbath mentioned in Leviticus 23:3—which occurs every week—all of a sudden becomes a High Sabbath. The "type" of Sabbath is simply not specified in the imprecise Hebrew of Leviticus 23:11, and we are forced to examine other Scriptures (i.e., Deuteronomy 16:9; Joshua 5:10-12) to formulate a more well-rounded interpretation of what is being referred to.

4. The Apostle Paul said that Yeshua the Messiah was the firstfruits of the resurrection—and he was a Pharisee:

The Apostle Paul is the one who writes the Corinthians, "Messiah has been raised from the dead, the first fruits of those who are asleep" (1 Corinthians 15:20). Paul is the one who associates some level of prophetic fulfillment to the firstfruits offering, the ceremony that begins the counting of the *omer* during the Festival of Unleavened Bread, with the resurrection of Yeshua. David H. Stern remarks in his *Jewish New Testament Commentary*, "Sha'ul probably wrote this letter between *Pesach* (5:6-8) and *Shavu'ot* (16:8), during the season for presenting the **firstfruits** of the harvest at the Temple (Leviticus 23:9-15)."[eee]

We need to temper Paul's words in 1 Corinthians with his own testimony before the Sanhedrin in Acts 23:6: "Brethren, I am a Pharisee, a son of Pharisees; I am on trial for the hope and resurrection of the dead!" The Greek *egō Pharisaios eimi* (ἐγὼ Φαρισαῖος εἰμι), appearing in the present active indicative tense, makes it abundantly clear that *Paul actively considered himself a Pharisee* the day that he made these remarks. *Halachically* the observance of *Shavuot* counting from after the High Sabbath of the Festival of Unleavened Bread, was a major division between the Pharisees and Sadducees of Yeshua's time. If we can accept Paul's testimony before the Sanhedrin as being accurate, then we can safely conclude that he observed *Shavuot* with the Pharisaic party (cf. Acts 20:16; 1 Corinthians 16:8). He had no problem writing that Yeshua fulfilled the prophetic typology of firstfruits, while at the same time being a Pharisee and recognizing that the firstfruits offering would be made on the 16th of Nisan.

Likewise, we have to remember Yeshua's own words in Matthew 23:2-3: "The scribes and the Pharisees have seated themselves in the chair of Moses; therefore all that they tell you, do and observe, but do not do according to their deeds; for they say *things* and do not do *them*." While Yeshua does issue some imperatives against the hypocrisy of the Pharisaic leaders in Matthew 23, He nevertheless instructs His followers to take their *halachic* lead from (many of) the Pharisaic rulings. We have justified course, then, to observe *Shavuot* as Messianic Believers with the remainder

---

[eee] Stern, *Jewish New Testament Commentary*, 488.

of the worldwide Jewish community on 06 Sivan—and not a date of our own choosing—along with the rest of the appointed times.

5. Following the Pharisaic method of determining *Shavuot* does not subtract from Yeshua's prophetic fulfillment of the firstfruits offering:

It is commonly asserted among advocates of the Saddusaical reckoning for *Shavuot* that beginning the *omer* count immediately after Passover, after the High Sabbath of Unleavened Bread, subtracts from Yeshua's prophetic fulfillment of the firstfruits offering. Specifically, because the counting of the *omer* can occur on any day of the week via the Pharisaical reckoning for *Shavuot*, it is believed among some to take away from Yeshua's "Sunday morning resurrection."

First of all, it should be noted that one can legitimately challenge the concept of a "Sunday morning resurrection" as Matthew 28:1 indicates that the Marys left to visit Yeshua's tomb *opse de sabbatōn* ('Οψὲ δὲ σαββάτων) or "late on the Sabbath day" (American Standard Version), meaning Saturday evening. Secondly, we all recognize that Yeshua's resurrection was three days and nights (Matthew 12:40) after His death. Counting back from Saturday evening, this places Yeshua's death on Thursday afternoon. Following this would seemingly have been the first day of Unleavened Bread (Friday), and then the first day of the *omer* count (Saturday) to be immediately followed by Yeshua's resurrection that evening. Yeshua would have been dead three days and nights: Thursday day/night, Friday day/night, and Saturday day/night.[fff]

This chronology *could* place Yeshua's resurrection immediately after the offering up of the *omer* (assuming that the Pharisees would allow for the sheaf waving to commence on an actual Sabbath, which was debated in ancient times; cf. b.*Menachot* 63, 65, 72). Some Messianics who follow the Saddusaical method may have difficulty with seeing how Yeshua could possibly fulfill this prophetic typology, were He not resurrected on the specific "day" of the firstfruits offering. *If* He was resurrected after the waving of the sheaf, our answer to this lies in understanding that Yeshua's sacrifice in prophetic fulfillment of Passover also fulfills the sacrifice in fulfillment of *Yom Kippur*—a holiday that occurs over seven months after Passover. This is a major theme of the Epistle to the Hebrews, and it forces the able interpreter to conclude that prophetic fulfillment in Scripture is often more "fluidic" than his or her Western mind is accustomed to understanding. Hegg observes,

"The parallel between first fruits and resurrection exists regardless of which day one calculates the beginning of counting the omer. The idea that events must happen simultaneously in order to be seen as valid fulfillment simply cannot be sustained from a biblical standpoint. As an example, Yeshua surely fulfills the picture of Yom Kippur and the sacrifice made on that day, but the timing of His death is not remotely close to the observance of Yom Kippur. The first fruits themselves, when understood within the overall festival, point to the fulfillment in Yeshua's resurrection, not necessarily that He rose on the same day that the sheaf was waved. For the lesson of first fruits is that more is to come: as the first of the harvest is brought to the Lord, the hope is that a great abundance is to follow. This is a parallel to Yeshua's resurrection, and as the first fruits from the dead the point

---

[fff] For a further discussion, consult Chapter 9, "The Last Seder and Yeshua's Passover Chronology."

is that many more will follow. Like barley brought in from the new crop, so Yeshua is the first to rise from the dead of His own accord. As such, He guarantees the full harvest of all who are His. This is the connection to the first fruits, and it does not require simultaneous events."[ggg]

If the offering of firstfruits occurred immediately before Yeshua's resurrection, it does not at all mean that He does not fulfill the prophetic typology of the firstfruits offering via His resurrection. To insist on such binary 0s and 1s precision is a product of a Twenty-First Century mind, but not a Jewish mind of the First Century.

Advocates of the Saddusaical view do not answer the question of how the Apostles commemorated the resurrection in the years following, and whether they remembered it on the *day* of the week—or the *date*—on which it occurred. While many Messianics may be agreed on when things happened the year of Yeshua's atoning sacrifice, how this was commemorated in the early Messianic community in later years—and consequently what we should do today—is a matter of considerable divergence.

It is notable that a sect known as the Quartodecimans, from the Eastern Christian Church of the Second-Fourth Centuries, followed a tradition of celebrating Easter three days after the Jewish Passover, and they saw no problem with commemorating the resurrection on *any day of the week*.[hhh] Once the Jewish community set the date for Passover, then claiming to follow a tradition from the Apostle John via Polycarp, the Quartodecimans would then count three days and that would be their date to celebrate Easter. However, the Council of Nicea decreed that a different date, the first Sunday after the vernal equinox, should be used to commemorate Easter. Susan E. Richardson's comments from *Holidays & Holy Days* confirm this:

> "...In A.D. 325, the Council of Nicea set aside a special day just to celebrate the Resurrection. The problem with an official day was deciding whether or not the Resurrection should be celebrated on a weekday or...on a Sunday.
> "Many felt that the date should continue to be based on the timing of the Resurrection during Passover. Once Jewish leaders determined the date of Passover each year, Christian leaders could set the date for Easter by figuring three days after Passover...
> "...As Christianity drew away from Judaism, some were reluctant to base the Christian celebration on the Jewish calendar."[iii]

Ironically, Messianics holding to a staunch view of a Saddusaical *Shavuot*—one that always occurs on a Sunday—have fallen into following a Church ruling that was designed to keep Christians away from the "Jewish Passover." Furthermore, it may actually detract from Yeshua's prophetic fulfillment of Passover. (Do note that Messianic Apologetics editor J.K. McKee's own reasoning against always commemorating a Sunday *Shavuot* has **nothing** to do with some vendetta against Christians who attend Church on Sunday, as this is another issue altogether, and the Lord surely moves where two or three are gathered together as stated in

---

[ggg] Hegg, "Counting the Omer."
[hhh] Cf. "Quartodecimans," in Bercot, 547.
[iii] Richardson, 58.

Matthew 18:20.) Instead of counting three days from the 14th of Nisan, the day of Passover, commemorating Yeshua's resurrection shortly after the High Sabbath of Unleavened Bread—some may have to count as many as five or six days between a Monday or Tuesday Passover and then a Sunday First Fruits. Would it not be better to follow a more accurate chronology of three days consistent with what Yeshua told us about His resurrection?

6. Following the Saddusaical method does not necessarily mean an emphasis on the resurrection:
Even though advocates of the Saddusaical determination for *Shavuot* may insist that they do not lose focus of Yeshua's resurrection—as they count the *omer* from Sunday (the supposed day of the week of Yeshua's resurrection when it originally took place)—it should be noted that the theology of the Sadducees is often not considered. The testimony of the Gospels and Acts is unanimous on the fact that the Sadducees ***did not believe*** in any kind of resurrection:

"For the Sadducees say that there is no resurrection, nor an angel, nor a spirit, but the Pharisees acknowledge them all" (Acts 23:8; cf. Matthew 22:23; Mark 12:18; Luke 20:27; Acts 23:6).

Also consider that in Acts 4, immediately following the outpouring of the Holy Spirit at *Shavuot*/Pentecost, it was the chief priests or Sadducees who harassed and detained the Apostles.

Theologically speaking, if we were to emphasize the resurrection as a definite teaching of Scripture—then why would we follow the *halachic* ruling of a First Century Jewish sect ***that denied the resurrection?*** The doctrine of resurrection was Pharisaical. Unfortunately, many Messianics who insist that the Saddusaical determination for *Shavuot* is proper often fall prey to the long-standing Christian belief that the Pharisees are the "bad guys," not realizing that Yeshua *never criticized* them for their basic theology, but instead their hypocritical attitudes. Furthermore, the Pharisaism of the Apostle Paul is often glossed over.[iii]

Between the two major Jewish sects in the First Century, following the Pharisaical (and consequently the traditional, modern Jewish) way of observing *Shavuot* actually affirms the reality of Yeshua's resurrection—as we place ourselves within a viable Jewish tradition that adhered to many of the spiritual ideas and concepts that evangelical Christians and Messianics today hold dear.

7. The Believers in Jerusalem are seen keeping *Shavuot* with the majority of the population, all of whom followed the Pharisaic method according to history:
The testimony of Acts is clear that the Apostles observed *Shavuot* with the majority of those Jews who had traveled from afar to attend:

"Now there were Jews living in Jerusalem, devout men from every nation under heaven...Parthians and Medes and Elamites, and residents of Mesopotamia, Judea and Cappadocia, Pontus and Asia, Phrygia and Pamphylia, Egypt and the districts of Libya around Cyrene, and visitors from Rome, both Jews and proselytes, Cretans and Arabs—we hear them in our *own* tongues speaking of the mighty deeds of God" (Acts 2:5, 9-11).

[iii] Consult the article "You Want to Be a Pharisee" by J.K. McKee.

Were these Jews assembled observing *Shavuot* according to the method of the Sadducees—or the Pharisees? Aside from the calendar debates that ensued in First Century Judaism, it is notable that the majority of Diaspora Jews were Pharisaical in their theology—often with their Diaspora synagogues planted by Pharisees. The historical record indicates that the Temple priesthood, in spite of their favoring the Saddusaical view, had to conform to the majority view and offer the sheaf offering on the 16th of Nisan, two days after Passover. The First Century historian Josephus attests,

> "**But on the second day of unleavened bread, which is the sixteenth day of the month**, they first partake of the fruits of the earth, for before that day they do not touch them… They take a handful of the ears, and dry them, then beat them small, and purge the barley from the bran; they then bring one tenth deal to the altar, to God; and, casting one handful of it upon the fire, they leave the rest for the use of the priest; and after this it is that they may publicly or privately reap their harvest. They also at this participation of the firstfruits of the earth, sacrifice a lamb, as a burnt offering to God" (*Antiquities of the Jews* 3.250-251).[kkk]

The Jewish philosopher Philo also confirms,

> "There is also a festival on the day of the paschal feast, **which succeeds the first day**, and this is named the sheaf, from what takes place on it; for the sheaf is brought to the altar as a first fruit both of the country which the nation has received for its own, and also of the whole land; so as to be an offering both for the nation separately, and also a common one for the whole race of mankind; and so that the people by it worship the living God, both for themselves and for all the rest of mankind, because they have received the fertile earth for their inheritance; for in the country there is no barren soil but even all those parts which appear to be stony and rugged are surrounded with soft veins of great depth, which, by reason of their richness, are very well suited for the production of living things" (*Special Laws* 2.162).[lll]

The historical record attests that the Pharisaic method for beginning the *omer* count was followed in the Jerusalem Temple in the First Century.

In response to this, many might argue that since the Saddusaical priesthood operated the Temple, only they would have the authority to control when and how *Shavuot* was commemorated. However, there are examples in Rabbinical literature of the contempt that the common people had for the Sadducees, as they were largely collaborators with the Roman occupiers of Judea, and how concessions did have to be made for those who favored Pharisaic traditions.

Consider that during the Second Temple period, a special water libation ceremony called *Simchat Beit ha-Sho'evah* (rejoicing of the house of water drawing) was practiced during the Feast of Tabernacles. This ceremony, referred to by Yeshua in the Gospels (John 7), was based on a Pharisaic interpretation of Isaiah

---

[kkk] *The Works of Josephus: Complete and Unabridged*, 96.
[lll] Philo Judaeus: *The Works of Philo: Complete and Unabridged*, trans. C.D. Yonge (Peabody, MA: Hendrickson, 1993), 583.

12:3, "Therefore you will joyously draw water from the springs of salvation," and was codified in the Mishnah:

"*The water libation:* How so? A golden flask, holding three *logs* in volume, did one fill with water from Siloam. [When] they reached the Water Gate, they blow a sustained, a quavering, and a sustained blast on the *shofar*. [The priest] went up on the ramp [at the south] and turned to his left [southwest]....R. Judah says, 'A *log* [of water] would one pour out as the water libation all eight days'" (m.*Sukkah* 4:9).[mmm]

Josephus notes that this custom was rejected by the Sadducees, and the violent reaction on one year, of the people who sided with the Pharisees:

"As to Alexander, his own people were seditious against him; for at a festival which was then celebrated, when he stood upon the altar, and was going to sacrifice, the nation rose upon him, and pelted him with citrons [which they then had in their hands, because] the law of the Jews, required that at the feast of tabernacles, everyone should have branches of the palm tree and citron tree; which thing we have elsewhere related. They also reviled him, as derived from a captive, and so unworthy of his dignity and of sacrificing" (*Antiquities of the Jews* 13.372; cf. b.*Sukkah* 48b).[nnn]

Alfred Edersheim holds the view that the Saddusaical priesthood, while adamant about their method of counting the *omer*, actually did have to offer up the sheaf of firstfruits in the Temple on 16 Nisan because the Pharisees had the masses on their side:

"The Pharisees held, that the time between Easter and Pentecost should be counted from the second day of the feast; the Sadducees insisted that it should commence with the literal 'Sabbath' after the festive day. But despite argument, the Sadducees had to join when the solemn procession went on the afternoon of the feast to cut down the 'first sheaf,' and to reckon Pentecost as did their opponents."[ooo]

The Jews who had come to Jerusalem to observe *Shavuot* in Acts—and hence hear the gospel message proclaimed—followed the Pharisaic lead. Notably, those from the Diaspora probably used the Greek LXX as their main Scripture, which likewise instructed them to follow the Pharisaic method.

8. What do you do with the method of the Essenes?

Even though the exegetical, theological, and historical evidence favors the counting of the *omer* and observance of *Shavuot* according to the Pharisaic method, it is interesting that the method of the First Century Essenes is often never considered by Messianics. While the theology of the early Messianic community had far, far more in common with the Pharisees than the Sadducees (in fact no Sadducee is ever recorded as having come to faith in Yeshua), there are strands of commonality with the Essenes who gave us the Dead Sea Scrolls. The Essenes did not deny the resurrection.

The Essenes interpreted "the day after the sabbath" in Leviticus 23:11 to actually be the weekly Sabbath following the week of Unleavened Bread, not the

---

[mmm] Neusner, *Mishnah*, 288.
[nnn] *The Works of Josephus: Complete and Unabridged*, 360.
[ooo] Edersheim, *Sketches of Jewish Social Life*, 220.
See Edersheim's further remarks in *The Temple*, pp 203-204.

Sabbath during the week of Unleavened Bread like the Sadducees. If we are basing our observance of *Shavuot* on theological commonality, while there is more evidence in favor of following the Pharisaic method than any other—why is the Essenic method often not mentioned or even considered? There is at least limited theological commonality between the early Messianic Believers and the Essenes—when compared to no theological commonality with the Sadducees.

Discussing this Issue with Fairness

The debate over whether the method of counting the *omer* via the Sadducees (and now the modern-day Karaites) or Pharisees—and which one is correct—is a debate going back 2,300 years, and it is doubtful that the emerging Messianic community will reach a solution in the short term. We should not consider it a salvation issue, though. **One day Yeshua the Messiah will return to sort it all out.** For the short term, the independent Messianic movement will probably not have cohesion on this issue (and many other issues, for that matter), and so we will need to learn how to moderate potential divisions. We will need to focus on the bigger issues that unite us during the Spring holiday season, and not divide over what are ultimately minor details.

The debate over counting the *omer* is probably a little more complicated than you originally thought. There is a great deal of information that is often left out of the deliberations by Saddusaical advocates, and there is often not a great deal of patience and forbearance that Pharisaical advocates have toward these non-traditionalists. How do we encourage a better way to investigate and analyze this issue in the future? How do we not leave important factors out of the conversation on how we are to count the *omer*? The burden of proof is actually more on the side of the Pharisaical advocates than the Saddusiacal advocates—not because of the data that clearly supports their view—but because of how they will treat those who fail to consider such data should they defiantly reject and brand it as "traditions of men."

Most who hold to the Saddusaical view have not examined the additional factors that play into one's examination of this issue—factors that have a more significant impact on other, and far more important aspects of our theology. In the Messianic community right now (2009), **we must have the proper attitude that allows for some variance and respects others whether they celebrate *Shavuot* in concurrence with or in modification of the standard Rabbinical calendar.** We have to be able to be constructive with those who hold to the Saddusaical point of view, and wish them God's blessings even if they do observe *Shavuot* on a date different from the rest of the Jewish and Messianic Jewish communities.

As today's Messianic movement grows and matures—and most especially as its hermeneutics improve—most in the future will be celebrating *Shavuot* in tandem with the worldwide Jewish community.

We should not favor the side of the Sadducees **not** out of any animosity toward the Christian Church or Sunday as a day of the week, because God can clearly perform miracles on *any day of the week He wants to*. (And be reminded, *Shavuot* will occur on a Sunday sooner or later according to the Pharisaical method.) We should not favor the Saddusaical method for counting the *omer* because it really does not employ a responsible hermeneutical approach. We have to be honest with the broad scale of data that supports the traditional method of observance, no different than how we would consider the same factors for issues that are far, far more important to our Messianic faith and the salvation we possess in Yeshua. If these interpretational factors are forgotten for a small issue like the counting of the *omer*, we will get into the habit of forgetting them when presented with **real salvation issues** like Yeshua's Messiahship. (And this has probably already occurred in far too many places already in the exegetical deliberations of various Messianic "teachers" and "leaders.")

Also for the long term, we should encourage a Quartodeciman style of remembering Yeshua's resurrection to emerge, as the traditional method of counting the *omer* for observing *Shavuot* wins out. This would likely be some kind of an intimate prayer service, where we reflect on His rising from the dead, immediately following the start of the *omer* count.

As we wait for more cohesion to come forth, in the meantime, each of us *must be united around the fact that He did resurrect*, even though some fail to recognize that the belief in resurrection is Pharisaical. Likewise, the primacy of loving one's neighbor above all other commandments is Pharisaical (b.*Shabbat* 31a). If we can love one another and be reasonable, then we can work out the debate of counting the *omer* in an appropriate manner that brings glory to God, and will accomplish His tasks in the Earth.[ppp]

What do you believe about speaking in tongues? What occurred on the Day of Pentecost when the Holy Spirit was poured out?

The issue about speaking in "tongues" is as much a debate in mainstream Christianity as it is in the Messianic movement. There are people in the Messianic movement today who come out of the varied charismatic movements, which frequently emphasize the gifts of the Spirit, speaking in tongues, and other so-called "signs and wonders." In our experience, many who come out of these backgrounds are some of the hardest to convince of Torah observance and the Messianic lifestyle, because many charismatics are of the opinion that they have "freedom in the Spirit," yet this freedom often goes beyond what is Scripturally defined for us. We are also continually reminded of the Messiah's warning to us, "For false messiahs and false prophets will appear and produce great signs and omens, to lead astray, if possible, even the elect" (Matthew 24:24, NRSV).

We are certainly not of the opinion that the "gifts are dead" and that the gifts of the Holy Spirit were only available to those in the First Century. *We are continuationists*,[qqq] but are also of the opinion that there has been gross misuse of the Spiritual gifts in recent years via some of the Pentecostal and charismatic groups that have popped up, and that we must return to a Scriptural foundation in what the Spiritual gifts actually are. God would not be doing a "new thing" in the world today that does not have some precedent or continuity with what is already seen in the Bible.

[ppp] For a further discussion of this issue, consult the article "Sadducees, Pharisees, and the Controversy of Counting the Omer" by J.K. McKee.

[qqq] Consult "The Charismatic Gifts Debate," in Gregory A. Boyd and Paul R. Eddy, eds., *Across the Spectrum: Understanding Issues in Evangelical Theology* (Grand Rapids: Baker Academic, 2002), pp 212-224.

Speaking in "tongues," as it is often manifested today in Christian assemblies and in some Messianic congregations, is often a person being "supernaturally empowered" to speak in some form of unintelligible gibberish. We certainly do not doubt the fact that we can be supernaturally empowered to speak in "groanings too deep for words" (Romans 8:26) or "groans that words cannot express" (NIV), as Paul calls them. But these groanings are only intended to be used when "the Spirit also helps our weakness; for we do not know how to pray as we should, but the Spirit Himself intercedes for *us*," and these "groanings too deep for words" (NASU) **are different** than what is commonly thought to be "speaking in tongues." These groanings could be called one's personal prayer language with God, and only used when one has an urgent prayer to say and does not know what to say, so the Spirit takes over.

Speaking in "tongues," as it is Biblically defined, is being supernaturally empowered to speak in an intelligible, foreign language that one does not know, or being supernaturally empowered to speak in one's native language and being heard by others in their native language which is different. We see this occur in the Book of Acts at *Shavuot*/Pentecost when the Holy Spirit was poured out upon those assembled: "And they were all filled of the Holy Spirit, and began to speak in other languages, as the Spirit gave *ability* to them to speak" (Acts 2:4, LITV). Acts 2:8 attests that those assembled said, "how do we hear each in our own dialect in which we were born?" (LITV). Those proclaiming the gospel at *Shavuot*/Pentecost not only were supernaturally empowered to speak or be heard in foreign languages, but were also speaking or being heard in the specific *regional dialects* of those assembled.

We believe that the gift of tongues is for today, but that it is not speaking in the meaningless gibberish that it is often credited as being. The Apostle Paul writes in 1 Corinthians 14:22, "So then tongues are for a sign, not to those who believe but to unbelievers; but prophecy *is for a sign*, not to unbelievers but to those who believe." This is because from the example given to us in Acts, the speaking in other languages occurred so that the good news of salvation in Messiah Yeshua could be proclaimed to those who needed it. This is why speaking in "tongues," or more correctly **languages**, is a sign for unbelievers.

KOSHER
YOUR
PLATE

MESSIANIC
SPRING HOLIDAY
HELPER

Kosher Your Plate for the Spring Holidays

The Spring holiday season involving *Purim*, Passover, and *Shavuot* is a time when we get to consider many different themes regarding God's deliverance of His people and being brought into His purpose. While this is a very serious time to ponder one's relationship with the Lord, we should certainly be joyful for His acts of salvation. There are many traditional, delicious foods often associated with the Spring appointed times that can add depth and dimension to your remembrance of them. There are also some recipes our family especially likes to bring out, enhancing our own commemoration.

Purim

Hamantashen Cookies
2 sticks of softened butter
2 cups of granulated sugar
2 large eggs
2 teaspoons vanilla extract
4 teaspoons baking powder
4 cups of white flour
filling: apricot preserves, orange marmalade, and strawberry preserves

Cut the butter into the sugar. Blend thoroughly, add eggs, and blend again. Add the flour – ½ cup at a time, blending it each time. Put the dough in the refrigerator overnight to chill. Roll the dough out to ¼ inch thick and cut circles with a 3-4 inch diameter cookie cutter (you can use the mouth of a glass also). Put a tablespoon of filling in the middle of each circle. Fold up the three sides of the circle to make a triangle, overlapping the sides and allowing some of the filling to show through in the middle. The cookies will look like little tricorn hats—a Haman hat! Bake at 375 degrees for about 10-15 minutes until the cookies are golden brown.

Passover

MAIN DISHES

Easy Cranberry Chicken
8 chicken breasts, skinless and boned
1 can whole berry cranberry sauce
1 envelop Lipton onion soup mix
1 small bottle French dressing

Put chicken in casserole dish. Stir cranberry sauce, soup mix, and French dressing together. Pour over the chicken. Bake at 350 degrees uncovered for one hour. Serve with rice.

Orange Baked Chicken
6 boneless chicken breasts
1/4 cup orange marmalade
1 cup matzah meal
1/2 teaspoon Italian seasoning

Wash the chicken, dry. Spread orange marmalade on both sides of the chicken. Mix the matzah meal with the seasoning in a dish and coat the chicken on both sides evenly. Place in a shallow dish 13" x 9" and cook at 400 degrees for 30 minutes or until cooked thoroughly. Serves 6.

Grilled Chicken
3 pounds cut up chicken

Marinate in Italian dressing for 1 hour. Grill over open flame until done. Serve with salad and bread. Serves 10

Chicken Marsala
6 boneless chicken breasts - flattened
1/2-cup matzah meal
1/4-teaspoon salt
1/4-teaspoon pepper
2 tablespoons olive oil
2 cloves garlic, finely chopped
1 cup sliced mushrooms
1/4 cup fresh parsley, chopped
1/2 cup Marsala wine

Flatten the chicken breasts. Mix meal, salt and pepper and coat chicken lightly. In frying pan, heat oil to medium-high and cook garlic, mushrooms, and parsley in it for 5 minutes, stirring often. Add chicken to pan and cook 8 minutes, turning once, until brown. Add wine and cook 8-10 minutes longer, or until chicken is no longer pink in the middle.

Lemon-Fried Chicken
1 chicken – cut into pieces
1/8 - cup fresh lemon juice
1/8 - teaspoon garlic salt
cooking oil
1/4 - teaspoon salt
1/8 - teaspoon dried thyme
1/8 - teaspoon dried marjoram
1/8 - teaspoon pepper
3/8 - cup matzah meal
1/2 - teaspoon grated lemon rind
1/2 - teaspoon paprika

Wash the chicken, dry. Place in a shallow dish and cover with lemon juice, ¼ cup oil, garlic salt, salt, thyme, marjoram, pepper. Marinade in refrigerator for 2 hours. Remove and drain. Roll chicken in matzah meal, lemon rind, and paprika. Heat ½ cup oil in frying pan. Brown the chicken on all sides. Place in baking dish. Bake uncovered in a preheated 350 degree oven for 45-50 minutes, or until tender. Enjoy!

Grilled Passover Lamb
4-5 pound lamb roast

Prepare a lamb roast for cooking, by soaking it in saltwater so that all of the blood is drained out. Cut off the fat. Open up the meat so it is flat like a steak. You may cook it in one piece, or cut it in two. Rub garlic salt and pepper on the meat to your taste. Grill over an open flame until it is cooked to your liking. Our family cooks over a gas grill outdoors. The drippings from the fat might cause the fire to flame up, so have water available to dampen the flame up. When cooked, serve with your Passover meal!

Baked Passover Lamb
5 pound lamb roast
garlic salt & pepper

Prepare a lamb roast for cooking, by soaking it in saltwater so that all of the blood is drained out. Cut off the fat. Rub garlic salt and pepper on the meat to your taste. Place the lamb on a rack in a shallow roasting pan to keep it out of the drippings. Roast at 350 degrees for about 2 – 2 ½ hours, or until a meat thermometer reads between 160-170 degrees. Let the roast set for 15 minutes covered. Carve and serve!

Marinated Lamb for the Crock-Pot
5 pound lamb roast
2 cloves garlic
¼ cup kosher salt
2 tablespoons peppercorns, cracked
1 tablespoon rosemary
3 cups dry red wine

Prepare the lamb roast for cooking by soaking it in saltwater so that all the blood is drained out. Cut off all the fat. Cut the garlic into 6 slices, and place it into small slits in the meat. Salt and pepper all over. Place lamb in a large bowl with one cup of wine over it. Refrigerate overnight. Drain lamb and place in a crock-pot with the remaining wine. Cover and cook on high for 1 hour, then turn the heat down to low for 8-10 hours, turning at least once. When it is finished, cut into thin slices and serve as your main dish. Enjoy!

SIDE DISHES

Charoset
4 tart apples, cored, and grated
1 ½ cups chopped pecans or walnuts
3 tablespoons granulated sugar
½ teaspoon ground cinnamon
½ teaspoon ground ginger
1 ½ teaspoons grated lemon rind
3 tablespoons fresh lemon juice
Passover red wine

Combine all ingredients and blend with enough wine to give a spreading consistency. Makes 8-10 servings.

Matzah Ball Soup
2 eggs
¼ cup shortening
1 cup matzah meal
¼ - ½ cup water
1 teaspoon salt
dash of ground ginger and ground cinnamon

Mix the eggs, shortening, and matzah meal, beating well. Add water, salt, and mix to a stiff batter. Add the seasoning, cover, and chill for 2 hours. About 30 minutes before serving, wet hands with cold water to prevent sticking and form into balls. Drop the balls into boiling salted water, cover, and cook for 30 minutes. Drain and serve in a nice chicken based soup.

Baba Ghanauj
1 medium eggplant
3 tablespoons of tahini (sesame-seed paste)
¼ cup lemon juice
2 cloves of garlic, crushed
salt & pepper to taste
parsley sprigs to garnish

Cook the eggplant over a charcoal grill until the skin blackens and blisters. Peel and wash eggplant. Squeeze as much of the bitter juice out as possible. Combine all the ingredients, except parsley, in a blender or food processor. Blend them into a thick paste. Chill and serve with matzo.

Andy's Yummy Highlands Charoset
by Andy Carvin[a]

five medium red apples
one medium yellow apple
3/4 cup walnuts or pecan pieces
cinnamon
sugar
kosher red wine
Drambuie[b]

Begin by chopping or grating the apples in a large bowl. Some folks prefer to peel the apples, but I like them unpeeled (adds color to the final product). Incorporate the chopped nuts and half a cup of the red wine. Then mix in a teaspoon of cinnamon and a couple of teaspoons of sugar, to taste. Feel free to add more red wine. For that added bonus, toss in a shot of Drambuie. Then, add more red wine. You get the picture.

You can leave out the Drambuie, but then it's no longer Highlands Charoset...

Best when refrigerated and served the next day.

DESSERTS

Macaroons
1 3/4 cup Baker's grated coconut
2 tablespoons flour
3 egg whites
1/3 cup sugar
1/8 teaspoon salt
1/2 teaspoon almond extract

Combine coconut, sugar, flour, and salt. Stir in egg whites and extract. Mix well. Drop from teaspoon onto lightly greased baking sheets. Bake at 325 degrees for 25 minutes, or until brown. Remove from baking sheets at once. Makes 2 dozen!

Maggie's Matzah Crunch
2 sticks butter
1 ½ cups brown sugar
¾ to 1 cup semisweet chocolate chips
5 unsalted pieces of matzah

Preheat oven to 350. Line cookie sheet with parchment paper or aluminum foil, then spray with no stick spray as well. Line cookie sheet with a single layer of matzah. (Cut or break them to fit.)

In a saucepan over medium heat, melt butter and brown sugar. Slowly bring to a boil and let boil for 3 minutes. Pour directly over matzah and place in oven for 12

---

[a] Taken from <andycarvin.com/archives/2006/04/andys_yummy_highland.html>.
[b] Drambuie is a Scottish liqueur of whiskey, honey, and lots of mysterious spices.

to 15 minutes. **Watch carefully so as not to burn.** Remove from oven and sprinkle chocolate chips on top. When chips melt (just a couple of minutes) spread with a spatula.

Let cool, either on counter or in refrigerator/freezer. Break into chunks.

Meringue Cookies
3 egg whites
1 cup granulated sugar
1/4 teaspoon salt
1 teaspoon vanilla extract
3/4 cup chopped pecans

Mix egg whites, sugar, salt, and vanilla into top of a double boiler. Place over boiling water and beat with an electric hand mixer until the mixture stands in stiff peaks. Scrape the bottom and sides of pan while you mix with a rubber spatula. Stir in nuts. Drop heaping teaspoonfuls of dough on two lightly greased baking sheets. Cook one sheet at a time in a preheated 300 degree oven for 12-15 minutes, or until lightly browned. Makes about 3 ½ dozen cookies.

Passover Nut Cake
6 eggs
6 tablespoons granulated sugar
6 tablespoons matzo cake meal
1 tablespoon lemon juice
2/3 cups finely chopped pecans or walnuts
1/8 teaspoon salt
confectioner's sugar

Separate eggs and beat egg yolks until they are thick. Beat in granulated sugar and continue beating until the mixture is thick and creamy. Gradually stir in matzo cake meal. Stir in lemon juice and nuts. Beat egg whites with salt until they are stiff and fold them into the cake batter. Pour batter into an ungreased tube pan. Bake in preheated oven at 300 degrees for 45 minutes, then increase heat to 325 degrees for another 15 minutes—or until the top of the cake springs back when touched. Remove from oven and invert pan. Cool thoroughly, cut out of pan, and place on cake plate. Sprinkle with confectioner's sugar. Enjoy!

Shavuot

Creamy Cheesecake
Nutty crumb crust:
150 gr (5 oz.) simple cookies (to obtain 1-1/4 cups crumbs)
1/4 cup walnut *or* pecan halves
3 tbsp sugar
6 tbsp (a little less than 1/2 cup) unsalted butter melted

Cheese filling:
450 gr (16 oz.) cream cheese, cut into pieces and softened
1/2 cup sour cream
3/4 cup sugar

3 large eggs
grated rind of 1 large lemon
1 tsp vanilla extract

Sour-cream topping:
1-1 1/2 cups sour cream
3 tbsp sugar
1 tsp vanilla extract

Crust: Preheat oven to 160 C (350 F). Process cookies in a food processor to fine crumbs, or put them in a bag and crush them with a rolling pin. Measure 1-1/4 cups. Chop nuts. Mix crumbs with nuts and sugar. Add melted butter and mix well. Lightly butter a 23-cm (9 in.) springform pan. Press nut mixture in an even layer on bottom and about 2-2 1/2 cm (1 in.) up sides of pan. Bake 10 minutes. Remove and let cool completely. Leave oven at 160 C/350 F.

Filling: Beat cream cheese with sour cream at low speed until very smooth.

Gradually beat in sugar. Beat in eggs, one by one. Beat in lemon rind. If using a vanilla bean, scrape its seeds with point of a knife into cheese mixture; or stir in vanilla extract. Carefully pour filling into cooled crust and bake about 45 minutes or until firm in center. Remove from oven and cool for 15 minutes. Raise oven temperature to 200 C (390 F).

Topping: Mix together sour cream, sugar and vanilla. Carefully spread topping on cake in an even layer, without letting it drop over crust. Return cake to oven and bake 7 minutes. Remove from oven and cool to room temperature.

Refrigerate at least 2 hours before serving. (Cake can be kept 3 days in refrigerator.) Remove sides of springform pan just before serving. Serves: 8-10

Blintzes Casserole
FOR LAYERS ONE AND THREE:
6 eggs
1 1/2 cups sour cream
1/2 cup orange juice
1/3 cup sugar
1/2 margarine, melted
1 cup flour
2 tsp. baking powder

FOR LAYER TWO:
8 oz. softened cream cheese
1 egg
1 pint cottage cheese
1 tbsp. sugar
1 tsp. vanilla

Beat each mixture in a bowl. Pour half of top mixture into greased 9x13 baking dish. Spoon bottom mixture on and top with remaining batter from top. Bake 45-55 minutes at 350 degrees. Serve w/ sour cream or fruit (or pie filling).

Eggplant Parmesan

Israelis love eggplant (chatzil in Hebrew) because it is economical, versatile, easy to prepare, and delicious in many different forms. Eggplant Parmesan is an especially popular dish on Shavuot, when dairy foods are served. This is an easy-to-make recipe (with spaghetti sauce) for Eggplant Parmesan.

1 large or 2 medium eggplants
3 eggs
1 cup dry bread crumbs
3/4 cup oil
24 ounces spaghetti sauce
1/2 cup Parmesan cheese, grated
1/2 pound Mozzarella cheese, sliced

1. Peel eggplant. Cut eggplant into 1/4 to 1/2 inch slices.
2. Dip each slice of eggplant into eggs and then crumbs.
3. Saute breaded eggplant slices until brown on both sides.
4. Preheat oven to 350° F
5. In a baking dish, spread spaghetti sauce to cover the bottom. Place a layer of eggplant slices in the sauce. Sprinkle with mozzarella and Parmesan cheeses. Repeat with remaining ingredients, ending with the cheeses.
6. Bake, uncovered at 350° F for 30 minutes, or until cheese is melted.

Honey-Wheat Challah for Shavuot

This recipe is suited to be mixed in a bread machine

¾ cup lukewarm water
2 ¼ tablespoons olive oil
3 tablespoons honey
1 teaspoon sea salt
2 eggs, beaten
2 cups whole wheat bread flour
1 cup unbleached flour
1 packet or 1 ¼ teaspoons active dry yeast

Add ingredients to bread pan in order in which they are listed. Select dough setting on bread machine. After cycle is complete, remove dough with a rubber spatula. Place dough on floured surface. Separate into 6 equal sections and roll each into 6 same length strips. Make each strip thicker in the middle to give the bread a tapered look. Braid the strips. Let rise for 45 minutes or until doubled in size. Place on greased baking sheet or baking stone.

Optional: Brush with beaten egg yolk and sprinkle on sesame seeds.

Bake in a preheated oven at 350 degrees for 25-30 minutes. Yield: two small loaves for Shavuot

LITURGICAL RESOURCES

PURIM
PASSOVER
COUNTING THE OMER
SHAVUOT

The Role of Liturgy

Many people who are not only new to the Messianic movement, but have been a part of it for a while, are somewhat skeptical regarding the role of liturgical worship. Reciting traditional prayers and hymns is sometimes thought to be dead religion, a throwback to Yeshua's warning, "when you pray, do not heap up empty phrases as the Gentiles do, for they think that they will be heard for their many words" (Matthew 6:7), or even, "for a pretense [the scribes] make long prayers. They will receive the greater condemnation" (Mark 12:40). Only if prayers are offered spontaneously, without the use of a special book or tradition, is it believed that God will find them acceptable.

A person who is skeptical of liturgical prayer cannot be entirely blamed for such opinions. There may be childhood memories of attending a Roman Catholic mass where endless liturgies in an unintelligible language, Latin, were repeated over and over. You might know some things about the Protestant Reformation, which fought against the highly formalized religion of Catholicism that had led to a corrupt clergy and deceived laity, and how you can go right to God with your prayers and not need anything else. Or, you might simply find all formal liturgy to be boring and that it takes away from the joy of worshipping the Lord.

Does all formal liturgy rob from the presence of the Holy Spirit? I hope not! The largest book of the Bible, and perhaps one of the most spiritually uplifting, is the Book of Psalms—a text full of liturgical prayers, songs, pleas, and laments. It is said of the early Believers, "they devoted themselves to the apostles' teaching and fellowship, to the breaking of bread and the prayers" (Acts 2:42). Theologians recognize how early hymns about Yeshua (Philippians 2:5-11; Colossians 1:15-20) from the ancient Messianic community, made their way into the Apostolic epistles. And at our Lord's Passover *seder* we are reminded, "when they had sung a hymn, they went out to the Mount of Olives" (Matthew 26:30). While we often associate liturgy with "High Church" worship, it is undeniably a part of the Biblical tradition that must be honored.

What is the role of liturgy? Liturgy can help provide structure and order to a worship service. It by no means has to be repetitive, endless, and *all* of it in a language that the people worshipping do not understand. It is, rather, to help create an environment of reverence and respect. It is to remind us that we are being invited into the presence of God, and that there are some things that we need to be considering. Even today's Protestant churches, which would be considered the least liturgical in comparison to both the Jewish Synagogue and Roman Catholic Church, still employ a fair amount of liturgy in the native tongues of the people, to create a sense of reverence.

Being raised at the United States Naval Academy in Annapolis, Maryland, my family frequently attended Protestant services at the Chapel, and we would hear and recite liturgy derived from Scriptures like Psalm 107:22-24:

"And let them sacrifice the sacrifices of thanksgiving, and declare his works with rejoicing. They that go down to the sea in ships, that do business in great waters; these see the works of the LORD, and his wonders in the deep" (KJV).

When hearing this read, or declaring it with a congregation, you have to pause for a moment and remember that there are sailors and Marines who have sacrificed of themselves so that America might remain free. Tears might well up in your eyes as you recall a family member or friend presently serving in the armed forces, as you offer up a quiet prayer for their safety. You might remember a loved one who has died for the cause of freedom, and express thankfulness to God for how they gave their lives with honor.

This is the role of liturgy: **bringing us closer to a holy God in great awe and reverence.** We remember who we are as mortals in His sight, either hearing a compilation of important admonitions from His Word, or confessing them together in unison. We recall Moses' declaration to Ancient Israel, "Fear not, stand firm, and see the salvation of the LORD, which he will work for you today" (Exodus 14:13). We declare the goodness and infinite power of our Eternal King, and how grateful we are to receive His grace and mercy. Most liturgy employed in worship comes directly from the Holy Scriptures, so just as Bible readings should draw us into God's presence, so can special prayers and hymns draw us into His presence.

In the Jewish tradition, liturgy is a very important part of the worship service for *Shabbat* and the appointed times. It calls the people of God to attention, to remember who He is in their lives, where we as human beings have perhaps fallen short, and why we need His help. Messianic congregations, fellowships, and home groups, are experiencing a renaissance today as liturgical worship is being considered for the special power it possesses in helping us learn how to be reverent before Him. Far from being the product of dead religion, liturgical worship is being rightly recognized as an important part of not only the First Century *ekklēsia*, but something that has been used properly by many generations of Jews and Christians. Wanting to build upon this heritage, liturgy should play *a role* in the worship of Messianic Believers.

Each Messianic congregation or gathering, just like each person, is different—meaning that the liturgical needs and wants will vary from location to location. Some congregations focus their *Shabbat* services and observance of the appointed times almost entirely around liturgical worship, and others scarcely use it at all. Some want all of their liturgy to be delivered in Hebrew, others prefer a fair mix of Hebrew and English, and others prefer very little Hebrew and mostly English. Some have a designated cantor or *chazzan* deliver the prayers, and others have a variety of individuals involved. Whichever you choose, we wish the Lord's blessings on you!

We encourage you to incorporate liturgy as a vital component of your worship services, but not the only component. Likewise, if you have not considered how liturgy can give your worship structure, focus, and reverence, the appointed times can be an excellent season to experiment!

Using these Liturgies

Only you can decide how much or how little liturgy is needed to bring a sense of awe and reverence to your remembrance of the Spring appointed times. We encourage you to follow the traditional blessings used for this season in your family's observance, as well as some customary prayers and procedures for this special season. The selection of prayers that we have included, we ourselves have used in our family experience as Messianic Believers (both in congregational and home settings), and have felt that they add to the holiness of this time. You may wish to add more liturgy or Scripture readings to your remembrance, or use less should you only be able to observe the Spring appointed times in your home.

Not all of the liturgy in this section has been reproduced in Hebrew, but only those traditional prayers where an English translation is all that is usually provided in the Synagogue. You are encouraged to incorporate these resources into your remembrance of each of the Spring appointed times, as will meet the needs of your family or home congregation.

Liturgical Resources for the Spring Appointed Times

The liturgical prayers that we have reproduced in the *Messianic Spring Holiday Helper* have been derived and reproduced from a variety of traditional Jewish sources (as specifically noted). These are tools that would certainly be beneficial for your personal or congregational library, as you might want more information on the history of composition within the Jewish liturgical tradition, or to have a complete *siddur* with both Hebrew and English.

The Authorised Daily Prayer Book (ed. J.H. Hertz; New York: Bloch Publishing Company, 1960)
The Hertz *siddur* is a mainstay in many branches of Judaism (and as such we have seen it referred to in various Christian works). More like a reference book than an actual prayer book, it includes the standard liturgies for just about every aspect of traditional Jewish life. Not only does it include text in both English and Hebrew, but it also includes a great deal of explanation and commentary that will aid someone unfamiliar with the Jewish liturgical tradition.
The downside to this publication is that it was originally published in Britain in the early Twentieth Century, and uses a great number of Elizabethan-period terms that could be unfamiliar to the modern reader.

Siddur Sim Shalom for Shabbat and Festivals (ed. Jules Harlow; New York: Rabbinical Assembly, 2007)
This is a standard *siddur* used in Conservative/Masorti Judaism. It is very user friendly, and reflects a modern and engaged social perspective. It includes a wide variety of prayers and procedures for contemporary, American Jewish life. It is an excellent companion to the Hertz *siddur*, and uses modern English.

Complete ArtScroll Siddur, Nusach Ashkenaz (eds. Nosson Scherman and Meir Zlotowitz; Brooklyn: Mesorah Publications, 1984)
This is a standard Orthodox Jewish *siddur* produced for English-speaking Ashkenazic Jews. It includes a wide variety of both personal and congregational liturgical prayers, along with a great deal of references to Rabbinic literature. The downside to it is that it represents the broad array of Orthodox movements, and as such there are references in various places to Jewish mysticism and other traditions frowned upon by the more moderate branches of Judaism. It largely does not represent an engaged social perspective, and is not as easy to navigate as the Hertz *siddur* and *Siddur Sim Shalom* publications.

Seif Edition of the ArtScroll Transliterated Siddur: Sabbath and Festival (ed., et. al. Nosson Scherman; Brooklyn: Mesorah Publications, 1998)
This is a companion to the main ArtScroll Siddur, with many of the Hebrew prayers transliterated into English.

Before and After the Reading of the Megillah of Esther

The following procedure for reading the scroll of Esther is largely adapted from the Conservative Jewish resource *Siddur Sim Shalom.*

═══════════════════════════════════════

Reading from the Megillah, or scroll of Esther, is a traditional feature of the festival of Purim that should be observed when this special season is remembered. It would be entirely insufficient for people in a Messianic congregation or fellowship to simply have a Purim celebration with some kind of theatrical play, without also having heard from the Biblical account of Esther.

There may be a variety of ways how your Messianic congregation or fellowship chooses to remember Purim. The actual day of Purim is the 14th of Adar, * *and should your local Messianic community have its own meeting place or building, you then have no difficulty simply holding your Purim festivities on this date. This could include the reading of the Megillah, a traditional Purim play with noisemakers, and then a time for eating and fellowship afterward.*

Many Messianic congregations choose to remember Purim on the weekly Sabbath that is closest to the 14th of Adar, in able to include the most amount of people they can in the festivities. If your congregation or fellowship chooses to do this, then your Purim celebration needs to basically replace the format of your weekly Shabbat service. This might mean (completely) cutting out some of the worship time, and following a format of: reading from the Megillah, including a short teaching on the significance of Purim (10-15 mins.), † *and the Purim play. Afterward, your congregation can hold a large fellowship oneg with refreshments.* ‡

The following blessings are traditionally read before and after the reading of the Megillah of Esther. Even if you do not really have a Messianic congregation to attend, these blessings can be employed in your home commemoration, perhaps as members of your family read and discuss the Book of Esther.

For Purim

Leader: *This blessing is recited before the reading of the Megillah:*

Barukh atah Adonai,	בָּרוּךְ אַתָּה יְיָ
Eloheinu melekh ha'olam,	אֱלֹהֵינוּ מֶלֶךְ הָעוֹלָם
asher kidshanu	אֲשֶׁר קִדְּשָׁנוּ בְּמִצְוֹתָיו
b'mitzvotav v'tzivanu al	וְצִוָּנוּ עַל מִקְרָא מְגִלָּה
miqra Megillah.	

Praised are You Lord our God, who rules the universe, instilling in us the holiness of commandments by commanding us to read the scroll

---

* Adar II on leap years.

† Of course, there is also no reason why the themes of Esther or *Purim* cannot have been taught on during the preaching time for your weekly *Shabbat* service the week, if not during several weeks, before.

‡ Note that it is traditional in the Jewish community for a large amount of alcohol to be consumed during *Purim*. While our ministry does not at all promote a position of "prohibition," it would be best for alcohol to not be available at congregational gatherings—and be reserved only for any home observance.

Messianic Spring Holiday Helper

of Esther.

All:

Barukh atah Adonai,
Eloheinu melekh
ha'olam,
she'asah nisim
l'avoteinu b'yamim
ha'hem u'v'zman ha'zeh

בָּרוּךְ אַתָּה יְיָ
אֱלֹהֵינוּ מֶלֶךְ הָעוֹלָם
שֶׁעָשָׂה נִסִּים לַאֲבוֹתֵינוּ
בַּיָּמִים הָהֵם וּבַזְּמַן הַזֶּה

Praised are You Lord our God, who rules the universe,
accomplishing miracles for our ancestors from ancient days until our
time.

Barukh atah Adonai,
Eloheinu melekh
ha'olam, she'he'cheyanu
v'ki'yemanu v'higi'anu
la'zman ha'zeh.

בָּרוּךְ אַתָּה יְיָ
אֱלֹהֵינוּ מֶלֶךְ הָעוֹלָם
שֶׁהֶחֱיָנוּ וְקִיְּמָנוּ
וְהִגִּיעָנוּ לַזְּמַן הַזֶּה

Praised are You Lord our God, who rules the universe, granting us
life, sustaining us, and enabling us to reach this day.

Reading of the Megillah

In traditional Judaism, a small Hebrew scroll of Esther is now opened and recited
from, no different than the weekly canting of the Torah portion. While many
Messianic congregations possess a *sefer Torah*, not very many have a *Megillah
Esther*. If you have a scroll of Esther, by all means do read some of it from the
Hebrew. If you do not, then use a more standard printed version from a Hebrew
Tanach.

At this point in your congregational observance of *Purim*, you may choose to have
a few designated readers recite from an English version of Esther, notably from the
high points of the story. This should take no more than seven-twelve minutes.

After the Reading of the Megillah

All: *This blessing is recited after the reading of the Megillah:*

Praised are You Lord our God, who rules the universe, championing our cause, avenging the wrongs done to us, liberating us from our enemies, and bringing retribution upon our persecutors. Praised are You Lord, the saving God, who brings judgment upon Israel's oppressors.

Shoshanat Ya'akov

Shoshanat Ya'akov is the concluding section of an acrostic poem dating to early medieval times, celebrating God's deliverance of the Jewish people from the clutches of evil.

Shoshanat Ya'akov tzahalah
    v'samechah,
bir'otam yachad tekelet Mordekhai,
t'shu'atam hayita l'netzach, v'tiqvatam
    b'kol dor v'dor.
L'hodiya she'kol qovekha lo yevoshu,
v'lo yikalmu kol ha'hosim bakh.
Arur Haman asher bikesh l'abdi,
    barukh Mordekhai ha'Yehudi.
Arurah Zeresh eshet mafchidi, berukhah
    Esther meginnah b'adi,
v'gam Charvonah zakur l'tov.

שׁוֹשַׁנַּת יַעֲקֹב צָהֲלָה וְשָׂמֵחָה
בִּרְאוֹתָם יַחַד תְּכֵלֶת מָרְדְּכָי
תְּשׁוּעָתָם הָיִיתָ לָנֶצַח וְתִקְוָתָם
בְּכָל דוֹר וָדוֹר
לְהוֹדִיעַ שֶׁכָּל קֹוֶיךָ לֹא יֵבֹשׁוּ
וְלֹא יִכָּלְמוּ כָּל הַחוֹסִים בָּךְ
אָרוּר הָמָן אֲשֶׁר בִּקֵּשׁ לְאַבְּדִי
בָּרוּךְ מָרְדְּכַי הַיְּהוּדִי
אֲרוּרָה זֶרֶשׁ אֵשֶׁת מַפְחִידִי
בְּרוּכָה אֶסְתֵּר מְגִנָּה בַּעֲדִי
וְגַם חַרְבוֹנָה זָכוּר לַטּוֹב

The rose of Jacob beamed with joy
when they beheld Mordecai robed in royal blue.
You have always been our deliverance,
our hope in every generation.
Those who set their hope in You will never be put to shame.
Those who trust in You will never be confounded.
Cursed be Haman, who sought to destroy us;
blessed be Mordecai the Jew.
Cursed be Zeresh, the wife of the one who terrified us;
blessed be Esther our protector,
and may Harvonah* also be remembered for good.

---

* One of the king's chamberlains (Esther 7:9).

A Passover Haggadah for Messianic Believers

Anyone's remembrance of Passover will feature the *haggadah*, a retelling of the account of Ancient Israel's trials in Egypt, as God dispensed plagues and led His people to freedom by the shedding of the lamb's blood. The main feature of the *haggadah* is to provide a framework so that people remembering the Passover, on the evening of the 14th of Nisan, can really be impacted by the events in a very meaningful and powerful way. It is commonly recognized that in spite of the diversity of Judaism today, the Passover *seder* "is probably the most universally celebrated...ritual."[*] It is still something that even the most liberal turn to for guidance and instruction.

Picking the right *haggadah* for the needs of a congregation or family is not an easy task. It has been observed how "Jews continue to rewrite, revise, and add to its text, recasting it so as to maintain the haggadah's relevance to their lives."[†] Every different denomination of Judaism, and diverse sectors of the worldwide Jewish community, each have their own version of the Passover *haggadah*. There are *haggadot* which are intended to be used for only a few hours, and then those which are to last all night long. There are those for congregations and those for families. There are *haggadot* for those living in Israel, in North America, and elsewhere.

Not surprisingly, the broad Messianic community—and perhaps even down to each Messianic congregation and ministry—has its own variations on the *haggadah*. There are Messianic *haggadot* that are more like those seen in Orthodox Judaism, and those which are more similar to Conservative or Reform Judaism. Some are quite traditional, supplemented with references made to the Last Supper of Messiah Yeshua, and others completely break with tradition. Some Messianic *haggadot* are guides to how to make Passover a spiritually uplifting time for Believers, and others bear little difference with those in mainstream Judaism, with the exception of a few references to Yeshua.

When our family first started observing the Passover on an annual basis, the main resource we used was simply *The Messianic Passover Haggadah* by Barry and Steffi Rubin (Baltimore: Lederer, 1996), something that is still a mainstay in the Messianic movement. We have witnessed a variety of other similar *haggadot* published since, some which are longer, and some which are shorter. (As a ministry, various congregations and individuals have certainly given us copies of their different *haggadot*.) On the whole, though, we have found this to be a very useful and beneficial resource— being a fair balance of tradition and Messiah emphasis.

As our Messianic walk has progressed, we have wanted to integrate much more of the "storytelling" feature in our Passover observance, incorporating a bit more of the traditional liturgy and wanting to reflect more on the themes of the Exodus. By including more Hebrew readings and Scripture readings into the *seder*, other people in attendance—most especially welcome guests—get to participate, rather than just spectate and wait until the main meal is served. With the elements of the *seder* meal on the table, it is a good thing to encourage everyone at the table to do something to make them feel involved, so they can learn and be blessed!

---

[*] Joseph Tabory, *JPS Commentary on the Haggadah* (Philadelphia: Jewish Publication Society, 2008), xv.
[†] Ibid., xi.

The **Passover Haggadah** we have offered in this *Messianic Spring Holiday Helper* follows the same basic order of service as *The Messianic Passover Haggadah* we originally used. However, we have also taken into consideration the order of service seen in the Conservative Jewish *Passover Haggadah: The Feast of Freedom* (The Rabbinical Assembly, 1982), edited by Rachel Anne Rabinowicz, designed mainly for American homes. Also quite valuable is the *JPS Commentary on the Haggadah* (Philadelphia: Jewish Publication Society, 2008) by Joseph Tabory, which not only includes an introduction to the development of the traditional *seder* meal in the diverse traditions of Judaism found during Passover, but also offers many options that can enhance the *seder* meal (in particular, the home *seder* meal). You will find both of these to be useful reference tools in putting together your own *seder*, and in formulating customs that will make your Passover remembrance something both special and educational.

There are a variety of *haggadot* available, enabling for your *seder* meal to last anywhere between one hour and ninety minutes. This *haggadah* has purposefully been written to fit more in the two-and-a-half hour, with meal and teaching included, timeframe. There is a bit of teaching included in the *haggadah*, as the substance of both the Exodus and the Last Supper will be considered. While this *haggadah* can be amended with places for praise and worship, the *seder* meal is intended to be something where God's people can be taught—not be entertained with music and dance, which does take place at some Messianic congregational *seder*s.

The Passover Haggadah we have formulated should help you to not only make the *seder* a blessed time for you and your family, but also a time for your guests to want to open up the Scriptures, and dig into the redemptive themes of the Exodus for themselves! While the main feature of the Passover *seder* is being able to focus on the different elements of the meal, we have offered some teaching points and explanations for your reference, which can guide your home or congregational activities. Our purpose for remembering the Passover is not only to celebrate the deliverance of Ancient Israel from Egyptian bondage, but how our Messiah Yeshua is the Lamb of God who redeems us from slavery to sin.

Bedikat Chametz

Prior to the Passover, it is customary that all leavened items be removed from one's home (Exodus 12:15, 19; 13:7). These leavened items notably include things that have *chametz*, or yeast in them. While many of these items can simply be eaten several weeks in advance, or perhaps given away to food banks to help the homeless or less fortunate, you will still probably have a few items left over. It is a useful exercise to go about your home searching for such leavened items.

The lesson we learn from removing all *chametz* from our homes or dwellings is that we are to always be searching out our hearts. Even if born again Believers have been forgiven and redeemed from sin by the blood of Messiah Yeshua, it is still quite likely that we have sinful habits or behaviors that need to be removed (cf. 1 Corinthians 5:6-8). Just as a small amount of yeast can make many loaves of leavened bread (Galatians 5:9), so a small amount of sin—if not taken captive and removed—can lead to other, more serious issues.

In many homes, once all *chametz* has been removed, it is customary to then go outside and burn it. Frequently, parents will have already gone ahead and removed all leavened items, but will deliberately hide a few leavened items to search for with their children. Such a search will often be conducted with the aid of a wooden spoon and a candle, for the specific reason that "The spirit of man is the lamp of the LORD, searching all his innermost parts" (Proverbs 20:27).

The following blessing can be employed before and after your search for chametz.

Before the search for leaven, recite:

Barukh atah Adonai, Eloheinu melekh ha'olam, asher kidshanu b'mitzvotav v'tzivanu al b'aur chametz.

בָּרוּךְ אַתָּה יְיָ אלהֵינוּ מֶלֶךְ הָעוֹלָם אֲשֶׁר קִדְּשָׁנוּ בְּמִצְוֹתָיו וְצִוָּנוּ עַל בִּעוּר חָמֵץ

Praised are You, Lord our God, King of the universe who has sanctified us through His commandments, commanding us to remove all *chametz*.

After the search for leaven, recite:

All *chametz* in my possession which I have not seen or removed, or of which I am unaware, is hereby nullified and ownerless as the dust of the Earth.

Messianic Spring Holiday Helper

Preparing Our Hearts for the Seder

This is something that can be adapted by the leader(s) of your seder, as it is intended to introduce either your home or congregational gathering. Preferably, your seder has started right before sundown on the 14th of Nisan.†*

Leader:
Shalom and welcome to our Passover table! This evening we celebrate the deliverance of our forbearers in faith, the Ancient Israelites, from the clutches of Egyptian slavery. We remember the images of the Passover lamb, whose blood was painted on the doorframes of the Israelite homes, sparing them from the angel of death. We will be thinking about the Exodus of hundreds of thousands of the Israelites on to Mount Sinai to be given God's Torah (Law). But perhaps most important, as Messianic Believers we will see how these lessons force us to consider the work of Yeshua the Messiah (Jesus Christ), in being slain as the Passover Lamb, atoning for all human sin. We will also be having to recall the intimate Last Supper meal He held with His Disciples, prior to being betrayed, unjustly humiliated and condemned, and then crucified.

Now would be an appropriate time to read a short passage of Scripture, meaningful for your family or congregation during this season.

You should now offer a prayer to open the evening.

This would also be an appropriate time for those attending the congregational seder meal to greet one another, a time of handshaking lasting between 2-3 minutes, with one's immediate neighbors.

Leader *or* Designated Reader:‡
Let us prepare ourselves for our *seder* commemoration, as we remember the great salvation acts of our God: the Exodus of Ancient Israel, and the sacrifice of our Messiah Yeshua. According to long-standing tradition, "In every generation a person is duty-bound to regard himself as if he has personally gone forth from Egypt, since it is said," "You shall tell your son on that day, 'It is because of what the LORD did for me when I came out of Egypt'" (Exodus 13:8). "Therefore we are duty-bound to thank, praise, glorify, honor, extol, and bless him who did for our forefathers and for us all these miracles. He brought us forth from slavery to freedom, anguish to joy, mourning to festival, darkness to great light, subjugation to redemption, so we should say before him, Hallelujah" (m.*Pesachim* 10:5).

The same God who delivered Ancient Israel from Egypt, is the same Heavenly Father who gave of His only begotten Son so that none should suffer eternal banishment from Him (John 3:16). He is the same God who delivers us today from the trials we face, who cares for all of His human creatures, being gracious to them.

---

*If this is a home *seder*, we would strongly encourage both husband and wife to share the responsibilities as leaders, alternating back and forth throughout the order of the *haggadah*.

† Obviously due to life circumstances, not all families or congregations are able to hold their *seder* meal on the 14th of Nisan. Frequently in our experience, Messianic congregations will encourage their members to hold a home *seder* on the 14th of Nisan, usually with a congregational *seder* held the evening of the 15th of Nisan. Yet, congregational *seders* may be held later during the week of Unleavened Bread, should the Passover meal be opened to visitors, something often contingent on being able to procure a facility that has the right capacity (i.e., hotel ballroom). As always, the family and community emphasis for the Passover needs to be remembered (Exodus 12:3-4). Observing Passover alone is by no means ideal.

‡ While it would make sense for this designated reader to be a family member, this is not entirely necessary.

This evening, we will use this *haggadah* to tell the story of the Passover. The Passover has a critical message to each of us, be we the actual descendants of the Israelites or not. It speaks of God's miraculous intervention in history, and serves to help us all understand the salvation we have in Messiah Yeshua. As Messiah's followers, we are to not only be enriched by what we declare tonight, but we are to be encouraged to be men and women who take an active interest in the affairs of the needy, oppressed, and downtrodden. The message that the Passover and Exodus holds for us as Believers is one where we not only appreciate Yeshua's sacrifice for our sins, but where we manifest the power of that sacrifice in acts of deliverance for our fellow human beings. We are here to remember how our Lord told His Disciples, "I have earnestly desired to eat this Passover with you before I suffer" (Luke 22:15), almost thinking that He is here among us conducting this *seder* meal Himself.

It is most customary for those who are attending the Passover *seder* to be reclining in some way, completely different from the Ancient Israelites who had to eat their meal in haste (Exodus 12:11). Our Passover today is a memorial of what took place in ancient times, a recognition that we are all people granted freedom by a holy God, concerned with our needs. We recline at the Passover as we enjoy the freedom He has provided us, something that the Israelites at the original Passover had yet to be given. Frequently, those who recline during the *seder* may do so with some kind of pillows or an armchair, although seeing to an appropriate degree comfort for those at your *seder* meal is really what is intended.

Many leaders of the *seder* meal will don a white robe called a *kittel*. Some look at the color of white as representing freedom. Others look at the *kittel* as a kind of priestly garment. Messianic Believers may consider how the saints are depicted as those who wear white robes (Revelation 7:9, 13-14).

If a Passover *seder* leader chooses to not wear a *kittel*, then it is still most appropriate that all in attendance try to wear their best. Wearing one's best is a sign of not only royalty, representative of people who serve the King of Kings, but also one where people of freedom can demonstrate that they are blessed by Him. Wearing normal clothes for the *seder* meal can be taken as a sign of disrespect, for the purposes of remembering one's deliverance into freedom.

Messianic Spring Holiday Helper

The Seder Plate

Whether holding a congregational or home seder, *you may need to take a moment to point out some of the different elements that make up the meal. Direct the attention of your audience or guests to the seder plate, and the cups of wine they will be drinking of.* [*] *This would be the appropriate time to make mention of the hotness of the bitter herbs (typically horseradish).*

If this is the first Passover seder *some of your guests have ever participated in, make them be aware that the* haggadah *they are using, and the meal in which they are about to partake—is to educate them as to the Passover's significance. This is to be a very hands on experience, where they learn in a tangible way what God's salvation involves.*

The centerpiece of the Passover *seder* will be how various elements have been arranged on a particular plate. While the *seder* plate itself comes from the Middle Ages, its basis is in ancient history, when food for different courses would be brought in on separate plates, and placed before those eating. It is certainly practical to see all of the main elements of our *seder* before us throughout the evening, but the reason for placing them all together was likely derived from the thought that one Passover commandment is not important from another. It will be just as important for you to consider the role of *matzah*, as it will be for you to consider the *karpas* or *charoset*.

There are six main elements that appear on the Passover *seder* plate, which today is usually some kind of ceremonial platter:

1. *zeroah* - roasted lamb shankbone
2. *karpas* - green vegetable, usually parsley or lettuce
3. *charoset* – fruit mixture of chopped nuts, apples, wine, and spices
4. *beitzah* – roasted egg
5. *matzah* – unleavened bread[†]
6. salt water or vinegar – used in the dipping of the *karpas*

Also present on the Passover table will be three pieces of *matzah* on a plate or in a special bag, either in front of the *seder*'s leader, or off to the right of the *seder* plate. (This will be different from any other *matzah* that has been made available for normal eating throughout the meal.) There will be a cup for drinking wine (or grape juice). For a home *seder*, there should be enough wine available so that adults can drink four standard cups.[‡] Congregational *seder*'s may need to stretch out the amount of wine or grape juice consumed, informing attendees that their single cup should last them for their allotted four cups. (It might be useful to have a decanter of some kind available for the wine and grape juice, should any extra be required.) A cup for Elijah is also commonplace for later in the *seder* meal.

Each of the elements on the *seder* plate are intended to allow for participants' senses to get a feel for the message of the Passover and Exodus.

---

[*] If this is a large congregational *seder*, we would recommend that you use grape juice instead of alcoholic wine. It is much easier to employ wine at a home *seder* meal.

[†] A few Messianic congregations will actually make their own *matzah* for the Passover *seder*. We would strongly recommend that other than those with special health needs, that you purchase standard Jewish *matzah* that is made explicitly for Passover. It is an important way that Messianic Believers can express commonality with a Jewish community that is sometimes suspicious of them.

[‡] While many will prefer to drink either Manischewitz wine, or some other sweet Jewish table wine, it is not uncommon for people to drink either red or white wine for Passover. Notably, there are non-sweet wines that are made expressly for Passover, which you may wish to provide for your guests. Purchasing these wines is again another way that Messianic Believers can express commonality with the Jewish community.

Children should drink grape juice.

Lighting of the Festival Candles

In almost all Jewish tradition, a designated female lights the candles, whether they be for the weekly Shabbat or any of the appointed times.

Female Candle Lighter: As we kindle the festival lights, we pray for the illumination of the Spirit of God to bring great personal meaning to this, our Passover commemoration.

Barukh atah Adonai,
Eloheinu melekh ha'olam,
asher kidshanu
b'mitzvotav v'tzivanu
l'hadlik ner shel yom tov

בָּרוּךְ אַתָּה יְיָ
אֱלֹהֵינוּ מֶלֶךְ הָעוֹלָם
אֲשֶׁר קִדְּשָׁנוּ בְּמִצְוֹתָיו
וְצִוָּנוּ לְהַדְלִיק
נֵר שֶׁל יוֹם טוֹב

Barukh atah Adonai,
Eloheinu melekh ha'olam,
she'he'cheyanu
v'ki'yemanu v'higi'anu
la'zman ha'zeh.

בָּרוּךְ אַתָּה יְיָ
אֱלֹהֵינוּ מֶלֶךְ הָעוֹלָם
שֶׁהֶחֱיָנוּ וְקִיְּמָנוּ
וְהִגִּיעָנוּ לַזְּמָן הַזֶּה

Blessed are You Lord our God, King of the universe, who has sanctified our lives through His commandments, commanding (or, permitting)[*] us to kindle the festival lights.

Blessed are You Lord our God, King of the universe, for giving us life, for sustaining us, and for enabling us to celebrate this festival.

The Four Cups of Wine

By this time, you should have informed your guests or audience that they will be drinking of four cups of wine (or grape juice). In the event that you are having a congregational seder, they may have to be reminded that their single cup is to last for the total four cups.

Leader: "But the LORD said to Moses, 'Now you shall see what I will do to Pharaoh; for with a strong hand he will send them out, and with a strong hand he will drive them out of his land'" (Exodus 6:1).

As the Lord spoke these words of encouragement to Moses, He revealed to His servant the plan by which He would redeem the Israelites.

All: The Lord declared:

I will bring you out from under the yoke of the Egyptians...
I will free you from being slaves...
I will redeem you with an outstretched arm...
I will take you as My own people, and I will be your God...
Exodus 6:6-7

---

[*] The traditional rendering includes "commands," but if this is uncomfortable for you it can be replaced with "permits."

Messianic Spring Holiday Helper

Leader: At Passover, we remember these promises of redemption and
           relationship by drinking from our cups four times. With each cup, let
           us remember the union that God desires.

THE FIRST CUP
The Cup of Sanctification

Leader: Let us lift the first cup together and bless the name of the Lord!

All: I am ready to drink the first of the four cups. This recalls God's
           promise of redemption to the people Israel, as it says, "I will bring
           you out from under the burdens of the Egyptians" (Exodus 6:6).

           Barukh atah Adonai,   בָּרוּךְ אַתָּה יְיָ
           Eloheinu melekh   אֱלֹהֵינוּ מֶלֶךְ הָעוֹלָם
           ha'olam, borei p'ri   בּוֹרֵא פְּרִי הַגָּפֶן
           ha'gafen.

           Blessed are You, Lord our God, King of the universe, who creates
           the fruit of the vine.

           Blessed are You, Lord our God, King of the universe, who has
           chosen us and distinguished us by sanctifying us through His
           commandments. You have lovingly favored us with the Sabbath for
           rest, festivals for joy, seasons and holidays for happiness, among
           them this day of Passover, the season of liberation, a day of sacred
           assembly commemorating the Exodus from Egypt. You have chosen
           us, sanctifying us, and have granted us Your sacred festivals in joy
           and happiness. Praised are You, Lord who sanctifies the people Israel
           and the festival seasons.

Leader: As He began His final Passover *seder*, Yeshua the Messiah shared a
           cup with His Disciples, and said to them, "Take this, and divide it
           among yourselves. For I tell you that from now on I will not drink of
           the fruit of the vine until the kingdom of God comes" (Luke 22:17-
           18).

           Let us all drink of this, the first cup of Passover.
All:

           Barukh atah Adonai,   בָּרוּךְ אַתָּה יְיָ
           Eloheinu melekh   אֱלֹהֵינוּ מֶלֶךְ הָעוֹלָם
           ha'olam, she'he'cheyanu   שֶׁהֶחֱיָנוּ וְקִיְּמָנוּ
           v'ki'yemanu v'higi'anu   וְהִגִּיעָנוּ לַזְּמַן הַזֶּה
           la'zman ha'zeh.

           Blessed are You, Lord our God, King of the universe, for giving us
           life, sustaining us, and for enabling us to reach this season.

           Drink the first cup while reclining.

Urchatz (Hand Washing)

Designated Reader:	"Who shall ascend the hill of the LORD? And who shall stand in his holy place? He who has clean hands and a pure heart, who does not lift up his soul to what is false and does not swear deceitfully" (Psalm 24:3-4).
Leader:	*Leader lifts a basin of water; if holding a congregational seder, designated persons at various locations at the tables are to do so as well*

Let us now offer the bowl of water to one another and share in this hand-washing ceremony.

Leader and designated persons pass around bowl of water to others

Let us also reflect upon the gesture of humility and the lesson of commitment made by Messiah Yeshua, when, on the night of His Last Supper He laid aside His garments and girded Himself with a towel. As the Fourth Gospel tells us,

"Then he poured water into a basin and began to wash the disciples' feet and to wipe them with the towel that was wrapped around him...When he had washed their feet and put on his outer garments and resumed his place, he said to them, 'Do you understand what I have done to you? You call me Teacher and Lord, and you are right, for so I am. If I then, your Lord and Teacher, have washed your feet, you also ought to wash one another's feet'" (John 13:5, 12-14).

All: *The customary blessing is not recited as the bowl of water is passed around, and people symbolically put the tips of their fingers into the basin.*

Karpas (Parsley)

Designated Reader:	"During those many days the king of Egypt died, and the people of Israel groaned because of their slavery and cried out for help. Their cry for rescue from slavery came up to God" (Exodus 2:23).
Leader:	*Leader lifts a piece of parsley*

Passover is a holiday that comes in the springtime, when much of the world is becoming green with life. This vegetable, called *karpas*, represents life, created and sustained by Almighty God.

Leader lifts up the salt water (or in some cases, vinegar)

But life in Egypt for the Israelites was a life of pain, suffering, and tears, represented by this salt water (or, vinegar). Let us take a spring of parsley and dip it into the salt water, remember that life is sometimes immersed in tears.

All:

Barukh atah Adonai, Eloheinu melekh ha'olam, borei p'ri ha'adamah.

בָּרוּךְ אַתָּה יי
אֱלֹהֵינוּ מֶלֶךְ הָעוֹלָם
בּוֹרֵא פְּרִי הָאֲדָמָה

Blessed are You, Lord our God, King of the universe, who creates the fruit of the Earth.

Leader: Now let us, together, eat the *karpas*.

All: *Take a twig of parsley, dip it into the salt water, and then eat.*

Yachatz (Breaking of the Matzah)

At this point in the *seder* the leader will note the three pieces of *matzah* which have been sitting off to the side of the other Passover elements. The middle of the three pieces will be removed and broken in two. The larger of the two pieces will be wrapped in a white linen napkin and set aside to be the *afikoman*, to be eaten at the conclusion of the meal.

It is customary to hide the *afikoman*, and in some families it is held for ransom.

There are a variety of explanations in Jewish tradition as to what the three pieces of *matzah* together represent, as a "Unity." Some consider it to represent the Patriarchs Abraham, Isaac, and Jacob; the three orders of priests, Levites, and the general people of Israel; or the three parts of the Tanach: Law, Prophets, and Writings. Messianic Believers often connect this to the tri-unity of God, manifest to us in the Scriptures as Father, Son, and Holy Spirit. It is not difficult, then, to see a symbolic representation of the breaking of the second piece of *matzah*—"the "Son"—given the redemptive themes of the Passover.*

Leader: We will now break the second piece of *matzah* into two pieces, wrapping the larger of the two into this special linen napkin, placing it aside until later in our meal.

---

* *The Messianic Passover Haggadah* places the breaking of the *matzah* after the recital of the Four Questions, whereas the traditional *haggadah* has placed the *Yachatz* before the Maggid and Four Questions and the telling of the Passover story. This *haggadah* follows suit, acknowledging the Messianic significance of the breaking of the second piece of *matzah* into the *afikoman* at the end of the Exodus account.

Maggid[*]

The main part of the seder *meal now begins: a period of instruction and reflection. This will include an introduction to what these Passover elements mean, the questioning of small children, a retelling of the Exodus account in Biblical history and tradition, and for Messianic Believers what these things mean to us in light of the salvation we possess in Yeshua the Messiah.*

Leader: *Leader now uncovers the main selection of* matzah *available, directing people to make note of it.*

This is the bread of affliction which the Israelites ate in the land of Egypt. All who are hungry, let them enter and eat. All who are in need, let them come and commemorate Passover.

Now we are all here. Next year in the Land of Israel! Now we are enslaved. Next year we will be free.

It is our hope that next year all of the community of Israel, and indeed all of humanity, will be free, and so we utter an appropriate plea to God for those around the world who are persecuted and unfree.

Leader, or designated person, may want to offer a short prayer or direct the audience/guests in a short moment of silence, as we prepare to enter into the instructive period of the seder.

All: O Lord, our God and God of our ancestors, just as You took the Israelites from among the Egyptians and led them through the sea, so may You have mercy on our brothers and sisters, the House of Israel, whose who are distressed and those who are oppressed, wherever they may be. Save them. Lead them from narrow straights to abundant favor, from darkness to light, from enslavement to redemption, speedily, in our days, and let us say: Amen.

We especially pray that all we encounter can experience not only physical freedom and material blessing, but most importantly can experience the spiritual freedom and reconciliation available only through Your Son, Messiah Yeshua.

Mah Nishtanah (The Four Questions)

Leader: *Leader now directs the audience to a small child, or a group of several children, who have been chosen in advance to ask the Four Questions of Passover.[†]*

The Holy Scriptures anticipated that when Passover would be remembered among future generations, children would ask "What do you mean by this service?" (Exodus 12:26) or "What does this ceremony mean to you?" (NIV). Both parents and spiritual mentors alike have the responsibility to make sure that young people really do understand the salvation themes of the Passover *seder*. As our Lord

---

[*] Meaning "speaker" or "preacher."
[†] A single child being substituted with several children, can also be interjected with a group of children, who may have practiced in advance to sing the Four Questions.

Yeshua Himself taught, "Let the children come to me; do not hinder them, for to such belongs the kingdom of God" (Mark 10:14). These children make up the Kingdom of God every bit as much as adults, and not only do they have much to be taught this evening—but by their example of asking questions they too might teach the adults some things.

Child:

Recital or canting of the Four Questions in Hebrew is followed by the English.

Mah nishtanah ha'lailah ha'zeh m'kol-ha'leilot?

מַה נִּשְׁתַּנָּה הַלַּיְלָה הַזֶּה מִכָּל הַלֵּילוֹת

Shebekol ha'leilot anu okhlin chametz u'matzah. Ha'lailah ha'zeh kulo matzah?

שֶׁבְּכָל הַלֵּילוֹת אָנוּ אוֹכְלִין חָמֵץ וּמַצָּה הַלַּיְלָה הַזֶּה כֻּלּוֹ מַצָּה

Shebekol ha'leilot anu okhlin she'ar yeraqot. Ha'lailah ha'zeh maror?

שֶׁבְּכָל הַלֵּילוֹת אָנוּ אוֹכְלִין שְׁאָר יְרָקוֹת הַלַּיְלָה הַזֶּה מָרוֹר

Shebekol ha'leilot eiyn anu matbilin afilu pa'am echat. Ha'lailah ha'zeh sh'tei f'amim?

שֶׁבְּכָל הַלֵּילוֹת אֵין אָנוּ מַטְבִּילִין אֲפִילוּ פַּעַם אֶחָת הַלַּיְלָה הַזֶּה שְׁתֵּי פְעָמִים

Shebekol ha'leilot anu okhlin bein yoshvin u'vein mesubin. Ha'lailah ha'zeh kulanu mesubin?

שֶׁבְּכָל הַלֵּילוֹת אָנוּ אוֹכְלִין בֵּין יוֹשְׁבִין וּבֵין מְסֻבִּין הַלַּיְלָה הַזֶּה כֻּלָּנוּ מְסֻבִּין

Child *or*
Group of
Children:

How different this night is from all other nights!

On all other nights we eat either leavened or unleavened bread.
   Why, on this night, do we eat only unleavened bread?

On all other nights we eat all kinds of vegetables.
   Why, on this night, must we eat bitter herbs?

On all other nights we do not usually dip vegetables even once.
   Why, on this night, do we dip twice?

On all other nights we eat either sitting upright or reclining.
   Why, on this night, do we eat reclining?

All: Please tell us what these things all mean. We desire to all be instructed.

THE MEANING OF THE PASSOVER

The main feature of the *haggadah* is the retelling of the account of Passover and the Exodus, something that has been preceded by the asking of questions by children. All in attendance at the *seder* will get to hear what took place with the enslaving of the Ancient Israelites, their deliverance by God via Moses, and how God humiliated an ancient superpower.

For Messianic Believers, the significance of the *seder* goes beyond just understanding the blood covering of the Passover lamb over the Israelite homes, or the plagues upon Egypt. It is our job to be able to connect the original Passover actions with Yeshua the Messiah's own sacrificial work. After the telling of the story of the Exodus, it is incumbent upon us to be able to recognize how the Passover elements sat in front of the Twelve Disciples, as Yeshua was conducting the Last Supper. Yeshua gave His Disciples critical instruction and teaching, as He would be arrested and executed the following day.

Leader will want to direct audience or guests to this being the longest part of the seder. *As it will include a great deal of teaching, this is when people will definitely want to have their Bibles handy. They will hear a variety of passages read, which they will want to know for further reflection.*

We were slaves

Leader: We were slaves to Pharaoh in Egypt but the Lord our God brought us forth with a mighty hand and with an outstretched arm. And if the Holy One, praised be He, had not taken our ancestors out of Egypt, then we, and our children, and our children's children, would still be enslaved to Pharaoh in Egypt. Now even if all of us were scholars, even if all of us were sages, even if all of us were elders, even if all of us were learned in the Torah, it would still be our duty to tell the story of the Exodus from Egypt. Moreover, whoever elaborates upon the story of the Exodus deserves praise.

All: Praised be He who is everywhere.
Praised be He.
Praised be He who gave the Torah to His people Israel.
Praised be He.

The Four Children[*]

Designated Reader: The Torah alludes to four types of children: one who is wise, and who is wicked, one who is simple, and one who does not know how to ask.

All: **What does the wise child ask?**

Designated Reader: "What is the meaning of the testimonies and the statutes and the rules that the LORD our God has commanded you?" (Deuteronomy 6:20).

---

[*] It might be appropriate to specifically choose a female or mother for this part of the reading.

You should inform this child of all the laws of Passover, including the ruling that nothing should be eaten after the *afikoman*.

All:	**What does the wicked child ask?**
Designated Reader:	"What do *you* mean by this service?" (Exodus 12:26).

To "you" and not to "him." Since he removes himself from the community by denying God's role in the Exodus, shake him by replying, "It is because of what the LORD did for *me* when I came out of Egypt" (Exodus 13:8). "For me." Not for him. Had he been there, he would not have been redeemed.

All:	**What does the simple child ask?**
Designated Reader:	"What is this all about?" You should tell him, "By strength of hand the LORD brought us out of Egypt, from the house of slavery" (Exodus 13:14).

All:	**And as for the child who does not know how to ask, what do we do?**
Designated Reader:	You should open the discussion for him, as it is written, "It is because of what the LORD did for me when I came out of Egypt" (Exodus 13:8).

In the beginning

Designated Reader:	In the beginning our ancestors served idols, but then God embraced us so that we might serve Him, as it is written,

"And Joshua said to all the people, 'Thus says the LORD, the God of Israel, "Long ago, your fathers lived beyond the Euphrates, Terah, the father of Abraham and of Nahor; and they served other gods. Then I took your father Abraham from beyond the River and led him through all the land of Canaan, and made his offspring many. I gave him Isaac. And to Isaac I gave Jacob and Esau. And I gave Esau the hill country of Seir to possess, but Jacob and his children went down to Egypt"''' (Joshua 24:2-4).

Praised be He who keeps His promises to Israel. Praised be He who foresaw both our enslavement and our redemption when He made the covenant with our father Abraham (Genesis 15). As it is written,

"Then the LORD said to Abram, 'Know for certain that your offspring will be sojourners in a land that is not theirs and will be servants there, and they will be afflicted for four hundred years. But I will bring judgment on the nation that they serve, and afterward they shall come out with great possessions'" (Genesis 15:13-14).

All:	*each raises the cup of wine in thanksgiving*

It is this promise that has sustained our ancestors and us, for not just one enemy has arisen to destroy us; rather in every generation there are those who seek our destruction, but the Holy One, praised be He, saves us from their hands.

replace the cup

Torah and Midrash*

We have reached the heart of the *haggadah*. The verses read in this section will supply a succinct synopsis of the Exodus. Each phrase will be expanded, to expound each thought, citing Biblical chapter and verse to support and illustrate explanations.

This section refers to a single Designated Reader, although as many as four readers could be included. Leader will need to have chosen these different readers in advance, so that they will have already practiced reading their different selections before speaking them in a public audience or large home setting. This will be the most critical section of the entire haggadah *for your audience or guests to follow.*

It would be appropriate for those delivering this part of the teaching to be either teenagers or young adults.

Leader:
We are blessed this evening to have some able students of the Holy Scriptures with us, who will be delivering a teaching on the significance of the Passover and God's deliverance of Ancient Israel from Egypt. They will be delivering a short message from four verses from the Book of Deuteronomy, and some traditional views of them as seen in the *haggadah* for many centuries, which should enlighten our perspective of the events—or at least encourage us to do further examination of them when our *seder* is over.

Let us all read these verses together.

All:
"And you shall make response before the LORD your God, 'A wandering Aramean was my father. And he went down into Egypt and sojourned there, few in number, and there he became a nation, great, mighty, and populous. And the Egyptians treated us harshly and humiliated us and laid on us hard labor. Then we cried to the LORD, the God of our fathers, and the LORD heard our voice and saw our affliction, our toil, and our oppression. And the LORD brought us out of Egypt with a mighty hand and an outstretched arm, with great deeds of terror, with signs and wonders'" (Deuteronomy 26:5-8).

Designated Reader:
Deuteronomy 26:5
"And you shall make response before the LORD your God, 'A wandering Aramean was my father. And he went down into Egypt and sojourned there, few in number, and there he became a nation, great, mighty, and populous'" (Deuteronomy 26:5).

My father was a wandering Aramean, and he went down to Egypt. He was impelled, by force of the Divine word, as it is written, "Know for certain that your offspring will be sojourners in a land that is not theirs and will be servants there, and they will be afflicted for four hundred years" (Genesis 15:13).

With just a few people. As it is written, "Your fathers went down to Egypt seventy persons, and now the LORD your God has made you as numerous as the stars of heaven" (Deuteronomy 10:22).

And sojourned there. This teaches that our father Jacob did not go down to settle permanently in Egypt but rather sojourn there, as it is

---

* Or, a seeking out of what the various passages referred are supposed to mean.

written,

"They said to Pharaoh, 'We have come to sojourn in the land, for there is no pasture for your servants' flocks, for the famine is severe in the land of Canaan. And now, please let your servants dwell in the land of Goshen'" (Genesis 47:4).

And there he became a great nation. This teaches that the Israelites became easily identifiable there. They became unique, recognized as a distinct nation, through their observance of commandments. They were never suspected of unchastity or of slander; they did not change their names and they did not change their language.

Mighty and numerous. As it is written,

"But the people of Israel were fruitful and increased greatly; they multiplied and grew exceedingly strong, so that the land was filled with them" (Exodus 1:7).

Designated Reader:
Deuteronomy 26:6

"And the Egyptians treated us harshly and humiliated us and laid on us hard labor" (Deuteronomy 26:6).

The Egyptians dealt harshly with us. They were ungrateful, for they paid back in evil the kindnesses that Joseph had done for them, as it is written, "Now there arose a new king over Egypt, who did not know Joseph" (Exodus 1:8). He acted as if he did not want to know anything about Joseph.

Another interpretation: the Egyptians dealt harshly with us. They made us appear to be bad, for it is written that Pharaoh said to his people, "Behold, the people of Israel are too many and too mighty for us. Come, let us deal shrewdly with them, lest they multiply, and, if war breaks out, they join our enemies and fight against us and escape from the land" (Exodus 1:9-10).

And oppressed us. As it is written, "Therefore they set taskmasters over them to afflict them with heavy burdens. They built for Pharaoh store cities, Pithom and Raamses. So they ruthlessly made the people of Israel work as slaves" (Exodus 1:11, 13).

And they imposed hard labor upon us. They would impose a difficult task upon the weak and an easy task upon the strong, a light burden upon the young and a heavy burden upon the old. This work was without end and futile, for the Egyptians wanted to not only enslave them but also break their spirit.

Designated Reader:
Deuteronomy 26:7

"Then we cried to the LORD, the God of our fathers, and the LORD heard our voice and saw our affliction, our toil, and our oppression" (Deuteronomy 26:7).

We cried out to the Lord. As it is written, "During those many days the king of Egypt died, and the people of Israel groaned because of their slavery and cried out for help. Their cry for rescue from slavery came up to God" (Exodus 2:23).

The God of our ancestors. Because of the merit of our ancestors, we were redeemed from Egypt. As it is written, "And God heard their groaning, and God remembered his covenant with Abraham, with Isaac, and with Jacob" (Exodus 2:24).

And the Lord heard our plea. As it is written, "I have surely seen the affliction of my people who are in Egypt and have heard their cry because of their taskmasters. I know their sufferings, and I have come down to deliver them out of the hand of the Egyptians and to bring them up out of that land to a good and broad land, a land flowing with milk and honey, to the place of the Canaanites, the Hittites, the Amorites, the Perizzites, the Hivites, and the Jebusites" (Exodus 3:7-8). And as it is written, "I will be with him in trouble" (Psalm 91:15). And as it is written, "In all their affliction he was afflicted" (Isaiah 63:3).

And saw. What did He see? He saw that the Israelites had compassion for each other. When one of them finished his quota of bricks, he would help others.

Our affliction. This refers to the enforced separation of husbands and wives. The Egyptians decreed that men should sleep in the field and women should sleep in the city, in order to decrease their offspring. The women, however, would bring warm food to their husbands, and comfort them, saying, "They shall not succeed in subjugating us. In the end, the Holy One will redeem us." Thus in spite of the decree, they would be together and they did have children. Through the merit of the righteous women of that generation the Israelites were redeemed from Egypt.

Our misery. This refers to the drowning of the sons, for Pharaoh decreed, "Every son that is born to the Hebrews you shall cast into the Nile, but you shall let every daughter live" (Exodus 1:22). The Israelites would circumcise their sons in Egypt. The Egyptians would ask, "Why do you insist upon circumcising them? In a little while we shall throw them into the river." The Israelites would response, "Nevertheless we shall circumcise them."

And our oppression. This refers to the straw. For Pharaoh decreed, "You shall no longer give the people straw to make bricks, as in the past; let them go and gather straw for themselves" (Exodus 5:7). Whenever the Egyptians counted the bricks and found the quota unfilled, the Israelite overseers refused to deliver their fellow Israelites to the Egyptians. Instead, they submitted themselves, and willingly suffered the punishment in order to lighten the ordeal of the Israelites.

Designated Reader: *Deuteronomy 26:8*

"The LORD freed us from Egypt by a mighty hand, by an outstretched arm and awesome power, and by signs and portents" (Deuteronomy 26:8).

Then the Lord took us out of Egypt. Not by an angel. Nor by a seraph. Nor by a messenger. Rather, the Holy One Himself, in His glory, as it is written, "For I will pass through the land of Egypt that night, and I will strike all the firstborn in the land of Egypt, both man and beast; and on all the gods of Egypt I will execute judgments: I am the LORD" (Exodus 12:12).

"I will pass through the land of Egypt"—I am not an angel. "I will strike all the firstborn"—I am not a seraph. "On all the gods of Egypt I will execute judgments"—I am not a messenger. "I am the LORD"—and there is no other.

With a mighty hand an outstretched arm. When the Egyptians made the life of our ancestors bitter, the Holy One said, "I will redeem them," as it is written, "I will bring you out from under the burdens of the Egyptians, and I will deliver you from slavery to them, and I will redeem you with an outstretched arm and with great acts of judgment. I will take you to be my people, and I will be your God, and you shall know that I am the LORD your God, who has brought you out from under the burdens of the Egyptians" (Exodus 6:6-7).

With awesome power. This refers to Divine revelation, as it is written, "Or has any god ever attempted to go and take a nation for himself from the midst of another nation, by trials, by signs, by wonders, and by war, by a mighty hand and an outstretched arm, and by great deeds of terror, all of which the LORD your God did for you in Egypt before your eyes?" (Deuteronomy 4:34).

With signs. This refers to the staff, as it is written, "And take in your hand this staff, with which you shall do the signs" (Exodus 4:17).

Another interpretation: with signs. This refers to God's commandments. For they are an eternal sign that God saves and redeems, and a remembrance for all generations of the covenant between the Holy One and His people. This it is written, "And it shall be to you as a sign on your hand and as a memorial between your eyes, that the law of the LORD may be in your mouth. For with a strong hand the LORD has brought you out of Egypt" (Exodus 13:9).

And with wonders. This refers to the plagues, as it is written, "And I will show wonders in the heavens and on the earth, blood and fire and columns of smoke" (Joel 2:30[3:3]).

The Ten Plagues

Having now reviewed the background of the Passover and Exodus, the ten plagues that God dispensed upon Egypt will now be remembered in a visible demonstration. Each person will dip his or her finger into the cup of wine, and then onto a plate or napkin on the side.

Leader:

Esher makot hei'vi'
haKadosh barukh hu al
ha'Mitzrim b'Mitzrayim
v'eilu hein.

עֶשֶׂר מַכּוֹת הֵבִיא
הַקָּדוֹשׁ בָּרוּךְ הוּא עַל
הַמִּצְרִים בְּמִצְרַיִם וְאֵלּוּ
הֵן

All:

These are the ten plagues which the Holy One brought upon the Egyptians (Exodus 7:15-12:31).

Leader: *At the mentioning of each plague, remove a drop of wine from cup.*

dam – blood	דָּם
tzafar'dea – frogs	צְפַרְדֵּעַ
kinim – gnats	כִּנִּים
arov – insects	עָרֹב
dever – pestilence	דֶּבֶר
sh'chin – boils	שְׁחִין
barad – hail	בָּרָד
ar'beh – locusts	אַרְבֶּה
choshekh – darkness	חֹשֶׁךְ
makat b'khrorot – death of the firstborn	מַכַּת בְּכוֹרוֹת

Dayenu
It would have been enough

With measured and mounting jubilation, this lilting litany and song chronicles an extraordinary progression. It tells how God in His lovingkindness raised Ancient Israel, step by step, from the degradation of slavery to the heights of freedom as His chosen people. We express our thankfulness for every beneficent act, and we delight in the godly design that plotted Israel's path—via Sinai—to the Promised Land.

After reciting the Dayenu *affirmations, it is customary for the attendees, or a group of children, to then sing the* Dayenu *song which follows.*

This haggadah has all attendees of the seder speak forth the Dayenu *affirmations, although you may feel free to adapt it as your Leader or Designated Reader may speak out the litany, followed by attendees responding with* "Dayenu."

All: How many acts of kindness God has performed for us!

Had He taken us out of Egypt without carrying out judgments against the Egyptians – *Dayenu.*

Had He carried out judgments against the Egyptians without vanquishing their gods – *Dayenu.*

Had He vanquished their gods without dividing the sea for us – *Dayenu.*

Had He divided the sea for us without leading us across on dry land – *Dayenu.*

Had He led us across on dry land without taking care of us for forty years in the desert – *Dayenu.*

Had He taken care of us for forty years in the desert without feeding us manna – *Dayenu.*

Had He fed us manna without giving us *Shabbat* * – *Dayenu.*

---

* Hebrew for "Sabbath."

Had He given us *Sabbath* without bringing us to Mount Sinai –
Dayenu.

Had He brought us to Mount Sinai without giving us the Torah –
Dayenu.

Had He given us the Torah without leading us to the Land of Israel –
Dayenu.

Had He led us to the Land of Israel without building the Temple for
us – *Dayenu.*

How manifold and miraculous are the great deeds that our God has
performed for us, from taking us out of Egypt to building the
Temple.

DAYENU SONG

reproduced at end of Haggadah *along with music*[*]

Leader *or*
Designated
Reader:

When the king of Egypt was told that the people had fled, the mind
of Pharaoh and his servants was changed toward the people, and they
said, "What is this we have done, that we have let Israel go from
serving us?"...The Egyptians pursued them, all Pharaoh's horses and
chariots and his horsemen and his army, and overtook them
encamped at the sea...And the people of Israel went into the midst of
the sea on dry ground, the waters being a wall to them on their right
hand and on their left. The Egyptians pursued and went in after them
into the midst of the sea, all Pharaoh's horses, his chariots, and his
horsemen...The waters returned and covered the chariots and the
horsemen; of all the host of Pharaoh that had followed them into the
sea, not one of them remained...Then Miriam the prophetess, the
sister of Aaron, took a tambourine in her hand, and all the women
went out after her with tambourines and dancing. And Miriam sang
to them: "Sing to the LORD, for he has triumphed gloriously; the horse
and his rider he has thrown into the sea" (Exodus 14:5, 9, 22-23, 28;
15:20-21).

The Responsibility to Remember the Passover

Leader *or*
Designated
Reader:

Rabbi Gamaliel, teacher of the Apostle Paul, would say, "Whoever
has not referred to these three matters connected to the Passover has
not fulfilled his obligation, and these three are they: Passover,
unleavened bread, and bitter herbs" (m.*Pesachim* 10:5).

---

[*] Some of you may choose not to sing this song, or if unfamiliar in a home setting, may simply choose to play a
recording of it.

The Passover offering: Why did our ancestors eat the Passover offering at their *seder?* As a reminder that the Holy One, praised be He, passed over the Israelite dwellings in Egypt, as it is written, "It is the sacrifice of the LORD's Passover, for he passed over the houses of the people of Israel in Egypt, when he struck the Egyptians but spared our houses" (Exodus 12:27).

Matzah: Why do we eat it? To remind ourselves that even before the dough of our ancestors had time to rise, the supreme King of Kings, the Holy One, praised be He, revealed Himself and redeemed them, as it is written: "And they baked unleavened cakes of the dough that they had brought out of Egypt, for it was not leavened, because they were thrust out of Egypt and could not wait, nor had they prepared any provisions for themselves" (Exodus 12:37).

Maror: Why do we eat it? To remind ourselves that, as it is written, the Egyptians "made their lives bitter with hard service, in mortar and brick, and in all kinds of work in the field. In all their work they ruthlessly made them work as slaves" (Exodus 1:14).

All:

In each generation, every individual should feel as though he or she had actually been redeemed from Egypt, as it is said, "You shall tell your son on that day, 'It is because of what the LORD did for me when I came out of Egypt'" (Exodus 13:8). For the Holy One redeemed not only our ancestors; He redeemed us with them, as it is said, "And he brought us out from there, that he might bring us in and give us the land that he swore to give to our fathers" (Deuteronomy 6:23).

each raises the cup of wine in thanksgiving

Therefore, we must revere, exalt, extol, acclaim, adore and glorify God who performed all these miracles for our ancestors and for us. He took us
   from slavery to freedom
   from despair to joy
   from mourning to celebration
   from darkness to light
   from enslavement to redemption
and we sing before Him a new song. Halleluyah!

Praised are You, Lord our God, King of the universe who has redeemed us and our ancestors from Egypt, who has brought us to this night when we eat unleavened bread and bitter herbs. O Lord, our God and God of our ancestors, enable us to celebrate in peace other holy days and festivals, joyful in the rebuilding of Your city Jerusalem and joyful in Your service. We will sing a new song of thanks for our redemption and for our spiritual liberation. Praised are You, Lord, redeemer of the people Israel.

replace the cup

Messianic Spring Holiday Helper

The Cup of Instruction

All: I am ready to drink the second of the four cups. This recalls God's
        promise of redemption to the people Israel, as it says, "I will bring
        you out from under the burdens of the Egyptians" (Exodus 6:6).

        Barukh atah Adonai,   בְּרוּךְ אַתָּה יי
        Eloheinu melekh   אֱלֹהֵינוּ מֶלֶךְ הָעוֹלָם
        ha'olam, borei p'ri   בּוֹרֵא פְּרִי הַגָּפֶן
        ha'gafen.

        Blessed are You, Lord our God, King of the universe, who creates
        the fruit of the vine.

Yeshua: Our Passover Centerpiece

Leader: Having heard about the Ancient Israelites' deliverance from Egypt in
           the first Passover, none of us can deny the importance of how the
           Exodus plays a role in further Biblical history—and how those who
           read the Hebrew Scriptures (Old Testament) are supposed to
           remember God's salvation of the Israelites. The Prophets implored
           Israel to not forget God's previous deliverance of their ancestors, so
           that they might turn in repentance to the One who is indeed gracious
           and merciful!

           The blood of the lamb painted onto the doorframes of the Israelite
           houses, saving them from the plague of death, serves to point us to
           important scenes that we see in the Apostolic Scriptures (New
           Testament). We are reminded explicitly of how Yeshua the Messiah
           is "the Lamb of God, who takes away the sin of the world!" (John
           1:29). He was sacrificed and slain for us, without a bone broken, just
           like the Passover lamb (John 19:36; cf. Exodus 12:46; Numbers 9:12).
           The Apostle Paul would bid the Corinthians, "For Messiah, our
           Passover lamb, has been sacrificed. Let us therefore celebrate the
           festival, not with the old leaven, the leaven of malice and evil, but
           with the unleavened bread of sincerity and truth" (1 Corinthians 5:7b-
           8).

All: We have all gathered here to celebrate the feast! Show us, Heavenly
           Father, what this can teach us as those who have received salvation in
           Your Son, our Messiah Yeshua!

Leader: As we have all heard of the traditional *seder* meal, our attention has
           undoubtedly been on another meal, the Last Supper, which our Lord
           held with His Disciples on the night He was betrayed by Judas
           Iscariot. Yeshua said, "I have earnestly desired to eat this Passover
           with you before I suffer" (Luke 22:15). The room was prepared
           according to His instructions, and the Lord said how "I will not eat it
           until it is fulfilled in the kingdom of God" (Luke 22:16). He directed
           the attention of the Disciples to the elements of *matzah* and wine,
           representative of how His body would soon be broken, and His blood
           shed, to atone for the sins of all humanity. What the original Passover
           and Exodus from Egypt represented, Yeshua would now fulfill in His

very person. His single sacrifice would be able to atone for all sins: "he has appeared once for all at the end of the ages to put away sin by the sacrifice of himself" (Hebrews 9:26).

Yeshua's atoning work for us has done more than deliver us from the plague of death; His sacrifice has brought us reconciliation with God the Father, and the ability for us to have completely restored communion with our Creator.

But did the Disciples who participated in the Last Supper really know what was about to happen? Did they realize that their Rabbi would be betrayed, unjustly condemned, humiliated and beaten by Romans, and then have to suffer the agony of crucifixion—within the next day? With all of the elements of the *seder* before them, what did they have to reflect on—even long after the Messiah was resurrected? What kind of an impact did that Last Seder meal really have on Yeshua's Disciples, who were given the responsibility of continuing by passing on His teachings, and most especially the good news of His salvation? Did Yeshua's sacrifice render the original Passover and Exodus to be unimportant? Or did His sacrifice make these things even more important for us followers to comprehend?

The Apostle Paul wrote, "I do not want you to be unaware, brothers and sisters, that our ancestors were all under the cloud, and all passed through the sea" (1 Corinthians 10:1, NRSV). He communicated this to not only his fellow Jews, but also to Greeks and Romans who had received Israel's Messiah into their hearts. *All Messiah followers* are to identify with the theme of the original Passover, Exodus, and wilderness trek of Ancient Israel. Abraham, Issac, Jacob, Joseph, Moses, Aaron, Joshua, and all other figures of the Hebrew Scriptures are the spiritual forbearers of all those who acknowledge Yeshua as Savior. All Believers are a part of the Commonwealth of Israel (Ephesians 2:11-12), as all people must look to Israel's Messiah for their redemption and cleansing from sins.

All:

This evening, O Lord, teach us of things that we have forgotten or overlooked from Your Word. Help us to remember the themes of the Passover, so that we might truly understand the severity of our salvation in our Messiah Yeshua!

Help us to remove all of the leaven or sin from our hearts, and help us to once again make Your plan of redemptive history the foremost of our thoughts and discussions throughout the year.

Answering the Four Questions

Leader:	The children have asked us to answer what the four elements of the Passover mean: (1) the *matzah* or unleavened bread, (2) the bitter herbs, (3) dipping twice, and (4) why we recline. We have just allowed our *haggadah* to give us some instruction not only about the original Passover and the Israelites' Exodus from Egypt, but also how these elements all work together in understanding the salvation we have in Messiah Yeshua, and what He accomplished for us via His sacrifice.
All:	**It is both a duty and a privilege to have the four questions of Passover answered, and to declare of the mighty works of our faithful God.**
Leader *or* Designated Reader:	On all other nights we eat bread with leaven, but on Passover we eat only *matzah*, unleavened bread. As the Ancient Israelites fled from Egypt, they did not have time for their dough to rise. Instead, the hot desert sun baked it flat. But even more than that, the Scriptures teach us that leaven symbolizes sin. Paul wrote, "Clean out the old leaven so that you may be a new lump" (1 Corinthians 5:7a), admonishing Believers to see that all ungodly behavior be removed from their lives.
All:	**During this season of Passover, let us break our old habits of sin and selfishness, and begin a fresh, new, and holy life. Let us be concerned with serving the needs of others, and not putting ourselves first.**
Leader:	**THE UNLEAVENED BREAD**
	Leader lifts the plate with the three pieces of matzah
	This is the bread of affliction, the poor bread which our spiritual forbearers ate while in Egypt. Let all who are hungry come and eat. Let all who are in need share in the hope of Passover.
	Three pieces of *matzah* are wrapped together for Passover. There are various explanations for this ceremony. The Rabbis call these three a "Unity." Some consider it a unity of the Patriarchs—Abraham, Isaac, and Jacob. Others explain it as a unity of worship—the priests, the Levites, and the people of Israel. We who know Messiah can see in this the unique *tri*-unity of God—Father, Son, and Holy Spirit. Three in one. In the *matzah* we can see a picture of the Messiah. See how it is striped and appears scourged.
All:	**"But he was wounded for our transgressions; he was crushed for our iniquities; upon him was the chastisement that brought us peace, and with his stripes we are healed" (Isaiah 53:5).**
Leader:	Take good notice of how the *matzah* is pierced.
All:	**"And I will pour out on the house of David and the inhabitants of Jerusalem a spirit of grace and pleas for mercy, so that, when they look on me, on him whom they have pierced, they shall mourn for him, as one mourns for an only child..." (Zechariah 12:10; cf. John 19:37).**

Leader: Early in our *seder*, we took the middle piece of *matzah* here and broke it in two. The Messiah too was afflicted and broken. The half of this, the *afikoman*,˙ is wrapped in a white linen napkin, just as the Messiah's body was wrapped for burial. The *afikoman* is hidden from everyone, just as Yeshua's body was placed in a tomb, hidden for a time.

The *afikoman* will return so that we can complete our Passover *seder*, just as the sinless Messiah rose from the dead to ascend into Heaven.

the smaller piece of the broken second piece of matzah *is now broken into several pieces and shared with those at your table*

Let us now share a piece of this unleavened bread of Passover.

All:

Barukh atah Adonai,   בָּרוּךְ אַתָּה יְיָ
Eloheinu melekh   אֱלֹהֵינוּ מֶלֶךְ הָעוֹלָם
ha'olam, hamotzi lechem
min ha'eretz.   הַמּוֹצִיא לֶחֶם מִן הָאָרֶץ

Blessed are You, Lord our God, King of the universe, who brings forth bread from the Earth.

Leader: **THE BITTER HERBS**

Leader directs the attention of audience and guests to the dish of bitter herbs

On all other nights, we eat all kinds of vegetables, but on Passover we eat only *maror*, bitter herbs. As sweet as our lives are today, let us still remember how bitter life was for the Ancient Israelites in Egypt.

All: "...[T]he Egyptians were in dread of the people of Israel. So they ruthlessly made the people of Israel work as slaves and made their lives bitter with hard service, in mortar and brick, and in all kinds of work in the field. In all their work they ruthlessly made them work as slaves" (Exodus 1:12-14).

Leader: As we scoop some *maror* onto a piece of *matzah*, let us allow the bitter taste to cause us to shed tears of compassion for the sorrow that the Israelites knew thousands of years ago.

Let us also consider the sorrow that many people throughout the world are experiencing this evening as well, knowing neither the Passover's message of freedom from bondage—nor the salvation that we possess in Messiah Yeshua.

All:

Barukh atah Adonai,   בָּרוּךְ אַתָּה יְיָ
Eloheinu melekh   אֱלֹהֵינוּ מֶלֶךְ הָעוֹלָם
ha'olam, asher kidshanu   אֲשֶׁר קִדְּשָׁנוּ בְּמִצְוֹתָיו
b'mitzvotav v'tzivanu al
akhilat maror.   וְצִוָּנוּ עַל אֲכִילַת מָרוֹר

˙ There is academic discussion over the origin of the term *afikoman*, which most are agreed is derived from the Greek *epikomen*, likely meaning "dessert." Some have tried to connect this to meaning "he has arisen," connected to the resurrection of Messiah Yeshua (cf. Tabory, 15 fn#22).

Blessed are You, Lord our God, King of the universe, who has sanctified us by His commandments, commanding us to eat bitter herbs.

all eat piece of matzah *with* maror

Leader: **DIPPING TWICE**

On all other nights we do not dip our vegetables even once, but tonight we dip them twice. We have already dipped the parsley into the salt water.

Leader directs the attention of audience and guests to the dish of charoset *(fruit and nut mixture)*

The Ancient Israelites toiled to make treasure cities for Pharaoh, working in brick and clay. We remember this task in a mixture called *charoset* (or, *charoses*), made from chopped apples, honey, nuts, and wine. Let us scoop some bitter herbs onto a small piece of *matzah*. But this time, before we eat, let us dip the herbs into the sweet *charoset*.

The tradition of the *korekh*, eating a piece of *matzah* with both *charoset* and *maror* arose in Second Temple times. This is a reminder of the Temple and a reminder of the practice of Hillel. While the Temple was in existence, Hillel would make a sandwich of the Passover offering, with *matzah* and *maror*, and eat all three together, in fulfillment of the verse, "They shall eat it with unleavened bread and bitter herbs" (Numbers 9:11).

All: *all are to hold up* matzah *with the* maror *and* charoset

We dip the bitter herbs into *charoset* to remind ourselves that even the most bitter circumstances can be sweetened by the hope we have in God.

all now eat

Leader: We should be reminded how at the point in His Last Supper meal, the Lord declared how the one betraying Him, would also dip into the bowl.

All: "And as they were reclining at table and eating, Yeshua said, 'Truly, I say to you, one of you will betray me, one who is eating with me.' They began to be sorrowful and to say to him one after another, 'Is it I?' He said to them, 'It is one of the twelve, one who is dipping bread into the dish with me'" (Mark 14:18-20).

Leader: **RECLINING**

On all other nights we eat either sitting or reclining, but tonight we eat reclining.

The first Passover was celebrated by a people enslaved.

All: Once we were slaves, but now we are freed!

Leader: The Ancient Israelites were instructed to eat the Passover in haste, their loins girded, their staffs in their hands, their sandals upon their feet, awaiting departure from the bondage of Egypt. Today we may all recline and freely enjoy the Passover *seder*.

PASSOVER DINNER
Shulchan Orekh

The Passover Dinner can now begin. One eats and drinks, taking into consideration that one has to eat the final *matzah* known as the *afikoman* shortly following. During the Last Supper meal Yeshua held with His Disciples, it was near the close of their eating that He directed their attention to the bread and wine (Mark 14:22; Matthew 26:26).

Depending on the time constraints for your seder, it would be best that the actual period of serving the meal and then eating should be no more than an hour to seventy-five minutes. Endless times of talking among your attendees or guests should be discouraged.*

The Leader of the congregational seder will need to be one of the first people to eat, as any teaching or presentation delivered will need to begin as the meal is just over half or three-quarters finished. This Leader should present a short 15-20 minute teaching on an important theme of the Passover that the audience needs to hear. Given the teaching section from the haggadah that focuses largely on different Torah passages on the Passover, it would be best for the Leader to consider various themes from the Apostolic Scriptures that look to the Exodus. Also to be considered would be a part of Yeshua's suffering and sacrifice in fulfillment of Passover typology. If the part following the dinner is the "Lord's Supper," then the need to create an environment of reverence is quite apparent.

If the Leader is holding a home seder, the need for a teaching time is less important. Discussion during the dinner will likely focus around some part of the Passover, the sacrificial work of Messiah Yeshua, etc.

---

* If you are holding a Passover *seder* for your congregation, the advantages of having your meal catered, and having actual servers at a hotel or banquet hall—will cut back significantly on the time it takes for people to go through a buffet line.

Tzafun

In the traditional *seder*, the *afikoman* is simply eaten as though it is the dessert of the meal. After the meal, a piece of *matzah* about the size of an olive is eaten. Eating this small piece is to ensure that the taste of *matzah* be left in one's mouth.

Today's Messianic Believers widely agree that it was at this point in the Last Supper meal of Yeshua the Messiah, when the Lord made His Disciples take notice of some specific bread and wine: "Now as they were eating, Yeshua took bread, and after blessing it broke it and gave it to the disciples, and said, 'Take, eat; this is my body.' And he took a cup, and when he had given thanks he gave it to them, saying, 'Drink of it, all of you'" (Matthew 26:26-27). The broken bread and the cup of wine would cause them to consider how He would be soon be beaten, and how His shed blood would provide atonement for sins. The Lord spoke forth how, "This cup that is poured out for you is the new covenant in my blood" (Luke 22:20).

So important is understanding the elements of bread and wine, Yeshua taught, "Whoever feeds on my flesh and drinks my blood has eternal life, and I will raise him up on the last day" (John 6:54). In eating of the *afikoman* and drinking of the Cup of Redemption, we are called to remember the specific point in the *seder* meal when Yeshua interrupted the normal routine—and made His Disciples pay attention! He specifically asked them, "Do this in remembrance of me" (Luke 22:19). The Apostle Paul adds, "For as often as you eat this bread and drink the cup, you proclaim the Lord's death until he comes" (1 Corinthians 11:26).

In the Christian tradition, the bread we are about to eat and the wine we are about to drink make up the elements of the Eucharist,[*] or communion. Communion is generally something that is offered in the Christian Church a bit more frequently than once a year. While Messianic custom varies from congregation to congregation, our *seder* meal is to be very reverent and contemplative at this time. The *seder* Leader and hosts should make sure that before the eating of the *afikoman* and drinking the Cup of Redemption begins, all food items should be put away. There should be no conversation going on. We are to remember the severity of this moment: "Whoever, therefore, eats the bread or drinks the cup of the Lord in an unworthy manner will be guilty of profaning the body and blood of the Lord" (1 Corinthians 11:27).

It would be appropriate for the seder *Leader or a Designated Reader to offer a short selection of verses from either the Gospels or Paul's instruction in 1 Corinthians, on the elements of the Last Supper.*

If you have the ability to do so, it would be appropriate to lower the lighting level where your seder *is being held, as it will change the ambiance of the evening to one of spiritual severity.*

Leader: Previously in our *seder* we broke the second piece of *matzah*, and wrapped the larger of the two pieces in a white linen napkin. We now bring this *afikoman* forth, traditionally understood to be the desert portion of our meal. In eating it, we recognize that we have had our fill of unleavened bread.

Most importantly, we believe that it was at this point in His Last Supper meal, that Yeshua took the *afikoman*, broke it, and said those direct words, "Take, eat; this is my body...This is my body, which is given for you (Matthew 26:26; Luke 22:19).

According to Jewish tradition, the taste of the *afikoman* is something that should remain in the mouths of those who eat it. The Apostle Paul asks us the question, "The bread that we break, is it not a participation in the body of Messiah?" (1 Corinthians 10:16).

---

[*] Derived from the Greek *eucharistos*, meaning blessed or grateful.

All: The Lord Yeshua broke the *matzah* and gave thanks.

Barukh atah Adonai,   בָּרוּךְ אַתָּה יְיָ
Eloheinu melekh   אֱלֹהֵינוּ מֶלֶךְ הָעוֹלָם
ha'olam, hamotzi lechem
min ha'eretz.   הַמּוֹצִיא לֶחֶם מִן הָאָרֶץ

Blessed are You, Lord our God, King of the universe, who brings forth bread from the Earth.

Let us now eat this *matzah*, meditating on the broken body of the Lamb of God who takes away the sin of the world. Let us allow the taste to linger in our mouths.

all now eat the afikoman; *allow for a moment of silent meditation.*

The Cup of Redemption

Leader: After our Lord Yeshua broke *matzah* and passed it to His Disciples, He then directed their attention to a cup of wine, saying, "Drink of it, all of you, for this is my blood of the covenant, which is poured out for many for the forgiveness of sins" (Matthew 26:27-28). The Disciples largely had no idea that the next day their Rabbi would have endured the pain of the cross, being beaten and made to die in a most humiliating and agonizing way. So as we prepare to drink the third cup of our *seder*, the Apostle Paul rightly reminds us, "You cannot drink the cup of the Lord and the cup of demons" (1 Corinthians 10:21). Even if we have been drinking of the same cup all evening long, this wine we now consume reminds us of the shed blood that has secured us final redemption from sins.

In drinking of this cup, we are not only reminded of the Passover lamb whose shed blood would save the Ancient Israelite homes from the plague of death—but now how the shed blood of the Messiah has saved us from eternal banishment from our Creator.

All: I am ready to drink the third of the four cups. This recalls God's promise of redemption to the people Israel, as it says, "I will bring you out from under the burdens of the Egyptians" (Exodus 6:6).

I am also ready to drink of the Lord's cup, a memorial of Yeshua's shed blood for the atonement of my sins.

Barukh atah Adonai,   בָּרוּךְ אַתָּה יְיָ
Eloheinu melekh   אֱלֹהֵינוּ מֶלֶךְ הָעוֹלָם
ha'olam, borei p'ri
ha'gafen.   בּוֹרֵא פְּרִי הַגָּפֶן

Blessed are You, Lord our God, King of the universe, who creates the fruit of the vine.

all now drink the third cup; allow for a moment of silent meditation.

Messianic Spring Holiday Helper

Leader: We have now eaten of the *afikoman* and have drunk of the third cup.

All: "For as often as you eat this bread and drink the cup, you proclaim the Lord's death until he comes" (1 Corinthians 11:26).

Let us not forget this moment of our Passover *seder*, as we reflect on its significance throughout the rest of the year.

The Cup of Elijah

Having the Cup of Elijah, a fifth cup of wine, present at the Passover table, is doubtlessly rooted in the Biblical understanding, "Behold, I will send you Elijah the prophet before the great and awesome day of the LORD comes" (Malachi 4:5[3:23]). The presence of Elijah, in some form or fashion, will herald the salvation activity or judgment of God. Believers in Messiah Yeshua recognize that to some degree, John the Immerser (or Baptist) functioned in the same prophetic office as did Elijah (Matthew 11:14; Luke 1:17). We still believe, though, that more is to come as we approach the Second Coming of our Messiah, and the defeat of God's enemies on Earth.

The Cup of Elijah is filled (along with the fourth cup). The Leader fills Elijah's goblet, or passes it around the table so that every participant can add some wine from his or her own cup. During congregational seder, Leader only needs to fill Cup of Elijah at the main table, directing attention of audience.

Leader: This extra cup is for Elijah the Prophet. Traditionally in the home, it is at this time that one of the children will open the door to welcome Elijah to our *seder*.

child now gets up to open door

All: "Behold, I will send you Elijah the prophet before the great and awesome day of the LORD comes" (Malachi 4:5[3:23]).

Leader: It has been the hope of many generations that Elijah would come at Passover, to announce the coming of the Messiah, the Son of David.

All: The fifth cup of the evening belongs to Elijah. The first four cups represent our landmarks on the road to redemption; for God lightened our burdens, removed our burdens, took us out of Egypt and made us His people. Yet the Bible speaks of a fifth landmark: Israel's return to the Promised Land. For centuries, while the Land of Israel languished in foster care, the fifth cup would be a reminder of Elijah's promised coming and the future restoration. Today, Israel is now a sovereign Jewish state. A homeless people has been restored to its cherished homeland. Jerusalem, never forgotten in the bleak black night of exile, is once more Israel's capital.

As we consider the Cup of Elijah, we anticipate the further redemption and restoration that will come to all Israel: an age of enduring peace and tranquility on Planet Earth brought about by the Kingship of Yeshua the Messiah.

---

* With each person filling Elijah's Cup together, it denotes how we all are to play a role in Israel's corporate redemption and restoration.

Hallel

After Yeshua and His Disciples finished their Last Supper meal, it is recorded that they sang a hymn and went off to the Mount of Olives (Mark 14:26; Matthew 26:30). The Passover *seder* is traditionally closed with the reciting of Hallel, a consideration of Psalms 115-118.

Since Hallel will be recited during the Shabbat *service of the week of Passover (see* **Hallel for Passover**)*, you may wish to substitute a selection of Scripture readings with some music.* * *This would be an appropriate time to find a special, contemplative song to sing or offer to the Lord, based on Psalms 115-118, or the themes of these verses.* †

PSALMS 115-118 are now considered

Nishmat‡

Some passages of the *Nishmat* are as old as the Temple, or as old as the Talmud. Authorship of this piece of liturgy is obscure, attributed to different figures in Jewish history, among them Shimon ben Shetach, statesman-scholar of the Hasomean era. On every Sabbath and at every festival, this rhapsody of prayer and praise is recited in the Synagogue. §

We consider the *Nishmat* something appropriate for you to consider as the Passover *seder* concludes.

Designated Reader:	The breath of all that lives praises You, Lord our God. The force that drives all flesh exalts You, our King, always. Transcending space and time, You are God. Without You we have no other to rescue and redeem us, to save us and sustain us, to show us mercy in disaster and distress. God of all ages, God of all creatures, ceaselessly extolled, You guide the world with kindness, its creatures with compassion. God neither slumbers nor sleeps. You stir the sleeping, support the falling, free the fettered, raise those bowed down and give voice to the speechless. You alone do we acknowledge.

All: Could song fill our mouth as water fills the sea,
           And could joy flood our tongue like countless saves,
        Could our lips utter praise as limitless as sky,
           And could our eyes match the splendor of the sun,
        Could we soar with arms like eagle's wings,
           And run with the gentle grace of swiftest deer,
        Never could we fully state our gratitude
        For one ten-thousandth of the lasting love
           Which is Your precious blessing, dearest God,
           Granted to our ancestors and to us.

Designated Reader: From Egypt You redeemed us, from the house of bondage You delivered us. In famine You nourished us, in prosperity You sustained us. You rescued us from the sword, protected us from pestilence and

---

* Cf. Rachel Anne Rabinowicz, ed., *Passover Haggadah: The Feast of Freedom* (The Rabbinical Assembly,1982), pp 106-113.
† *The Messianic Passover Haggadah*, pp 30-31, considers Psalm 136:1-16, 26.
‡ Meaning, "breath," a part of the opening sentence of the liturgy.
§ Cf. *The Feast of Freedom*, pp 114-117.

saved us from severe and lingering disease. To this day Your compassion has helped us, Your kindness has not forsaken us. Never abandon us, Lord our God. These limbs which You formed for us, this soul-force which You breathed into us, this tongue which You set in our mouth, must thank, praise, extol, exalt and sing Your holiness and sovereignty. Every mouth shall thank You, every tongue shall pledge devotion. Every head shall bow to You, every knee shall bend to You, every heart shall revere You, every fiber of our being shall sing You glory, as the Psalmist sang: "All my bones shall say, 'O LORD, who is like you, delivering the poor from him who is too strong for him, the poor and needy from him who robs him?'" (Psalm 25:10). Who can equal you, who can be compared to You, great mighty, awesome, exalted God, Creator of Heaven and Earth? We extol You even as David sang: "Praise the LORD! Praise the LORD, O my soul!" (Psalm 146:1).

All: You are God through the vastness of Your power, great through the glory of Your name, mighty forever, awesome through Your awesome works. You are King, enthroned supreme.

Designated Reader: He inhabits eternity, sacred and exalted. As the Psalmist has written:

Rejoice in the Lord, you righteous. It is fitting for the upright to praise Him. By the mouth of the upright are You extolled, by the words of the righteous are You praised, by the tongue of the faithful are You acclaimed, in the heart of the saintly are You hallowed.

All: Among assembled throngs of the House of Israel in every generation Your name shall be glorified in song, our King. For it is the duty of all creatures, Lord our God and God of our ancestors, to thank, laud and glorify You, extolling, exalting, to add our own praise to the songs of David, Your anointed servant.

You shall always be praised, great and holy God, our King in Heaven and on Earth. Songs of praise and psalms of gratitude become You, acknowledging Your might and Your dominion. Yours are strength and sovereignty, sanctity, grandeur and glory always. We offer You our devotion, open our hearts in thanksgiving. Praised are You, Sovereign of wonders, crowned with adoration, delighting in mortal song and psalm, exalted King, eternal life of the universe.

THE FOURTH CUP
The Cup of Praise

All: I am ready to drink the final of the four cups. This recalls God's promise of redemption to the people Israel, as it says, "I will bring you out from under the burdens of the Egyptians" (Exodus 6:6).

Barukh atah Adonai,
Eloheinu melekh
ha'olam, borei p'ri
ha'gafen.

בָּרוּךְ אַתָּה יי
אֱלֹהֵינוּ מֶלֶךְ הָעוֹלָם
בּוֹרֵא פְּרִי הַגָּפֶן

Blessed are You, Lord our God, King of the universe, who creates the fruit of the vine.

We thank You for the Earth's bounty and the pleasing, spacious, desirable land which You gave our ancestors, that they might eat of its produce and be satisfied with its goodly yield. Lord our God, have mercy on Jerusalem Your city, on Zion the home of Your glory, and on the Temple. Fully restore Jerusalem soon and in our day, so that we may rejoice in its restoration and eat of the land's good fruit in abundance and praise You in holiness. Grant us joy on this Passover. We thank You for the land for the fruit of the vine. Praised are You, Lord, for the land and for the fruit of the vine.

Leader: Our Passover *seder* is now complete, just as our redemption is forever complete. Let us conclude with the traditional desire that we may celebrate Passover next year in Jerusalem!

All:

L'shanah ha'ba'ah   לַשָּׁנָה הַבָּאָה
b'Yerushalayim   בִּירוּשָׁלָיִם

Next year in Jerusalem!

Leader: Our *seder* has now ended with its history-laden rites. We have journeyed from Egypt on this storied night of nights. We bore witness, remembering the ancient promises of God for deliverance. We pray before Him that He would redeem this Earth from its sin, as He has pledged in His Word to do. Messiah Yeshua said, "For I tell you I will not eat it until it is fulfilled in the kingdom of God" (Luke 22:16). O Lord, we eagerly await that future time, when we can all celebrate the Passover with You in Your Kingdom—and remember all of Your acts of salvation and redemption!

Leader now offers a closing prayer as the seder *concludes*

THE DAYENU SONG

STANZA 1

Ilu hotzianu mimitzrayim,
v'lo asah vahem sh'fatim,
dayeinu!

אִלּוּ הוֹצִיאָנוּ מִמִּצְרַיִם

וְלֹא עָשָׂה בָּהֶם שְׁפָטִים

דַּיֵּנוּ

STANZA 2

Ilu asah vahem sh'fatim
v'lo asah be'eloheihem,
dayeinu!

אִלּוּ עָשָׂה בָּהֶם שְׁפָטִים

וְלֹא עָשָׂה בֵּאלֹהֵיהֶם

דַּיֵּנוּ

STANZA 3

Ilu asah be'eloheihem,
v'lo harag et b'choreihem,
dayeinu!

אִלּוּ עָשָׂה בֵּאלֹהֵיהֶם

וְלֹא הָרַג אֶת בְּכוֹרֵיהֶם

דַּיֵּנוּ

STANZA 4

Ilu harag et b'choreihem,
v'lo natan lanu et mamonam,
dayeinu!

אִלּוּ הָרַג אֶת בְּכוֹרֵיהֶם

וְלֹא נָתַן לָנוּ אֶת מָמוֹנָם

דַּיֵּנוּ

STANZA 5

Ilu natan lanu et mamonam,
v'lo kara lanu et hayam,
dayeinu!

אִלּוּ נָתַן לָנוּ אֶת מָמוֹנָם

וְלֹא קָרַע לָנוּ אֶת הַיָּם

דַּיֵּנוּ

STANZA 6

Ilu kara lanu et hayam,
v'lo he'eviranu v'tocho becharavah,
dayeinu!

אִלּוּ קָרַע לָנוּ אֶת הַיָּם

וְלֹא הֶעֱבִירָנוּ בְּתוֹכוֹ בֶּחָרְבָּה

דַּיֵּנוּ

STANZA 7

Ilu he'eviranu v'tocho becharavah,
v'lo shika tzareinu b'tocho,
dayeinu!

אִלּוּ הֶעֱבִירָנוּ בְּתוֹכוֹ בֶּחָרְבָּה

וְלֹא שָׁקַע צָרֵינוּ בְּתוֹכוֹ

דַּיֵּנוּ

STANZA 8

Ilu shika tzareinu b'tocho,
v'lo sipeik tzorkeinu bamidbar
   arba'im shana,
dayeinu!

אִלּוּ שָׁקַע צָרֵינוּ בְּתוֹכוֹ

וְלֹא סָפֵק צָרְכְנוּ בַּמִּדְבָּר

אַרְבָּעִים שָׁנָה

דַּיֵּנוּ

STANZA 9

Ilu sipeik tzorkeinu bamidbar
   arba'im shana,
v'lo he'echilanu et haman,
dayeinu!

אִלּוּ סָפֵק צָרְכֵינוּ בַּמִּדְבָּר

אַרְבָּעִים שָׁנָה

וְלֹא הֶאֱכִילָנוּ אֶת הַמָּן

דַּיֵּנוּ

STANZA 10
Ilu he'echilanu et haman,
v'lo natan lanu et hashabbat,
dayeinu!

אִלּוּ הֶאֱכִילָנוּ אֶת הַמָּן
וְלֹא נָתַן לָנוּ אֶת הַשַּׁבָּת
דַּיֵּנוּ

STANZA 11
Ilu natan lanu et hashabbat,
v'lo keirvanu lifnei har sinai,
dayeinu!

אִלּוּ נָתַן לָנוּ אֶת הַשַּׁבָּת
וְלֹא קֵרְבָנוּ לִפְנֵי הַר סִינַי
דַּיֵּנוּ

STANZA 12
Ilu keirvanu lifnei har sinai,
v'lo natan lanu et hatorah,
dayeinu!

אִלּוּ קֵרְבָנוּ לִפְנֵי הַר סִינַי
וְלֹא נָתַן לָנוּ אֶת הַתּוֹרָה
דַּיֵּנוּ

STANZA 13
Ilu natan lanu et hatorah,
v'lo hichnisanu l'eretz yisra'eil,
dayeinu!

אִלּוּ נָתַן לָנוּ אֶת הַתּוֹרָה
וְלֹא הִכְנִיסָנוּ לְאֶרֶץ יִשְׂרָאֵל
דַּיֵּנוּ

STANZA 14
Ilu hichnisanu l'eretz yisra'eil,
v'lo vanah lanu et beit hamikdash,
dayeinu!

אִלּוּ הִכְנִיסָנוּ לְאֶרֶץ יִשְׂרָאֵל
וְלֹא בָּנָה לָנוּ אֶת בֵּית הַמִּקְדָּשׁ
דַּיֵּנוּ

ENGLISH TRANSLATION of DAYENU

STANZA 1
If He had brought us out from Egypt,
and had not carried out judgments
   against them—
Dayenu, it would have sufficed!

STANZA 2
If He had carried out judgments
   against them,
and not against their idols—
Dayenu, it would have sufficed!

STANZA 3
If He had destroyed their idols,
and had not smitten their first-born—
Dayenu, it would have sufficed!

STANZA 4
If He had smitten their first-born,
and had not given us their wealth—
Dayenu, it would have sufficed!

STANZA 5
If He had given us their wealth,
and had not split the sea for us—
Dayenu, it would have sufficed!

STANZA 6
If He had split the sea for us,
and had not taken us through it on
dry land—
Dayenu, it would have sufficed!

STANZA 7
If He had taken us through the sea on
   dry land,
and had not drowned our oppressors in
   it—
Dayenu, it would have sufficed!

STANZA 8
If He had drowned our oppressors
   in it,
and had not supplied our needs in
   the desert for forty years—
   Dayenu, it would have sufficed!

STANZA 9
If He had supplied our needs in the
desert for forty years,
and had not fed us the manna—
Dayenu, it would have sufficed!

STANZA 10
If He had fed us the manna,
and had not given us the Shabbat—
Dayenu, it would have sufficed!

STANZA 11
If He had given us the Shabbat,
and had not brought us before Mount
   Sinai—
   Dayenu, it would have sufficed!

STANZA 12
If He had brought us before Mount
   Sinai,
and had not given us the Torah—
Dayenu, it would have sufficed!

STANZA 13
If He had given us the Torah,
and had not brought us into the land of
   Israel—
Dayenu, it would have sufficed!

STANZA 14
If He had brought us into the land
   of Israel,
and not built for us the Holy
   Temple—
Dayenu, it would have sufficed!

Hallel for Passover

Hallel is recited for the traditional morning services in the synagogue during the week Passover.* The Hallel Psalms recall for us the celebration of Festivals in the Temple. Through them we express our gratitude and joy for Divine providence. God's concern for us is reflected in our past redemption and deliverance, inspiring us to express our faith in the future.

On the last six days of Passover, the opening sections of Psalms 115 and 116 are omitted. This is known as Chatzi Hallel.

Cantor: Praised are You Lord our God, who rules the universe, instilling in us the holiness of commandments, by commanding us to recite Hallel.

Cantor:†
congregation speaks italics

Psalm 113:
Praise the LORD!
Praise, O servants of the LORD, praise the name of the LORD! Blessed be the name of the LORD from this time forth and forevermore!
From the rising of the sun to its setting, the name of the LORD is to be praised! The LORD is high above all nations, and his glory above the heavens!
Who is like the LORD our God, who is seated on high, who looks far down on the heavens and the earth?
He raises the poor from the dust and lifts the needy from the ash heap, to make them sit with princes, with the princes of his people.
He gives the barren woman a home, making her the joyous mother of children. Praise the LORD!

Cantor:
congregation speaks italics

Psalm 114:
When Israel went out from Egypt, the house of Jacob from a people of strange language, Judah became his sanctuary, Israel his dominion.
The sea looked and fled; Jordan turned back. The mountains skipped like rams, the hills like lambs.
What ails you, O sea, that you flee? O Jordan, that you turn back? O mountains, that you skip like rams? O hills, like lambs?
Tremble, O earth, at the presence of the Lord, at the presence of the God of Jacob, who turns the rock into a pool of water, the flint into a spring of water.

Cantor:
congregation speaks italics

Psalm 115:1-11:
Not to us, O LORD, not to us, but to your name give glory, for the sake of your steadfast love and your faithfulness!
Why should the nations say, "Where is their God?" Our God is in the heavens; he does all that he pleases.
Their idols are silver and gold, the work of human hands. They have mouths, but do not speak; eyes, but do not see.
They have ears, but do not hear; noses, but do not smell. They have hands, but do not feel; feet, but do not walk;
and they do not make a sound in their throat. Those who make them become like them; so do all who trust in them.

---

* It is most unlikely that your Messianic congregation or fellowship has some kind of prayer service every day. The Hallel can simply be adopted, then, for personal meditation and reflection.
† Because a total of nine Psalm selections are read, your congregation or fellowship may wish to have a number of Designated Readers help lead in the Hallel.

O Israel, trust in the LORD! He is their help and their shield.
O house of Aaron, trust in the LORD! He is their help and their shield.
You who fear the LORD, trust in the LORD! He is their help and their shield.

Cantor:
congregation speaks italics

Psalm 115:12-18:
The LORD has remembered us; he will bless us; he will bless the house of Israel;
he will bless the house of Aaron; he will bless those who fear the LORD, both the small and the great.
May the LORD give you increase, you and your children! May you be blessed by the LORD, who made heaven and earth!
The heavens are the LORD's heavens, but the earth he has given to the children of man.
The dead do not praise the LORD, nor do any who go down into silence.*
But we will bless the LORD from this time forth and forevermore. Praise the LORD!

Cantor:
congregation speaks italics

Psalm 116:1-11:
I love the LORD, because he has heard my voice and my pleas for mercy. Because he inclined his ear to me, therefore I will call on him as long as I live.
The snares of death encompassed me; the pangs of Sheol laid hold on me; I suffered distress and anguish.
Then I called on the name of the LORD: "O LORD, I pray, deliver my soul!"
Gracious is the LORD, and righteous; our God is merciful.
The LORD preserves the simple; when I was brought low, he saved me.
Return, O my soul, to your rest; for the LORD has dealt bountifully with you.
For you have delivered my soul from death, my eyes from tears, my feet from stumbling; I will walk before the LORD in the land of the living.
I believed, even when I spoke, "I am greatly afflicted"; I said in my alarm, "All mankind are liars."

Cantor:
congregation speaks italics

Psalm 116:12-19:
What shall I render to the LORD for all his benefits to me?
I will lift up the cup of salvation and call on the name of the LORD, I will pay my vows to the LORD in the presence of all his people.
Precious in the sight of the LORD is the death of his saints.
O LORD, I am your servant; I am your servant, the son of your maidservant. You have loosed my bonds. I will offer to you the sacrifice of thanksgiving and call on the name of the LORD.
I will pay my vows to the LORD in the presence of all his people,
in the courts of the house of the LORD, in your midst, O Jerusalem. Praise the LORD!

Cantor:

Psalm 117:
Praise the LORD, all nations! Extol him, all peoples! For great is his steadfast love toward us, and the faithfulness of the LORD endures forever. Praise the LORD!

---

* Editor's note: This is in reference to public worship in the Temple.

Cantor:
congregation speaks
italics

Psalm 118:1-20:

The beginning of the Hodu is canted in Hebrew

Hodu l'ADONAI ki tov, ki
l'olam chasdo.

הוֹדוּ לַיהוָה כִּי־טוֹב
כִּי לְעוֹלָם חַסְדּוֹ

Oh give thanks to the LORD, for he is good; for his steadfast love
endures forever! Let Israel say, "His steadfast love endures forever."
Let the house of Aaron say, "His steadfast love endures forever." Let
those who fear the LORD say, "His steadfast love endures forever."

Out of my distress I called on the LORD; the LORD answered me and
set me free. The LORD is on my side; I will not fear. What can man do
to me?
The LORD is on my side as my helper; I shall look in triumph on
those who hate me.
It is better to take refuge in the LORD than to trust in man. It is better
to take refuge in the LORD than to trust in princes.
All nations surrounded me; in the name of the LORD I cut them off!
They surrounded me, surrounded me on every side; in the name of
the LORD I cut them off!
They surrounded me like bees; they went out like a fire among
thorns; in the name of the LORD I cut them off! I was pushed hard,
so that I was falling, but the LORD helped me.
The LORD is my strength and my song; he has become my salvation.
Glad songs of salvation are in the tents of the righteous: "The right
hand of the LORD does valiantly, the right hand of the LORD exalts,
the right hand of the LORD does valiantly!"
I shall not die, but I shall live, and recount the deeds of the LORD.
The LORD has disciplined me severely, but he has not given me over
to death.
Open to me the gates of righteousness, that I may enter through them
and give thanks to the LORD.
This is the gate of the LORD; the righteous shall enter through it.

Cantor:
congregation speaks
italics

Psalm 118:21-29:
I thank you that you have answered me and have become my
salvation.
The stone that the builders rejected has become the cornerstone.
This is the LORD 's doing; it is marvelous in our eyes.

cantor reads these lines first, then followed by the congregation
This is the day that the LORD has made; let us rejoice and be glad
in it. Save us, we pray, O LORD! O LORD, we pray, give us
success!

Ana ADONAI hoshi'ah na

אָנָּא יְהוָה הוֹשִׁיעָה נָּא

Ana ADONAI hatzlichah na.

אָנָּא יְהוָה הַצְלִיחָה נָּא

Blessed is he who comes in the name of the LORD! We bless you
from the house of the LORD.
The LORD is God, and he has made his light to shine upon us. Bind

the festal sacrifice with cords, up to the horns of the altar!
You are my God, and I will give thanks to you; you are my God; I will extol you.
Oh give thanks to the LORD, for he is good; for his steadfast love endures forever!

Cantor: May all Creation praise You, Lord our God. May the pious, the righteous who do Your will, and all Your people, the House of Israel, join in acclaiming You with joyous song. May they praise, revere, adore, extol, exalt and sanctify Your glory, our Sovereign. To You it is good to chant praise; to Your glory it is fitting to sing. You are God, from age to age, everlastingly. Praised are You Lord, Sovereign acclaimed with songs of praise.

Counting the Omer to Shavuot

The following procedure for remembering the counting of the *omer*, for the seven weeks between Passover and *Shavuot*, is largely adapted from the Conservative Jewish resource *Siddur Sim Shalom*. This is something that you can read yourself, as you reflect and meditate on the work of God during each day of the fifty-day *omer* count.

The "omer" (literally "sheaf") refers to an offering from the new barley crop, brought to the ancient Temple, on the 16th of Nisan, a ceremony associated with the Festival of Unleavened Bread. Omer has come to be the name of the period between Passover and Shavuot. By counting these days (sefriat ha'omer), we recall Ancient Israel's liberation from enslavement, commemorated by Passover—along with God's gift of the Torah, commemorated at Shavuot. As we count the omer, our hearts turn to the revelation of God's Torah, so essential for our spiritual guidance and instruction. We count the days between Passover and Shavuot to heighten our anticipation of celebrating the giving of God's Law to His people, the event that gives meaning to Ancient Israel's liberation and calling by Him, and which continues to mold His people today.

Day-by-Day Counting

I am ready to fulfill the command of counting the *omer*, as it is ordained in the Torah: "And from the day on which you bring the sheaf of elevation offering—the day after the sabbath—you shall count off seven weeks. They must be complete: you must count until the day after the seventh week—fifty days" (Leviticus 23:15-16a, NJPS).

Barukh atah Adonai, Eloheinu melekh ha'olam, asher kidshanu b'mitzvotav v'tzivanu al sefriat ha'omer.

בָּרוּךְ אַתָּה יְיָ אֱלֹהֵינוּ מֶלֶךְ הָעוֹלָם אֲשֶׁר קִדְּשָׁנוּ בְּמִצְוֹתָיו וְצִוָּנוּ עַל סְפִירַת הָעֹמֶר

Praised are You Lord our God, who rules the universe, instilling in us the holiness of commandments by commanding us to count the *omer*.

the following is now repeated on the appropriate day of the omer counting:

1.	Today is **1 day** of the Omer.	*16 Nisan*
2.	Today is **2 days** of the Omer.	*17 Nisan*
3.	Today is **3 days** of the Omer.	*18 Nisan*
4.	Today is **4 days** of the Omer.	*19 Nisan*
5.	Today is **5 days** of the Omer.	*20 Nisan*
6.	Today is **6 days** of the Omer.	*21 Nisan*
7.	Today is **7 days** of the Omer. *eighth night of Unleavened Bread*	*22 Nisan*
8.	Today is **8 days—a week and one day** of the Omer.	*23 Nisan*
9.	Today is **9 days—a week and two days** of the Omer.	*24 Nisan*

10.	Today is 10 days—a week and three days of the Omer.	25 *Nisan*
11.	Today is 11 days—a week and four days of the Omer.	26 *Nisan*
12.	Today is 12 days—a week and five days of the Omer.	27 *Nisan* *Yom Ha'Shoah*
13.	Today is 13 days—a week and six days of the Omer.	28 *Nisan*
14.	Today is 14 days—two weeks of the Omer.	29 *Nisan*
15.	Today is 15 days—two weeks and one day of the Omer.	30 *Nisan*
16.	Today is 16 days—two weeks and two days of the Omer.	01 *Iyar*
17.	Today is 17 days—two weeks and three days of the Omer.	02 *Iyar*
18.	Today is 18 days—two weeks and four days of the Omer.	03 *Iyar*
19.	Today is 19 days—two weeks and five days of the Omer.	04 *Iyar*
20.	Today is 20 days—two weeks and six days of the Omer.	05 *Iyar* *Yom Ha'Atzmaut*
21.	Today is 21 days—three weeks of the Omer.	06 *Iyar*
22.	Today is 22 days—three weeks and one day of the Omer.	07 *Iyar*
23.	Today is 23 days—three weeks and two days of the Omer.	08 *Iyar*
24.	Today is 24 days—three weeks and three days of the Omer.	09 *Iyar*
25.	Today is 25 days—three weeks and four days of the Omer.	10 *Iyar*
26.	Today is 26 days—three weeks and five days of the Omer.	11 *Iyar*
27.	Today is 27 days—three weeks and six days of the Omer.	12 *Iyar*
28.	Today is 28 days—four weeks of the Omer.	13 *Iyar*
29.	Today is 29 days—four weeks and one day of the Omer.	14 *Iyar*
30.	Today is 30 days—four weeks and two days of the Omer.	15 *Iyar*
31.	Today is 31 days—four weeks and three days of the Omer.	16 *Iyar*
32.	Today is 32 days—four weeks and four days of the Omer.	17 *Iyar*
33.	Today is 33 days—four weeks and five days of the Omer.	18 *Iyar*
34.	Today is 34 days—four weeks and six days of the Omer.	19 *Iyar*
35.	Today is 35 days—five weeks of the Omer	20 *Iyar*
36.	Today is 36 days—five weeks and one day of the Omer.	21 *Iyar*
37.	Today is 37 days—five weeks and two days of the Omer.	22 *Iyar*
38.	Today is 38 days—five weeks and three days of the Omer.	23 *Iyar*

39.	Today is 39 days—five weeks and four days of the Omer.	24 Iyar
40.	Today is 40 days—five weeks and five days of the Omer.*	25 Iyar
41.	Today is 41 days—five weeks and six days of the Omer.	26 Iyar
42.	Today is 42 days—six weeks of the Omer.	27 Iyar
43.	Today is 43 days—six weeks and one day of the Omer.	28 Iyar *Yom Yerushalayim*
44.	Today is 44 days—six weeks and two days of the Omer.	29 Iyar
45.	Today is 45 days—six weeks and three days of the Omer.	01 Sivan
46.	Today is 46 days—six weeks and four days of the Omer.	02 Sivan
47.	Today is 47 days—six weeks and five days of the Omer.	03 Sivan
48.	Today is 48 days—six weeks and six days of the Omer.	04 Sivan
49.	Today is 49 days—seven weeks of the Omer.	05 Sivan *Erev Shavuot*

These prayers can be reflected on during each day of the Omer.

Blessed is everyone who fears the LORD, who walks in his ways! You shall eat the fruit of the labor of your hands; you shall be blessed, and it shall be well with you. Your wife will be like a fruitful vine within your house; your children will be like olive shoots around your table. Behold, thus shall the man be blessed who fears the LORD. The LORD bless you from Zion! May you see the prosperity of Jerusalem all the days of your life! May you see your children's children! Peace be upon Israel! (Psalm 128).

Our personal journeys in life are marked by enslavements and liberations, revelations, and promised lands. Just as we marked the approach of significant moments in our own lives, so we count the days in the life of our people. As we pause to recall the Israelites' bond with the soil, their dependance on its fertility, and their gratitude for the annual harvest of grain, we also give thanks to God for renewing for us a year of life and of blessing.

---

* On the year of His crucifixion and resurrection, it would have been at about this point that Yeshua ascended into Heaven (Acts 1:3).

Hallel for Shavuot

Hallel is recited on Shavuot. The Hallel Psalms recall for us the celebration of Festivals in the Temple. Through them we express our gratitude and joy for Divine providence. God's concern for us in reflected in our past redemption and deliverance, inspiring us to express our faith in the future.

Cantor: Praised are You Lord our God, who rules the universe, instilling in us the holiness of commandments, by commanding us to recite Hallel.

Cantor:[*]
congregation speaks italics

Psalm 113:
Praise the LORD!
> *Praise, O servants of the LORD, praise the name of the LORD!*
> *Blessed be the name of the LORD from this time forth and*
> *forevermore!*

From the rising of the sun to its setting, the name of the LORD is to be praised! The LORD is high above all nations, and his glory above the heavens!
> *Who is like the LORD our God, who is seated on high, who looks far*
> *down on the heavens and the earth?*

He raises the poor from the dust and lifts the needy from the ash heap, to make them sit with princes, with the princes of his people.
> *He gives the barren woman a home, making her the joyous mother of*
> *children. Praise the LORD!*

Cantor:
congregation speaks italics

Psalm 114:
When Israel went out from Egypt, the house of Jacob from a people of strange language, Judah became his sanctuary, Israel his dominion.
> *The sea looked and fled; Jordan turned back. The mountains*
> *skipped like rams, the hills like lambs.*

What ails you, O sea, that you flee? O Jordan, that you turn back? O mountains, that you skip like rams? O hills, like lambs?
> *Tremble, O earth, at the presence of the Lord, at the presence of the*
> *God of Jacob, who turns the rock into a pool of water, the flint into a*
> *spring of water.*

Cantor:
congregation speaks italics

Psalm 115:1-11:
Not to us, O LORD, not to us, but to your name give glory, for the sake of your steadfast love and your faithfulness!
> *Why should the nations say, "Where is their God?" Our God is in*
> *the heavens; he does all that he pleases.*

Their idols are silver and gold, the work of human hands. They have mouths, but do not speak; eyes, but do not see.
> *They have ears, but do not hear; noses, but do not smell. They have*
> *hands, but do not feel; feet, but do not walk;*

and they do not make a sound in their throat. Those who make them become like them; so do all who trust in them.
> *O Israel, trust in the LORD! He is their help and their shield.*

O house of Aaron, trust in the LORD! He is their help and their shield.
> *You who fear the LORD, trust in the LORD! He is their help and their*
> *shield.*

---

[*] Because a total of nine Psalm selections are read, your congregation or fellowship may wish to have a number of Designated Readers help lead in the Hallel.

Cantor:
congregation speaks italics

Psalm 115:12-18:
The LORD has remembered us; he will bless us; he will bless the house of Israel;
he will bless the house of Aaron; he will bless those who fear the LORD, both the small and the great.
May the LORD give you increase, you and your children! May you be blessed by the LORD, who made heaven and earth!
The heavens are the LORD's heavens, but the earth he has given to the children of man.
The dead do not praise the LORD, nor do any who go down into silence.*
But we will bless the LORD from this time forth and forevermore. Praise the LORD!

Cantor:
congregation speaks italics

Psalm 116:1-11:
I love the LORD, because he has heard my voice and my pleas for mercy. Because he inclined his ear to me, therefore I will call on him as long as I live.
The snares of death encompassed me; the pangs of Sheol laid hold on me; I suffered distress and anguish.
Then I called on the name of the LORD: "O LORD, I pray, deliver my soul!"
Gracious is the LORD, and righteous; our God is merciful.
The LORD preserves the simple; when I was brought low, he saved me.
Return, O my soul, to your rest; for the LORD has dealt bountifully with you.
For you have delivered my soul from death, my eyes from tears, my feet from stumbling; I will walk before the LORD in the land of the living.
I believed, even when I spoke, "I am greatly afflicted"; I said in my alarm, "All mankind are liars."

Cantor:
congregation speaks italics

Psalm 116:12-19:
What shall I render to the LORD for all his benefits to me?
I will lift up the cup of salvation and call on the name of the LORD, I will pay my vows to the LORD in the presence of all his people.
Precious in the sight of the LORD is the death of his saints.
O LORD, I am your servant; I am your servant, the son of your maidservant. You have loosed my bonds. I will offer to you the sacrifice of thanksgiving and call on the name of the LORD.
I will pay my vows to the LORD in the presence of all his people,
in the courts of the house of the LORD, in your midst, O Jerusalem. Praise the LORD!

Cantor:

Psalm 117:
Praise the LORD, all nations! Extol him, all peoples! For great is his steadfast love toward us, and the faithfulness of the LORD endures forever. Praise the LORD!

---

* Editor's note: This is in reference to public worship in the Temple.

Cantor:
congregation speaks
italics

Psalm 118:1-20

The beginning of the Hodu is canted in Hebrew

Hodu l'ADONAI ki tov, ki
l'olam chasdo.

הוֹדוּ לַיהוָה כִּי־טוֹב
כִּי לְעוֹלָם חַסְדּוֹ

Oh give thanks to the LORD, for he is good; for his steadfast love
endures forever! Let Israel say, "His steadfast love endures forever."
Let the house of Aaron say, "His steadfast love endures forever." Let
those who fear the LORD say, "His steadfast love endures forever."

Out of my distress I called on the LORD; the LORD answered me and
set me free. The LORD is on my side; I will not fear. What can man do
to me?
The LORD is on my side as my helper; I shall look in triumph on
those who hate me.
It is better to take refuge in the LORD than to trust in man. It is better
to take refuge in the LORD than to trust in princes.
All nations surrounded me; in the name of the LORD I cut them off!
They surrounded me, surrounded me on every side; in the name of
the LORD I cut them off!
They surrounded me like bees; they went out like a fire among
thorns; in the name of the LORD I cut them off! I was pushed hard,
so that I was falling, but the LORD helped me.
The LORD is my strength and my song; he has become my salvation.
Glad songs of salvation are in the tents of the righteous: "The right
hand of the LORD does valiantly, the right hand of the LORD exalts,
the right hand of the LORD does valiantly!"
I shall not die, but I shall live, and recount the deeds of the LORD.
The LORD has disciplined me severely, but he has not given me over
to death.
Open to me the gates of righteousness, that I may enter through them
and give thanks to the LORD.
This is the gate of the LORD; the righteous shall enter through it.

Cantor:
congregation speaks
italics

Psalm 118:21-29:
I thank you that you have answered me and have become my
salvation.
The stone that the builders rejected has become the cornerstone.
This is the LORD 's doing; it is marvelous in our eyes.

cantor reads these lines first, then followed by the congregation
This is the day that the LORD has made; let us rejoice and be glad
in it. Save us, we pray, O LORD! O LORD, we pray, give us
success!

Ana ADONAI hoshi'ah na

אָנָא יְהוָה הוֹשִׁיעָה נָּא

Ana ADONAI hatzlichah na.

אָנָא יְהוָה הַצְלִיחָה נָא

Blessed is he who comes in the name of the LORD! We bless you
from the house of the LORD.
The LORD is God, and he has made his light to shine upon us. Bind

the festal sacrifice with cords, up to the horns of the altar!
You are my God, and I will give thanks to you; you are my God; I will extol you.
Oh give thanks to the LORD, for he is good; for his steadfast love endures forever!

Cantor:

May all Creation praise You, Lord our God. May the pious, the righteous who do Your will, and all Your people, the House of Israel, join in acclaiming You with joyous song. May they praise, revere, adore, extol, exalt and sanctify Your glory, our Sovereign. To You it is good to chant praise; to Your glory it is fitting to sing. You are God, from age to age, everlastingly. Praised are You Lord, Sovereign acclaimed with songs of praise.

About the Editor

Margaret McKee Huey is one of the founders of Outreach Israel Ministries (OIM) and serves on its Board as the Office Manager.

Margaret is a multi-talented woman who exemplifies what a Proverbs 31 woman should be. Besides handling the business responsibilities of OIM and editing assignments with our publications, she operates an internationally known needlework sampler design business that she founded in 1985. Yet, she still finds time to successfully invest in raising her three children.

In addition to her business acumen, Margaret is spiritually gifted as an evangelist. She was actively involved in evangelism through the *Walk to Emmaus*, *Chrysalis Program* and the *Lay Witness Mission* while in the United Methodist Church. When asked what Biblical character she most identifies with, she demurely responds, "why John the Baptist, of course." The passion of her heart is communicating the "Gospel According to the Torah." In an inspiring and convicting way, she not only helps you understand the sacrifice of Yeshua and your salvation, but also helps you understand the mercy of the Holy One as one follows His Torah.

Margaret comes from a long line of Methodist preachers and teachers. Although raised in a Christian home, she did not come to true saving faith until the age of 30. She was immediately drawn into an appreciation of Israel, the Jewish people, understanding that Yeshua was the Messiah of Israel and even celebrating the Seder Passover with her first husband, Kim McKee, at their Methodist church beginning in 1986.

Lamentably, in 1992 Margaret was widowed at the age of 39 with the responsibility for three young children. This unexpected tragedy did not detour her from her relationship with God, but instead prompted her into even greater dependency upon Him as her provider and comforter. As a result of her life experiences, she is gifted in grief counseling and deliverance issues.

Margaret is the editor for the upcoming Messianic cookbook, *Kosher Your Plate*, as well as editor for the *Messianic Helper Series*. Some of the titles for this series include: *Messianic Winter Holiday Helper*, *Messianic Spring Holiday Helper*, *Messianic Fall Holiday Helper*, and the *Messianic Sabbath Helper*.

Margaret is a graduate of Vanderbilt University with a Bachelor of Science degree in Geology. She is the wife of William Mark Huey and the mother of John McKee, Jane McKee, and Maggie Willetts, and now resides in Dallas, Texas. She is a member of Eitz Chaim Messianic Jewish Synagogue.

Margaret can be reached via Outreach Israel Ministries.

E-mail: margaret@outreachisrael.net

Contributors to this Volume

William Mark Huey became a Believer in the Messiah of Israel in 1978, but it was a Zola Levitt tour to Israel in 1994 with his wife Margaret, which sparked an ardent search for answers about the Hebraic and Jewish Roots of our faith, and the significance of the Torah, Biblical festivals, and the seventh-day Sabbath/*Shabbat*—among other things. By 1995, his family became members of a Messianic Jewish congregation in Dallas, Texas, and their pursuit for truth intensified. Within a year, Mark formed a conference-producing enterprise called "The Remnant Exchange," and began hosting prophecy conferences and seminars with increasing Messianic understanding and emphasis. Mark's business experience, owning a commercial real estate brokerage company, coupled with Margaret's ownership of a cross-stitch design company, led them to form a ministry consulting business which worked with a variety of Messianic ministries from 1997-2002. Mark and Margaret have dedicated their lives to serving the Lord in order to use their God-given gifts, talents, and abilities to advance His Kingdom until the Messiah returns.

By 2002, after years of exposure to tangible evidence that the prophesied "restoration of all things" (Acts 3:21) was becoming a reality, the impetus to focus energy and attention on Israel, the people, the Land, and Torah-centered Messianic teachings merged together. The outcome was the formation of **Outreach Israel Ministries**, of which Mark serves as Director, and Margaret as Business Manager. *From the beginning of Outreach Israel Ministries, the need to educate and to minister to the expanding number of Messianics has always been at the heart of the mission.* The merger with TNN Online in 2003 (now **Messianic Apologetics**) substantially enhanced the capabilities. Today, both Outreach Israel Ministries and Messianic Apologetics have a significant role to play in aiding the people of the broad Messianic movement, in the theological and spiritual issues that they face—as many Jewish people are coming to faith in Israel's Messiah, and many evangelical Christians embrace their faith heritage in Israel's Scriptures in tangibly new ways.

Mark Huey also serves as the National Director of **March of Remembrance**, which facilitates memorial prayer walks of Jewish, Christian, and Messianic people to remember the Holocaust. Mark and Margaret Huey both cherish the privilege to be a responsible part of coordinating national March of Remembrance events which honor Holocaust survivors and descendants. They believe that March of Remembrance is one of many ministry vehicles which have been called to facilitate the eventual reconciliation between Jewish and non-Jewish people, who are ardent followers of the God of Abraham, Isaac, and Jacob.

Over the past thirty years, Mark has organized, produced, and/or participated in conferences, seminars, and ministry related events as an exhortative speaker, and is the author of a number of books which focus on encouraging others to embrace the Hebraic and Jewish roots of our faith. These include the commentaries, *TorahScope, Volumes I, II, & III, TorahScope Haftarah Exhortations, TorahScope Apostolic Scriptures Reflections*, and the devotionals, *Counting the Omer and Sayings of the Fathers: A Messianic Perspective on the Pirkei Avot.*

Mark is a graduate of Vanderbilt University with a B.A. in history, with graduate studies toward a master's degree in aviation management completed at Embry-Riddle Aeronautical University. Mark has served in leadership roles at Messianic congregations and fellowships, as an elder at Beit Yisrael Congregation in

Orlando, FL (2005-2010), and as both an ordained *shammash* (deacon) and elder at Eitz Chaim Messianic Jewish Synagogue of Richardson, TX (2014-present). Mark and Margaret Huey currently reside in Dallas, TX and have five grown children and two grandchildren.

John Kimball McKee is an integral part of Outreach Israel Ministries, and serves as the editor of Messianic Apologetics, an Internet website that specializes in a wide variety of Biblical topics. He has grown up in a family which has been in constant pursuit of God's truth, and has been exposed to things of the Lord since infancy. Since 1995 he came to the realization of the post-tribulational return of the Messiah for His own and the importance of the Jewish and Hebraic Roots of our faith. He is a graduate of the University of Oklahoma (Class of 2003) with a B.A. in political science, and holds an M.A. in Biblical Studies from Asbury Theological Seminary (Class of 2009). He is a 2009 recipient of the Zondervan Biblical Languages Award for Greek. John holds memberships in the Evangelical Theological Society, the Evangelical Philosophical Society, and Christians for Biblical Equality, and is a longtime supporter of the perspectives and views of the Creationist ministry of Reasons to Believe.

John is an apologist for the Creator God and in helping people understand their faith heritage in Ancient Israel and Second Temple Judaism. Much of his ministry in the past has been campus based to the multitudes in evangelical Christianity who are associated with a wide variety of Protestant denominations and persuasions. John has introduced college students to things that are Messianic such as the original Hebrew name of our Savior, Yeshua HaMashiach (Jesus the Messiah), a name that he has known since 1983.

John's testimony before his Christian friends at college challenged much of their previous thinking about the whole of the Holy Scriptures and the need to follow the commandments of the Most High. His college peers asked him many varied questions: Why do you not believe in the pre-trib rapture? What do you think of the *Left Behind* books? Why do you observe the seventh-day Sabbath? Why do you eat kosher? Why do you wear a beard? Why do you celebrate the feasts of Israel? Why will you use a *tallit* and wrap *tefillin*/phylacteries during private prayer? Why do you consult original Hebrew and Greek language texts of the Bible? Why don't you come to church with us on Sunday? This led John into Messianic apologetics and the defense of our faith. John strives to be one who is committed to a life of holiness and methodical Bible study, as a person who has a testimony of being born again and who sincerely desires to obey the Lord.

Since the 1990s, John's ministry has capitalized on the Internet's ability to reach people all over this planet. He has spoken with challenging, probing, and apologetic articles to a wide Messianic audience, and those Christians who are interested in Messianic beliefs. In the past decade (2005-2014), John has positioned himself as a well-needed, moderate and Centrist voice, in a Messianic movement which is trying to determine its purpose, relevance, and mission to modern society—a voice striving to sit above much of the posturing, maneuvering, and religious politics of the broad Messianic spectrum. Given his generational family background in evangelical Christian ministry, as well as in academics and the military, John carries a strong burden to assist in the development and maturation of our emerging Messianic theology and spirituality, so that we might truly know the mission of God. John has had the profound opportunity since 1997 to engage many in dialogue, so that they will consider the questions he postulates, as his only agenda is to be as Scripturally sound as possible. John believes in demonstrating a great deal of honor and respect to both his evangelical Christian, Wesleyan and Reformed heritage, as well as to the Jewish Synagogue, and together allowing the strengths and virtues of both Judaism and Christianity to be employed for the Lord's plan for the Messianic movement in the long term future.

J.K. McKee is author of numerous books, dealing with a wide range of topics that are important for today's Messianic Believers. He has also written many articles on theological issues, and is presently focusing his attention on Messianic commentaries of various books of the Bible.

J.K. McKee is the son of the late K. Kimball McKee (1951-1992) and Margaret Jeffries McKee Huey (1953-), and stepson of William Mark Huey (1951-), who married his mother in 1994, and is the executive director of Outreach Israel Ministries.

John has a very strong appreciation for those who have preceded him. His father, Kimball McKee, was a licensed lay minister in the Kentucky Conference of the United Methodist Church, and was a very strong evangelical Christian, most appreciable of the Jewish and Hebraic Roots of the faith. Among his many ministry pursuits, Kim brought the Passover *seder* to Christ United Methodist Church in Florence, KY, was a Sunday school teacher, and was extremely active in the Walk to Emmaus, leading the first men's walk in Madras, India in 1991. John is the grandson of the late William W. Jeffries (1914-1989), who served as a professor at the United States Naval Academy in Annapolis, MD from 1942-1989, notably as the museum director and founder of what is now the William W. Jeffries Memorial Archives in the Nimitz Library. John is the great-grandson of Bishop Marvin A. Franklin (1894-1972), who served as a minister and bishop of the Methodist Church, throughout his ministry serving churches in Georgia, Florida, Alabama, and Mississippi. Bishop Franklin was President of the Council of Bishops from 1959-1960. John is also the third cousin of the late Charles L. Allen (1913-2005), formerly the senior pastor of Grace Methodist Church of Atlanta, GA and First Methodist Church of Houston, TX, and author of numerous books, notably including *God's Psychiatry*. Among all of his forbearers, though, he considers his personality to be most derived from his late paternal grandfather, George Kenneth McKee (1903-1978), and his maternal grandmother, Mary Ruth Franklin Jeffries (1919-).

J.K. McKee is a native of the Northern Kentucky/Greater Cincinnati, OH area. He has also lived in Dallas, TX, Norman, OK, Kissimmee-St. Cloud, FL, and Roatán, Honduras, Central America. He presently resides in Dallas, TX, and is a member in good standing at Eitz Chaim Messianic Jewish Synagogue.

On social media, J.K. McKee can be friended on Facebook at **facebook.com/JKMMessianic**, and followed on Twitter **@JKMMessianic**.

Bibliography

Articles
Arav, Rami. "Hermon, Mount," in *ABD*.
Buchanan, G.W. "Judas Iscariot," in *ISBE*.
Burge, G.M. "'I Am' Sayings," in *Dictionary of Jesus and the Gospels*.
Campbell, J.Y. "Perfection," in *IDB*.
Casey, Maurice. "The Date of the Passover Sacrifices and Mark 14:12" in <u>Tyndale Bulletin</u> Vol. 48. No. 2 (1997).
Chamblin, J.K. "Psychology," in *Dictionary of Paul and His Letters*.
"firstfruits," in *Dictionary of Judaism in the Biblical Period*.
Frankel, Rafael. "Tabor, Mount," in *ABD*.
Glasser, A.F. "Pentecost," in *ISBE*.
Gregg, D. Larry. "Easter," in *EDB*.
Green, J.B. "Death of Jesus," in *Dictionary of Jesus and the Gospels*.
Greenberg, M. "Scourging," in *IDB*.
"Haggadah of Passover," in *Dictionary of Judaism in the Biblical Period*.
Hegg, Tim. (2002). *Counting the Omer: An Inquiry into the Divergent Methods of the 1st Century Judaisms. Torah Resource*. Retrieved 12 March, 2007, from <http://www.torahresource.com>.
_____. (2009). *The Chronology of the Crucifixion: A Comparison of the Gospel Accounts. Torah Resource*. Retrieved 22 January, 2010, from <http://www.torahresource.com>.
Hoskins, Paul M. "Deliverance from Death by the True Passover Lamb: A Significant Aspect of the Fulfillment of the Passover in the Gospel of John" in <u>Journal of the Evangelical Theological Society</u> Vol. 52 No. 2 (2009).
Jacobs, Louis. "Purim," in *EJ*.
Kitchen, K.A. "Exodus, The," in *ABD*.
Liverani, M. "Ugarit; Ugaritic," in *ISBE*.
Lohse, E. "*sábbaton*," in *TDNT*.
Longenecker, R.N. "Preparation, Day of," in *ISBE*.
Marshall, I.H. "Lamb of God," in *Dictionary of Jesus and the Gospels*.
Nunnally, W.E. "Preparation, Day of," in *ISBE*.
O'Collins, Gerald G. "Crucifixion," in *ABD*.
Petersen, Lorman M. "Pilate," in *NIDB*.
Pfeiffer, Charles F. "Exodus," in *NIDB*.
Rigsby, R.O. "Firstfruits," in *Dictionary of the Old Testament Pentateuch*.
Scott, Jack B. "'ēl," in *TWOT*.
Sherwin-White, A.N. "Pilate, Pontius," in *ISBE*.
Stein, R.H. "Last Supper," in *Dictionary of Jesus and the Gospels*.
Walton, J.H. "Exodus, Date of," in *Dictionary of the Old Testament Pentateuch*.

Bible Versions and Study Bibles
American Standard Version (New York: Thomas Nelson & Sons, 1901).
Barker, Kenneth L., ed., et. al. *NIV Study Bible* (Grand Rapids: Zondervan, 2002).
Berlin, Adele, and Marc Zvi Brettler, eds. *The Jewish Study Bible*, NJPS (Oxford: Oxford University Press, 2004).
Esposito, Paul W. *The Apostles' Bible, An English Septuagint Version* (http://www.apostlesbible.com/).
God's Game Plan: The Athlete's Bible 2007, HCSB (Nashville: Serendipity House Publishers, 2007).
Green, Jay P., trans. *The Interlinear Bible*. (Lafayette, IN: Sovereign Grace Publishers, 1986).
Harrelson, Walter J., ed., et. al. *New Interpreter's Study Bible*, NRSV (Nashville: Abingdon, 2003).
Holman Christian Standard Bible (Nashville: Broadman & Holman, 2004).
Holy Bible, Contemporary English Version (New York: American Bible Society, 1995).
Holy Bible, King James Version (edited 1789).
Holy Bible, New International Version (Grand Rapids: Zondervan, 1978).
LaHaye, Tim, ed. *Tim LaHaye Prophecy Study Bible*, KJV (Chattanooga: AMG Publishers, 2000).
May, Herbert G., and Bruce M. Metzger, eds. *The New Oxford Annotated Bible With the Apocrypha*, RSV (New York: Oxford University Press, 1977).

New American Standard Bible (La Habra, CA: Foundation Press Publications, 1971).
New American Standard, Updated Edition (Anaheim, CA: Foundation Publications, 1995).
New King James Version (Nashville: Thomas Nelson, 1982).
New Revised Standard Version (National Council of Churches of Christ, 1989).
Packer, J.I., ed. *The Holy Bible, English Standard Version* (Wheaton, IL: Crossway Bibles, 2001).
Ryrie, Charles C., ed. *The Ryrie Study Bible*, New American Standard (Chicago: Moody Press, 1978).
Scherman, Nosson, and Meir Zlotowitz, eds. *ArtScroll Tanach* (Brooklyn: Mesorah Publications, 1996).
Siewert, Frances E., ed. *The Amplified Bible* (Grand Rapids: Zondervan, 1965).
Stern, David H., trans. *Jewish New Testament* (Clarksville, MD: Jewish New Testament Publications, 1995).
_____, trans. *Complete Jewish Bible* (Clarksville, MD: Jewish New Testament Publications, 1998).
Tanakh: The Holy Scriptures (Philadelphia: Jewish Publication Society, 1999).
The Holy Bible, Revised Standard Version (Nashville: Cokesbury, 1952).
Young, Robert, trans. *Young's Literal Translation*.
Zodhiates, Spiros, ed. *Hebrew-Greek Key Study Bible*, NASB (Chattanooga: AMG Publishers, 1994).

Books
Bacchiocchi, Samuele. *From Sabbath to Sunday* (Rome: Pontifical Gregorian University Press, 1977).
Bauckham, Richard. *Jesus and the God of Israel* (Grand Rapids: Eerdmans, 2008).
Berkowitz, Ariel and D'vorah. *Torah Rediscovered* (Lakewood, CO: First Fruits of Zion, 1996).
_____. *Take Hold* (Littleton, CO: First Fruits of Zion, 1999).
Bowman, Jr., Robert M., and J. Ed Komoszewski. *Putting Jesus in His Place: The Case for the Deity of Christ* (Grand Rapids: Kregel, 2007).
Boyd, Gregory A., and Paul R. Eddy, eds. *Across the Spectrum: Understanding Issues in Evangelical Theology* (Grand Rapids: Baker Academic, 2002).
Brown, Michael. *Our Hands Are Stained With Blood* (Shippensburg, PA: Destiny Image, 1990).
_____. *Answering Jewish Objections to Jesus, Volume 3: Messianic Prophecy Objections* (Grand Rapids: Baker Books, 2003).
Bruce, F.F. *New Testament History* (New York: Doubleday, 1969).
Carson, D.A., ed. *From Sabbath to Lord's Day* (Eugene, OR: Wipf and Stock, 1999).
_____, and Douglas J. Moo. *An Introduction to the New Testament*, second edition (Grand Rapids: Zondervan, 2005).
Cassuto, Umberto. *The Documentary Hypothesis and the Composition of the Pentateuch* (Jerusalem and New York: Shalem Press, 2006).
Cohen, Mitchell, and Nicole Fermon, eds. *Princeton Readings in Political Thought* (Princeton, NJ: Princeton University Press, 1996).
Cooper, John W. *Body, Soul & Life Everlasting: Biblical Anthropology and the Monism-Dualism Debate* (Grand Rapids: Eerdmans, 1989).
Dewsnap Meinhardt, Molly, ed. *Jesus: The Last Day* (Washington, D.C.: Biblical Archaeology Society, 2003).
Dillard, Raymond B., and Tremper Longman III. *An Introduction to the Old Testament* (Grand Rapids: Zondervan, 1994).
Dunn, James D.G. *The New Perspective on Paul* (Grand Rapids: Eerdmans, 2005).
Edersheim, Alfred. *Sketches of Jewish Social Life* (Peabody, MA: Hendrickson, 1994).
_____. *The Temple: Its Ministry and Services* (Peabody, MA: Hendrickson, 1994).
Edgar, Brian. *The Message of the Trinity* (Downers Grove, IL: InterVarsity, 2004).
Egan, Hope. *Holy Cow! Does God Care About What We Eat?* (Littleton, CO: First Fruits of Zion, 2005).
Fee, Gordon D., and Douglas Stuart. *How to Read the Bible for All Its Worth* (Grand Rapids: Zondervan, 2003).
Friedman, David. *They Loved the Torah* (Baltimore: Lederer Books, 2001).
Goldingay, John. *Old Testament Theology: Israel's Gospel* (Downers Grove, IL: InterVarsity, 2003).
Gundry, Robert H. *The Church and the Tribulation* (Grand Rapids: Zondervan, 1973).
_____. *First the Antichrist* (Grand Rapids: Baker Books, 1997).
Guthrie, Donald. *New Testament Introduction* (Downers Grove, IL: InterVarsity, 1990).
Hamp, Douglas. *Discovering the Language of Jesus* (Santa Ana, CA: Calvary Chapel Publishing, 2005).
Harrison, R.K. *Introduction to the Old Testament* (Grand Rapids: Eerdmans, 1969).
Hegg, Tim. *Introduction to Torah Living* (Tacoma, WA: TorahResource, 2002).
_____. *The Letter Writer: Paul's Background and Torah Perspective* (Littleton, CO: First Fruits of Zion, 2002).

_____. *It is Often Said: Comments and Comparisons of Traditional Christian Theology and Hebraic Thought*, 2 vols. (Littleton, CO: First Fruits of Zion, 2003).

_____. *Fellow Heirs: Jews & Gentiles Together in the Family of God* (Littleton, CO: First Fruits of Zion, 2003).

Huey, William Mark, and J.K. McKee. *Hebraic Roots: An Introductory Study* (Kissimmee, FL: TNN Press, 2003, 2009).

Hunt, Dave. *How Close Are We?* (Eugene, OR: Harvest House, 1993).

Juster, Daniel C. *Growing to Maturity* (Denver: The Union of Messianic Jewish Congregations Press, 1987).

_____. *Jewish Roots* (Shippensburg, PA: Destiny Image, 1995).

Kaiser, Walter C. *Toward Old Testament Ethics* (Grand Rapids: Zondervan, 1983).

_____. *The Old Testament Documents: Are They Reliable and Relevant?* (Downers Grove, IL: InterVarsity, 2001).

_____. *The Promise-Plan of God: A Biblical Theology of the Old and New Testaments* (Grand Rapids: Zondervan, 2008).

Kaiser, Walter C., Peter H. Davids, F.F. Bruce, and Manfred T. Brauch. *Hard Sayings of the Bible* (Downers Grove, IL: InterVarsity, 1996).

Kaiser, Walter C., and Moisés Silva. *An Introduction to Biblical Hermeneutics* (Grand Rapids: Zondervan, 1994).

Kitchen, K.A. *The Bible in Its World: The Bible & Archaeology Today* (Eugene, OR: Wipf & Stock, 1977).

_____. *On the Reliability of the Old Testament* (Grand Rapids: Eerdmans, 2003).

Koster, C.J. *Come Out of Her, My People* (Northriding, South Africa: Institute for Scripture Research, 1996).

Ladd, George Eldon. *The Blessed Hope* (Grand Rapids: Eerdmans, 1956).

Lancaster, D. Thomas. *The Mystery of the Gospel: Jew and Gentile in the Eternal Purpose of God* (Littleton, CO: First Fruits of Zion, 2003).

_____. *Restoration: Returning the Torah of God to the Disciples of Jesus* (Littleton, CO: First Fruits of Zion, 2005).

Levitt, Zola. *The Seven Feasts of Israel* (Dallas: Zola Levitt Ministries, 1979).

McKee, J.K. *The New Testament Validates Torah* (Kissimmee, FL: TNN Press, 2004, 2008).

_____. *James for the Practical Messianic* (Kissimmee, FL: TNN Press, 2005).

_____. *Hebrews for the Practical Messianic* (Kissimmee, FL: TNN Press, 2006).

_____. *A Survey of the Apostolic Scriptures for the Practical Messianic* (Kissimmee, FL: TNN Press, 2006).

_____. *Philippians for the Practical Messianic* (Kissimmee, FL: TNN Press, 2007).

_____. *When Will the Messiah Return?*, academic edition (Kissimmee, FL: TNN Press, 2007).

_____. *Galatians for the Practical Messianic*, second edition (Kissimmee, FL: TNN Press, 2007).

_____. *A Survey of the Tanach for the Practical Messianic* (Kissimmee, FL: TNN Press, 2008).

_____. *Ephesians for the Practical Messianic* (Kissimmee, FL: TNN Press, 2008).

_____. *Colossians and Philemon for the Practical Messianic* (Kissimmee, FL: TNN Press, 2010).

_____. *Acts 15 for the Practical Messianic* (Kissimmee, FL: TNN Press, 2010).

Morey, Robert A. *Death and the Afterlife* (Minneapolis: Bethany House, 1984).

Richardson, Susan E. *Holidays & Holy Days* (Ann Arbor, MI: Servant Publications, 2001).

Russell, Brian D. *The Song of the Sea: the Date of Composition and Influence of Exodus 15: 1-21* (New York: Peter Lang, 2007).

Scarlata, Robin, and Linda Pierce. *A Family Guide to the Biblical Holidays with Activities for all Ages* (Madison, TN: Family Christian Press, 1997).

Stern, David H. *Restoring the Jewishness of the Gospel* (Clarksville, MD: Jewish New Testament Publications, 1990).

_____. *Messianic Jewish Manifesto* (Clarksville, MD: Jewish New Testament Publications, 1992).

Stevens, R. Paul. *The Other Six Days* (Grand Rapids: Eerdmans, 1999).

Thompson, David L. *Bible Study That Works* (Nappanee, IN: Evangel Publishing House, 1994).

Walzer, Michael. *Exodus and Revolution* (New York: Daniel Doron, 1979).

Wilson, Marvin R. *Our Father Abraham* (Grand Rapids: Eerdmans, 1989).

Wright, Christopher J.H. *The Mission of God: Unlocking the Bible's Grand Narrative* (Downers Grove, IL: IVP Academic, 2006).

Wright, N.T. *What Saint Paul Really Said* (Grand Rapids: Eerdmans, 1997).

_____. *Paul in Fresh Perspective* (Minneapolis: Fortress Press, 2005).

_____. *Surprised by Hope: Rethinking Heaven, the Resurrection, and the Mission of the Church* (New York: HarperCollins, 2008).

Christian Reference Sources and Cited Commentaries

Alexander, T. Desmond, and David W. Baker, eds. *Dictionary of the Old Testament Pentateuch* (Downers Grove, IL: InterVarsity, 2003).

Arnold, Bill T., and H.G.M. Williamson, eds. *Dictionary of the Old Testament Historical Books* (Downers Grove, IL: InterVarsity, 2005).

Beasley-Murray, George R. *Word Biblical Commentary: John*, Vol 36 (Waco, TX: Word Books, 1987).

Bercot, David W., ed. *A Dictionary of Early Christian Beliefs* (Peabody, MA: Hendrickson, 1998).

Bettenson, Henry, and Chris Maunder, eds. *Documents of the Christian Church* (Oxford: Oxford University Press, 1999).

Bromiley, Geoffrey, ed. *International Standard Bible Encyclopedia*, 4 vols. (Grand Rapids: Eerdmans, 1988).

Bruce, F.F. *New International Commentary on the New Testament: The Epistle to the Hebrews* (Grand Rapids: Eerdmans, 1990).

Buttrick, George, ed., et. al. *The Interpreter's Dictionary of the Bible*, 4 vols. (Nashville: Abingdon, 1962).

Cairns, Alan. *Dictionary of Theological Terms* (Greenville, SC: Ambassador Emerald International, 2002).

Crim, Keith, ed. *Interpreter's Dictionary of the Bible: Supplementary Volume* (Nashville: Abingdon, 1976).

Dunn, James D.G. *New International Greek Testament Commentary: The Epistles to the Colossians and to Philemon* (Grand Rapids: Eerdmans, 1996).

_____, and John W. Rogerson, eds. *Eerdmans Commentary on the Bible* (Grand Rapids: Eerdmans, 2003).

Durham, John I. *Word Biblical Commentary: Exodus*, Vol. 3 (Waco, TX: Word Books, 1987).

Evans, Craig A., and Stanley E. Porter, eds. *Dictionary of New Testament Background* (Downers Grove, IL: InterVarsity, 2000).

Fee, Gordon D. *New International Commentary on the New Testament: Paul's Letter to the Philippians* (Grand Rapids: Eerdmans, 1995).

France, R.T. *Tyndale New Testament Commentaries: Matthew* (Grand Rapids: Eerdmans, 1985).

_____. *New International Commentary on the New Testament: The Gospel of Matthew* (Grand Rapids: Eerdmans, 2007).

Freedman, David Noel, ed. *Anchor Bible Dictionary*, 6 vols. (New York: Doubleday, 1992).

Gaebelein, Frank E., ed. et. al. *Expositor's Bible Commentary*, 12 vols. (Grand Rapids: Zondervan, 1976-1992).

Geisler, Norman L., ed. *Baker Encyclopedia of Christian Apologetics* (Grand Rapids: Baker, 1999).

Green, Joel B., Scot McKnight, and I. Howard Marshall, eds. *Dictionary of Jesus and the Gospels* (Downers Grove, IL: InterVarsity, 1992).

Grenz, Stanley J., David Guretzki, and Cherith Fee Nordling. *Pocket Dictionary of Theological Terms* (Downers Grove, IL: InterVarsity, 1999).

Guelich, Robert A. *Word Biblical Commentary: Mark 1-8:26*, Vol. 34a (Dallas: Word Books, 1989).

Guthrie, D. and J.A. Motyer, eds. *The New Bible Commentary Revised* (Grand Rapids: Eerdmans, 1970).

Harrison, Everett F., ed. *Baker's Dictionary of Theology* (Grand Rapids: Baker Book House, 1960).

Hawthorne, Gerald F. *Word Biblical Commentary: Philippians*, Vol. 43 (Waco, TX: Word Books, 1983).

_____, Ralph P. Martin, and Daniel G. Reid, eds. *Dictionary of Paul and His Letters* (Downers Grove, IL: InterVarsity, 1993).

Keck, Leander E., ed. et. al. *New Interpreter's Bible*, Vol 8 (Nashville: Abingdon, 1995).

Keener, Craig S. *The IVP Bible Background Commentary: New Testament* (Downers Grove, IL: InterVarsity, 1993).

_____. *IVP New Testament Commentary Series: Matthew* (Downers Grove, IL: InterVarsity, 1997).

Keil, C., and F. Delitzsch, eds. *Commentary on the Old Testament*, 10 vols.

Kerr, Hugh T., ed. *Readings in Christian Thought* (Nashville: Abingdon, 1990).

Laymon, Charles M., ed. *The Interpreter's One-Volume Commentary on the Bible* (Nashville: Abingdon, 1971).

Longman III, Tremper, and Peter Enns, eds. *Dictionary of the Old Testament Wisdom, Poetry & Writings* (Downers Grove, IL: InterVarsity, 2008).

Martin, Ralph P., and Peter H. Davids, eds. *Dictionary of the Later New Testament & Its Developments* (Downers Grove, IL: InterVarsity, 1997).

Moo, Douglas J. *Pillar New Testament Commentary: The Letters to the Colossians and to Philemon* (Grand Rapids: Eerdmans, 2008).

Morris, Leon. *Tyndale New Testament Commentaries: 1 Corinthians* (Grand Rapids: Eerdmans, 1987).

Nolland, John. *New International Greek Testament Commentary: The Gospel of Matthew* (Grand Rapids: Eerdmans, 2005).

Peterson, David G. *Pillar New Testament Commentary: The Acts of the Apostles* (Grand Rapids: Eerdmans, 2009).

Roberts, Alexander, and James Donaldson, eds. *The Apostolic Fathers*, American Edition.

Schaff, Philip. *History of the Christian Church*, 8 vols. (Grand Rapids: Eerdmans, 1995).

Tenney, Merrill C., ed. *The New International Dictionary of the Bible* (Grand Rapids: Zondervan, 1987).

The Book of Common Prayer (New York: Oxford University Press, 1990).

Thiselton, Anthony C. *New International Greek Testament Commentary: The First Epistle to the Corinthians* (Grand Rapids: Eerdmans, 2000).

Unger, Merrill F. *Unger's Bible Handbook* (Chicago: Moody Press, 1967).

Walton, John H., and Victor H. Matthews and Mark W. Chavalas. *The IVP Bible Background Commentary: Old Testament* (Downers Grove, IL: InterVarsity, 2000).

Wesley, John. *Explanatory Notes Upon the New Testament*, reprint (Peterborough, UK: Epworth Press, 2000).

Greek Language Resources

Aland, Kurt, et. al. *The Greek New Testament, Fourth Revised Edition* (Stuttgart: Deutche Bibelgesellschaft/United Bible Societies, 1998).

Balme, Maurice, and Gilbert Lawall. *Athenaze: An Introduction to Ancient Greek*, Book I (New York and Oxford: Oxford University Press, 1990).

Black, David Allan. *Learn to Read New Testament Greek*, expanded edition (Nashville: Broadman & Holman, 1994).

Brenton, Sir Lancelot C. L., ed & trans. *The Septuagint With Apocrypha* (Peabody, MA: Hendrickson, 1999).

Bromiley, Geoffrey W., ed. *Theological Dictionary of the New Testament*, abridged (Grand Rapids: Eerdmans, 1985).

Brown, Robert K., and Philip W. Comfort, trans. *The New Greek-English Interlinear New Testament* (Carol Stream, IL: Tyndale House, 1990).

Danker, Frederick William, ed., et. al. *A Greek-English Lexicon of the New Testament and Other Early Christian Literature*, third edition (Chicago: University of Chicago Press, 2000).

Liddell, Henry George, and Robert Scott, eds. *Liddell and Scott's Greek-English Lexicon*, abridged (Oxford: Clarendon Press, 1953).

Metzger, Bruce M. *A Textual Commentary on the Greek New Testament* (London and New York: United Bible Societies, 1975).

Nestle, Erwin, and Kurt Aland, eds. *Novum Testamentum Graece, Nestle-Aland 27th Edition* (Stuttgart: Deutche Bibelgesellschaft, 1993).

Nestle-Aland Greek-English New Testament, NE27-RSV (Stuttgart: United Bible Societies/Deutche Bibelgesellschaft, 1981).

Newman, Jr., Barclay M. *A Concise Greek-English Dictionary of the New Testament* (Stuttgart: United Bible Societies/Deutche Bibelgesellschaft, 1971).

Rahlfs, Alfred, ed. *Septuaginta* (Stuttgart: Deutche Bibelgesellschaft, 1979).

Rogers, Cleon L., Jr., and Cleon L. Rogers III. *The New Linguistic and Exegetical Key to the Greek New Testament* (Grand Rapids: Zondervan, 1998).

Thayer, Joseph H. *Thayer's Greek-English Lexicon of the New Testament* (Peabody, MA: Hendrickson, 2003).

Vine, W.E. *Vine's Expository Dictionary of New Testament Words* (Nashville: Thomas Nelson, 1968).

Wallace, Daniel B. *Greek Grammar Beyond the Basics* (Grand Rapids: Zondervan, 1996).

Zodhiates, Spiros, ed. *Complete Word Study Dictionary: New Testament* (Chattanooga: AMG Publishers, 1993).

Hebrew Language Resources

Arnold, Bill T., and John H. Choi. *A Guide to Biblical Hebrew Syntax* (New York: Cambridge University Press, 2003).

Baker, Warren, and Eugene Carpenter, eds. *Complete Word Study Dictionary: Old Testament* (Chattanooga: AMG Publishers, 2003).

Brown, Francis, S.R. Driver, and Charles A. Briggs. *Hebrew and English Lexicon of the Old Testament* (Oxford: Clarendon Press, 1979).

Davidson, Benjamin. *The Analytical Hebrew and Chaldee Lexicon* (Grand Rapids: Zondervan, 1970).

Dotan, Aron, ed. *Biblia Hebraica Leningradensia* (Peabody, MA: Hendrickson, 2001).

Elliger, Karl, and Wilhelm Rudolph, et. al., eds. *Biblica Hebraica Stuttgartensia* (Stuttgart: Deutche Bibelgesellschaft, 1977).

Gabe, Eric S., ed. *New Testament in Hebrew and English* (Hitchin, UK: Society for Distributing the Hebrew Scriptures, 2000).

Harris, R. Laird, Gleason L. Archer, Jr., and Bruce K. Waltke, eds. *Theological Wordbook of the Old Testament* (Chicago: Moody Press, 1980).

Holladay, William L., ed. *A Concise Hebrew and Aramaic Lexicon of the Old Testament* (Leiden, the Netherlands: E.J. Brill, 1988).

Jastrow, Marcus. *Dictionary of the Targumim, Talmud Bavli, Talmud Yerushalmi, and Midrashic Literature* (New York: Judaica Treasury, 2004).

Kelley, Page H., Daniel S. Mynatt, and Timothy G. Crawford, eds. *The Masorah of Biblia Hebraica Stuttgartensia* (Grand Rapids: Eerdmans, 1998).

Koehler, Ludwig, and Walter Baumgartner, eds. *The Hebrew & Aramaic Lexicon of the Old Testament*, 2 vols. (Leiden, the Netherlands: Brill, 2001).

Seow, C.L. *A Grammar for Biblical Hebrew*, revised edition (Nashville: Abingdon, 1995).

Tov, Emanuel. *Textual Criticism of the Hebrew Bible* (Minneapolis: Fortress Press, 1992).

תורה נביאים כתובים והברית החדשה (Jerusalem: Bible Society in Israel, 1991).

Unger, Merrill F., and William White. *Nelson's Expository Dictionary of the Old Testament* (Nashville: Thomas Nelson, 1980).

Historical Sources

Bettenson, Henry, and Chris Maunder, eds. *Documents of the Christian Church* (Oxford: Oxford University Press, 1999).

Davies, W.W. *The Codes of Hammurabi and Moses* (Berkeley, CA: Apocryphile Press, 2006).

Eusebius: *Ecclesiastical History*, trans. C.F. Cruse (Peabody, MA: Hendrickson, 1998).

Funk & Wagnall's New Encyclopedia, 29 vols. (Rand McNally, 1990).

Irvin, Dale T., and Scott W. Sunquist. *History of the World Christian Movement*, Vol. 1 (Maryknoll, NY: Orbis Books, 2001).

Josephus, Flavius: *The Works of Josephus: Complete and Unabridged*, trans. William Whiston (Peabody, MA: Hendrickson, 1987).

Judaeus, Philo: *The Works of Philo: Complete and Unabridged*, trans. C.D. Yonge (Peabody, MA: Hendrickson, 1993).

Kerr, Hugh T., ed. *Readings in Christian Thought* (Nashville: Abingdon, 1990).

Parker, Simon B., ed. *Ugaritic Narrative Poetry* (Atlanta: Society of Biblical Literature, 1997).

Shanks, Hershel, ed. *Ancient Israel: From Abraham to the Roman Destruction of the Temple* (Washington, D.C.: Biblical Archaeology Society, 1999).

Jewish Reference Sources and Cited Commentaries

Cohen, A. *Soncino Chmash* (Brooklyn: Soncino Press, 1983).

Cohen, Abraham. *Everyman's Talmud: The Major Teachings of the Rabbinic Sages* (New York: Schoken, 1995).

Eisenberg, Ronald L. *The JPS Guide to Jewish Traditions* (Philadelphia: Jewish Publication Society, 2004).

Encyclopaedia Judaica. MS Windows 9x. Brooklyn: Judaica Multimedia (Israel) Ltd, 1997.

Hertz, J.H., ed. *Pentateuch & Haftorahs* (London: Soncino, 1960).

_____. ed. *The Authorised Daily Prayer Book*, revised (New York: Bloch Publishing Company, 1960).

Kolatch, Alfred J. *The Jewish Book of Why* (Middle Village, NY: Jonathan David Publishers, 1981).

_____. *The Second Jewish Book of Why* (Middle Village, NY: Jonathan David Publishers, 1985).

Lieber, David L., ed. *Etz Hayim: Torah and Commentary* (New York: Rabbinical Assembly, 2001).

Neusner, Jacob, trans. *The Mishnah: A New Translation* (New Haven and London: Yale University Press, 1988).

_____, ed. *The Tosefta: Translated from the Hebrew With a New Introduction*, 2 vols. (Peabody, MA: Hendrickson, 2002).

_____, and William Scott Green, eds. *Dictionary of Judaism in the Biblical Period* (Peabody, MA: Hendrickson, 2002).

Rabinowicz, Rachel Anne. *Passover Haggadah: The Feast of Freedom* (The Rabbinical Assembly, 1982).

Rubin, Barry and Steffi. *The Messianic Passover Haggadah* (Baltimore: Lederer, 1996).

Sarna, Nahum M. *JPS Torah Commentary: Genesis* (Philadelphia: Jewish Publication Society, 1989).

_____. *JPS Torah Commentary: Exodus* (Philadelphia: Jewish Publication Society, 1991).

Scherman Nosson, and Meir Zlotowitz, eds. *The Complete ArtScroll Siddur: Nusach Ashkenaz* (Brooklyn: Mesorah Publications, 1984).

Scherman, Nosson, ed. et. al., *Seif Edition of the ArtScroll Transliterated Siddur: Sabbath and Festival* (Brooklyn: Mesorah Publications, 1998).

———————, ed. et. al. *The ArtScroll Chumash, Stone Edition*, 5th ed. (Brooklyn: Mesorah Publications, 2000).

Spieler, Marlena. *Jewish Cooking: The Traditions, Techniques, Ingredients, and Recipes* (London: Hermes House, 2003).

Tabory, Joseph. *JPS Commentary on the Haggadah* (Philadelphia: Jewish Publication Society, 2008).

Messianic Reference Sources
Stern, David H. *Jewish New Testament Commentary* (Clarksville, MD: Jewish New Testament Publications, 1995).

Miscellaneous Texts and Lexicons
Young, Robert. *Young's Analytical Concordance to the Bible* (Grand Rapids: Eerdmans, 1977).

Software Programs
BibleWorks 5.0. MS Windows 9x. Norfolk: BibleWorks, LLC, 2002. CD-ROM.

BibleWorks 7.0. MS Windows XP. Norfolk: BibleWorks, LLC, 2006. CD-ROM.

E-Sword 7.6.1. MS Windows 9x. Franklin, TN: Equipping Ministries Foundation, 2005.

E-Sword 8.0.8. MS Windows 9x. Franklin, TN: Equipping Ministries Foundation, 2008.

Judaic Classics Library II. MS Windows 3.1. Brooklyn: Institute for Computers in Jewish Life, 1996. CD-ROM.

Libronix Digital Library System 1.0d: Church History Collection. MS Windows XP. Garland, TX: Galaxie Software. 2002.

QuickVerse 6.0. MS Windows 95. Hiawatha, IA: Parsons Technology, 1999. CD-ROM.

The Essential Christian Library. MS-Windows 95. Coeur d'Alene, ID: Packard Technologies, 1998. CD-ROM.

World Book 2003. CD-ROM, Chicago: World Book, Inc., 2003.

Messianic Apologetics is dedicated to producing high quality, doctrinally sound, challenging, and fair-minded publications and resources for Twenty-First Century Messianic people. Our broad faith community faces any number of issues requiring resolution—from newcomers to the Messianic movement and those who have been involved for many years. The books, studies, commentaries, and analyses provided by Messianic Apologetics intend to aid the legitimate needs of today's Messianic people, so they can have the answers they seek in their walk with the Messiah of Israel.

Titles are available for purchase at **amazon.com**.

www.outreachisrael.net or at

Hebraic Roots: An Introductory Study
is Messianic Apologetics' main, best-selling publication, that offers a good overview of the Messianic movement and Messianic lifestyle that can be used for individual or group study in twelve easy lessons

Introduction to Things Messianic
is an excellent companion to *Hebraic Roots*, which goes into substantially more detail into the emerging theology of the Messianic movement, specific areas of Torah observance, and aspects of faith such as salvation and eschatology

The Messianic Helper series, edited by Margaret McKee Huey, includes a series of books with instructional information on how to have a Messianic home, including holiday celebration guides. After reading both *Hebraic Roots* and *Introduction to Things Messianic,* these are the publications you need to read!

Messianic Spring Holiday Helper
is a guide to assist you during the Spring holiday season, analyzing the importance of *Purim,* Passover and Unleavened Bread, *Shavuot,* and the non-Biblical holiday of Easter

Messianic Fall Holiday Helper
is a guide for the Fall holiday season of *Yom Teruah/Rosh HaShanah, Yom Kippur,* and *Sukkot,* along with reflective teachings and exhortations

Messianic Winter Holiday Helper
is a guide to help you during the Winter holiday season, addressing the significance of *Chanukah,* the period of the Maccabees, and the non-Biblical holiday of Christmas

Messianic Sabbath Helper
is a guide that will help you make the seventh-day Sabbath a delight, discussing how to keep *Shabbat,* common Jewish traditions associated with *Shabbat,* the history of the transition to Sunday that occurred in early Christianity, respecting those in the past who kept a "Sunday Sabbath," and an extensive analysis of Biblical passages from the Tanach (OT) and Apostolic Scriptures (NT) about the Sabbath, rest, and their relevance to modern-day Messiah followers
> also available is the five-chapter mini-book excerpt **Shabbat: Sabbath for Messianic Believers,** intended as a congregational handout

Messianic Kosher Helper
is a guide discussing various aspects of the kosher dietary laws, clean and unclean meats, common Jewish traditions associated with kashrut, common claims made that these are no longer important for Believers, and an extensive analysis of Biblical passages from the Tanach (OT) and Apostolic Scriptures (NT) about the Torah's dietary laws and their relevance
> also available is the five-chapter mini-book excerpt **Kashrut: Kosher for Messianic Believers**, intended as a congregational handout

Messianic Torah Helper
is a guide that weighs the different perspectives of the Pentateuch present in Jewish and Christian theology, considers the role of the Law for God's people, and how today's Messianics can fairly approach issues of *halachah* and tradition in their Torah observance

Outreach Israel Ministries director **Mark Huey** has written Torah commentaries and reflections that are thought provoking and very enlightening for Messianic Believers today.

TorahScope Volume I
is a compilation workbook of insightful commentaries on the weekly Torah and Haftarah portions

TorahScope Volume II
is a second compilation workbook of expanded commentaries on the weekly Torah and Haftarah portions

TorahScope Volume III
is a third compilation workbook of expanded commentaries on the weekly Torah and Haftarah portions, specifically concentrating on the theme of faith

TorahScope Haftarah Exhortations
is a compilation workbook of insightful commentaries on the specific, weekly Haftarah portions, designed to be used to compliment the weekly Torah reading

TorahScope Apostolic Scripture Reflections
is a compilation workbook of insightful reflections on suggested readings from the Apostolic Scriptures or New Testament, designed to be used to compliment the weekly Torah and Haftarah readings

Counting the Omer: A Daily Devotional Toward Shavuot
is a daily devotional with fifty succinct reflections from Psalms, guiding you during the season between the festivals of Passover and Pentecost

Sayings of the Fathers: A Messianic Perspective on Pirkei Avot
is a daily devotional for two years of reflection on the Mishnah tractate *Pirkei Avot*, introducing you to some of the key views present in the Apostolic period as witnessed by the Jewish Sages (intended to be read during the counting of the *omer*)

Messianic Apologetics editor **J.K. McKee** has written on Messianic theology and practice, including studies on Torah observance, the end-times, and commentaries that are helpful to those who have difficult questions to answer.

The New Testament Validates Torah
Does the New Testament Really Do Away With the Law?
is a resource examining a wide variety of Biblical passages, discussing whether or not the Torah of Moses is really abolished in the New Testament

Torah In the Balance, Volume I
The Validity of the Torah and Its Practical Life Applications
examines the principal areas of a Torah observant walk of faith for the newcomer, including one's spiritual motives

Torah In the Balance, Volume II
The Set-Apart Life in Action—The Outward Expressions of Faith
examines many of the finer areas of Torah observance, which has a diversity of interpretations and applications as witnessed in both mainstream Judaism and the wide Messianic community

Confronting Critical Issues
An Analysis of Subjects that Affects the Growth and Stability
of the Emerging Messianic Movement
compiles a variety of articles and analyses that directly confront negative teachings and trends that have been witnessed in the broad Messianic community in the past decade

Messianic Apologetics has produced a variety of **Messianic commentaries** on various books of the Bible under the "for the Practical Messianic" byline. These can be used in an individual, small group, or congregational study.

general commentaries:
A Survey of the Tanach for the Practical Messianic
A Survey of the Apostolic Scriptures for the Practical Messianic

specific book commentaries:
Acts 15 for the Practical Messianic
Romans for the Practical Messianic
1 Corinthians for the Practical Messianic
2 Corinthians for the Practical Messianic (coming 2016)
Galatians for the Practical Messianic
Ephesians for the Practical Messianic
Philippians for the Practical Messianic
Colossians and Philemon for the Practical Messianic
The Pastoral Epistles for the Practical Messianic
1&2 Thessalonians for the Practical Messianic
James for the Practical Messianic
Hebrews for the Practical Messianic

Additional Materials Available From Messianic Apologetics

One of the goals of Messianic Apologetics is to always be in the mode of producing more cutting edge materials, addressing head on some of the theological and spiritual issues facing our emerging Messianic movement. In addition to our current array of available and soon-to-be available publications, the following are a selection of **Future Projects**, in various stages of planning and pre-production, most of which involve research at the present time (2015-2016). Look for their release sometime over the next two to five years and beyond.

Salvation on the Line: The Nature of Yeshua and His Divinity
by J.K. McKee

will be a lengthy study defending Yeshua the Messiah as God, evaluating the state of Christology in the broad Messianic movement, and intends to examine a wide array of Bible passages, mainly to be compiled into two volumes: (I) Gospels and Acts; (II) The General Epistles, The Pauline Epistles, The Later New Testament

After the Afterlife: Messianic Engagement With Heaven, Hell, and the Resurrection of the Dead

will be a compilation of teaching about the intermediate state, eternal punishment, the philosophy of future resurrection, and will evaluate the Messianic movement's strengths and weaknesses regarding human composition

Made in the USA
San Bernardino, CA
01 February 2016